ASPEN

2010-2011 Supplement

National Security Law
Fourth Edition

and

Counterterrorism Law

Stephen Dycus
Professor of Law
Vermont Law School

William C. Banks
Board of Advisors Distinguished Professor
Syracuse University

Peter Raven-Hansen
Glen Earl Weston Research Professor of Law
George Washington University

Wolters Kluwer
Law & Business

AUSTIN   BOSTON   CHICAGO   NEW YORK   THE NETHERLANDS

Aspen Publishers
Attn: Permissions Department
76 Ninth Avenue, 7th Floor
New York, NY   10011-5201

To contact Customer Care, e-mail customer.service@aspenpublishers.com,
call 1-800-234-1660, fax 1-800-901-9075, or mail correspondence to:

Aspen Publishers
Attn: Order Department
PO Box 990
Frederick, MD 21705

Printed in the United States of America.

1 2 3 4 5 6 7 8 9 0

ISBN 978-0-7355-9862-1

About Wolters Kluwer Law & Business

Wolters Kluwer Law & Business is a leading provider of research information and workflow solutions in key specialty areas. The strengths of the individual brands of Aspen Publishers, CCH, Kluwer Law International and Loislaw are aligned within Wolters Kluwer Law & Business to provide comprehensive, in-depth solutions and expert-authored content for the legal, professional and education markets.

CCH was founded in 1913 and has served more than four generations of business professionals and their clients. The CCH products in the Wolters Kluwer Law & Business group are highly regarded electronic and print resources for legal, securities, antitrust and trade regulation, government contracting, banking, pension, payroll, employment and labor, and healthcare reimbursement and compliance professionals.

Aspen Publishers is a leading information provider for attorneys, business professionals and law students. Written by preeminent authorities, Aspen products offer analytical and practical information in a range of specialty practice areas from securities law and intellectual property to mergers and acquisitions and pension/benefits. Aspen's trusted legal education resources provide professors and students with high-quality, up-to-date and effective resources for successful instruction and study in all areas of the law.

Kluwer Law International supplies the global business community with comprehensive English-language international legal information. Legal practitioners, corporate counsel and business executives around the world rely on the Kluwer Law International journals, loose-leafs, books and electronic products for authoritative information in many areas of international legal practice.

Loislaw is a premier provider of digitized legal content to small law firm practitioners of various specializations. Loislaw provides attorneys with the ability to quickly and efficiently find the necessary legal information they need, when and where they need it, by facilitating access to primary law as well as state-specific law, records, forms and treatises.

Wolters Kluwer Law & Business, a unit of Wolters Kluwer, is headquartered in New York and Riverwoods, Illinois. Wolters Kluwer is a leading multinational publisher and information services company.

Contents

Contents

Preface

The spate of developments in the national security law and counter-terrorism fields continues almost unabated. These developments present both challenges and opportunities for students and teachers alike. Our job here is to explore the critical role of lawyers in providing for the nation's security, while also protecting the freedoms for which we are prepared to fight and die. Because no subject in law is more dynamic, we have to work hard to keep current. (We discuss events in the news at the beginning of every day's class.) In the process, however, we gain a special insight into the workings of law and government, and into the responsibility of lawyers to help keep us safe and free.

This year's Supplement includes excerpts from the recently published National Security Strategy, as well as a letter from President Obama regarding war powers, to help frame many of the issues addressed in our courses. Also included here are the latest in a long series of decisions about national security letters (*Doe v. Holder (Doe VI)*), a case involving the use of the material witness statute to detain a terrorist suspect (*Al-Kidd v. Ashcroft*), a case about profiling of suspected terrorists (*Farag v. United States*), two recent cases interpreting and applying the Supreme Court's *Boumediene* decision (*Al Maqaleh v. Gates* (D.C. Cir.) and *Al-Bihani v. Obama* (D.C. Cir.)), and the Supreme Court's ruling on First Amendment challenges to one of the material support statutes (*Holder v. Humanitarian Law Project*). In addition, you will find here a letter from Attorney General Holder explaining the rationale for handling terrorist suspects within the criminal justice system, the final report of the Guantanamo Review Task Force, the Military Commissions Act of 2009, and a new executive order on classification of national security information.

This Supplement serves two closely related casebooks: *National Security Law (4th ed.)* and *Counterterrorism Law*. This Preface is followed immediately by two Teacher's Guides, one for each book, which indicate the placement of supplemental materials in each case-book. Each document is accompanied by a reference to one or both casebooks. For example, the decision in *Tabbaa v. Chertoff* appears with this instruction: **[NSL p. 613, insert after Note 9. CTL p. 238, insert after Note 10.]**. "NSL" refers to *National Security Law (4th ed.)*, "CTL" to *Counterterrorism Law*.

We expect the rapid pace of developments to continue for the foreseeable future. As notable events occur, we will continue to document them by posting edited new materials on the websites for the two casebooks, from which they may be downloaded by teachers and shared with students. The website for *National Security Law (4th ed.)* is at http://www.aspenlawschool.com/books/dycus_nationalsecurity/; for *Counterterrorism Law* at http://www.aspenlawschool.com/books/dycus_counterterrorism/.

In an effort to keep this Supplement to a manageable size, we have moved two replacement chapters to the websites – one dealing with the organization and coordination of counterterrorism investigations (NSL Chapter 22 and CTL Chapter 8), the other with tort suits against terrorists and their sponsors (CTL Chapter 23) – from which they may be downloaded.

These chapters, along with materials in this Supplement, as well as more recent developments, will ultimately be incorporated into the pending fifth edition of *National Security Law* and second edition of *Counterterrorism Law*, which are scheduled for publication in 2011.

As always, we are extremely grateful to our adopters, fellow members of the National Security Law Section of the Association of American Law Schools, fellow members of the editorial board of the *Journal of National Security Law & Policy*, fellow casebook authors (our collaborators in building the field), and our many friends in the national security community. We also wish to thank our research assistants: Andrea Masselli at Syracuse University College of Law; Josh Weiss at George Washington University Law Center; and Daniel Bougie, Daniel Burke, Caitlin Morgenstern, and Alexandra Sherertz at Vermont Law School. Thanks are due as well to our production editor, Darren Kelly, for his help in preparing this Supplement. Finally, we are grateful to Eric Holt, Barbara Roth, and Carol McGeehan of Aspen Publishers for their continued encouragement and support.

Stephen Dycus
William C. Banks
Peter Raven-Hansen

July 21, 2010

Teacher's Guide for National Security Law (4th Edition)

Chapter 16. Other Legal Problems in the Intelligence Field

Chapter 19. Congressional Authority for National Security Surveillance

Chapter 20. Third-Party Records and Data Mining

Chapter 21. Screening for Security

Chapter 22. Organization and Coordination of Counterterrorism Investigations

Chapter 23. Surveillance Abroad

Chapter 24. Civil Detention of Terrorist Suspects

Chapter 25. Suspending the Great Writ

Chapter 26. Military Detention

Chapter 27. Interrogating Terrorist Suspects

Chapter 28. Criminalizing Terrorism and Material Support

Chapter 29. Secret Evidence

Chapter 30. Trial by Military Commission

Chapter 32. The Domestic Role of the Armed Forces

Chapter 33. Regulating Access to National Security Information

Chapter 34. Statutory Access
to National Security Information

Chapter 35. Access to National Security
Information in Civil Litigation

Chapter 36. Restraining Unauthorized
Disclosures of National Security Information

Chapter 37. Restraints on Publication of
National Security Information

* * *

Teacher's Guide for Counterterrorism Law

Chapter 8. Organizing and Coordinating Counterterrorism Investigations

Chapter 9. Investigating Abroad

Chapter 10. Civil Detention of Terrorist Suspects

Chapter 11. Suspending the Great Writ

Chapter 12. Military Detention of Terrorist Suspects

Chapter 13. Interrogating Terrorist Suspects

Chapter 14. Extraordinary Rendition

Chapter 15. Criminalizing Treason, Terrorism, and Material Support

Chapter 17. Trying Suspected Terrorists as Criminals

Chapter 18. Trying Suspected Terrorists in Military Courts

Chapter 21. The Military's Domestic Role in Counterterrorism

Chapter 23. Suing Terrorists and Their Supporters

Table of Cases

* * *

[NSL p. 5, insert at the end of Chapter 1. CTL p. 38, insert at the end of Chapter 1.]

National Security Strategy
May 2010
available at http://www.whitehouse.gov/sites/default/
files/rss_viewer/national_security_strategy.pdf

I. Overview of National Security Strategy

At the dawn of the 21st century, the United States of America faces a broad and complex array of challenges to our national security. Just as America helped to determine the course of the 20th century, we must now build the sources of American strength and influence, and shape an international order capable of overcoming the challenges of the 21st century.

The World as It Is, A Strategy for the World We Seek

To succeed, we must face the world as it is. The two decades since the end of the Cold War have been marked by both the promise and perils of change. The circle of peaceful democracies has expanded; the specter of nuclear war has lifted; major powers are at peace; the global economy has grown; commerce has stitched the fate of nations together; and more individuals can determine their own destiny. Yet these advances have been accompanied by persistent problems. Wars over ideology have given way to wars over religious, ethnic, and tribal identity; nuclear dangers have proliferated; inequality and economic instability have intensified; damage to our environment, food insecurity, and dangers to public health are increasingly shared; and the same tools that empower individuals to build enable them to destroy. . . .

III. Advancing Our Interests . . .

Disrupt, Dismantle, and Defeat Al-Qa'ida and its Violent Extremist Affiliates in Afghanistan, Pakistan, and Around the World

The United States is waging a global campaign against al-Qa'ida and its terrorist affiliates. To disrupt, dismantle and defeat al-Qa'ida and its affiliates, we are pursuing a strategy that protects our homeland, secures the world's most dangerous weapons and material, denies al-Qa'ida safe haven, and builds positive partnerships with Muslim communities around the world. Success requires a broad, sustained, and integrated campaign that judiciously applies every tool of American power—both military and civilian—as well as the concerted efforts of like-minded states and multilateral institutions.

We will always seek to delegitimize the use of terrorism and to isolate those who carry it out. Yet this is not a global war against a tactic—terrorism or a religion—Islam. We are at war with a specific network, al-Qa'ida, and its terrorist affiliates who support efforts to attack the United States, our allies, and partners.

Prevent Attacks on and in the Homeland: To prevent acts of terrorism on American soil, we must enlist all of our intelligence, law enforcement, and homeland security capabilities. We will continue to integrate and leverage state and major urban area fusion centers that have the capability to share classified information; establish a nationwide framework for reporting suspicious activity; and implement an integrated approach to our counterterrorism information systems to ensure that the analysts, agents, and officers who protect us have access to all relevant intelligence throughout the government. We are improving information sharing and cooperation by linking networks to facilitate Federal, state, and local capabilities to seamlessly exchange messages and information, conduct searches, and collaborate. We are coordinating better with foreign partners to identify, track, limit access to funding, and prevent terrorist travel. Recognizing the inextricable link between domestic and transnational security, we will collaborate bilaterally, regionally, and through international institutions to promote global efforts to prevent terrorist attacks.

Strengthen Aviation Security: We know that the aviation system has been a particular target of al-Qa'ida and its affiliates. We must continue to bolster aviation security worldwide through a focus on increased information collection and sharing, stronger passenger vetting and screening measures, the development and development of advanced screening technologies, and cooperation with the international community to strengthen aviation security standards and efforts around the world.

Deny Terrorists Weapons of Mass Destruction: To prevent acts of terrorism with the world's most dangerous weapons, we are dramatically accelerating and intensifying efforts to secure all vulnerable nuclear materials by the end of 2013, and to prevent the spread of nuclear weapons. We will also take actions to safeguard knowledge and capabilities in the life and chemical sciences that could be vulnerable to misuse.

Deny Al-Qa'ida the Ability to Threaten the American People, Our Allies, Our Partners and Our Interests Overseas: Al-Qa'ida and its allies must not be permitted to gain or retain any capacity to plan and launch international terrorist attacks, especially against the U.S. homeland. Al Qa'ida's core in Pakistan remains the most dangerous component of the larger network, but we also face a growing threat from the group's allies worldwide. We must deny these groups the ability to conduct operational plotting from any locale, or to recruit, train, and position operatives, including those from Europe and North America.

Afghanistan and Pakistan: This is the epicenter of the violent extremism practiced by al Qa'ida. The danger from this region will only grow if its security slides backward, the Taliban controls large swaths of Afghanistan, and al-Qa'ida is allowed to operate with impunity. To prevent future attacks on the United States, our allies, and partners, we must work with others to keep the pressure on al-Qa'ida and increase the security and capacity of our partners in this region.

In Afghanistan, we must deny al-Qa'ida a safe haven, deny the Taliban the ability to overthrow the government, and strengthen the capacity of Afghanistan's security forces and government so that they can take lead responsibility for Afghanistan's future. Within Pakistan, we are working with the government to address the local, regional, and global threat from violent extremists.

We will achieve these objectives with a strategy comprised of three components.

- First, our military and International Security Assistance Force (ISAF) partners within Afghanistan are targeting the insurgency, working to secure key population centers, and increasing efforts to train Afghan security forces. These military resources will allow us to create the conditions to transition to Afghan responsibility. In July 2011, we will begin reducing our troops responsibly, taking into account conditions on the ground. We will continue to advise and assist Afghanistan's Security Forces so that they can succeed over the long term.

- Second, we will continue to work with our partners, the United Nations, and the Afghan Government to improve accountable and effective governance. As we work to advance our strategic partnership with the Afghan Government, we are focusing assistance on supporting the President of Afghanistan and those ministries, governors, and local leaders who combat corruption and deliver for the people. Our efforts will be based upon performance, and we will measure progress. We will also target our assistance to areas that can make an immediate and enduring impact in the lives of the Afghan people, such as agriculture, while supporting the human rights of all of Afghanistan's people—women and men. This will support our long-term commitment to a relationship between our two countries that supports a strong, stable, and prosperous Afghanistan.

•   Third, we will foster a relationship with Pakistan founded upon mutual interests and mutual respect. To defeat violent extremists who threaten both of our countries, we will strengthen Pakistan's capacity to target violent extremists within its borders, and continue to provide security assistance to support those efforts. To strengthen Pakistan's democracy and development, we will provide substantial assistance responsive to the needs of the Pakistani people, and sustain a long-term partnership committed to Pakistan's future. The strategic partnership that we are developing with Pakistan includes deepening cooperation in a broad range of areas, addressing both security and civilian challenges, and we will continue to expand those ties through our engagement with Pakistan in the years to come.

Deny Safe Havens and Strengthen At-Risk States: Wherever al-Qa'ida or its terrorist affiliates attempt to establish a safe haven—as they have in Yemen, Somalia, the Maghreb, and the Sahel—we will meet them with growing pressure. We also will strengthen our own network of partners to disable al-Qa'ida's financial, human, and planning networks; disrupt terrorist operations before they mature; and address potential safe-havens before al-Qa'ida and its terrorist affiliates can take root. These efforts will focus on information-sharing, law enforcement cooperation, and establishing new practices to counter evolving adversaries. We will also help states avoid becoming terrorist safe havens by helping them build their capacity for responsible governance and security through development and security sector assistance.

Deliver Swift and Sure Justice: To effectively detain, interrogate, and prosecute terrorists, we need durable legal approaches consistent with our security and our values. We adhere to several principles: we will leverage all available information and intelligence to disrupt attacks and dismantle al-Qa'ida and affiliated terrorist organizations; we will bring terrorists to justice; we will act in line with the rule of law and due process; we will submit decisions to checks and balances and accountability; and we will insist that matters of detention and secrecy are addressed in a manner consistent with our Constitution and laws. To deny violent extremists one of their most potent recruitment tools, we will close the prison at Guantanamo Bay.

Resist Fear and Overreaction: The goal of those who perpetrate terrorist attacks is in part to sow fear. If we respond with fear, we allow violent extremists to succeed far beyond the initial impact of their attacks, or attempted attacks—altering our society and enlarging the standing of al-Qa'ida and its terrorist affiliates far beyond its actual reach. Similarly, overreacting in a way that creates fissures between America and certain regions or religions will undercut our leadership and make us less safe.

Contrast Al-Qa'ida's Intent to Destroy with Our Constructive Vision: While violent extremists seek to destroy, we will make clear our intent to build. We are striving to build bridges among people of different faiths and regions. We will continue to work to resolve the Arab-Israeli conflict, which has long been a source of tension. We will continue to stand up for the universal rights of all people, even for those with whom we disagree. We are developing new partnerships in Muslim communities around the world on behalf of health, education, science, employment, and innovation. And through our broader emphasis on Muslim engagement, we will communicate our commitment to support the aspirations of all people for security and opportunity. Finally, we reject the notion that al-Qa'ida represents any religious authority. They are not religious leaders, they are killers; and neither Islam nor any other religion condones the slaughter of innocents.

Use of Force

Military force, at times, may be necessary to defend our country and allies or to preserve broader peace and security, including by protecting civilians facing a grave humanitarian crisis. We will draw on diplomacy, development, and international norms and institutions to help resolve disagreements, prevent conflict, and maintain peace, mitigating where possible the need for the use of force. This means credibly underwriting U.S. defense commitments with tailored approaches to deterrence and ensuring the U.S. military continues to have the necessary capabilities across all domains—land, air, sea, space, and cyber. It also includes helping our allies and partners build capacity to fulfill their responsibilities to contribute to regional and global security.

While the use of force is sometimes necessary, we will exhaust other options before war whenever we can, and carefully weigh the costs and risks of action against the costs and risks of inaction. When force is necessary, we will continue to do so in a way that reflects our values and strengthens our legitimacy, and we will seek broad international support, working with such institutions as NATO and the U.N. Security Council.

The United States must reserve the right to act unilaterally if necessary to defend our nation and our interests, yet we will also seek to adhere to standards that govern the use of force. Doing so strengthens those who act in line with international standards, while isolating and weakening those who do not. We will also outline a clear mandate and specific objectives and thoroughly consider the consequences —intended and unintended—of our actions. And the United States will take care when sending the men and women of our Armed Forces into harm's way to ensure they have the leadership, training, and equipment they require to accomplish their mission. . . .

[NSL p. 254, insert at end of page.]

Letter from the President to the Speaker of the House of Representatives and the President Pro Tempore of the Senate Regarding the War Powers Report
December 16, 2009
http://www.whitehouse.gov/the-press-office/letter-president-regarding-war-powers-report

Dear Madam Speaker: (Dear Mr. President:)

I am providing this supplemental consolidated report, prepared by my Administration and consistent with the War Powers Resolution (Public Law 93-148), as part of my efforts to keep the Congress informed about global deployments of U.S. Armed Forces equipped for combat. This supplemental report covers ongoing U.S. contingency operations overseas.

Since October 7, 2001, the United States has conducted combat operations in Afghanistan against al-Qa'ida terrorists and their Taliban supporters, and has deployed various combat-equipped forces to a number of locations in the Central, Pacific, European, Southern, and Africa Command areas of operation in support of those and other overseas operations. These operations and deployments remain ongoing and were previously reported consistent with Public Law 107-40 and the War Powers Resolution.

In response to the terrorist threat, I will direct additional measures, as necessary, in the exercise of the right of the United States to self-defense and to protect U.S. citizens and interests. Such measures may include short-notice deployments of special operations and other forces for sensitive operations in various locations throughout the world. It is not possible to know at this time the precise scope or the duration of the deployments of U.S. Armed Forces necessary to counter the terrorist threat to the United States.

United States Armed Forces, with the assistance of numerous international partners, continue to conduct the U.S. campaign to pursue al-Qa'ida terrorists and to eliminate support to al-Qa'ida. These operations have been successful in seriously degrading al-Qa'ida's capabilities. United States Armed Forces, with the assistance of numerous international partners, brought an end to the Taliban's leadership of Afghanistan. Our forces are actively pursuing and engaging remaining al-Qa'ida and Taliban fighters in Afghanistan. The total number of U.S. forces in Afghanistan is approximately 68,000, of which over 34,000 are assigned to the International Security Assistance Force (ISAF) in Afghanistan. The U.N. Security Council authorized ISAF in U.N. Security Council Resolution 1386 on December 20, 2001, and has reaffirmed its authorization since that time, most recently for a 12-month period from October 13, 2009, in U.N. Security Council Resolution 1890 on October 8, 2009. The mission of ISAF, under NATO command and in partnership with the Government of the Islamic Republic of Afghanistan, is to conduct population-centric counterinsurgency operations, enable expanded and effective Afghan National Security Forces, and support improved governance and development in order to protect the Afghan people and provide a secure environment for sustainable security. Presently, 43 nations contribute to ISAF, including all 28 NATO Allies.

The United States continues to detain several hundred al-Qa'ida and Taliban fighters who are believed to pose a continuing threat to the United States and its interests. The combat-equipped forces deployed since January 2002 to Naval Base, Guantanamo Bay, Cuba, in the U.S. Southern Command area of operation, continue to conduct secure detention operations for the approximately 230 detainees at Guantanamo Bay under Public Law 107-40 and consistent with principles of the law of war.

The U.N. Security Council authorized a Multinational Force (MNF) in Iraq, under unified command, in U.N. Security Council Resolution 1511 on October 16, 2003, and reaffirmed its authorization in U.N. Security Council Resolution 1546 on June 8, 2004, U.N. Security Council Resolution 1637 on November 8, 2005, U.N. Security Council Resolution 1723 on November 28, 2006, and U.N. Security Council Resolution 1790 on December 18, 2007; the authorization was not renewed in 2009. Since the expiration of the authorization and mandate for the MNF in U.N. Security Council Resolution 1790 on December 31, 2008, U.S. forces have continued operations to support Iraq in its efforts to maintain security and stability in Iraq pursuant to the bilateral Agreement Between the United States of America and the Republic of Iraq on the Withdrawal of United States Forces from Iraq and the Organization of Their Activities during Their Temporary Presence in Iraq, which entered into force on January 1, 2009. These contributions have included, but have not been limited to, assisting in building the capability of the Iraqi security forces, supporting the development of Iraq's political institutions, improving local governance, enhancing ministerial capacity, and providing critical humanitarian and reconstruction assistance to the Iraqis. The United States contribution of forces to the Iraq mission fluctuates over time, depending on the conditions in theater as determined by the commanders on the ground; the present U.S. contribution is approximately 116,000 U.S. military personnel.

In furtherance of U.S. efforts against terrorists who pose a continuing and imminent threat to the United States, its friends, its allies, and our forces abroad, the United States continues to work with partners around the globe. These efforts include the deployment of U.S. combat-equipped forces to assist in enhancing the counterterrorism capabilities of our friends and allies. United States combat-equipped forces continue to be located in the Horn of Africa region.

In addition, the United States continues to conduct maritime interception operations on the high seas in the areas of responsibility of all of the geographic combatant commands. These maritime operations are aimed at stopping the movement, arming, and financing of international terrorists.

As noted in previous reports regarding U.S. contributions in support of peacekeeping efforts in Kosovo, the U.N. Security Council authorized Member States to establish a NATO-led Kosovo Force (KFOR) in U.N. Security Council Resolution 1244 on June 10, 1999. The original mission of KFOR was to monitor, verify, and, when necessary, enforce compliance with the Military Technical Agreement between NATO and the then Federal Republic of Yugoslavia (now Serbia), while maintaining a safe and secure environment. Today, KFOR deters renewed hostilities and, with local authorities and international institutions, contributes to the maintenance of a safe and secure environment.

Currently, 24 NATO Allies contribute to KFOR. Eight non-NATO countries also participate by providing military and other support personnel. The United States contribution to KFOR is about 1,475 U.S. military personnel, or approximately 11 percent of the total strength of approximately 12,500 personnel. The United States forces participating in KFOR have been assigned to the eastern region of Kosovo, but also have operated in other areas of the country based on mission requirements. For U.S. KFOR forces, as for KFOR generally, helping to maintain a safe and secure environment and freedom of movement remain the principal military tasks. KFOR operates under NATO command and control and rules of engagement, and coordinates with and supports the European Union (EU)-led International Civilian Office and the EU Rule of Law Mission, within its means and capabilities. KFOR provides a security presence in towns, villages, and the countryside, and organizes checkpoints and patrols in key areas to provide security, to protect all segments of Kosovo's population, and to help instill a feeling of confidence across all ethnic communities throughout Kosovo. NATO periodically conducts formal reviews of KFOR's mission. These reviews provide a basis for assessing current force levels, future requirements, and recommendations for adjustments to KFOR's force structure and eventual withdrawal. NATO adopted the Joint Operations Area plan to regionalize and rationalize its force structure in the Balkans.

The Kosovo Police has primary responsibility for public safety and policing throughout Kosovo. KFOR also offers as-needed security assistance in response to civil unrest. KFOR augments security in particularly sensitive areas or in response to particular threats as events on the ground dictate.

In January 2009, the Government of Kosovo established the Kosovo Security Force (KSF). Separately, the Government of Kosovo began the process of dissolving the Kosovo Protection Corps (KPC). The KSF is a lightly armed, civilian-led security force that provides crisis response, explosive ordnance disposal, and civil protection. The newly formed Ministry for the Kosovo Security Force provides civilian oversight and control for the KSF. KFOR provides technical and policy guidance to the KSF and assists with recruiting for new members, chairing selection boards that identify former KPC members suitable for service in the

KSF, supervising NATO standard training programs for new recruits, and coordinating KSF equipment purchases and donations.

I have directed the participation of U.S. Armed Forces in all of these operations pursuant to my constitutional authority to conduct the foreign relations of the United States and as Commander in Chief and Chief Executive. Officials of my Administration and I communicate regularly with the leadership and other Members of Congress with regard to these deployments, and we will continue to do so.

Sincerely,
Barack Obama

[NSL p. 315. Insert before Notes and Questions.]

Senate Select Committee on Intelligence, Report on Whether Public Statements Regarding Iraq by U.S. Government Officials Were Substantiated by Intelligence Information
S. Rep. No. 110-345 (2008)
available at http://intelligence.senate.gov/pdfs/110345.pdf

[In June 2008, the Senate Select Committee on Intelligence issued its final report on the relationship between available intelligence and the Bush administration's public statements concerning justifications for the war in Iraq. The report, which runs 172 pages, and which includes fascinating details about the work of the intelligence agencies, is briefly excerpted here.]

I. Scope and Methodology

(U) This report's scope, as agreed to unanimously by the Committee on February 12, 2004, is to assess "whether public statements and reports and testimony regarding Iraq by U.S. Government officials made between the Gulf War period and the commencement of Operation Iraqi Freedom were substantiated by intelligence information."

(U) In order to complete this task, the Committee decided to concentrate its analysis on the statements that were central to the nation's decision to go to war. Specifically, the Committee chose to review five major policy speeches by key Administration officials regarding the threats posed by Iraq, Iraqi weapons of mass destruction programs, Iraqi ties to terrorist groups, and possible consequences of a US invasion of Iraq. . . .

(U) These speeches are the best representations of how the Bush Administration communicated intelligence analysis to the Congress, the American people, and the international community. They are also fairly comprehensive in scope, so evaluations about whether a particular statement in a speech was substantiated can be extrapolated to cover similar statements made at similar times. The Committee believes that these speeches would have been subject to careful review inside the White House and most were also reviewed by the intelligence community. . . .

(U) The Committee selected particular statements from these speeches that pertained to eight categories: nuclear weapons, biological weapons, chemical weapons, weapons of mass destruction (generally), methods of delivery, links to terrorism, regime intent, and assessments about the post-war situation in Iraq. The report is organized along these eight categories . . . .

(U) To conduct this review, the Committee assembled hundreds of intelligence reports produced prior to March 19, 2003 in an effort to understand the state of intelligence analysis at the time of various speeches and statements. . . .

(U) Furthermore, the Committee reviewed only finished analytic intelligence documents, with few exceptions. This did not include intelligence reports "from the field" or less formal communications between intelligence agencies and other parts of the Executive Branch.

(U) The Committee has attempted to note where disagreements existed within the Intelligence Community and where different reporting could substantiate different interpretations. . . .

(U) In addition to examining the question of whether public statements were substantiated by the underlying intelligence, the Committee's review also addressed the extent to which statements were incomplete and where relevant Intelligence Community assessments were not made part of the public discourse. A public statement that selectively uses only that intelligence that supports a particular policy position while ignoring or disregarding intelligence that either weakens or contradicts the position may be accurate on its face but present a slanted picture nonetheless. . . .

II. Nuclear Weapons

- "The Iraqi regime has in fact been very busy enhancing its capabilities in the field of chemical and biological agents. And they continue to pursue the nuclear program they began so many years ago." – *Vice President Richard Cheney, Nashville, Tennessee, August 26, 2002* . . .

- "But Saddam Hussein has defied all these efforts and continues to develop weapons of mass destruction. The first time we may be completely certain he has a – nuclear weapons is when, God forbids, he uses one." – *President George W. Bush, Address to the United Nations General Assembly, September 12, 2002* . . .

- "Facing clear evidence of peril we cannot wait for the final proof – the smoking gun – that could come in the form of a mushroom cloud." – *President George W. Bush, Cincinnati, Ohio, October 7, 2002* . . .

- "The British government has learned that Saddam Hussein recently sought significant quantities of uranium from Africa. Our intelligence sources tell us that he has attempted to purchase high-strength aluminum tubes suitable for nuclear weapons production." – *President George W. Bush, State of the Union Address, January 29, 2003*

- "We have no indication that Saddam Hussein has ever abandoned his nuclear weapons program. On the contrary, we have more than a decade of proof that he remains determined to acquire nuclear weapons." – *Secretary of State Colin Powell, Address to the United Nations Security Council, February 5, 2003* . . .

(U) In major policy speeches the President, the Vice President and the Secretary of State indicated that the Iraqi government had an active nuclear weapons program. The President and the Secretary of State both indicated that this nuclear weapons program had continued even while international weapons inspectors were in Iraq. . . .

(U) In the late 1990s and early 2000s, the intelligence community produced a number of coordinated assessments regarding possible Iraqi nuclear programs. These assessments consistently concluded that the

International Atomic Energy Agency (IAEA) and the United Nations Special Commission (UNSCO) had destroyed or neutralized Iraq's pre-Gulf War nuclear infrastructure, and that Iraq did not appear to have reconstituted its nuclear weapons program.

(U) These assessments were also consistent in assessing that Iraq had maintained some of the intellectual capital and physical infrastructure necessary for a nuclear weapons program, and that Iraq continued to procure "dual-use" technologies, with both nuclear and non-nuclear potential uses. They agreed that if Iraq decided to restart a nuclear weapons program, with proper foreign assistance it could produce enough fissile material for a nuclear weapon within five to seven years, and that if Iraq in some way acquired adequate fissile material from a foreign source, it could produce a nuclear weapon within one year. . . .

(U) The intelligence community's collective judgment that Iraq did not appear to have reconstituted its nuclear weapons program did not change until the publication of the October 2002 NIE on Iraqi WMD programs . . . . However, some individual agencies shifted their perspectives before this point. In April 2001, the CIA noted that Iraq's attempts to purchase high-strength aluminum tubes and other dual-use equipment suggested that a reconstitution effort might be underway. This judgment was included in several other CIA assessments. In August 2002 the CIA published a paper on Iraqi WMD capabilities . . . which concluded that these procurement activities indicated that the Iraqi government had restarted its nuclear weapons program.

(U) The Defense Intelligence Agency produced several similar assessments in 2002 . . . .

(U) The Department of Energy (DOE) disagreed with the CIA's conclusions regarding the aluminum tubes, and assessed that it was more likely that the tubes were intended for a different use, such as a conventional rocket program. . . .

(U) The Department of State's Bureau of Intelligence and Research (State/INR) disagreed with the CIA that Iraq had restarted a nuclear weapons program, and concurred with the DOE that the aluminum tubes were probably intended for other purposes. . . .

[Most of the analysis of public statements and intelligence concerning an Iraqi nuclear weapons program, along with similar analyses of other WMD programs, delivery systems, and links to terrorists, is omitted here.]

Conclusions

(U) **Conclusion 1**: Statements by the President, Vice President, Secretary of State and the National Security Advisor regarding a possible Iraqi nuclear weapons program were generally substantiated by intelligence community estimates, but did not convey the substantial disagreements that existed in the intelligence community. . . .

(U) **Conclusion 2**: Statements in the major speeches analyzed, as well as additional statements, regarding Iraq's possession of biological agent, weapons, production capability, and use of mobile biological laboratories were substantiated by intelligence information. Intelligence assessments from the late 1990s through early 2003 consistently stated that Iraq retained biological warfare agent and the capability to produce more. . . . Policymakers did not discuss intelligence gaps in Iraq's biological weapons programs, which were explicit in the October 2002 NIE. . . .

(U) **Conclusion 3**: Statements in the major speeches analyzed, as well additional statements, regarding Iraq's possession of chemical weapons were substantiated by intelligence information.

Intelligence assessments . . . stated that Iraq had retained up to 100 metric tons of its chemical weapons stockpile. The October 2002 NIE provided a range of 100 to 500 metric tons of chemical weapons.

(U) **Conclusion 4**: Statements by the President and Vice President prior to the October 2002 National Intelligence Estimate regarding Iraq's chemical weapons production capability and activities did not reflect the intelligence community's uncertainties as to whether such production was ongoing.

The intelligence community assessed that Saddam Hussein wanted to have chemical weapons production capability and that Iraq was seeking to hide such capability in its dual use chemical industry. Intelligence assessments, especially prior to the October 2002 NIE, clearly stated that analysts could not confirm that production was ongoing.

(U) **Conclusion 5**: Statements by the President, Vice President, Secretary of State and Secretary of Defense regarding Iraq's possession of weapons of mass destruction were generally substantiated by intelligence information, though many statements made regarding ongoing production prior to late 2002 reflected a higher level of certainty than the intelligence judgments themselves.

Many senior policymaker statements in early and mid-2002 claimed that there was no doubt that the Iraqi government possessed or was producing weapons of mass destruction. While the intelligence community assessed at this time that the Iraqi regime possessed some chemical and biological munitions, most reports produced prior to fall 2002 cited intelligence gaps regarding production and expressed room for doubt about whether production was ongoing. Prior to late 2002, the intelligence community did not collectively assess with any certainty that Iraq was actively producing any weapons of mass destruction. . . .

(U) **Conclusion 10**: Statements in the major speeches analyzed, as well additional statements, regarding Iraq's support for terrorist groups other than al-Qa'ida were substantiated by intelligence information.

The intelligence community reported regularly on Iraq's safe harbor and financial support for Palestinian rejectionist groups, the Abu Nidal Organization, and others. The February 2002 NIE fully supported the claim that Iraq had, and would continue, to support terrorist groups.

(U) **Conclusion 11**: Statements that Iraq provided safe haven for Abu Musab al-Zargawi and other al-Qa'ida-related terrorist members were substantiated by the intelligence assessments.

Intelligence assessments noted Zargawi's presence in Iraq and his ability to travel and operate within the country. . . .

(U) **Conclusion 12**: Statements and implications by the President and Secretary of State suggesting that Iraq and al-Qa'ida had a partnership, or that Iraq had provided al-Qa'ida with weapons training, were not substantiated by the intelligence.

Intelligence assessments, including multiple CIA reports and the November 2002 NIE, dismissed the claim that Iraq and al-Qa'ida were cooperating partners. . . .

(U) **Conclusion 15**: Statements by the President and the Vice President indicating that Saddam Hussein was prepared to give weapons of mass destruction to terrorist groups for attacks against the United States were contradicted by available intelligence information. . . . The October 2002 National Intelligence Estimate assessed that Saddam Hussein did not have nuclear weapons, and was unwilling to conduct terrorist attacks against the US using conventional, chemical or biological weapons at that time, in part because he feared that doing so would give the US a stronger case for war with Iraq. This judgment was echoed by both earlier and later intelligence community assessments. All of these assessments noted that gauging Saddam's intentions was quite difficult, and most suggested that he would be more likely to initiate hostilities if he felt that a US invasion was imminent. . . .

[Additional views of Senators Rockefeller, Feinstein, Feingold, Hagel, and Snowe are omitted.]

Minority Views of Vice Chairman Bond and Senators Chambliss, Hatch, and Burr

This majority-only written report by the Senate Intelligence Committee is a great disappointment to us and an unfortunate commentary on the political nature of intelligence oversight in the Congress today. . . . We have rarely seen such a poorly handled congressional investigation . . . .

. . . As the Committee's Phase I report showed, it was the intelligence that was faulty. In the cases in which the majority concluded that statements were not substantiated by intelligence or did not convey fully the intelligence community's analysis, it is clear that either the words of the policymakers in question or the body of intelligence available at the time were distorted in order to make these false charges. . . .

In the nuclear area, for example, the majority report's first conclusion notes that policymakers' statements about Iraq's nuclear activities were substantiated by intelligence, but the majority concludes that some statements did not convey disagreements that existed within the intelligence community. Many Democrats in Congress also discussed Iraq's nuclear efforts during the Iraq war debate and in other venues and similarly did not describe disagreements within the intelligence community. . . .

[Additional minority views of Senators Warner, Chambliss, Bond, Hatch, and Burr are omitted.]

[NSL p. 397. Replace Executive Order No. 12,333 with the following amended executive order.]

Executive Order No. 12,333
United States Intelligence Activities
(as amended by Executive Order Nos. 13,284 (2003),
13,355 (2004), and 13,470 (2008))
73 Fed. Reg. 45,325 (July 30, 2008)

Timely, insightful, and accurate information about the activities, capabilities, plans, and intentions of foreign powers, organizations, and persons and their agents, is essential to the national security of the United States. All reasonable and lawful means must be used to ensure that the United States will receive the best intelligence possible. For that purpose, by virtue of the authority vested in me by the Constitution and the laws of the United States of America, including the National Security Act of 1947, as amended, and as President of the United States of America, in order to provide for the effective conduct of United States intelligence activities and the protection of constitutional rights, it is hereby ordered as follows:

PART 1. *Goals, Directions, Duties, and Responsibilities with Respect to United States Intelligence Efforts*

1.1 *Goals.* The United States intelligence effort shall provide the President, the National Security Council, and the Homeland Security Council with the necessary information on which to base decisions concerning the development and conduct of foreign, defense, and economic policies, and the protection of United States national interests from foreign security threats. All departments and agencies shall cooperate fully to fulfill this goal.

(a) All means, consistent with applicable Federal law and this order, and with full consideration of the rights of United States persons, shall be used to obtain reliable intelligence information to protect the United States and its interests. . . .

(g) All departments and agencies have a responsibility to prepare and to provide intelligence in a manner that allows the full and free exchange of information, consistent with applicable law and presidential guidance.

1.2 *The National Security Council.*

(a) *Purpose.* The National Security Council (NSC) shall act as
the highest ranking executive branch entity that provides support to
the President for review of, guidance for, and direction to the
conduct of all foreign intelligence, counterintelligence, and covert
action, and attendant policies and programs.

(b) *Covert Action and Other Sensitive Intelligence Operations.*
The NSC shall consider and submit to the President a policy
recommendation, including all dissents, on each proposed covert
action and conduct a periodic review of ongoing covert action
activities, including an evaluation of the effectiveness and consistency with current national policy of such activities and consistency
with applicable legal requirements. The NSC shall perform such
other functions related to covert action as the President may direct,
but shall not undertake the conduct of covert actions. The NSC shall
also review proposals for other sensitive intelligence operations.

1.3 *Director of National Intelligence.* Subject to the authority,
direction, and control of the President, the Director of National Intelligence (Director) shall serve as the head of the Intelligence Community,
act as the principal adviser to the President, to the NSC, and to the
Homeland Security Council for intelligence matters related to national
security, and shall oversee and direct the implementation of the National
Intelligence Program and execution of the National Intelligence Program
budget. The Director will lead a unified, coordinated, and effective
intelligence effort. In addition, the Director shall, in carrying out the
duties and responsibilities under this section, take into account the views
of the heads of departments containing an element of the Intelligence
Community and of the Director of the Central Intelligence Agency.

(a) Except as otherwise directed by the President or prohibited by
law, the Director shall have access to all information and intelligence
described in section 1.5(a) of this order. For the purpose of access to
and sharing of information and intelligence, the Director: . . .

(2) Shall develop guidelines for how information or
intelligence is provided to or accessed by the Intelligence
Community in accordance with section 1.5(a) of this order, and
for how the information or intelligence may be used and shared
by the Intelligence Community. All guidelines developed in
accordance with this section shall be approved by the Attorney
General and, where applicable, shall be consistent with guidelines issued pursuant to section 1016 of the Intelligence Reform

and Terrorism Protection Act of 2004 (Public Law 108-458) (IRTPA).

(b) In addition to fulfilling the obligations and responsibilities prescribed by the Act, the Director:

(1) Shall establish objectives, priorities, and guidance for the Intelligence Community to ensure timely and effective collection, processing, analysis, and dissemination of intelligence, of whatever nature and from whatever source derived; . . .

(3) Shall oversee and provide advice to the President and the NSC with respect to all ongoing and proposed covert action programs;

(4) In regard to the establishment and conduct of intelligence arrangements and agreements with foreign governments and international organizations:

(A) May enter into intelligence and counterintelligence arrangements and agreements with foreign governments and international organizations;

(B) Shall formulate policies concerning intelligence and counterintelligence arrangements and agreements with foreign governments and international organizations; and

(C) Shall align and synchronize intelligence and counterintelligence foreign relationships among the elements of the Intelligence Community to further United States national security, policy, and intelligence objectives; . . .

(6) Shall establish common security and access standards for managing and handling intelligence systems, information, and products, with special emphasis on facilitating:

(A) The fullest and most prompt access to and dissemination of information and intelligence practicable, assigning the highest priority to detecting, preventing, preempting, and disrupting terrorist threats and activities against the United States, its interests, and allies; and

(B) The establishment of standards for an interoperable information sharing enterprise that facilitates the sharing of intelligence information among elements of the Intelligence Community;

(7) Shall ensure that appropriate departments and agencies have access to intelligence and receive the support needed to perform independent analysis;

(8) Shall protect, and ensure that programs are developed to protect, intelligence sources, methods, and activities from unauthorized disclosure;

(9) Shall, after consultation with the heads of affected departments and agencies, establish guidelines for Intelligence Community elements for:

(A) Classification and declassification of all intelligence and intelligence-related information classified under the authority of the Director or the authority of the head of a department or Intelligence Community element; . . .

(14) Shall have ultimate responsibility for production and dissemination of intelligence produced by the Intelligence Community and authority to levy analytic tasks on intelligence production organizations within the Intelligence Community, in consultation with the heads of the Intelligence Community elements concerned; . . .

(16) Shall ensure the timely exploitation and dissemination of data gathered by national intelligence collection means, and ensure that the resulting intelligence is disseminated immediately to appropriate government elements, including military commands;

(17) Shall determine requirements and priorities for, and manage and direct the tasking, collection, analysis, production, and dissemination of, national intelligence by elements of the Intelligence Community, including approving requirements for collection and analysis and resolving conflicts in collection requirements and in the tasking of national collection assets of Intelligence Community elements (except when otherwise directed by the President or when the Secretary of Defense exercises collection tasking authority under plans and arrangements approved by the Secretary of Defense and the Director); . . .

(20) Shall ensure, through appropriate policies and procedures, the deconfliction, coordination, and integration of all intelligence activities conducted by an Intelligence Community element or funded by the National Intelligence Program. In accordance with these policies and procedures:

(A) The Director of the Federal Bureau of Investigation shall coordinate the clandestine collection of foreign intelligence collected through human sources or through human-enabled means and counterintelligence activities inside the United States;

(B) The Director of the Central Intelligence Agency shall coordinate the clandestine collection of foreign intelligence collected through human sources or through human-enabled means and counterintelligence activities outside the United States;

(C) All policies and procedures for the coordination of counterintelligence activities and the clandestine collection of foreign intelligence inside the United States shall be subject to the approval of the Attorney General; and

(D) All policies and procedures developed under this section shall be coordinated with the heads of affected departments and Intelligence Community elements; . . .

(c) The Director's exercise of authorities in the Act and this order shall not abrogate the statutory or other responsibilities of the heads of departments of the United States Government or the Director of the Central Intelligence Agency. Directives issued and actions taken by the Director in the exercise of the Director's authorities and responsibilities to integrate, coordinate, and make the Intelligence Community more effective in providing intelligence related to national security shall be implemented by the elements of the Intelligence Community, provided that any department head whose department contains an element of the Intelligence Community and who believes that a directive or action of the Director violates the requirements of section 1018 of the IRTPA or this subsection shall bring the issue to the attention of the Director, the NSC, or the President for resolution in a manner that respects and does not abrogate the statutory responsibilities of the heads of the departments.

(d) Appointments to certain positions.

(1) The relevant department or bureau head shall provide recommendations and obtain the concurrence of the Director for the selection of: the Director of the National Security Agency, the Director of the National Reconnaissance Office, the Director of the National Geospatial-Intelligence Agency, the Under Secretary of Homeland Security for Intelligence and Analysis, the Assistant Secretary of State for Intelligence and Research, the Director of the Office of Intelligence and Counterintelligence of the Department of Energy, the Assistant Secretary for Intelligence and Analysis of the Department of the Treasury, and the Executive Assistant Director for the National Security Branch of the Federal Bureau of Investigation. If the Director

does not concur in the recommendation, the department head may not fill the vacancy or make the recommendation to the President, as the case may be. If the department head and the Director do not reach an agreement on the selection or recommendation, the Director and the department head concerned may advise the President directly of the Director's intention to withhold concurrence. . . .

(e) Removal from certain positions.

(1) Except for the Director of the Central Intelligence Agency, whose removal the Director may recommend to the President, the Director and the relevant department head shall consult on the removal, or recommendation to the President for removal, as the case may be, of: the Director of the National Security Agency, the Director of the National Geospatial-Intelligence Agency, the Director of the Defense Intelligence Agency, the Under Secretary of Homeland Security for Intelligence and Analysis, the Assistant Secretary of State for Intelligence and Research, and the Assistant Secretary for Intelligence and Analysis of the Department of the Treasury. If the Director and the department head do not agree on removal, or recommendation for removal, either may make a recommendation to the President for the removal of the individual. . . .

1.4. *The Intelligence Community.* Consistent with applicable Federal law and with the other provisions of this order, and under the leadership of the Director, as specified in such law and this order, the Intelligence Community shall:

(a) Collect and provide information needed by the President and, in the performance of executive functions, the Vice President, the NSC, the Homeland Security Council, the Chairman of the Joint Chiefs of Staff, senior military commanders, and other executive branch officials and, as appropriate, the Congress of the United States;

(b) In accordance with priorities set by the President, collect information concerning, and conduct activities to protect against, international terrorism, proliferation of weapons of mass destruction, intelligence activities directed against the United States, international criminal drug activities, and other hostile activities directed against the United States by foreign powers, organizations, persons, and their agents;

(c) Analyze, produce, and disseminate intelligence; . . .

(f) Protect the security of intelligence related activities, information, installations, property, and employees by appropriate means, including such investigations of applicants, employees, contractors, and other persons with similar associations with the Intelligence Community elements as are necessary; . . .

(i) Perform such other functions and duties related to intelligence activities as the President may direct.

1.5. *Duties and Responsibilities of the Heads of Executive Branch Departments and Agencies.* The heads of all departments and agencies shall:

(a) Provide the Director access to all information and intelligence relevant to the national security or that otherwise is required for the performance of the Director's duties, to include administrative and other appropriate management information, except such information excluded by law, by the President, or by the Attorney General acting under this order at the direction of the President;

(b) Provide all programmatic and budgetary information necessary to support the Director in developing the National Intelligence Program;

(c) Coordinate development and implementation of intelligence systems and architectures and, as appropriate, operational systems and architectures of their departments, agencies, and other elements with the Director to respond to national intelligence requirements and all applicable information sharing and security guidelines, information privacy, and other legal requirements; . . .

(f) Ensure that all elements within the department or agency comply with the provisions of Part 2 of this order, regardless of Intelligence Community affiliation, when performing foreign intelligence and counterintelligence functions; . . .

(h) Inform the Attorney General, either directly or through the Federal Bureau of Investigation, and the Director of clandestine collection of foreign intelligence and counterintelligence activities inside the United States not coordinated with the Federal Bureau of Investigation;

(i) Pursuant to arrangements developed by the head of the department or agency and the Director of the Central Intelligence Agency and approved by the Director, inform the Director and the Director of the Central Intelligence Agency, either directly or through his designee serving outside the United States, as appropriate, of clandestine collection of foreign intelligence collected through human sources or through human-enabled means outside the United States that has not been coordinated with the Central Intelligence Agency; . . .

1.6. *Heads of Elements of the Intelligence Community.* The heads of elements of the Intelligence Community shall:

    (a) Provide the Director access to all information and intelligence relevant to the national security or that otherwise is required for the performance of the Director's duties, to include administrative and other appropriate management information, except such information excluded by law, by the President, or by the Attorney General acting under this order at the direction of the President;

    (b) Report to the Attorney General possible violations of Federal criminal laws by employees and of specified Federal criminal laws by any other person as provided in procedures agreed upon by the Attorney General and the head of the department, agency, or establishment concerned, in a manner consistent with the protection of intelligence sources and methods, as specified in those procedures;

    (c) Report to the Intelligence Oversight Board, consistent with Executive Order 13462 of February 29, 2008, and provide copies of all such reports to the Director, concerning any intelligence activities of their elements that they have reason to believe may be unlawful or contrary to executive order or presidential directive;

    (d) Protect intelligence and intelligence sources, methods, and activities from unauthorized disclosure in accordance with guidance from the Director;

    (e) Facilitate, as appropriate, the sharing of information or intelligence, as directed by law or the President, to State, local, tribal, and private sector entities;

    (f) Disseminate information or intelligence to foreign governments and international organizations under intelligence or counterintelligence arrangements or agreements established in accordance with section 1.3(b)(4) of this order; . . .

    (h) Ensure that the inspectors general, general counsels, and agency officials responsible for privacy or civil liberties protection for their respective organizations have access to any information or intelligence necessary to perform their official duties.

1.7. *Intelligence Community Elements.* Each element of the Intelligence Community shall have the duties and responsibilities specified below, in addition to those specified by law or elsewhere in this order. Intelligence Community elements within executive departments shall serve the information and intelligence needs of their respective heads of departments and also shall operate as part of an integrated Intelligence Community, as provided in law or this order.

(a) The Central Intelligence Agency. The Director of the Central Intelligence Agency shall:

(1) Collect (including through clandestine means), analyze, produce, and disseminate foreign intelligence and counterintelligence;

(2) Conduct counterintelligence activities without assuming or performing any internal security functions within the United States;

(3) Conduct administrative and technical support activities within and outside the United States as necessary for cover and proprietary arrangements;

(4) Conduct covert action activities approved by the President. No agency except the Central Intelligence Agency (or the Armed Forces of the United States in time of war declared by the Congress or during any period covered by a report from the President to the Congress consistent with the War Powers Resolution, Public Law 93-148) may conduct any covert action activity unless the President determines that another agency is more likely to achieve a particular objective;

(5) Conduct foreign intelligence liaison relationships with intelligence or security services of foreign governments or international organizations consistent with section 1.3(b)(4) of this order;

(6) Under the direction and guidance of the Director, and in accordance with section 1.3(b)(4) of this order, coordinate the implementation of intelligence and counterintelligence relationships between elements of the Intelligence Community and the intelligence or security services of foreign governments or international organizations; and

(7) Perform such other functions and duties related to intelligence as the Director may direct. . . .

(c) The National Security Agency. The Director of the National Security Agency shall:

(1) Collect (including through clandestine means), process, analyze, produce, and disseminate signals intelligence informa-

tion and data for foreign intelligence and counterintelligence purposes to support national and departmental missions;

(2) Establish and operate an effective unified organization for signals intelligence activities, except for the delegation of operational control over certain operations that are conducted through other elements of the Intelligence Community. No other department or agency may engage in signals intelligence activities except pursuant to a delegation by the Secretary of Defense, after coordination with the Director;

(3) Control signals intelligence collection and processing activities, including assignment of resources to an appropriate agent for such periods and tasks as required for the direct support of military commanders;

(4) Conduct administrative and technical support activities within and outside the United States as necessary for cover arrangements;

(5) Provide signals intelligence support for national and departmental requirements and for the conduct of military operations; . . .

(g) Intelligence Elements of the Federal Bureau of Investigation. Under the supervision of the Attorney General and pursuant to such regulations as the Attorney General may establish, the intelligence elements of the Federal Bureau of Investigation shall:

(1) Collect (including through clandestine means), analyze, produce, and disseminate foreign intelligence and counterintelligence to support national and departmental missions, in accordance with procedural guidelines approved by the Attorney General, after consultation with the Director;

(2) Conduct counterintelligence activities; and

(3) Conduct foreign intelligence and counterintelligence liaison relationships with intelligence, security, and law enforcement services of foreign governments or international organizations in accordance with sections 1.3(b)(4) and 1.7(a)(6) of this order. . . .

(j) The Office of the Director of National Intelligence. The Director shall collect (overtly or through publicly available sources), analyze, produce, and disseminate information, intelligence, and counterintelligence to support the missions of the Office of the Director of National Intelligence, including the National Counterterrorism Center, and to support other national missions. . . .

1.10. *The Department of Defense.* The Secretary of Defense shall:

(a) Collect (including through clandestine means), analyze, produce, and disseminate information and intelligence and be responsive to collection tasking and advisory tasking by the Director;

(b) Collect (including through clandestine means), analyze, produce, and disseminate defense and defense related intelligence and counterintelligence, as required for execution of the Secretary's responsibilities;

(c) Conduct programs and missions necessary to fulfill national, departmental, and tactical intelligence requirements;

(d) Conduct counterintelligence activities in support of Department of Defense components and coordinate counterintelligence activities in accordance with section 1.3(b)(20) and (21) of this order;

(e) Act, in coordination with the Director, as the executive agent of the United States Government for signals intelligence activities; . . .

PART 2. *Conduct of Intelligence Activities* . . .

2.2. *Purpose.* . . . Set forth below are certain general principles that, in addition to and consistent with applicable laws, are intended to achieve the proper balance between the acquisition of essential information and protection of individual interests. Nothing in this Order shall be construed to apply to or interfere with any authorized civil or criminal law enforcement responsibility of any department or agency.

2.3. *Collection of Information.* Elements of the Intelligence Community are authorized to collect, retain or disseminate information concerning United States persons only in accordance with procedures established by the head of the Intelligence Community element concerned . . . and approved by the Attorney General . . . after consultation with the Director. Those procedures shall permit collection, retention, and dissemination of the following types of information: . . .

(b) Information constituting foreign intelligence or counterintelligence, including such information concerning corporations or other commercial organizations. Collection within the United States of foreign intelligence not otherwise obtainable shall be undertaken by the Federal Bureau of Investigation (FBI) or, when significant foreign intelligence is sought, by other authorized elements of the Intelligence Community, provided that no foreign intelligence collection by such elements may be undertaken for the purpose of acquiring information concerning the domestic activities of United States persons; . . .

(e) Information needed to protect foreign intelligence or counterintelligence sources, methods, and activities from unauthorized disclosure. Collection within the United States shall be undertaken by the FBI except that other elements of the Intelligence Community may also collect such information concerning present or former employees, present or former intelligence element contractors or their present or former employees, or applicants for such employment or contracting; . . .

2.4. *Collection Techniques.* Elements of the Intelligence Community shall use the least intrusive collection techniques feasible within the United States or directed against United States persons abroad. Elements of the Intelligence Community are not authorized to use such techniques as electronic surveillance, unconsented physical searches, mail surveillance, physical surveillance, or monitoring devices unless they are in accordance with procedures established by the head of the Intelligence Community element concerned or the head of a department containing such element and approved by the Attorney General, after consultation with the Director. Such procedures shall protect constitutional and other legal rights and limit use of such information to lawful governmental purposes. These procedures shall not authorize:

(a) The Central Intelligence Agency (CIA) to engage in electronic surveillance within the United States except for the purpose of training, testing, or conducting countermeasures to hostile electronic surveillance;

(b) Unconsented physical searches in the United States by elements of the Intelligence Community other than the FBI, except for:

(1) Searches by counterintelligence elements of the military services directed against military personnel within the United States or abroad for intelligence purposes, when authorized by a military commander empowered to approve physical searches for law enforcement purposes, based upon a finding of probable cause to believe that such persons are acting as agents of foreign powers; and

(2) Searches by CIA of personal property of non-United States persons lawfully in its possession;

(c) Physical surveillance of a United States person in the United States by elements of the Intelligence Community other than the FBI, except for:

(1) Physical surveillance of present or former employees, present or former intelligence element contractors or their present or former employees, or applicants for any such employment or contracting; and

(2) Physical surveillance of a military person employed by a non-intelligence element of a military service; and

(d) Physical surveillance of a United States person abroad to collect foreign intelligence, except to obtain significant information that cannot reasonably be acquired by other means.

2.5. *Attorney General Approval.* The Attorney General hereby is delegated the power to approve the use for intelligence purposes, within the United States or against a United States person abroad, of any technique for which a warrant would be required if undertaken for law enforcement purposes, provided that such techniques shall not be undertaken unless the Attorney General has determined in each case that there is probable cause to believe that the technique is directed against a foreign power or an agent of a foreign power. The authority delegated pursuant to this paragraph, including the authority to approve the use of electronic surveillance as defined in the Foreign Intelligence Surveillance Act of 1978, as amended, shall be exercised in accordance with that Act.

2.6. *Assistance to Law Enforcement and Other Civil Authorities.* Elements of the Intelligence Community are authorized to: . . .

(b) Unless otherwise precluded by law or this Order, participate in law enforcement activities to investigate or prevent clandestine intelligence activities by foreign powers, or international terrorist or narcotics activities; . . .

2.7. *Contracting.* Elements of the Intelligence Community are authorized to enter into contracts or arrangements for the provision of goods or services with private companies or institutions in the United States and need not reveal the sponsorship of such contracts or arrangements for authorized intelligence purposes. Contracts or arrangements with academic institutions may be undertaken only with the consent of appropriate officials of the institution.

2.8. *Consistency with Other Laws.* Nothing in this Order shall be construed to authorize any activity in violation of the Constitution or statutes of the United States.

2.9. *Undisclosed Participation in Organizations Within the United States.* No one acting on behalf of elements of the Intelligence Community may join or otherwise participate in any organization in the United States on behalf of any element within the Intelligence Community without disclosing such person's intelligence affiliation to appropriate officials of the organization, except in accordance with procedures established by the head of the Intelligence Community element concerned or the head of a department containing such element and approved by the Attorney General, after consultation with the Director. Such participation shall be authorized only if it is essential to achieving lawful purposes as determined by the Intelligence Community element head or designee. No such participation may be undertaken for the purpose of influencing the activity of the organization or its members except in cases where:

(a) The participation is undertaken on behalf of the FBI in the course of a lawful investigation; or

(b) The organization concerned is composed primarily of individuals who are not United States persons and is reasonably believed to be acting on behalf of a foreign power. . . .

2.11. *Prohibition on Assassination.* No person employed by or acting on behalf of the United States Government shall engage in, or conspire to engage in, assassination.

2.12. *Indirect Participation.* No element of the Intelligence Community shall participate in or request any person to undertake activities forbidden by this Order.

2.13. *Limitation on Covert Action.* No covert action may be conducted which is intended to influence United States political processes, public opinion, policies, or media.

PART 3. *General Provisions*

3.1. *Congressional Oversight.* The duties and responsibilities of the Director and the heads of other departments, agencies, elements, and entities engaged in intelligence activities to cooperate with the Congress in the conduct of its responsibilities for oversight of intelligence activities shall be implemented in accordance with applicable law, including title V of the [National Security Act of 1947, as amended]. The requirements of applicable law, including title V of the [National

Security Act of 1947, as amended], shall apply to all covert action
activities as defined in this Order. . . .

3.5. *Definitions.* For the purposes of this Order, the following terms
shall have these meanings:

(a) *Counterintelligence* means information gathered and
activities conducted to identify, deceive, exploit, disrupt, or protect
against espionage, other intelligence activities, sabotage, or
assassinations conducted for or on behalf of foreign powers,
organizations, or persons, or their agents, or international terrorist
organizations or activities.

(b) *Covert action* means an activity or activities of the United
States Government to influence political, economic, or military
conditions abroad, where it is intended that the role of the United
States Government will not be apparent or acknowledged publicly,
but does not include:

(1) Activities the primary purpose of which is to acquire
intelligence, traditional counterintelligence activities, traditional
activities to improve or maintain the operational security of
United States Government programs, or administrative activities;

(2) Traditional diplomatic or military activities or routine
support to such activities;

(3) Traditional law enforcement activities conducted by
United States Government law enforcement agencies or routine
support to such activities; or

(4) Activities to provide routine support to the overt
activities (other than activities described in paragraph (1), (2), or
(3)) of other United States Government agencies abroad.

(c) *Electronic surveillance* means acquisition of a nonpublic
communication by electronic means without the consent of a person
who is a party to an electronic communication or, in the case of a
nonelectronic communication, without the consent of a person who
is visibly present at the place of communication, but not including
the use of radio direction-finding equipment solely to determine the
location of a transmitter. . . .

(e) *Foreign intelligence* means information relating to the
capabilities, intentions, or activities of foreign governments or
elements thereof, foreign organizations, foreign persons, or
international terrorists.

(f) *Intelligence* includes foreign intelligence and counterintelligence.

(g) *Intelligence activities* means all activities that elements of the Intelligence Community are authorized to conduct pursuant to this order.

(h) *Intelligence Community* and agencies within the Intelligence Community refers to:

    (1) The Office of the Director of National Intelligence;

    (2) The Central Intelligence Agency;

    (3) The National Security Agency;

    (4) The Defense Intelligence Agency;

    (5) The National Geospatial-Intelligence Agency;

    (6) The National Reconnaissance Office;

    (7) The other offices within the Department of Defense for the collection of specialized national foreign intelligence through reconnaissance programs;

    (8) The intelligence and counterintelligence elements of the Army, the Navy, the Air Force, and the Marine Corps;

    (9) The intelligence elements of the Federal Bureau of Investigation;

    (10) The Office of National Security Intelligence of the Drug Enforcement Administration;

    (11) The Office of Intelligence and Counterintelligence of the Department of Energy;

    (12) The Bureau of Intelligence and Research of the Department of State;

    (13) The Office of Intelligence and Analysis of the Department of the Treasury;

    (14) The Office of Intelligence and Analysis of the Department of Homeland Security;

    (15) The intelligence and counterintelligence elements of the Coast Guard; and

    (16) Such other elements of any department or agency as may be designated by the President, or designated jointly by the Director and the head of the department or agency concerned, as an element of the Intelligence Community.

(i) *National Intelligence and Intelligence Related to National Security* means all intelligence, regardless of the source from which derived and including information gathered within or outside the United States, that pertains, as determined consistent with any guidance issued by the President, or that is determined for the purpose of access to information by the Director in accordance with section 1.3(a)(1) of this order, to pertain to more than one United

States Government agency; and that involves threats to the United States, its people, property, or interests; the development, proliferation, or use of weapons of mass destruction; or any other matter bearing on United States national or homeland security.

(j) *The National Intelligence Program* means all programs, projects, and activities of the Intelligence Community, as well as any other programs of the Intelligence Community designated jointly by the Director and the head of a United States department or agency or by the President. Such term does not include programs, projects, or activities of the military departments to acquire intelligence solely for the planning and conduct of tactical military operations by United States Armed Forces. . . .

NOTES AND QUESTIONS

[NSL p. 400. Replace the introductory paragraph to Notes and Questions with the following material.]

The July 30, 2008, amendment to Executive Order No. 12,333 made many significant revisions to the original Reagan order that require changes to the cross-references in some of the following notes and questions, as well as some changes to the answers. Nevertheless, questions concerning the evolution of the order and the control over the intelligence community that it asserts remain valid and relevant and have therefore been retained. References to the "Reagan order" should simply be read as references to amended Executive Order 12,333, except where the supplemental material refers to the "original Reagan order."

Preamble language typically sets forth the presumed authority for the prescriptions that follow. Precisely what constitutional or statutory authority empowered the President to promulgate this executive order?

[NSL p. 402. Add "DNI" to the entities listed in Note 2.]

[NSL p. 402. In Note 3, replace "§3.4(h)" with "§3.5(b)," and replace the second paragraph of the Note with the following material.]

The Ford and Carter executive orders, unlike the original Reagan order, formally included the Justice Department in the covert action decision-making process. What role, if any, is assigned the Attorney General in covert action approval by the amended order? What other provisions does it make for lawyers to participate in the intelligence activities it addresses? Does their involvement really matter if the President is free to ignore their advice?

[NSL p. 403. Delete Note 1.]

[NSL p. 403. Replace the text of Note 4 with the following material.]

Section 1.7(a)(3) of the amended order provides that the CIA may "conduct administrative and technical support activities within and outside the United States as necessary for cover and proprietary arrangements." What kinds of activities does this provision contemplate?

[NSL p. 403. Replace the text of Note 5 with the following material.]

The original Reagan order listed seven entities in the "intelligence community." The amended order now lists fifteen. §3.5(h). Some have simply been renamed or subdivided in the re-organization of the community. Others are new, however, or have been assigned expanded roles that merit their identification as parts of the community. Is the list broad enough to cover all entities conducting intelligence activities? Do you think that the apparent expansion of the intelligence community is permanent, or merely a transient by-product of the war on terrorism? Is the apparent expansion likely to improve the community's performance? Or enhance the likelihood that its activities will comply with U.S. law or American principles?

[NSL p. 404. Replace the text of Note 6 with the following material.]

Look closely at §3.5(b). Does it provide a clear and workable definition of covert action? How would you synthesize the criteria the entire amended order sets out for the approval of covert action? Does any problematic covert activity escape the definition or the criteria?

[NSL p. 410. Replace the text of Note 1 with the following material.]

The original Reagan order stated that only the CIA could conduct "special" (i.e., covert) activities unless the President determined that "another agency is more likely to achieve a particular objective." Could the NSC legitimately have carried out the arms sales and Contra supply missions without such a presidential determination? Do you see any

practical difference in the language of §1.7(a)(4) of the order as amended
in 2008? What is the effect of §1.2(b) of the amended order?

**[NSL p. 444. Replace the excerpt of Executive Order No. 12,333 with
§1.7(c) of the amended order, reproduced *supra* p. 17.]**

[NSL p. 556, CTL p. 174. Add the following decision after Note 9.]

In re Directives [Redacted Text]* Pursuant to Section 105B of the Foreign Intelligence Surveillance Act

Foreign Intelligence Surveillance Court of Review, 2008
551 F.3d 1004

[After a FISC judge decided in May 2007 not to continue approval of
what had been the TSP under FISC supervision, the Bush administration
urged Congress to pass statutory authorization for its program. In
August 2007, Congress enacted the Protect America Act, Pub. L. No.
110-55, 121 Stat. 552, which permitted the DNI and the Attorney
General to authorize collection of foreign intelligence concerning
persons reasonably believed to be outside the United States, without
obtaining an order from the FISC, even if one party to the communication was a U.S. citizen inside the United States. The Protect America
Act expired by its own terms in February 2008, leading to the enactment
on July 10, 2008, of the FISA Amendments Act, referred to in this
decision and excerpted below. This decision was rendered on August 22,
2008, but only published in redacted form on January 12, 2009.]

SELYA, Chief Judge. This petition for review stems from directives
issued to the petitioner [redacted text] pursuant to a now-expired set of
amendments to the Foreign Intelligence Surveillance Act of 1978
(FISA), [50 U.S.C.A. §§1801-1871 (West 2003 & Supp. 2008)]. Among
other things, those amendments, known as the Protect America Act of
2007 (PAA), Pub. L. No. 110-55, 121 Stat. 552, authorized the United
States to direct communications service providers to assist it in acquiring
foreign intelligence when those acquisitions targeted third persons (such
as the service provider's customers) reasonably believed to be located

---

* The text and footnotes that have been redacted from this opinion contain
classified information.

outside the United States. Having received [redacted text] such
directives, the petitioner challenged their legality before the Foreign
Intelligence Surveillance Court (FISC). When that court found the
directives lawful and compelled obedience to them, the petitioner
brought this petition for review. . . .

I. THE STATUTORY FRAMEWORK

On August 5, 2007, Congress enacted the PAA, codified in pertinent
part at 50 U.S.C. §§1805a to 1805c, as a measured expansion of FISA's
scope. Subject to certain conditions, the PAA allowed the government to
conduct warrantless foreign intelligence surveillance on targets
(including United States persons) "reasonably believed" to be located
outside the United States.[1] 50 U.S.C. §1805b(a). This proviso is of
critical importance here.

Under the new statute, the Director of National Intelligence (DNI)
and the Attorney General (AG) were permitted to authorize, for periods
of up to one year, "the acquisition of foreign intelligence information
concerning persons reasonably believed to be outside the United States"
if they determined that the acquisition met five specified criteria. *Id.*
These criteria included (i) that reasonable procedures were in place to
ensure that the targeted person was reasonably believed to be located
outside the United States; (ii) that the acquisitions did not constitute
electronic surveillance;[2] (iii) that the surveillance would involve the
assistance of a communications service provider; (iv) that a significant
purpose of the surveillance was to obtain foreign intelligence
information; and (v) that minimization procedures in place met the
requirements of 50 U.S.C. §1801(h). *Id.* §1805b(a)(1)-(5). Except in
limited circumstances (not relevant here), this multi-part determination
was required to be made in the form of a written certification "supported
as appropriate by affidavit of appropriate officials in the national security
field." *Id.* §1805b(a). Pursuant to this authorization, the DNI and the
AG were allowed to issue directives to "person[s]"—a term that includes

---

1. We refer to the PAA in the past tense because its provisions expired on
February 16, 2008.

2. The PAA specifically stated, however, that "[n]othing in the definition of
electronic surveillance . . . shall be construed to encompass surveillance directed
at a person reasonably believed to be located outside of the United States." 50
U.S.C. §1805a.

agents of communications service providers—delineating the assistance
needed to acquire the information. *Id.* §1805b(e); *see id.*§1805b(a)(3).

The PAA was a stopgap measure. By its terms, it sunset[ted] on
February 16, 2008. Following a lengthy interregnum, the lapsed
provisions were repealed on July 10, 2008, through the instrumentality of
the FISA Amendments Act of 2008, Pub. L. No. 110-261, §403, 122
Stat. 2436, 2473 (2008). But because the certifications and directives
involved in the instant case were issued during the short shelf life of the
PAA, they remained in effect. *See* FISA Amendments Act of 2008
§404(a)(1). We therefore assess the validity of the actions at issue here
through the prism of the PAA.

[redacted text]

II. BACKGROUND

Beginning in [redacted text] 2007, the government issued directives
to the petitioner commanding it to assist in warrantless surveillance of
certain customers [redacted text and footnote]. These directives were
issued pursuant to certifications that purported to contain all the
information required by the PAA.

The certifications require certain protections above and beyond those
specified by the PAA. For example, they require the AG and the
National Security Agency (NSA) to follow the procedures set out under
Executive Order 12333 §2.5, 46 Fed. Reg. 59,941, 59,951 (Dec. 4,
1981), before any surveillance is undertaken. Moreover, affidavits
supporting the certifications spell out additional safeguards to be
employed in effecting the acquisitions. This last set of classified
procedures has not been included in the information transmitted to the
petitioner. In essence, as implemented, the certifications permit
surveillances conducted to obtain foreign intelligence for national
security purposes when those surveillances are directed against foreign
powers or agents of foreign powers reasonably believed to be located
outside the United States.

The . . . petitioner . . . refused to comply with the directives. On
[redacted text], the government moved to compel compliance.
Following amplitudinous briefing, the FISC handed down a meticulous
opinion validating the directives and granting the motion to compel. . . .

III. ANALYSIS . . .

B. *The Fourth Amendment Challenge.* . . .

The petitioner's remonstrance has two main branches. First, it
asserts that the government, in issuing the directives, had to abide by the
requirements attendant to the Warrant Clause of the Fourth Amendment.
Second, it argues that even if a foreign intelligence exception to the
warrant requirements exists and excuses compliance with the Warrant
Clause, the surveillances mandated by the directives are unreasonable
and, therefore, violate the Fourth Amendment. The petitioner limits each
of its claims to the harm that may be inflicted upon United States
persons.

1. *The Nature of the Challenge.*

As a threshold matter, the petitioner asserts that its Fourth
Amendment arguments add up to a facial challenge to the PAA. The
government contests this characterization, asserting that the petitioner
presents only an as-applied challenge. We agree with the government. . . .

We . . . deem the petitioner's challenge an as-applied challenge and
limit our analysis accordingly. This means that, to succeed, the
petitioner must prove more than a theoretical risk that the PAA could on
certain facts yield unconstitutional applications. Instead, it must
persuade us that the PAA is unconstitutional as implemented here.

2. *The Foreign Intelligence Exception.*

The recurrent theme permeating the petitioner's arguments is the
notion that there is no foreign intelligence exception to the Fourth
Amendment's Warrant Clause. The FISC rejected this notion, positing
that our decision in *In re Sealed Case* [310 F.3d 717, 721 (FISA Ct. Rev.
2002)] confirmed the existence of a foreign intelligence exception to the
warrant requirement.

While the *Sealed Case* court avoided an express holding that a
foreign intelligence exception exists by assuming arguendo that whether
or not the warrant requirements were met, the statute could survive on
reasonableness grounds, *see* 310 F.3d at 741-42, we believe that the
FISC's reading of that decision is plausible.

The petitioner argues correctly that the Supreme Court has not
explicitly recognized such an exception; indeed, the Court reserved that

question in *United States v. United States District Court (Keith)*, 407 U.S. 297, 308-09 (1972). But the Court has recognized a comparable exception, outside the foreign intelligence context, in so-called "special needs" cases. In those cases, the Court excused compliance with the Warrant Clause when the purpose behind the governmental action went beyond routine law enforcement and insisting upon a warrant would materially interfere with the accomplishment of that purpose. *See, e.g., Vernonia Sch. Dist. 47J v. Acton*, 515 U.S. 646, 653 (1995) (upholding drug testing of high-school athletes and explaining that the exception to the warrant requirement applied "when special needs, beyond the normal need for law enforcement, make the warrant and probable-cause requirement[s] impracticable" (quoting *Griffin v. Wisconsin*, 483 U.S. 868, 873 (1987))); *Skinner v. Ry. Labor Execs. Ass'n*, 489 U.S. 602, 620 (1989) (upholding regulations instituting drug and alcohol testing of railroad workers for safety reasons); *cf. Terry v. Ohio*, 392 U.S. 1, 23-24 (1968) (upholding pat-frisk for weapons to protect officer safety during investigatory stop).

The question, then, is whether the reasoning of the special needs cases applies by analogy to justify a foreign intelligence exception to the warrant requirement for surveillance undertaken for national security purposes and directed at a foreign power or an agent of a foreign power reasonably believed to be located outside the United States. Applying principles derived from the special needs cases, we conclude that this type of foreign intelligence surveillance possesses characteristics that qualify it for such an exception.

For one thing, the purpose behind the surveillances ordered pursuant to the directives goes well beyond any garden-variety law enforcement objective. It involves the acquisition from overseas foreign agents of foreign intelligence to help protect national security. Moreover, this is the sort of situation in which the government's interest is particularly intense.

The petitioner has a fallback position. Even if there is a narrow foreign intelligence exception, it asseverates, a definition of that exception should require the foreign intelligence purpose to be the primary purpose of the surveillance. For that proposition, it cites the Fourth Circuit's decision in *United States v. Truong Dinh Hung*, 629 F.2d 908, 915 (4th Cir. 1980). That dog will not hunt.

This court previously has upheld as reasonable under the Fourth Amendment the Patriot Act's substitution of "a significant purpose" for the talismanic phrase "primary purpose." . . . In our view the more appropriate consideration is the programmatic purpose of the surveillances and whether—as in the special needs cases—that programmatic purpose involves some legitimate objective beyond ordinary crime control.

Under this analysis, the surveillances authorized by the directives easily pass muster. Their stated purpose centers on garnering foreign intelligence. There is no indication that the collections of information are primarily related to ordinary criminal-law enforcement purposes. Without something more than a purely speculative set of imaginings, we cannot infer that the purpose of the directives (and, thus, of the surveillances) is other than their stated purpose.

We add, moreover, that there is a high degree of probability that requiring a warrant would hinder the government's ability to collect time-sensitive information and, thus, would impede the vital national security interests that are at stake. *See, e.g., Truong Dinh Hung,* 629 F.2d at 915 (explaining that when the object of a surveillance is a foreign power or its collaborators, "the government has the greatest need for speed, stealth, and secrecy"). [redacted text] Compulsory compliance with the warrant requirement would introduce an element of delay, thus frustrating the government's ability to collect information in a timely manner. [redacted text]

For these reasons, we hold that a foreign intelligence exception to the Fourth Amendment's warrant requirement exists when surveillance is conducted to obtain foreign intelligence for national security purposes and is directed against foreign powers or agents of foreign powers reasonably believed to be located outside the United States.

3. *Reasonableness.*

This holding does not grant the government carte blanche: even though the foreign intelligence exception applies in a given case, governmental action intruding on individual privacy interests must comport with the Fourth Amendment's reasonableness requirement. Thus, the question here reduces to whether the PAA, as applied through the directives, constitutes a sufficiently reasonable exercise of governmental power to satisfy the Fourth Amendment.

. . . To determine the reasonableness of a particular governmental action, an inquiring court must consider the totality of the circumstances. *Samson v. California,* 547 U.S. 843, 848 (2006); *Tennessee v. Garner,* 471 U.S. 1, 8-9 (1985). This mode of approach takes into account the nature of the government intrusion and how the intrusion is implemented. The more important the government's interest, the greater the intrusion that may be constitutionally tolerated.

The totality of the circumstances model requires the court to balance the interests at stake. If the protections that are in place for individual privacy interests are sufficient in light of the governmental interest at stake, the constitutional scales will tilt in favor of upholding the government's actions. If, however, those protections are insufficient to alleviate the risks of government error and abuse, the scales will tip toward a finding of unconstitutionality.

Here, the relevant governmental interest—the interest in national security—is of the highest order of magnitude. See Haig v. Agee, 453 U.S. 280, 307 (1981); In re Sealed Case, 310 F.3d at 746. Consequently, we must determine whether the protections afforded to the privacy rights of targeted persons are reasonable in light of this important interest.

At the outset, we dispose of two straw men—arguments based on a misreading of our prior decision in Sealed Case. First, the petitioner notes that we found relevant six factors contributing to the protection of individual privacy in the face of a governmental intrusion for national security purposes. See In re Sealed Case, 310 F.3d at 737-41 (contemplating prior judicial review, presence or absence of probable cause, particularity, necessity, duration, and minimization). On that exiguous basis, it reasons that our decision there requires a more rigorous standard for gauging reasonableness.

This is a mistaken judgment. In Sealed Case, we did not formulate a rigid six-factor test for reasonableness. That would be at odds with the totality of the circumstances test that must guide an analysis in the precincts patrolled by the Fourth Amendment. We merely indicated that the six enumerated factors were relevant under the circumstances of that case.

Second, the petitioner asserts that our Sealed Case decision stands for the proposition that, in order to gain constitutional approval, the PAA procedures must contain protections equivalent to the three principal warrant requirements: prior judicial review, probable cause, and particularity. That is incorrect. What we said there—and reiterate today—is that the more a set of procedures resembles those associated with the traditional warrant requirements, the more easily it can be determined that those procedures are within constitutional bounds. We therefore decline the petitioner's invitation to reincorporate into the foreign intelligence exception the same warrant requirements that we already have held inapplicable.

Having placed *Sealed Case* into perspective, we turn to the
petitioner's contention that the totality of the circumstances demands a
finding of unreasonableness here. That contention boils down to the idea
that the protections afforded under the PAA are insufficiently analogous
to the protections deemed adequate in *Sealed Case* because the PAA
lacks (i) a particularity requirement, (ii) a prior judicial review
requirement for determining probable cause that a target is a foreign
power or an agent of a foreign power, and (iii) any plausible proxies for
the omitted protections. For good measure, the petitioner suggests that
the PAA's lack of either a necessity requirement or a reasonable
durational limit diminishes the overall reasonableness of surveillances
conducted pursuant thereto.

The government rejoins that the PAA, as applied here, constitutes
reasonable governmental action. It emphasizes both the protections
spelled out in the PAA itself and those mandated under the certifications
and directives. This matrix of safeguards comprises at least five
components: targeting procedures, minimization procedures, a procedure
to ensure that a significant purpose of a surveillance is to obtain foreign
intelligence information, procedures incorporated through Executive
Order 12333 §2.5, and [redacted text] procedures [redacted text] outlined
in an affidavit supporting the certifications.

The record supports the government. Notwithstanding the parade of
horribles trotted out by the petitioner, it has presented no evidence of any
actual harm, any egregious risk of error, or any broad potential for abuse
in the circumstances of the instant case. Thus, assessing the intrusions at
issue in light of the governmental interest at stake and the panoply of
protections that are in place, we discern no principled basis for
invalidating the PAA as applied here. In the pages that follow, we
explain our reasoning.

The petitioner's arguments about particularity and prior judicial
review are defeated by the way in which the statute has been applied.
When combined with the PAA's other protections, the [redacted text]
procedures and the procedures incorporated through the Executive Order
are constitutionally sufficient compensation for any encroachments.

The [redacted text] procedures [redacted text] are delineated in an ex
parte appendix filed by the government. They also are described, albeit
with greater generality, in the government's brief. [redacted text]
Although the PAA itself does not mandate a showing of particularity, *see*
50 U.S.C. §1805b(b), this pre-surveillance procedure strikes us as
analogous to and in conformity with the particularity showing
contemplated by *Sealed Case*. 310 F.3d at 740. [redacted text]

The procedures incorporated through section 2.5 of Executive Order 12333, made applicable to the surveillances through the certifications and directives, serve to allay the probable cause concern. That section states in relevant part:

> The Attorney General hereby is delegated the power to approve the use for intelligence purposes, within the United States or against a United States person abroad, of any technique for which a warrant would be required if undertaken for law enforcement purposes, provided that such techniques shall not be undertaken unless the Attorney General has determined in each case that there is *probable cause* to believe that the technique is directed against *a foreign power or an agent of a foreign power.*

46 Fed. Reg. at 59,951 (emphasis supplied). Thus, in order for the government to act upon the certifications, the AG first had to make a determination that probable cause existed to believe that the targeted person is a foreign power or an agent of a foreign power. Moreover, this determination was not made in a vacuum. The AG's decision was informed by the contents of an application made pursuant to Department of Defense (DOD) regulations. *See* DOD, Procedures Governing the Activities of DOD Intelligence Components that Affect United States Persons, DOD 5240.1-R, Proc. 5, Pt. 2.C (Dec.1982). Those regulations required that the application include a statement of facts demonstrating both probable cause and necessity. *See id.* They also required a statement of the period—not to exceed 90 days—during which the surveillance was thought to be required.[7] *See id.*

[redacted text and footnote]

The petitioner's additional criticisms about the surveillances can be grouped into concerns about potential abuse of executive discretion and concerns about the risk of government error (including inadvertent or incidental collection of information from non-targeted United States persons). We address these groups of criticisms sequentially.

The petitioner suggests that, by placing discretion entirely in the hands of the Executive Branch without prior judicial involvement, the

---

7. At oral argument, the government augmented this description, stating that, under the DOD procedure, the NSA typically provides the AG with a two-to-three-page submission articulating the facts underlying the determination that the person in question is an agent of a foreign power; that the National Security Division of the Department of Justice writes its own memorandum to the AG; and that an oral briefing of the AG ensues.

procedures cede to that Branch overly broad power that invites abuse. But this is little more than a lament about the risk that government officials will not operate in good faith. That sort of risk exists even when a warrant is required. In the absence of a showing of fraud or other misconduct by the affiant, the prosecutor, or the judge, a presumption of regularity traditionally attaches to the obtaining of a warrant.

Here—where an exception affords relief from the warrant requirement—common sense suggests that we import the same presumption. Once we have determined that protections sufficient to meet the Fourth Amendment's reasonableness requirement are in place, there is no justification for assuming, in the absence of evidence to that effect, that those prophylactic procedures have been implemented in bad faith.

Similarly, the fact that there is some potential for error is not a sufficient reason to invalidate the surveillances. [redacted text]

Equally as important, some risk of error exists under the original FISA procedures—procedures that received our imprimatur in *Sealed Case,* 310 F.3d at 746. A prior judicial review process does not ensure that the types of errors complained of here [redacted text] would have been prevented.

It is also significant that effective minimization procedures are in place. These procedures serve as an additional backstop against identification errors as well as a means of reducing the impact of incidental intrusions into the privacy of non-targeted United States persons. The minimization procedures implemented here are almost identical to those used under FISA to ensure the curtailment of both mistaken and incidental acquisitions. These minimization procedures were upheld by the FISC in this case, and the petitioner stated at oral argument that it is not quarreling about minimization but, rather, about particularity. Thus, we see no reason to question the adequacy of the minimization protocol.

The petitioner's concern with incidental collections is overblown. It is settled beyond peradventure that incidental collections occurring as a result of constitutionally permissible acquisitions do not render those acquisitions unlawful. *See, e.g., United States v. Kahn,* 415 U.S. 143, 157-58, (1974). The government assures us that it does not maintain a database of incidentally collected information from non-targeted United States persons, and there is no evidence to the contrary. On these facts, incidentally collected communications of non-targeted United States persons do not violate the Fourth Amendment.

To the extent that the petitioner may be concerned about the adequacy of the targeting procedures, it is worth noting that those procedures include provisions designed to prevent errors. [redacted text] Furthermore, a PAA provision codified at 50 U.S.C. §1805b(d) requires the AG and the DNI to assess compliance with those procedures and to report to Congress semi-annually.

4. *A Parting Shot.*

The petitioner fires a parting shot. It presented for the first time at oral argument a specific privacy concern that could possibly arise under the directives. This parting shot may have been waived by the failure to urge it either before the FISC or in the petitioner's pre-argument filings in this court. We need not probe that point, however, because the petitioner is firing blanks: no issue falling within this description has arisen to date. Were such an issue to arise, there are safeguards in place that may meet the reasonableness standard. We do, however, direct the government promptly to notify the petitioner if this issue arises under the directives.

The foregoing paragraph is a summary of our holding on this issue. We discuss with greater specificity the petitioner's argument, the government's safeguards, and our order in the classified version of this opinion.

5. *Recapitulation.*

After assessing the prophylactic procedures applicable here, including the provisions of the PAA, the affidavits supporting the certifications, section 2.5 of Executive Order 12333, and the declaration mentioned above, we conclude that they are very much in tune with the considerations discussed in *Sealed Case.* Collectively, these procedures require a showing of particularity, a meaningful probable cause determination, and a showing of necessity. They also require a durational limit not to exceed 90 days—an interval that we previously found reasonable.[11] *See In re Sealed Case,* 310 F.3d at 740. Finally, the

---

11. This time period was deemed acceptable because of the use of continuing minimization procedures. *In re Sealed Case,* 310 F.3d at 740. Those minimization procedures are nearly identical to the minimization procedures employed in this case. *See* text *supra.*

risks of error and abuse are within acceptable limits and effective minimization procedures are in place.

Balancing these findings against the vital nature of the government's national security interest and the manner of the intrusion, we hold that the surveillances at issue satisfy the Fourth Amendment's reasonableness requirement.

IV. CONCLUSION

Our government is tasked with protecting an interest of utmost significance to the nation—the safety and security of its people. But the Constitution is the cornerstone of our freedoms, and government cannot unilaterally sacrifice constitutional rights on the altar of national security. Thus, in carrying out its national security mission, the government must simultaneously fulfill its constitutional responsibility to provide reasonable protections for the privacy of United States persons. The judiciary's duty is to hold that delicate balance steady and true.

We believe that our decision to uphold the PAA as applied in this case comports with that solemn obligation. In that regard, we caution that our decision does not constitute an endorsement of broad-based, indiscriminate executive power. Rather, our decision recognizes that where the government has instituted several layers of serviceable safeguards to protect individuals against unwarranted harms and to minimize incidental intrusions, its efforts to protect national security should not be frustrated by the courts. This is such a case.

We need go no further. The decision granting the government's motion to compel is affirmed; the petition for review is denied and dismissed; and the motion for a stay is denied as moot.

So Ordered.

ORDER

Whereas,

1. An opinion that addresses and resolves issues of statutory and constitutional significance has been filed under seal;

2. It would serve the public interest and the orderly administration of justice to publish this opinion;

3. Publication of an unredacted opinion would disclose materials that have been properly classified by the Executive Branch;

4. Redactions, after consultation with the Executive Branch, can be made to exclude such classified materials without distorting the content of the discussion of the statutory and constitutional issues;

5. Such redactions have been made by the Court;

It Is Hereby Ordered that:

1. The redacted opinion shall be published . . . .

2. Notwithstanding the publication of the redacted opinion, the parties and their counsel, and any agent of, or other person(s) working in concert with, any party or counsel, shall continue to handle and safeguard all classified information pertaining to this case in accordance with applicable security requirements and regulations and applicable orders issued by this Court or the FISC. . . .

[NSL p. 556, CTL p. 174. Insert after *In re Directives [Redacted Text].*]

FISA Amendments Act of 2008
Pub. L. No. 110-261, 122 Stat. 2436

[Section 101 of the 2008 Act struck Title VII of FISA as it existed (containing the expired Protect America Act), and added the following new Title VII:]

TITLE VII – ADDITIONAL PROCEDURES REGARDING CERTAIN PERSONS OUTSIDE THE UNITED STATES. . . .

§702. Procedures for Targeting Certain Persons Outside the United States Other than United States Persons.

(a) Authorization – Notwithstanding any other provision of law, upon the issuance of an order in accordance with subsection (i)(3) or a determination under subsection (c)(2), the Attorney General and the Director of National Intelligence may authorize jointly, for a period of up to 1 year from the effective date of the authorization, the targeting of persons reasonably believed to be located outside the United States to acquire foreign intelligence information.

(b) Limitations – An acquisition authorized under subsection (a) –

(1) may not intentionally target any person known at the time of acquisition to be located in the United States;

(2) may not intentionally target a person reasonably believed to be located outside the United States if the purpose of such acquisition is to target a particular, known person reasonably believed to be in the United States;

(3) may not intentionally target a United States person reasonably believed to be located outside the United States;

(4) may not intentionally acquire any communication as to which the sender and all intended recipients are known at the time of the acquisition to be located in the United States; and

(5) shall be conducted in a manner consistent with the fourth amendment to the Constitution of the United States.

(c) Conduct of Acquisition –

(1) In General – An acquisition authorized under subsection (a) shall be conducted only in accordance with –

(A) the targeting and minimization procedures adopted in accordance with subsections (d) and (e); and

(B) upon submission of a certification in accordance with subsection (g), such certification.

(2) Determination – A determination under this paragraph and for purposes of subsection (a) is a determination by the Attorney General and the Director of National Intelligence that exigent circumstances exist because, without immediate implementation of an authorization under subsection (a), intelligence important to the national security of the United States may be lost or not timely acquired and time does not permit the issuance of an order pursuant to subsection (i)(3) prior to the implementation of such authorization. . . .

(4) Construction – Nothing in title I shall be construed to require an application for a court order under such title for an acquisition that is targeted in accordance with this section at a person reasonably believed to be located outside the United States.

(d) Targeting Procedures –

(1) Requirement to Adopt – The Attorney General, in consultation with the Director of National Intelligence, shall adopt targeting procedures that are reasonably designed to –

(A) ensure that any acquisition authorized under subsection (a) is limited to targeting persons reasonably believed to be located outside the United States; and

(B) prevent the intentional acquisition of any communication as to which the sender and all intended recipients are known at the time of the acquisition to be located in the United States.

(2) Judicial Review – The procedures adopted in accordance with paragraph (1) shall be subject to judicial review pursuant to subsection (i).

(e) Minimization Procedures –

(1) Requirement to Adopt – The Attorney General, in consultation with the Director of National Intelligence, shall adopt minimization procedures that meet the definition of minimization procedures under section 101(h) or 301(4), as appropriate, for acquisitions authorized under subsection (a).

(2) Judicial Review – The minimization procedures adopted in accordance with paragraph (1) shall be subject to judicial review pursuant to subsection (i).

(f) Guidelines for Compliance with Limitations –

(1) Requirement to Adopt – The Attorney General, in consultation with the Director of National Intelligence, shall adopt guidelines to ensure –

(A) compliance with the limitations in subsection (b); and

(B) that an application for a court order is filed as required by this Act.

(2) Submission of Guidelines – The Attorney General shall provide the guidelines adopted in accordance with paragraph (1) to –

(A) the congressional intelligence committees;

(B) the Committees on the Judiciary of the Senate and the House of Representatives; and

(C) the Foreign Intelligence Surveillance Court.

(g) Certification –

(1) In General –

(A) Requirement – Subject to subparagraph (B), prior to the implementation of an authorization under subsection (a), the Attorney General and the Director of National Intelligence shall provide to the Foreign Intelligence Surveillance Court a written certification and any supporting affidavit, under oath and under seal, in accordance with this subsection.

(B) Exception – If the Attorney General and the Director of National Intelligence make a determination under subsection (c)(2) and time does not permit the submission of a certification under this subsection prior to the implementation of an authorization under subsection (a), the Attorney General and the Director of National Intelligence shall submit to the Court a certification for such authorization as soon as practicable but in no event later than 7 days after such determination is made.

(2) Requirements – A certification made under this subsection shall –

(A) attest that –

(i) there are procedures in place that have been approved, have been submitted for approval, or will be submitted with the certification for approval by the Foreign Intelligence Surveillance Court that are reasonably designed to –

(I) ensure that an acquisition authorized under subsection (a) is limited to targeting persons reasonably believed to be located outside the United States; and

(II) prevent the intentional acquisition of any communication as to which the sender and all intended recipients are known at the time of the acquisition to be located in the United States;

(ii) the minimization procedures to be used with respect to such acquisition –

(I) meet the definition of minimization procedures under section 101(h) or 301(4), as appropriate; and

(II) have been approved, have been submitted for approval, or will be submitted with the certification for approval by the Foreign Intelligence Surveillance Court;

(iii) guidelines have been adopted in accordance with subsection (f) to ensure compliance with the limitations in subsection (b) and to ensure that an application for a court order is filed as required by this Act;

(iv) the procedures and guidelines referred to in clauses (i), (ii), and (iii) are consistent with the requirements of the fourth amendment to the Constitution of the United States;

(v) a significant purpose of the acquisition is to obtain foreign intelligence information;

(vi) the acquisition involves obtaining foreign intelligence information from or with the assistance of an electronic communication service provider; and

(vii) the acquisition complies with the limitations in subsection (b);

(B) include the procedures adopted in accordance with subsections (d) and (e);

(C) be supported, as appropriate, by the affidavit of any appropriate official in the area of national security who is –

(i) appointed by the President, by and with the advice and consent of the Senate; or

(ii) the head of an element of the intelligence community;

(D) include –

(i) an effective date for the authorization that is at least 30 days after the submission of the written certification to the court; or

(ii) if the acquisition has begun or the effective date is less than 30 days after the submission of the written certification to the court, the date the acquisition began or the effective date for the acquisition; and

(E) if the Attorney General and the Director of National Intelligence make a determination under subsection (c)(2), include a statement that such determination has been made. . . .

(6) Review – A certification submitted in accordance with this subsection shall be subject to judicial review pursuant to subsection (i).

(h) Directives and Judicial Review of Directives –

(1) Authority – With respect to an acquisition authorized under subsection (a), the Attorney General and the Director of National Intelligence may direct, in writing, an electronic communication service provider to –

(A) immediately provide the Government with all information, facilities, or assistance necessary to accomplish the acquisition in a manner that will protect the secrecy of the acquisition and produce a minimum of interference with the services that such electronic communication service provider is providing to the target of the acquisition; . . .

(3) Release from Liability – No cause of action shall lie in any court against any electronic communication service provider for providing any information, facilities, or assistance in accordance with a directive issued pursuant to paragraph (1).

(4) Challenging of Directives –

(A) Authority to Challenge – An electronic communication service provider receiving a directive issued pursuant to paragraph (1) may file a petition to modify or set aside such

directive with the Foreign Intelligence Surveillance Court, which
shall have jurisdiction to review such petition. . . .

(5) Enforcement of Directives –

(A) Order to Compel – If an electronic communication
service provider fails to comply with a directive issued pursuant
to paragraph (1), the Attorney General may file a petition for an
order to compel the electronic communication service provider
to comply with the directive with the Foreign Intelligence
Surveillance Court, which shall have jurisdiction to review such
petition. . . .

(6) Appeal –

(A) Appeal to the Court of Review – The Government or an
electronic communication service provider receiving a directive
issued pursuant to paragraph (1) may file a petition with the
Foreign Intelligence Surveillance Court of Review for review of
a decision issued pursuant to paragraph (4) or (5). . . .

(B) Certiorari to the Supreme Court – The Government or an
electronic communication service provider receiving a directive
issued pursuant to paragraph (1) may file a petition for a writ of
certiorari for review of a decision of the Court of Review issued
under subparagraph (A). . . .

(i) Judicial Review of Certifications and Procedures –

(1) In General –

(A) Review by the Foreign Intelligence Surveillance Court –
The Foreign Intelligence Surveillance Court shall have
jurisdiction to review a certification submitted in accordance
with subsection (g) and the targeting and minimization
procedures adopted in accordance with subsections (d) and (e),
and amendments to such certification or such procedures. . . .

(2) Review – The Court shall review the following:

(A) Certification – A certification submitted in accordance
with subsection (g) to determine whether the certification
contains all the required elements.

(B) Targeting Procedures – The targeting procedures
adopted in accordance with subsection (d) to assess whether the
procedures are reasonably designed to –

(i) ensure that an acquisition authorized under subsection
(a) is limited to targeting persons reasonably believed to be
located outside the United States; and

(ii) prevent the intentional acquisition of any
communication as to which the sender and all intended

recipients are known at the time of the acquisition to be located in the United States.

(C) Minimization Procedures – The minimization procedures adopted in accordance with subsection (e) to assess whether such procedures meet the definition of minimization procedures under section 101(h) or section 301(4), as appropriate.

(3) Orders –

(A) Approval – If the Court finds that a certification submitted in accordance with subsection (g) contains all the required elements and that the targeting and minimization procedures adopted in accordance with subsections (d) and (e) are consistent with the requirements of those subsections and with the fourth amendment to the Constitution of the United States, the Court shall enter an order approving the certification and the use, or continued use in the case of an acquisition authorized pursuant to a determination under subsection (c)(2), of the procedures for the acquisition.

(B) Correction of Deficiencies – If the Court finds that a certification submitted in accordance with subsection (g) does not contain all the required elements, or that the procedures adopted in accordance with subsections (d) and (e) are not consistent with the requirements of those subsections or the fourth amendment to the Constitution of the United States, the Court shall issue an order directing the Government to, at the Government's election and to the extent required by the Court's order –

(i) correct any deficiency identified by the Court's order not later than 30 days after the date on which the Court issues the order; or

(ii) cease, or not begin, the implementation of the authorization for which such certification was submitted. . . .

(4) Appeal –

(A) Appeal to the Court of Review – The Government may file a petition with the Foreign Intelligence Surveillance Court of Review for review of an order under this subsection. . . .

(D) Certiorari to the Supreme Court – The Government may file a petition for a writ of certiorari for review of a decision of the Court of Review issued under subparagraph (A). . . .

(l) Assessments and Reviews –

(1) Semiannual Assessment – Not less frequently than once every 6 months, the Attorney General and Director of National

Intelligence shall assess compliance with the targeting and minimization procedures adopted in accordance with subsections (d) and (e) and the guidelines adopted in accordance with subsection (f) and shall submit each assessment to –

    (A) the Foreign Intelligence Surveillance Court; and

    (B) consistent with the Rules of the House of Representatives, [and] the . . . Rules of the Senate . . . –

        (i) the congressional intelligence committees; and

        (ii) the Committees on the Judiciary of the House of Representatives and the Senate.

(2) Agency Assessment – The Inspector General of the Department of Justice and the Inspector General of each element of the intelligence community authorized to acquire foreign intelligence information under subsection (a), with respect to the department or element of such Inspector General –

    (A) are authorized to review compliance with the targeting and minimization procedures adopted in accordance with subsections (d) and (e) and the guidelines adopted in accordance with subsection (f); . . . [and]

    (D) shall provide each such review to –

        (i) the Attorney General;

        (ii) the Director of National Intelligence; and

        (iii) consistent with the Rules of the House of Representatives, [and] the . . . Rules of the Senate. . . –

            (I) the congressional intelligence committees; and

            (II) the Committees on the Judiciary of the House of Representatives and the Senate.

(3) Annual Review –

    (A) Requirement to Conduct – The head of each element of the intelligence community conducting an acquisition authorized under subsection (a) shall conduct an annual review to determine whether there is reason to believe that foreign intelligence information has been or will be obtained from the acquisition. The annual review shall provide, with respect to acquisitions authorized under subsection (a) –

        (i) an accounting of the number of disseminated intelligence reports containing a reference to a United States-person identity; . . .

        (iii) the number of targets that were later determined to be located in the United States and, to the extent possible, whether communications of such targets were reviewed; and

(iv) a description of any procedures developed by the head of such element of the intelligence community and approved by the Director of National Intelligence to assess, in a manner consistent with national security, operational requirements and the privacy interests of United States persons . . . .

(C) Provision of Review – The head of each element of the intelligence community that conducts an annual review under subparagraph (A) shall provide such review to –

(i) the Foreign Intelligence Surveillance Court;

(ii) the Attorney General;

(iii) the Director of National Intelligence; and

(iv) consistent with the Rules of the House of Representatives, [and] the . . . Rules of the Senate . . . –

(I) the congressional intelligence committees; and

(II) the Committees on the Judiciary of the House of Representatives and the Senate.

§703. Certain Acquisitions Inside the United States Targeting United States Persons Outside the United States.

(a) Jurisdiction of the Foreign Intelligence Surveillance Court –

(1) in General – The Foreign Intelligence Surveillance Court shall have jurisdiction to review an application and to enter an order approving the targeting of a United States person reasonably believed to be located outside the United States to acquire foreign intelligence information, if the acquisition constitutes electronic surveillance or the acquisition of stored electronic communications or stored electronic data that requires an order under this Act, and such acquisition is conducted within the United States.

(2) Limitation – If a United States person targeted under this subsection is reasonably believed to be located in the United States during the effective period of an order issued pursuant to subsection (c), an acquisition targeting such United States person under this section shall cease unless the targeted United States person is again reasonably believed to be located outside the United States while an order issued pursuant to subsection (c) is in effect. Nothing in this section shall be construed to limit the authority of the Government to seek an order or authorization under, or otherwise engage in any activity that is authorized under, any other title of this Act.

(b) Application –

(1) In General – Each application for an order under this section shall be made by a Federal officer in writing upon oath or affirmation to a judge having jurisdiction under subsection (a)(1). Each application shall require the approval of the Attorney General based upon the Attorney General's finding that it satisfies the criteria and requirements of such application, as set forth in this section, and shall include –

(A) the identity of the Federal officer making the application;

(B) the identity, if known, or a description of the United States person who is the target of the acquisition;

(C) a statement of the facts and circumstances relied upon to justify the applicant's belief that the United States person who is the target of the acquisition is –

(i) a person reasonably believed to be located outside the United States; and

(ii) a foreign power, an agent of a foreign power, or an officer or employee of a foreign power;

(D) a statement of proposed minimization procedures that meet the definition of minimization procedures under section 101(h) or 301(4), as appropriate;

(E) a description of the nature of the information sought and the type of communications or activities to be subjected to acquisition;

(F) a certification made by the Attorney General or an official specified in section 104(a)(6) that –

(i) the certifying official deems the information sought to be foreign intelligence information;

(ii) a significant purpose of the acquisition is to obtain foreign intelligence information;

(iii) such information cannot reasonably be obtained by normal investigative techniques;

(iv) designates the type of foreign intelligence information being sought according to the categories described in section 101(e); . . .

(G) a summary statement of the means by which the acquisition will be conducted and whether physical entry is required to effect the acquisition;

(H) the identity of any electronic communication service provider necessary to effect the acquisition, provided that the application is not required to identify the specific facilities, places, premises, or property at which the acquisition authorized under this section will be directed or conducted; . . . [and]

(J) a statement of the period of time for which the acquisition is required to be maintained, provided that such period of time shall not exceed 90 days per application. . . .

(c) Order –

(1) Findings – Upon an application made pursuant to subsection (b), the Foreign Intelligence Surveillance Court shall enter an ex parte order as requested or as modified by the Court approving the acquisition if the Court finds that – . . .

(B) on the basis of the facts submitted by the applicant, for the United States person who is the target of the acquisition, there is probable cause to believe that the target is –

(i) a person reasonably believed to be located outside the United States; and

(ii) a foreign power, an agent of a foreign power, or an officer or employee of a foreign power; . . .

(D) the application that has been filed contains all statements and certifications required by subsection (b) and the certification or certifications are not clearly erroneous on the basis of the statement made under subsection (b)(1)(F)(v) and any other information furnished under subsection (b)(3).

(2) Probable Cause – In determining whether or not probable cause exists for purposes of paragraph (1)(B), a judge having jurisdiction under subsection (a)(1) may consider past activities of the target and facts and circumstances relating to current or future activities of the target. No United States person may be considered a foreign power, agent of a foreign power, or officer or employee of a foreign power solely upon the basis of activities protected by the first amendment to the Constitution of the United States.

(3) Review –

(A) Limitation on Review – Review by a judge having jurisdiction under subsection (a)(1) shall be limited to that required to make the findings described in paragraph (1). . . .

(6) Duration – An order approved under this subsection shall be effective for a period not to exceed 90 days and such order may be renewed for additional 90-day periods upon submission of renewal applications meeting the requirements of subsection (b). . . .

(d) Emergency Authorization – [This provision substantially repeats the authority set out in FISA §105, 50 U.S.C. §1805, except that it extends from 48 hours to 7 days the time for the Attorney General to apply for a judicial order after authorizing acquisition in an emergency.]

(e) Release From Liability – No cause of action shall lie in any court against any electronic communication service provider for providing any information, facilities, or assistance in accordance with an order or request for emergency assistance issued pursuant to subsection (c) or (d), respectively.

(f) Appeal –

(1) Appeal to the Foreign Intelligence Surveillance Court of Review – The Government may file a petition with the Foreign Intelligence Surveillance Court of Review for review of an order issued pursuant to subsection (c). . . .

(2) Certiorari to the Supreme Court – The Government may file a petition for a writ of certiorari for review of a decision of the Court of Review issued under paragraph (1). . . .

(g) Construction – Except as provided in this section, nothing in this Act shall be construed to require an application for a court order for an acquisition that is targeted in accordance with this section at a United States person reasonably believed to be located outside the United States.

§704. Other Acquisitions Targeting United States Persons Outside the United States.

(a) Jurisdiction and Scope –

(1) Jurisdiction – The Foreign Intelligence Surveillance Court shall have jurisdiction to enter an order pursuant to subsection (c).

(2) Scope – No element of the intelligence community may intentionally target, for the purpose of acquiring foreign intelligence information, a United States person reasonably believed to be located outside the United States under circumstances in which the targeted United States person has a reasonable expectation of privacy and a warrant would be required if the acquisition were conducted inside the United States for law enforcement purposes, unless a judge of the Foreign Intelligence Surveillance Court has entered an order with respect to such targeted United States person or the Attorney General has authorized an emergency acquisition pursuant to subsection (c) or (d), respectively, or any other provision of this Act. . . .

(b) Application – Each application for an order under this section shall be made by a Federal officer in writing upon oath or affirmation to a judge having jurisdiction under subsection (a)(1). Each application shall require the approval of the Attorney General based upon the

Attorney General's finding that it satisfies the criteria and requirements of such application as set forth in this section and shall include – . . .

(3) a statement of the facts and circumstances relied upon to justify the applicant's belief that the United States person who is the target of the acquisition is –

(A) a person reasonably believed to be located outside the United States; and

(B) a foreign power, an agent of a foreign power, or an officer or employee of a foreign power; . . .

(5) a certification made by the Attorney General, an official specified in section 104(a)(6), or the head of an element of the intelligence community that –

(A) the certifying official deems the information sought to be foreign intelligence information; and

(B) a significant purpose of the acquisition is to obtain foreign intelligence information; . . . [and]

(7) a statement of the period of time for which the acquisition is required to be maintained, provided that such period of time shall not exceed 90 days per application.

[§704(c)-(e) generally repeats the requirements of §703(c)-(f).] . . .

§705. Joint Applications and Concurrent Authorizations.

(a) Joint Applications and Orders – If an acquisition targeting a United States person under section 703 or 704 is proposed to be conducted both inside and outside the United States, a judge having jurisdiction under section 703(a)(1) or 704(a)(1) may issue simultaneously, upon the request of the Government in a joint application complying with the requirements of sections 703(b) and 704(b), orders under sections 703(c) and 704(c), as appropriate.

(b) Concurrent Authorization – If an order authorizing electronic surveillance or physical search has been obtained under section 105 or 304, the Attorney General may authorize, for the effective period of that order, without an order under section 703 or 704, the targeting of that United States person for the purpose of acquiring foreign intelligence information while such person is reasonably believed to be located outside the United States. . . .

§707. Congressional Oversight.

(a) Semiannual Report – Not less frequently than once every 6 months, the Attorney General shall fully inform, in a manner consistent with national security, the congressional intelligence committees and the Committees on the Judiciary of the Senate and the House of Representatives, consistent with the Rules of the House of Representatives, [and] the . . . Rules of the Senate . . . concerning the implementation of this title. . . .

[Section 102(a) of the 2008 Act amended Title I of FISA by adding at the end the following new section:]

STATEMENT OF EXCLUSIVE MEANS BY WHICH ELECTRONIC SURVEILLANCE AND INTERCEPTION OF CERTAIN COMMUNICATIONS MAY BE CONDUCTED

§112. (a) Except as provided in subsection (b), the procedures of chapters 119, 121, and 206 of title 18, United States Code, and this Act shall be the exclusive means by which electronic surveillance and the interception of domestic wire, oral, or electronic communications may be conducted.

(b) Only an express statutory authorization for electronic surveillance or the interception of domestic wire, oral, or electronic communications, other than as an amendment to this Act or chapters 119, 121, or 206 of title 18, United States Code, shall constitute an additional exclusive means for the purpose of subsection (a).

[Section 102(b) of the 2008 Act provided conforming amendments to FISA §109(a), 50 U.S.C. §1809(a), which criminalizes violations of FISA.]

[Section 102(c) of the 2008 Act amended FISA §105, 50 U.S.C. §1805, extending from 48 hours to 7 days the time to apply for a judicial order if the Attorney General authorizes electronic surveillance in an emergency.] . . .

[Sections 107 and 108 of the 2008 Act provided conforming amendments to FISA's physical search provisions and to its provisions for emergency pen registers and trap and trace devices.] . . .

[Section 110(a)(1) of the 2008 Act amended FISA §101(a), 50 U.S.C. §1801(a), by adding the following new definition of a "foreign power":]

(7) an entity not substantially composed of United States persons that is engaged in the international proliferation of weapons of mass destruction.

[Section 110(a)(2) of the 2008 Act amended FISA §101(b)(1), 50 U.S.C. §1801(b)(1), by adding the following new definitions of "agent of a foreign power," to include "any person other than a United States person, who":]

(D) engages in the international proliferation of weapons of mass destruction, or activities in preparation therefor; or
(E) engages in the international proliferation of weapons of mass destruction, or activities in preparation therefor for or on behalf of a foreign power; or

[Section 110(a)(3) of the 2008 Act amended FISA §101(e)(1)(B), 50 U.S.C. §1801(e)(1)(B), which offers one definition of "foreign intelligence information," by striking "sabotage or international terrorism" and inserting "sabotage, international terrorism, or the international proliferation of weapons of mass destruction."] . . .

[Section 201 of the 2008 Act amended FISA as it existed by adding the following new title:]

TITLE VIII – PROTECTION OF PERSONS ASSISTING THE GOVERNMENT

§801. Definitions.

In this title:
(1) Assistance – The term "assistance" means the provision of, or the provision of access to, information (including communication contents, communications records, or other information relating to a customer or communication), facilities, or another form of assistance. . . .

§802. Procedures for Implementing Statutory Defenses.

(a) Requirement for Certification – Notwithstanding any other provision of law, a civil action may not lie or be maintained in a Federal or State court against any person for providing assistance to an element of the intelligence community, and shall be promptly dismissed, if the Attorney General certifies to the district court of the United States in which such action is pending that –

(1) any assistance by that person was provided pursuant to an order of the court established under section 103(a) directing such assistance;

(2) any assistance by that person was provided pursuant to a certification in writing under section 2511(2)(a)(ii)(B) or 2709(b) of title 18, United States Code;

(3) any assistance by that person was provided pursuant to a directive under section 102(a)(4), 105B(e), as added by section 2 of the Protect America Act of 2007 (Public Law 110-55), or 702(h) directing such assistance;

(4) in the case of a covered civil action, the assistance alleged to have been provided by the electronic communication service provider was –

(A) in connection with an intelligence activity involving communications that was –

(i) authorized by the President during the period beginning on September 11, 2001, and ending on January 17, 2007; and

(ii) designed to detect or prevent a terrorist attack, or activities in preparation for a terrorist attack, against the United States; and

(B) the subject of a written request or directive, or a series of written requests or directives, from the Attorney General or the head of an element of the intelligence community (or the deputy of such person) to the electronic communication service provider indicating that the activity was –

(i) authorized by the President; and

(ii) determined to be lawful; or

(5) the person did not provide the alleged assistance.

(b) Judicial Review –

(1) Review of Certifications – A certification under subsection (a) shall be given effect unless the court finds that such certification

is not supported by substantial evidence provided to the court pursuant to this section. . . .

[Section 301 of the 2008 Act requires that the Inspectors General of agencies that participated in the TSP complete a comprehensive review of the program and provide a preliminary report to congressional committees within 60 days after enactment and a final report within 1 year of enactment.] . . .

[NSL p. 559, CTL p. 177. Insert after Note 2.]

Warshak v. United States
United States Court of Appeals, 6th Circuit, 2007
490 F.3d 455
vacated on ripeness grounds, 532 F.3d 521
(6th Cir. 2008) (en banc)

BOYCE F. MARTIN, JR., Circuit Judge. The government appeals the district court's entry of a preliminary injunction, prohibiting it from seizing "the contents of any personal e-mail account maintained by an Internet Service Provider in the name of any resident of the Southern District of Ohio without providing the relevant account holder or subscriber prior notice and an opportunity to be heard on any complaint, motion, or other pleading seeking issuance of such an order." For the reasons discussed below, we largely affirm the district court's decision, requiring only that the preliminary injunction be slightly modified on remand.

I. . . .

[During a criminal investigation of Steven Warshak for mail and wire fraud, money laundering, and related federal offenses, the government obtained an order from a United States Magistrate Judge directing an internet service provider ("ISP") to turn over to government agents information pertaining to Warshak's e-mail account, including (1) customer account information, such as application information, "account identifiers," "[b]illing information to include bank account numbers," contact information, and "[any] other information pertaining to the customer, including set up, synchronization, etc."; (2) "[t]he contents of wire or electronic communications (not in electronic storage unless greater than 181 days old) that were placed or stored in directories or files owned or controlled" by the ISP; and (3) "[a]ll Log files and backup tapes." At a later date, Warshak was informed of the order and sought an injunction prohibiting future searches. The district court issued a preliminary injunction.]

The gist of this remedy appears to be that when a hearing is required and the e-mail account holder is given an opportunity in court to resist the disclosure of information, any resulting order is more like a subpoena than a search warrant. Therefore the standard necessary to obtain an order under the [Stored Communications Act (SCA), 18 U.S.C. §§2701-2712] – that the government introduce "specific and articulable facts showing that there are reasonable grounds to believe that the contents" of the e-mail to be seized "are relevant and material to an ongoing criminal investigation" [18 U.S.C. §2705(d)] – is permissible as the functional equivalent of a subpoena given the subject's ability to contest the order in court. Because this standard is lower than the probable cause standard necessary to obtain a search warrant, it is sufficient to justify a warrantless search only in instances where notice is provided to the account holder.

The government appeals from the district court's ruling. . . .

III. . . .

B. Likelihood of Success on the Merits: Probable Cause versus Reasonableness and Fourth Amendment Implications of SCA Orders

1. Probable Cause versus Reasonableness

With respect to the merits of the preliminary injunction, the government argues that court orders issued under section 2703 are not searches but rather compelled disclosures, akin to subpoenas. As a result, according to the government, the more stringent showing of probable cause, a prerequisite to the issuance of a warrant under the Fourth Amendment, is inapplicable, and an order under section 2703 need only be supported by a showing of "reasonable relevance."

The government is correct that "whereas the Fourth Amendment mandates a showing of probable cause for the issuance of search warrants, subpoenas are analyzed only under the Fourth Amendment's general reasonableness standard." *Doe v. United States*, 253 F.3d 256, 263-64 (6th Cir. 2001). As this Court has explained, "[o]ne primary reason for this distinction is that, unlike 'the immediacy and intrusiveness of a search and seizure conducted pursuant to a warrant[,]' the reasonableness of an administrative subpoena's command can be contested in federal court before being enforced." *Id.* at 264 (quoting *In re Subpoena Duces Tecum*, 228 F.3d 341, 347-49 (4th Cir. 2000)); *see also Donovan v. Lone Steer*, 464 U.S. 408, 415 (1984). The government is also correct that this principle extends to subpoenas to third-parties – that is, entities other than the subject of the investigation, like NuVox and Yahoo in this case. *See United States v. Phibbs*, 999 F.2d 1053, 1077 (6th Cir. 1993).

Phibbs makes explicit, however, a necessary Fourth Amendment caveat to the rule regarding third-party subpoenas: the party challenging the subpoena has "standing to dispute [its] issuance on Fourth Amendment grounds" if he can "demonstrate that he had a legitimate expectation of privacy attaching to the records obtained." *Id.*; *see also United States v. Miller*, 425 U.S. 435, 444 (1976) ("**Since no Fourth Amendment interests of the depositor are implicated here,** this case is governed by the general rule that the issuance of a subpoena to a third party to obtain the records of that party does not violate the rights of a defendant." (emphasis added)). This language reflects the rule that where the party challenging the disclosure has voluntarily disclosed his records to a third party, he maintains no expectation of privacy in the disclosure vis-a-vis that individual, and assumes the risk of that person disclosing (or being compelled to disclose) the shared information to the authorities. *See, e.g., United States v. Jacobsen*, 466 U.S. 109, 117 (1984) ("[W]hen an individual reveals private information to another, he assumes the risk that his confidant will reveal that information to the authorities, and if that occurs the Fourth Amendment does not prohibit governmental use of that information.").

Combining this disclosure to a third party with the government's ability to subpoena the third party alleviates any need for the third-party subpoena to meet the probable cause requirement, if the challenger has not maintained an expectation of privacy with respect to the individual being compelled to make the disclosure. For example, in *Phibbs,* the documents in question were credit card and phone records that were "readily accessible to employees during the normal course of business." 999 F.2d at 1078. A similar rationale was employed by the Supreme Court in *Miller.* 425 U.S. at 442 ("The checks are not confidential communications but negotiable instruments to be used in commercial transactions. All of the documents obtained, including financial statements and deposit slips, contain only information voluntarily conveyed to the banks and exposed to their employees in the ordinary

course of business."). *See also SEC v. Jerry T. O'Brien, Inc.*, 467 U.S.
735, 743 (1984) ("When a person communicates information to a third
party even on the understanding that the communication is confidential,
he cannot object if the third party conveys that information or records
thereof to law enforcement authorities."). The government's compelled
disclosure argument, while relevant, therefore begs the critical question
of whether an e-mail user maintains a reasonable expectation of privacy
in his e-mails vis-a-vis the party who is subject to compelled disclosure –
in this instance, the ISPs. If he does not, as in *Phibbs* or *Miller,* then the
government must meet only the reasonableness standard applicable to
compelled disclosures to obtain the material. If, on the other hand, the
e-mail user does maintain a reasonable expectation of privacy in the
content of the e-mails with respect to the ISP, then the Fourth
Amendment's probable cause standard controls the e-mail seizure.

2. Reasonable expectation of privacy in e-mail content

Two amici curiae convincingly analogize the privacy interest that
e-mail users hold in the content of their e-mails to the privacy interest in
the content of telephone calls, recognized by the Supreme Court in its
line of cases involving government eavesdropping on telephone
conversations. *See Smith v. Maryland*, 442 U.S. 735 (1979); *Katz v.
United States*, 389 U.S. 347 (1967); *Berger v. New York*, 388 U.S. 41
(1967). In *Berger* and *Katz,* telephone surveillance that intercepted the
content of a conversation was held to constitute a search, because the
caller "is surely entitled to assume that the words he utters into the
mouthpiece will not be broadcast to the world," and therefore cannot be
said to have forfeited his privacy right in the conversation. *Katz,* 389
U.S. at 352. This is so even though "[t]he telephone conversation itself
must be electronically transmitted by telephone company equipment, and
may be recorded or overheard by the use of other company equipment."
Smith, 442 U.S. at 746 (Stewart, J., dissenting). On the other hand, in
Smith, the Court ruled that the use of [a] pen register, installed at the
phone company's facility to record the numbers dialed by the telephone
user, did not amount to a search. This distinction was due to the fact that
"a pen register differs significantly from the listening device employed in
Katz, for pen registers do not acquire the *contents* of communications."
442 U.S. at 741 (emphasis in original).

The distinction between *Katz* and *Miller* makes clear that the
reasonable expectation of privacy inquiry in the context of shared
communications must necessarily focus on two narrower questions than

the general fact that the communication was shared with another. First, we must specifically identify the party with whom the communication is shared, as well as the parties from whom disclosure is shielded. Clearly, under *Katz,* the mere fact that a communication is shared with another person does not entirely erode all expectations of privacy, because otherwise eavesdropping would never amount to a search. It is true, however, that by sharing communications with someone else, the speaker or writer assumes the risk that it could be revealed to the government by that person, or obtained through a subpoena directed to that person. *See Miller,* 425 U.S. at 443 ("[T]he Fourth Amendment does not prohibit the obtaining of information revealed to a third party and conveyed by him to Government authorities."). The same does not necessarily apply, however, to an intermediary that merely has the ability to access the information sought by the government. Otherwise phone conversations would never be protected, merely because the telephone company can access them; letters would never be protected, by virtue of the Postal Service's ability to access them; the contents of shared safe deposit boxes or storage lockers would never be protected, by virtue of the bank or storage company's ability to access them.

The second necessary inquiry pertains to the precise information actually conveyed to the party through whom disclosure is sought or obtained. This distinction provides the obvious crux for the different results in *Katz* and *Smith,* because although the conduct of the telephone user in *Smith* "may have been calculated to keep the *contents* of his conversation private, his conduct was not and could not have been calculated to preserve the privacy of the number he dialed." 442 U.S. at 743. Like the depositor in *Miller,* the caller in *Smith* "assumed the risk" of the phone company disclosing the records that he conveyed to it. *Id.* Yet this assumption of the risk is limited to the specific information conveyed to the service provider, which in the telephone context excludes the content of the conversation. It is apparent, therefore, that although the government can compel disclosure of a shared communication from the party with whom it was shared, it can only compel disclosure of the specific information to which the subject of its compulsion has been granted access. It cannot, on the other hand, bootstrap an intermediary's limited access to one part of the communication (e.g., the phone number) to allow it access to another part (the content of the conversation).

This focus on the specific information shared with the subject of compelled disclosure applies with equal force in the e-mail context. Compelled disclosure of subscriber information and related records through the ISP might not undermine the e-mail subscriber's Fourth Amendment interest under *Smith,* because like the information obtained through the pen register in *Smith* and like the bank records in *Miller,* subscriber information and related records are records of the service provider as well, and may likely be accessed by ISP employees in the normal course of their employment. Consequently, the user does not maintain the same expectation of privacy in them vis-a-vis the service provider, and a third party subpoena to the service provider to access information that is shared with it likely creates no Fourth Amendment problems. The combined precedents of *Katz* and *Smith,* however, recognize a heightened protection for the **content** of the communications. Like telephone conversations, simply because the phone company or the ISP **could** access the content of e-mails and phone calls, the privacy expectation in the content of either is not diminished, because there is a societal expectation that the ISP or the phone company will not do so as a matter of course.

Similarly, under both *Miller* and *Katz,* if the government in this case had received the content of Warshak's e-mails by subpoenaing the person with whom Warshak was e-mailing, a Fourth Amendment challenge brought by Warshak would fail, because he would not have maintained a reasonable expectation of privacy vis-a-vis his e-mailing partners. *See Phibbs,* 999 F.2d at 1077. But this rationale is inapplicable where the party subpoenaed is not expected to access the content of the documents, much like the phone company in *Katz.* Thus, as Warshak argues, the government could not get around the privacy interest attached to a private letter by simply subpoenaing the postal service with no showing of probable cause, because unlike in *Phibbs,* postal workers would not be expected to read the letter in the normal course of business. *See Ex parte Jackson,* 96 U.S. 727, 733 (1878) ("No law of Congress can place in the hands of officials connected with the postal service any authority to invade the secrecy of letters and such sealed packages in the mail; and all regulations adopted as to mail matter of this kind must be in subordination to the great principle embodied in the fourth amendment of the Constitution."). Similarly, a bank customer maintains an expectation of privacy in a safe deposit box to which the bank lacks access (as opposed to bank records, like checks or account statements), and the government could not compel disclosure of the contents of the safe deposit box only by subpoenaing the bank.

This analysis is consistent with other decisions that have addressed an individual's expectation of privacy in particular electronic communications. In *Guest v. Leis,* 255 F.3d 325, 333 (6th Cir. 2001), we concluded that users of electronic bulletin boards lacked an expectation of privacy in material posted on the bulletin board, as such materials were "intended for publication or public posting." Of course the public disclosure of material to an untold number of readers distinguishes bulletin board postings from e-mails, which typically have a limited, select number of recipients. *See also Jackson,* 96 U.S. at 733 ("[A] distinction is to be made between different kinds of mail matter, – between what is intended to be kept free from inspection, such as letters, and sealed packages subject to letter postage; and what is open to inspection, such as newspapers, magazines, pamphlets, and other printed matter, purposely left in a condition to be examined."). Although we stated that an e-mail sender would "lose a legitimate expectation of privacy in an e-mail that had already reached its recipient," analogizing such an e-mailer to "a letter-writer," this diminished privacy is only relevant with respect to the recipient, as the sender has assumed the risk of disclosure by or through the recipient. *Id.* at 333 (citing *United States v. King,* 55 F.3d 1193, 1196 (6th Cir. 1995)). *Guest* did not hold that the mere use of an intermediary such as an ISP to send and receive e-mails amounted to a waiver of a legitimate expectation of privacy.

Other courts have addressed analogous situations where electronic communications were obtained based on the sender's use of a computer network. In *United States v. Simons,* the Fourth Circuit held that a government employee lacked a reasonable expectation of privacy in electronic files on his office computer, in light of the employer's policy that explicitly notified the employee of its intention to "audit, inspect, and monitor" his computer files. 206 F.3d 392, 398 (4th Cir. 2000). In light of this explicit policy, the employee's belief that his files were private was not objectively reasonable. *Id.* On the other hand, in *United States v. Heckenkamp,* the Ninth Circuit held that a university student did have a reasonable expectation of privacy in his computer files even though he "attached [his computer] to the university network," because the "university policies do not eliminate Heckenkamp's expectation of privacy in his computer." 482 F.3d 1142, 1147 (9th Cir. 2007). Although the university did "establish limited instances in which university administrators may access his computer in order to protect the university's systems," this exception fell far short of a blanket monitoring or auditing policy, and the Ninth Circuit deemed it insufficient to waive the user's expectation of privacy.

Heckenkamp and *Simons* provide useful bookends for the question before us, regarding when the use of some intermediary provider of computer and e-mail services – be it a commercial ISP, a university, an employer, or another type of entity – amounts to a waiver of the user's reasonable expectation of privacy in the content of the e-mails with respect to that intermediary. In instances where a user agreement explicitly provides that e-mails and other files will be monitored or audited, as in *Simons,* the user's knowledge of this fact may well extinguish his reasonable expectation of privacy. Without such a statement, however, the service provider's control over the files and ability to access them under certain limited circumstances will not be enough to overcome an expectation of privacy, as in *Heckenkamp.*

Turning to the instant case, we have little difficulty agreeing with the district court that individuals maintain a reasonable expectation of privacy in e-mails that are stored with, or sent or received through, a commercial ISP. The content of e-mail is something that the user "seeks to preserve as private," and therefore "may be constitutionally protected." *Katz,* 389 U.S. at 351. It goes without saying that like the telephone earlier in our history, e-mail is an ever-increasing mode of private communication, and protecting shared communications through this medium is as important to Fourth Amendment principles today as protecting telephone conversations has been in the past. *See Katz,* 389 U.S. at 352 ("To read the Constitution more narrowly is to ignore the vital role that the public telephone has come to play in private communication.").

The government asserts that ISPs have the contractual right to access users' e-mails. The district court's ruling was based on its willingness to credit Warshak's contrary factual argument that "employees of commercial ISPs [do not] open and read – [nor do] their subscribers reasonably expect them to open and read – individual subscriber e-mails as a matter of course." This factual determination tracks the language from *Miller* and *Phibbs* that suggests a privacy interest in records held by a third party is only undermined where the documents are accessed by the third party or its employees "in the ordinary course of business." *Miller,* 425 U.S. at 442. Moreover, as explained in the Ninth Circuit's decision in *Heckenkamp,* mere accessibility is not enough to waive an expectation of privacy. *See Heckenkamp,* 482 F.3d at 1147 (holding that university policies establishing "limited instances in which university administrators may access [the user's] computer in order to protect the university's systems" was insufficient to eliminate an expectation of privacy); *see also Katz,* 389 U.S. at 351 ("[W]hat [a pay phone user] seeks to preserve as private, **even in an area accessible to the public,** may be constitutionally protected." (emphasis added)). Where a user agreement calls for regular auditing, inspection, or monitoring of e-mails, the expectation may well be different, as the potential for an administrator to read the content of e-mails in the account should be apparent to the user. *See Simons,* 206 F.3d at 398. Where there is such an arrangement, compelled disclosure by means of an SCA order at the ISP would be akin to the third party subpoena directed at a bank, as in *Miller* and *Jerry T. O'Brien.* In contrast, the terms of service in question here, which the government has cited to in both the district court and this Court, clearly provide for access only in limited circumstances, rather than wholesale inspection, auditing, or monitoring of e-mails.[7] Because the ISP's right to access e-mails under these user agreements is reserved for extraordinary circumstances, much like the university policy in *Heckenkamp,* it is similarly insufficient to undermine a user's expectation of privacy. For now, the government has made no showing that e-mail content is regularly accessed by ISPs, or that users are aware of such access of content.

The government also insists that ISPs regularly screen users' e-mails for viruses, spam, and child pornography. Even assuming that this is true, however, such a process does not waive an expectation of privacy in the content of e-mails sent through the ISP, for the same reasons that the terms of service are insufficient to waive privacy expectations. The government states that ISPs "are developing technology that will enable them to scan user images" for child pornography and viruses. The government's statement that this process involves "technology," rather than manual, human review, suggests that it involves a computer searching for particular terms, types of images, or similar indicia of wrongdoing that would not disclose the content of the e-mail to any person at the ISP or elsewhere, aside from the recipient. But the reasonable expectation of privacy of an e-mail user goes to the **content** of the e-mail message. The fact that a computer scans millions of e-mails for signs of pornography or a virus does not invade an individual's content-based privacy interest in the e-mails and has little

---

7. *See* Gov't Br. at 34 (citing Yahoo terms of service which allow access where "reasonably necessary to: (a) comply with legal process; (b) enforce the [Terms of Service]; (c) respond to claims that any Content violates the rights of third parties; (d) respond to your requests for customer service; or (e) protect the rights, property or personal safety of Yahoo!, its users and the public."). As amicus Electronic Frontier Foundation points out, each instance involves outside prompting for an ISP to review content, and does not occur in the normal course of business. This type of accessibility by the service provider was rejected as diminishing the expectation of privacy in *Katz,* as well as in *Heckenkamp.*

bearing on his expectation of privacy in the content. In fact, these screening processes are analogous to the post office screening packages for evidence of drugs or explosives, which does not expose the content of written documents enclosed in the packages. The fact that such screening occurs as a general matter does not diminish the well-established reasonable expectation of privacy that users of the mail maintain in the packages they send.

It is also worth noting that other portions of the SCA itself strongly support an e-mail user's reasonable expectation of privacy in the content of his e-mails. Section 2701 prohibits unauthorized users from accessing e-mails. Section 2702 generally prohibits an ISP from disclosing e-mail content without the permission of the user. Further, section 2703 makes it easier for the government to get an order requiring the disclosure of records and subscriber information, in which the user does not maintain a privacy interest vis-a-vis the ISP, than to obtain an order requiring the disclosure of content. The statute also requires a warrant to search the content of e-mails that have been stored for 180 days or less. 18 U.S.C. [2]703(a). Thus, even though the contested exception in section 2703(b) creates tension with the Fourth Amendment's requirements for a warrant, independent provisions support the proposition that a user maintains a reasonable expectation of privacy in the content of his e-mails.

The government's compelled disclosure argument is initially on point, but fails to address adequately the caveat relating to a party's maintenance of a reasonable expectation of privacy in documents in the custody of a third party. A warrant based on probable cause would not have been necessary had the government subpoenaed Warshak or given him prior notice of its intent to seek an SCA order, because the need for this higher showing would be offset by his ability to obtain judicial review before producing any e-mails. *See Phibbs,* 999 F.2d at 1077 ("The subpoena has to be 'sufficiently limited in scope, relevant in purpose, and specific in directive so that compliance [would] not be unreasonable.' If it is a subpoena duces tecum, the government does not have to secure a judicial warrant before service is effectuated. Nonetheless, 'the subpoenaed party [must be able to] obtain judicial review of the reasonableness of the demand prior to suffering penalties for refusing to comply.'") (citing *See v. City of Seattle,* 387 U.S. 541, 544 (1967)). The same rationale would apply if the government subpoenaed a third party that had access to the content of the e-mails, and against whom Warshak had no claim of privacy, such as the recipient of one of his e-mails. By the same token, an SCA order that provided notice to the ISP alone, and not to the user, would be appropriate in the limited instances where the user had waived his expectation of privacy with respect to the ISP, such as where the government can show that auditing, monitoring, or inspection are expressly provided for in the terms of service, or where the user has e-mailed content directly to the ISP. Where the third party is not expected to access the e-mails in the normal course of business, however, the party maintains a reasonable expectation of privacy, and subpoenaing the entity with mere custody over the documents is insufficient to trump the Fourth Amendment warrant requirement.

The district court enjoined the United States "from seizing, pursuant to court order under 18 U.S.C. §2703(d), the contents of any personal e-mail account maintained by an Internet Service Provider in the name of any resident of the Southern District of Ohio without providing the relevant account holder or subscriber prior notice and an opportunity to be heard. . . ." Our discussion above necessitates one modification to this injunction, which counsel for Warshak agreed at oral argument would be appropriate. If the government can show, based on specific facts, that an e-mail account holder has waived his expectation of privacy vis-a-vis the ISP, compelled disclosure of e-mails through notice to the ISP alone would be appropriate. This is a narrow modification, however, as a right to access e-mails in an account only in certain limited circumstances would not be sufficient. Rather, the government must show that the ISP or other intermediary clearly established and utilized the right to inspect, monitor, or audit the content of e-mails, or otherwise had content revealed to it. In such cases the SCA order will operate as the functional equivalent of a third party subpoena, allowing disclosure through a party that has total access to the documents in question. On remand, therefore, the preliminary injunction shall allow seizures of e-mail in three situations: (1) if the government obtains a search warrant under the Fourth Amendment, based on probable cause and in with the particularity requirement; (2) if the government provides notice to the account holder in seeking an SCA order, according him the same judicial review he would be allowed were he to be subpoenaed; or (3) if the government can show specific, articulable facts, demonstrating that an ISP or other entity has complete access to the e-mails in question and that it actually relies on and utilizes this access in the normal course of business, sufficient to establish that the user has waived his expectation of privacy with respect to that entity, in which case compelled disclosure may occur if that entity is afforded notice and an opportunity to be heard. . . .

IV.

The district court correctly determined that e-mail users maintain a reasonable expectation of privacy in the content of their e-mails, and we agree that the injunctive relief it crafted was largely appropriate, although we find necessary one modification. On remand, the preliminary injunction should be modified to prohibit the United States from seizing the contents of a personal e-mail account maintained by an ISP in the name of any resident of the Southern District of Ohio, pursuant to a court order issued under 18 U.S.C. §2703(d), without either (1) providing the relevant account holder or subscriber prior notice and an opportunity to be heard, or (2) making a fact-specific showing that the account holder maintained no expectation of privacy with respect to the ISP, in which case only the ISP need be provided prior notice and an opportunity to be heard.

[NSL p. 581, insert after Note 7. CTL p. 200, insert after Note 8.]

John Doe, Inc. v. Mukasey (*Doe V*)
United States Court of Appeals for the Second Circuit, 2008
549 F.3d 861

JON O. NEWMAN, Circuit Judge: This appeal concerns challenges to the constitutionality of statutes regulating the issuance by the Federal Bureau of Investigation ("FBI") of a type of administrative subpoena generally known as a National Security Letter ("NSL") to electronic communication service providers ("ECSPs"). *See* 18 U.S.C. §§2709, 3511 (collectively "the NSL statutes). . . . Primarily at issue on this appeal are challenges to the provisions (1) prohibiting the recipient from disclosing the fact that an NSL has been received, *see* 18 U.S.C. §2709(c), and (2) structuring judicial review of the nondisclosure requirement, *see id.*§3511(b). . . .

Background . . .

Amendments to the NSL statutes. While appeals in *Doe I* and *Doe [II]* were pending, Congress amended the NSL statutes in two respects. *See* USA Patriot Improvement and Reauthorization Act of 2005, §§115, 116(a), Pub. L. No. 109-177, 120 Stat. 192, 211-14 (Mar. 9, 2006) ("the Reauthorization Act"), *amended by* USA Patriot Act Additional Reauthorizing Amendments Act of 2006, §4(b), Pub. L. No. 109-178,

120 Stat. 278, 280 (Mar. 9, 2006) ("Additional Reauthorization Act"), codified at 18 U.S.C.A. §2709(c) (West Supp. 2008). . . . The Reauthorization Act amended subsection 2709(c) by replacing the single paragraph of former subsection 2709(c) with four subdivisions, the fourth of which was amended by the Additional Reauthorization Act. We consider below the text of amended subsection 2709(c), which is set out in the margin.[7] Second, in the Reauthorization Act, Congress added provisions for judicial review, now codified in section 3511, to permit the recipient of an NSL to petition a United States district court for an

---

7. Subsection 2709(c), as amended by the Additional Reauthorization Act, provides:

(c) Prohibition of certain disclosure.—

(1) If the Director of the Federal Bureau of Investigation, or his designee in a position not lower than Deputy Assistant Director at Bureau headquarters or a Special Agent in Charge in a Bureau field office designated by the Director, certifies that otherwise there may result a danger to the national security of the United States, interference with a criminal, counterterrorism, or counterintelligence investigation, interference with diplomatic relations, or danger to the life or physical safety of any person, no wire or electronic communications service provider, or officer, employee, or agent thereof, shall disclose to any person (other than those to whom such disclosure is necessary to comply with the request or an attorney to obtain legal advice or legal assistance with respect to the request) that the Federal Bureau of Investigation has sought or obtained access to information or records under this section.

(2) The request shall notify the person or entity to whom the request is directed of the nondisclosure requirement under paragraph (1).

(3) Any recipient disclosing to those persons necessary to comply with the request or to an attorney to obtain legal advice or legal assistance with respect to the request shall inform such person of any applicable nondisclosure requirement. Any person who receives a disclosure under this subsection shall be subject to the same prohibitions on disclosure under paragraph (1).

(4) At the request of the Director of the Federal Bureau of Investigation or the designee of the Director, any person making or intending to make a disclosure under this section shall identify to the Director or such designee the person to whom such disclosure will be made or to whom such disclosure was made prior to the request, except that nothing in this section shall require a person to inform the Director or such designee of the identity of an attorney to whom disclosure was made or will be made to obtain legal advice or legal assistance with respect to the request under subsection (a).

18 U.S.C.A. §2709(c) (West Supp. 2008). . . .

order modifying or setting aside the NSL, *see* 18 U.S.C.A. §3511(a)
(West Supp. 2008), and the nondisclosure requirement, *see id.* §3511(b).
The NSL may be modified if "compliance would be unreasonable,
oppressive, or otherwise unlawful." *Id.* §3511(a). The nondisclosure
requirement, which prohibits disclosure by the NSL recipient of the fact
that the FBI has sought or obtained access to the requested information,
may be modified or set aside, upon a petition filed by the NSL recipient,
id. §3511(b)(1), if the district court "finds that there is no reason to
believe that disclosure may endanger the national security of the United
States" or cause other of the enumerated harms (worded slightly
differently from subsection 2709(c)(1)), *see id.* §3511(b)(2), (3). The
nondisclosure requirement further provides that if the Attorney General
or senior governmental officials certify that disclosure may endanger the
national security or interfere with diplomatic relations, such certification
shall be treated as "conclusive" unless the court finds that the
certification was made "in bad faith." *Id.* . . .

   The District Court's second decision. On September 6, 2007, the
District Court issued its second opinion, ruling, on cross-motions for
summary judgment, that, despite the amendments to the NSL statutes,
subsections 2709(c) and 3511(b) are facially unconstitutional, *see id.* at
387, and that the Defendants-Appellants are enjoined from issuing NSLs
under section 2709 and enforcing the provisions of subsections 2709(c)
and 3511(b), *see id.* at 425-26. . . .

   [The district court held that the nondislosure requirement constituted
a "prior restraint" under First Amendment law, requiring "strict scrutiny"
by the court. Acknowledging that national security is a compelling state
interest, the district court held that the nondisclosure provisions vested
executive officials with broad discretion without necessary procedural
safeguards. It also found that the statutory amendments violated the First
Amendment and the separation of powers by prescribing judicial review
procedures and a judicial review standard inconsistent with strict scrutiny
and by permitting nondisclosure orders that are not narrowly tailored in
scope or duration.]

Discussion . . .

I. Applicable Principles

   The First Amendment principles relevant to the District Court's
rulings are well established, although their application to the statutory
provisions at issue requires careful consideration. A judicial order

"forbidding certain communications when issued in advance of the time that such communications are to occur" is generally regarded as a "prior restraint." A content-based restriction is subject to review under the standard of strict scrutiny, requiring a showing that the restriction is "narrowly tailored to promote a compelling Government interest." *United States v. Playboy Entertainment Group, Inc.,* 529 U.S. 803, 813 (2000).

Where expression is conditioned on governmental permission, such as a licensing system for movies, the First Amendment generally requires procedural protections to guard against impermissible censorship. *See Freedman* [*v. Maryland,* 380 U.S. 51, 58 (1965)]. *Freedman* identified three procedural requirements: (1) any restraint imposed prior to judicial review must be limited to "a specified brief period"; (2) any further restraint prior to a final judicial determination must be limited to "the shortest fixed period compatible with sound judicial resolution"; and (3) the burden of going to court to suppress speech and the burden of proof in court must be placed on the government.

Once constitutional standards have been authoritatively enunciated, Congress may not legislatively supercede them. . . .

The national security context in which NSLs are authorized imposes on courts a significant obligation to defer to judgments of Executive Branch officials. . . .

The last set of principles implicated by the Plaintiffs' constitutional challenges concerns the somewhat related issues of judicial interpretation of unclear statutes, judicial revision of constitutionally defective statutes, and judicial severance of constitutionally invalid provisions from otherwise valid provisions. It is well established that courts should resolve ambiguities in statutes in a manner that avoids substantial constitutional issues.

Less clear is the authority of courts to revise a statute to overcome a constitutional defect. Of course, it is the province of the Legislative Branch to legislate. But in limited circumstances the Supreme Court has undertaken to fill in a statutory gap arising from the invalidation of a portion of a statute. . . .

III. The Interpretation of the NSL Statutes . . .

. . . [S]ubsection 2709(c) specifies what senior FBI officials must certify to trigger the nondisclosure requirement, and subsection 3511(b) specifies, in similar but not identical language, what a district court must find in order to modify or set aside such a requirement. Senior FBI officials must certify that in the absence of a nondisclosure requirement "there may result a danger to the national security of the United States, interference with a criminal, counterterrorism, or counterintelligence investigation, interference with diplomatic relations, or danger to the life or physical safety of any person." 18 U.S.C. §2709(c)(1). Upon challenge by an NSL recipient, a district court may modify or set aside a nondisclosure requirement "if it finds that there is no reason to believe that disclosure may endanger the national security of the United States, interfere with a criminal, counterterrorism, or counterintelligence investigation, interfere with diplomatic relations, or endanger the life or physical safety of any person." *Id.*§3511(b)(2).

These provisions present three issues for interpretation: (1) what is the scope of the enumerated harms? (2) what justifies a nondisclosure requirement? and (3) which side has the burden of proof?. . .

[The government made concessions on each of these questions.]

Under the principles outlined above, we are satisfied that we may accept the Government's concessions on all three matters of statutory interpretation without trenching on Congress's prerogative to legislate. We will therefore construe subsection 2709(c)(1) to mean that the enumerated harms must be related to "an authorized investigation to protect against international terrorism or clandestine intelligence activities," 18 U.S.C. §2709(b)(1), (2), and construe subsections 3511(b)(2) and (3) to place on the Government the burden to persuade a district court that there is a good reason to believe that disclosure may result in one of the enumerated harms, and to mean that a district court, in order to modify or set aside a nondisclosure order, must find that such a good reason exists.

IV. Constitutionality of the NSL Statutes

(a) *Basic approach.* Turning to the First Amendment issues with respect to the NSL statutes as thus construed, we believe that the proper path to decision lies between the broad positions asserted by the parties. Although the nondisclosure requirement is in some sense a prior restraint, as urged by the Plaintiffs, it is not a typical example of such a restriction for it is not a restraint imposed on those who customarily wish to exercise rights of free expression, such as speakers in public fora, distributors of literature, or exhibitors of movies. And although the nondisclosure requirement is triggered by the content of a category of information, that category, consisting of the fact of receipt of an NSL and some related details, is far more limited than the broad categories of information that have been at issue with respect to typical content-based restrictions.

On the other hand, we do not accept the Government's contentions that the nondisclosure requirement can be considered to satisfy First Amendment standards based on analogies to secrecy rules applicable to grand juries, judicial misconduct proceedings, and certain interactions between individuals and governmental entities. The justification for grand jury secrecy inheres in the nature of the proceedings. As the Supreme Court has noted, such secrecy serves several interests common to most such proceedings, including enhancing the willingness of witnesses to come forward, promoting truthful testimony, lessening the risk of flight or attempts to influence grand jurors by those about to be indicted, and avoiding public ridicule of those whom the grand jury declines to indict.

Although these interests do not warrant a prohibition on disclosure of a witness's own testimony after the term of the grand jury has ended, they generally suffice to maintain grand jury secrecy against First Amendment claims to divulge information a witness obtained through participation in the grand jury process. Unlike the grand jury proceeding, as to which interests in secrecy arise from the nature of the proceeding, the nondisclosure requirement of subsection 2709(c) is imposed at the demand of the Executive Branch under circumstances where secrecy might or might not be warranted, depending on the circumstances alleged to justify such secrecy. . . .

The nondisclosure requirement of subsection 2709(c) is not a typical prior restraint or a typical content-based restriction warranting the most rigorous First Amendment scrutiny. On the other hand, the Government's analogies to nondisclosure prohibitions in other contexts do not persuade us to use a significantly diminished standard of review. In any event, John Doe, Inc., has been restrained from publicly expressing a category of information, albeit a narrow one, and that information is relevant to intended criticism of a governmental activity. *See Gentile v. State Bar of Nevada*, 501 U.S. 1030, 1034 (1991) ("There is no question that speech critical of the exercise of the State's power lies at the very center of the First Amendment."); *Landmark [Communications, Inc. v. Virginia*, 435 U.S. 829, 838 (1978)] ("Whatever differences may exist about interpretations of the First Amendment, there is practically universal agreement that a major purpose of that Amendment was to protect the free discussion of governmental affairs.") (internal quotation marks omitted).

The panel is not in agreement as to whether, in this context, we should examine subsection 2709(c) under a standard of traditional strict scrutiny or under a standard that, in view of the context, is not quite as "exacting" a form of strict scrutiny, *Seattle Times [Co. v. Rhinehart*, 467 U.S. 20, 33 (1984)]. Ultimately, this disagreement has no bearing on our disposition because, as we discuss below, the only two limitations on NSL procedures required by First Amendment procedural standards would be required under either degree of scrutiny. We note that, for purposes of the litigation in this Court, the Government has conceded that strict scrutiny is the applicable standard.

(b) *Strict scrutiny.* Under strict scrutiny review, the Government must demonstrate that the nondisclosure requirement is "narrowly tailored to promote a compelling Government interest," *Playboy Entertainment,* 529 U.S. at 813, and that there are no "less restrictive alternatives [that] would be at least as effective in achieving the legitimate purpose that the statute was enacted to serve," *Reno v. ACLU,* 521 U.S. 844, 874 (1997). Since "[i]t is obvious and unarguable that no governmental interest is more compelling than the security of the Nation," *Haig v. Agee,* 453 U.S. 280, 307 (1981) (internal quotation marks omitted), the principal strict scrutiny issue turns on whether the narrow tailoring requirement is met, and this issue, as the District Court observed, essentially concerns the process by which the nondisclosure requirement is imposed and tested.

With subsections 2709(c) and 3511(b) interpreted as set forth above, *see* Part III, *supra,* two aspects of that process remain principally at issue: the absence of a requirement that the Government initiate judicial review of the lawfulness of a nondisclosure requirement and the degree of deference a district court is obliged to accord to the certification of senior governmental officials in ordering nondisclosure.

(i) *Absence of requirement that the Government initiate judicial review.* The Plaintiffs alleged, and the District Court agreed, that the third *Freedman* procedural requirement applies to the NSL statutes, requiring the Government to initiate judicial review of its imposition of a nondisclosure requirement. . . .

Instead of determining whether, as the Government contends, a burden of initiating litigation can prevent application of the third *Freedman* procedural safeguard, we consider an available means of minimizing that burden, use of which would substantially avoid the Government's argument. The Government could inform each NSL recipient that it should give the Government prompt notice, perhaps within ten days, in the event that the recipient wishes to contest the nondisclosure requirement. Upon receipt of such notice, the Government could be accorded a limited time, perhaps 30 days, to initiate a judicial review proceeding to maintain the nondisclosure requirement, and the proceeding would have to be concluded within a prescribed time, perhaps 60 days. In accordance with the first and second *Freedman* safeguards, the NSL could inform the recipient that the nondisclosure requirement would remain in effect during the entire interval of the recipient's decision whether to contest the nondisclosure requirement, the Government's prompt application to a court, and the court's prompt adjudication on the merits. The NSL could also inform the recipient that the nondisclosure requirement would remain in effect if the recipient declines to give the Government notice of an intent to challenge the requirement or, upon a challenge, if the Government prevails in court. If the Government is correct that very few NSL recipients have any interest in challenging the nondisclosure requirement (perhaps no more than three have done so thus far), this "reciprocal notice procedure" would nearly eliminate the Government's burden to initiate litigation (with a corresponding minimal burden on NSL recipients to defend numerous lawsuits). Thus, the Government's litigating burden can be substantially minimized, and the resulting slight burden is not a reason for precluding application of the third *Freedman* safeguard.

The Government's second argument for not applying *Freedman*'s third safeguard relies on an attempt to analogize the nondisclosure requirement in NSLs to nondisclosure requirements imposed in the context of pre-existing interaction with a governmental activity. Unlike the movies subject to licensing in *Freedman,* which were created independently of governmental activity, the information kept secret by an NSL, the Government contends, is "information that the recipient learns by (and only through) his participation in the [G]overnment's own investigatory processes." Although the governmental interaction distinction has validity with respect to the litigant obtaining discovery material in *Seattle Times* and the former CIA employees seeking to disclose sensitive material in *[United States v.] Marchetti* [466 F.2d 1309 (4th Cir. 1972)], and *Snepp* [v. *United States,* 444 U.S. 507 (1980)], we think it has no application to an ECSP with no relevant governmental interaction prior to receipt of an NSL. The recipient's "participation" in the investigation is entirely the result of the Government's action. . . .

Third, the Government seeks to avoid *Freedman*'s third requirement on the ground that the risk of administrative error "is significantly smaller under [sub]section 2709(c) than under licensing schemes like the one in *Freedman.*" Although the risk of error may be smaller, it remains

sufficient to require a judicial review procedure that conforms to
Freedman. The OIG [Office of Inspector General, Dept. of Justice]
Report concluded that "'the FBI used NSLs in violation of applicable NSL
statutes, Attorney General Guidelines, and internal FBI policies.'" . . .

The availability of a minimally burdensome reciprocal notice
procedure for governmental initiation of judicial review and the
inadequacy of the Government's attempts to avoid the third *Freedman*
safeguard persuade us that this safeguard, normally required where strict
scrutiny applies, must be observed. Therefore, in the absence of
Government-initiated judicial review, subsection 3511(b) is not narrowly
tailored to conform to First Amendment procedural standards. We
conclude, as did the District Court, that subsection 3511(b) does not
survive either traditional strict scrutiny or a slightly less exacting
measure of such scrutiny.

(ii) *Deference to administrative discretion.* The Plaintiffs
contended, and the District Court agreed, that the judicial review
contemplated by subsection 3511(b) authorizes a degree of deference to
the Executive Branch that is inconsistent with First Amendment
standards. Although acknowledging that "national security is a
compelling interest justifying nondisclosure in certain situations," the
District Court faulted the review provision in several respects. First, the
Court stated that the statute "requires the court to blindly credit a finding
that there 'may' be a reason – potentially any conceivable and not
patently frivolous reason – for it to believe disclosure will result in a
certain harm." *Id.* Our construction of the statute, however, avoids that
concern. As indicated above, *see* Part III, *supra,* we interpret subsection
3511(b) to place on the Government the burden to show a "good" reason
to believe that disclosure may result in an enumerated harm, *i.e.,* a harm
related to "an authorized investigation to protect against international
terrorism or clandestine intelligence activities," 18 U.S.C. §2709(b)(1),
(2), and to place on a district court an obligation to make the "may
result" finding only after consideration, albeit deferential, of the
Government's explanation concerning the risk of an enumerated harm.

Assessing the Government's showing of a good reason to believe
that an enumerated harm may result will present a district court with a
delicate task. While the court will normally defer to the Government's
considered assessment of *why* disclosure in a particular case may result
in an enumerated harm related to such grave matters as international
terrorism or clandestine intelligence activities, it cannot, consistent with
strict scrutiny standards, uphold a nondisclosure requirement on a
conclusory assurance that such a likelihood exists. In this case, the

director of the FBI certified that "the disclosure of the NSL itself or its contents may endanger the national security of the United States." To accept that conclusion without requiring some elaboration would "cast Article III judges in the role of petty functionaries, persons required to enter as a court judgment an executive officer's decision, but stripped of capacity to evaluate independently whether the executive's decision is correct." *Gutierrez de Martinez v. Lamagno,* 515 U.S. 417, 426 (1995).

In showing why disclosure would risk an enumerated harm, the Government must at least indicate the nature of the apprehended harm and provide a court with some basis to assure itself (based on *in camera* presentations where appropriate) that the link between disclosure and risk of harm is substantial. As the Government acknowledges, "Nothing in [subs]ection 3511(b) would require a district court to confine judicial review to the FBI's necessarily unelaborated public statement about the need for nondisclosure. The provisions in [subs]ections 3511(d) and (e) for *ex parte* and *in camera* review provide a ready mechanism for the FBI to provide a more complete explanation of its reasoning, and the court is free to elicit such an explanation as part of the review process."

We have every confidence that district judges can discharge their review responsibility with faithfulness to First Amendment considerations and without intruding on the prerogative of the Executive Branch to exercise its judgment on matters of national security. Such a judgment is not to be second-guessed, but a court must receive some indication that the judgment has been soundly reached. As the Supreme Court has noted in matters of similar gravity, the Constitution "envisions a role for all three branches when individual liberties are at stake." *Hamdi v. Rumsfeld,* 542 U.S. 507, 536 (2004).

The District Court's second reason for considering the judicial review procedure of subsection 3511(b) deficient was a perceived preclusion of a court's authority, when presented with a "plausible, reasonable, and specific" enumerated harm, to balance "the potential harm against the particular First Amendment interest raised by a particular challenge." We see no deficiency in this regard. The balance sought by the District Court is an important aspect of judicial review of prior restraints. That is why we have interpreted the statutory standard to permit a nondisclosure requirement only upon an adequate demonstration that a good reason exists reasonably to apprehend a risk of an enumerated harm, and have expressly read the enumerated harms as being linked to international terrorism or clandestine intelligence activities. As a result of this interpretation, the balance sought by the District Court is now inherent in the statutory standard. A demonstration of a reasonable likelihood of potential harm, related to international terrorism or clandestine intelligence activities, will virtually always outweigh the First Amendment interest in speaking about such a limited and particularized occurrence as the receipt of an NSL and will suffice to maintain the secrecy of the fact of such receipt.

The District Court's third objection to the judicial review procedure is far more substantial. The Court deemed inconsistent with strict scrutiny standards the provision of subsections 3511(b)(2) and (b)(3) specifying that a certification by senior governmental officials that disclosure may "endanger the national security of the United States or interfere with diplomatic relations . . . shall be treated as conclusive unless the court finds that the certification was made in bad faith." 18 U.S.C. §3511(b)(2). We agree.

There is not meaningful judicial review of the decision of the Executive Branch to prohibit speech if the position of the Executive Branch that speech would be harmful is "conclusive" on a reviewing court, absent only a demonstration of bad faith. To accept deference to that extraordinary degree would be to reduce strict scrutiny to no scrutiny, save only in the rarest of situations where bad faith could be shown. Under either traditional strict scrutiny or a less exacting application of that standard, some demonstration from the Executive Branch of the need for secrecy is required in order to conform the nondisclosure requirement to First Amendment standards. The fiat of a governmental official, though senior in rank and doubtless honorable in the execution of official duties, cannot displace the judicial obligation to enforce constitutional requirements. "Under no circumstances should the Judiciary become the handmaiden of the Executive." *United States v. Smith,* 899 F.2d 564, 569 (6th Cir. 1990).

V. Remedy

To recapitulate our conclusions, we (1) construe subsection 2709(c) to permit a nondisclosure requirement only when senior FBI officials certify that disclosure may result in an enumerated harm that is related to "an authorized investigation to protect against international terrorism or clandestine intelligence activities," (2) construe subsections 3511(b)(2) and (b)(3) to place on the Government the burden to show that a good reason exists to expect that disclosure of receipt of an NSL will risk an enumerated harm, (3) construe subsections 3511(b)(2) and (b)(3) to mean that the Government satisfies its burden when it makes an adequate demonstration as to why disclosure in a particular case may result in an enumerated harm, (4) rule that subsections 2709(c) and 3511(b) are unconstitutional to the extent that they impose a nondisclosure requirement without placing on the Government the burden of initiating judicial review of that requirement, and (5) rule that subsections 3511(b)(2) and (b)(3) are unconstitutional to the extent that, upon such review, a governmental official's certification that disclosure may endanger the national security of the United States or interfere with diplomatic relations is treated as conclusive.

Implementing these conclusions requires us to apply the principles of judicial interpretation and limited revision of statutes and consider the related issue of severance discussed in Part I, *supra*. We are satisfied that conclusions (1), (2), and (3) fall within our judicial authority to interpret statutes to avoid constitutional objections or conform to constitutional requirements. Conclusions (4) and (5) require further consideration.

We deem it beyond the authority of a court to "interpret" or "revise" the NSL statutes to create the constitutionally required obligation of the Government to initiate judicial review of a nondisclosure requirement. However, the Government might be able to assume such an obligation without additional legislation. As we discussed in Part IV(b)(i), *supra,* the Government's concern about the potentially substantial burden of initiating litigation can be readily alleviated by use of the reciprocal notice procedure we have suggested. . . .

In view of these possibilities, we need not invalidate the entirety of the nondisclosure requirement of subsection 2709(c) or the judicial review provisions of subsection 3511(b). Although the conclusive presumption clause of subsections 3511(b)(2) and (b)(3) must be stricken, we invalidate subsection 2709(c) and the remainder of subsection 3511(b) only to the extent that they fail to provide for Government-initiated judicial review. The Government can respond to this partial invalidation ruling by using the suggested reciprocal notice procedure. With this procedure in place, subsections 2709(c) and 3511(b) would survive First Amendment challenge. . . .

Conclusion

Accordingly, for all the foregoing reasons, subsections 2709(c) and 3511(b) are construed in conformity with this opinion and partially invalidated only to the extent set forth in this opinion, the injunction is modified as set forth in this opinion, and the judgment of the District

Court is affirmed in part, reversed in part, and remanded for further proceedings consistent with this opinion.

[NSL p. 581, CTL p. 200. Insert the following two decisions, *Doe VI* and *Doe VII*, after *John Doe, Inc. v. Mukasey (Doe V)*.]

Doe v. Holder *(Doe VI)*
United States District Court for the Southern District of New York, 2009
665 F. Supp. 2d 426

VICTOR MARRERO, District Judge. . . . The discrete issue presently before this Court is whether the Government is justified in continuing to require nondisclosure of a National Security Letter ("NSL") issued to Doe. Following remand, the Government submitted an ex parte, in camera filing under seal, consisting of a classified sworn Declaration (the "Declaration"), dated June 16, 2009, made by a Supervisory Special Agent of the Federal Bureau of Investigation ("FBI"). . . .

II. DISCUSSION

B. Nondisclosure of the NSL . . .

. . . On the basis of an in camera review of the Government's classified Declaration, this Court finds that there is no genuine issue of material fact as to whether the Government's justification meets the standard set forth by the Second Circuit. The Court is persuaded that the Government has demonstrated that a good reason exists to believe that disclosure may result in a harm related to an authorized ongoing investigation to protect against international terrorism or clandestine intelligence activities. Also, as required by *John Doe, Inc. [v. Mukasey,* 549 F.3d 861 (2d Cir. 2008)]*, the Government has demonstrated to the satisfaction of the Court that the link between disclosure and the risk of harm is substantial.

Plaintiffs contend that even if the Government can satisfy its burden as to non-disclosure of the NSL, there is no continuing need for non-disclosure of John Doe's identity. The Court disagrees. Plaintiffs' contention that revealing John Doe's identity would "add only the most marginal information about the government's investigation," is not persuasive. The Court finds, on the basis of its in camera inspection of the Declaration, that there is a reasonable likelihood that knowledge of Doe's identity could inform the Government's target that he or she is still under active investigation. This result would be even more likely if this Court were to partially lift the NSL's nondisclosure requirement. The outcome of such a course would be to identify an active investigation as requiring continuing nondisclosure while simultaneously providing information that could be useful to the Government's target. The Supreme Court, in upholding non-disclosure of intelligence information by the Central Intelligence Agency under apposite circumstances, has cautioned that "bits and pieces" of data "may aid in piecing together bits of other information even when the individual piece is not of obvious importance in itself." *CIA v. Sims,* 471 U.S. 159, 178 (1985). The Court therefore finds that the Government has carried its burden as to the nondisclosure of Doe's identity.

Finally, Plaintiffs seek disclosure of the NSL Attachment, arguing that it demonstrates abuse of the FBI's NSL power and is a matter of public concern. The Government opposes this request on the grounds that disclosure of the NSL Attachment is being raised for the first time in this litigation and is not within the scope of the present proceeding. For the purposes of this motion, the Court treats the NSL Attachment as part of the NSL issued to Doe and thus denies Plaintiffs' motion to lift the nondisclosure requirement as to the NSL Attachment. Plaintiff has not identified any authority to support its contention that the NSL Attachment should be considered separately. Nor does the Court find any reason to disaggregate the NSL into component parts.

C. First Amendment

The Court notes that this ruling does not constitute a permanent bar on the NSL's disclosure. *See John Doe, Inc.,* at 883-84 (stating that NSL nondisclosure requirement is subject to annual challenges as provided by §3511(b)); *Doe v. Gonzales,* 449 F.3d 415, 422 (2d Cir. 2006) ("A permanent ban on speech seems highly unlikely to survive the test of strict scrutiny, one where the government must show that the statute is narrowly tailored to meet a compelling government interest.") (Cardamone, J., concurring) (*citing Ashcroft v. ACLU,* 542 U.S. 656, 665-66 (2004)). As articulated by the Second Circuit in *John Doe, Inc.,* and previously by this Court in *Doe I* [*Doe v. Ashcroft,* 334 F. Supp. 2d 471 (S.D.N.Y. 2004)] and *Doe II* [*Doe v. Gonzales,* 386 F. Supp. 2d 66 (D. Conn. 2004)], NSL non-disclosure orders implicate First Amendment interests fundamental to our Constitution. The First Amendment requires that a nondisclosure order be maintained only as long as it is "narrowly tailored to promote a compelling Government interest," *John Doe, Inc.,*

549 F.3d at 878 (*quoting United States v. Playboy Entm't Group*, 529 U.S. 803, 813 (2000)), and that there are no "less restrictive alternatives [that] would be at least as effective in achieving the legitimate purpose that the statute was enacted to serve." *Id.* (*quoting Reno v. ACLU*, 521 U.S. 844, 874 (1997)). Subsection 3511(b) provides that NSL recipients can challenge the nondisclosure requirement annually. Plaintiffs therefore possess the right to challenge the nondisclosure order again in the future if it remains necessary to do so. As provided by the Second Circuit, in the event subsequent challenges are raised, the standards and burden of proof articulated in *John Doe, Inc.* will apply.

III. ORDER

For the reasons stated above, it is hereby ordered that [the] motion . . . of plaintiffs John Doe ("Doe"), the American Civil Liberties Union, and the American Civil Liberties Union Foundation . . . to lift the nondisclosure requirement of the National Security Letter issued to Doe is DENIED. Defendants Eric Holder, in his official capacity as Attorney General of the United States, Robert Mueller, in his official capacity as Director of the Federal Bureau of Investigation, and Valerie E. Caproni, in her official capacity as General Counsel to the Federal Bureau of Investigation . . . are hereby permitted to enforce the nondisclosure provisions of 18 U.S.C. §2709(c) and 18 U.S.C. §3511(b) as applied to the National Security Letter issued to Doe . . . .

So ordered.

Doe v. Holder *(Doe VII)*
United States District Court for the Southern District of New York, 2010
2010 WL 1253522

VICTOR MARRERO, District Judge. . . . [In this decision, the court considered plaintiff's motion for reconsideration of the court's earlier order authorizing nondisclosure of an attachment to the National Security Letter issued to Doe. It ordered the disclosure of material it found to be within the scope of information that the Patriot Act authorized the FBI to obtain by use of NSLs or of material that the FBI publicly acknowledged requesting previously by NSL. This information included the name, address, telephone number, account number, email address and billing information of a subscriber. But it refused to order disclosure of the rest of the Attachment.]

... Specifically, the Court finds that the Government has demonstrated a reasonable likelihood that disclosure of the Attachment in its entirety could inform current targets of law enforcement investigations, including the particular target of the Government's ongoing inquiry in this action, as well as, potentially, future targets, as to certain types of records and other materials the Government seeks through national security investigations employing NSLs. The Government has made a plausible showing that public access to such information could provide knowledge about current FBI activities as well as valuable insights into the agency's investigative methods that could produce the harms the NSL statute sought to safeguard against. . . .

... The Supreme Court, in upholding nondisclosure of intelligence information by the Central Intelligence Agency under analogous circumstances, has recognized that risks of what "may" happen have bearing upon and may be factored in resolving government claims for nondisclosure, cautioning that "bits and pieces of data *may* aid in piecing together bits of other information even when the individual piece is not of obvious importance in itself," *CIA v. Sims,* 471 U.S. 159 (1985) (emphasis added).

The Supreme Court's observation in *Sims* reflects practical wisdom drawn from everyday experience. Individuals intent on carrying out illegal activities often manage to remain outside the reach of the law, one step ahead of the police and forearmed by resourceful monitoring of the information the government gathers through law enforcement methods and technologies. By common sense analogy, were John Dillinger handed pieces of the bank's blueprints showing directions to the vault, he very well "may" or "could" find his way to the spot marked "X," or if tipped that the cops have staked lookouts at the scene, he "might" avoid the job altogether. To reasonably demonstrate the likelihood of that deduction would not demand giant leaps of conjecture. Yet, under Plaintiffs' theory in the case at hand, any risk of future harm from compelled disclosure of police surveillance information under these circumstances would be dismissed as purely speculative and unjustified. Consequently, to show that the projected law enforcement concerns are genuine essentially would require that at least some clues about the police's surveillance plans be revealed first and then wait and see whether the feared harm does indeed materialize. The Court finds no thing in First Amendment doctrine; or in logic, reason or practical experience, that would compel such an outcome. Accordingly, the Court finds that the Government has carried its burden as to the nondisclosure of portions of the Attachment. . . .

[NSL p. 590. Substitute for *MacWade v. Kelly* (S.D.N.Y.).]

MacWade v. Kelly
United States Court of Appeals, Second Circuit, 2006
460 F.3d 260

[The New York City subway system, with 26 interconnected lines and 468 passenger stations operating 24 hours a day, is the most heavily used subway in the United States. Experts assert that transportation systems like it are attractive targets for terrorist bombings because they carry large numbers of people. An attack could produce huge casualties, as well as causing widespread economic consequences and public fear. Following the March 11, 2004, Madrid commuter train bombings that killed more than 200 persons, another 2004 train bombing in Moscow that killed 40, and the London subway bombings in July 2005, killing 52 persons, the New York City subway system adopted a random "container inspection program" to address the threat of an explosive device being taken into the subway in a carry-on container or backpack.]

STRAUB, Circuit Judge. We consider whether the government may employ random, suspicionless container searches in order to safeguard mass transportation facilities from terrorist attack. The precise issue before us is whether one such search regime, implemented on the New York City subway system, satisfies the special needs exception to the Fourth Amendment's usual requirement of individualized suspicion. We hold that it does. . . .

BACKGROUND

I. *The Subway System and the Container Inspection Program*

. . . A "checkpoint" consists of a group of uniformed police officers standing at a folding table near the row of turnstiles disgorging onto the train platform. At the table, officers search the bags of a portion of subway riders entering the station.

In order to enhance the Program's deterrent effect, the NYPD selects the checkpoint locations "in a deliberative manner that may appear random, undefined, and unpredictable." In addition to switching checkpoint locations, the NYPD also varies their number, staffing, and scheduling so that the "deployment patterns . . . are constantly shifting." While striving to maintain the veneer of random deployment, the NYPD bases its decisions on a sophisticated host of criteria, such as fluctuations in passenger volume and threat level, overlapping coverage provided by its other counter-terrorism initiatives, and available manpower.

The officers assigned to each checkpoint give notice of the searches and make clear that they are voluntary. Close to their table they display a large poster notifying passengers that "backpacks and other containers [are] subject to inspection." The Metropolitan Transportation Authority, which operates the subway system, makes similar audio announcements in subway stations and on trains. A supervising sergeant at the checkpoint announces through a bullhorn that all persons wishing to enter the station are subject to a container search and those wishing to avoid the search must leave the station. Although declining the search is not by itself a basis for arrest, the police may arrest anyone who refuses to be searched and later attempts to reenter the subway system with the uninspected container.

Officers exercise virtually no discretion in determining whom to search. The supervising sergeant establishes a selection rate, such as every fifth or tenth person, based upon considerations such as the number of officers and the passenger volume at that particular checkpoint. The officers then search individuals in accordance with the established rate only.

Once the officers select a person to search, they limit their search as to scope, method, and duration. As to scope, officers search only those containers large enough to carry an explosive device, which means, for example, that they may not inspect wallets and small purses. Further, once they identify a container of eligible size, they must limit their inspection "to what is minimally necessary to ensure that the . . . item does not contain an explosive device," which they have been trained to recognize in various forms. They may not intentionally look for other contraband, although if officers incidentally discover such contraband, they may arrest the individual carrying it.[8] Officers may not attempt to read any written or printed material. Nor may they request or record a passenger's personal information, such as his name, address, or demographic data.

The preferred inspection method is to ask the passenger to open his bag and manipulate his possessions himself so that the officer may

---

8. At oral argument counsel for defendants informed us that thus far there have been no arrests for general crimes stemming from the seizure of non-explosive contraband discovered during a search conducted pursuant to the Program.

determine, on a purely visual basis, if the bag contains an explosive device. If necessary, the officer may open the container and manipulate its contents himself. Finally, because officers must conduct the inspection for no "longer than necessary to ensure that the individual is not carrying an explosive device," a typical inspection lasts for a matter of seconds. . . .

DISCUSSION . . .

II. *The Special Needs Doctrine*

. . . As the Fourth Amendment's text makes clear, the concept of reasonableness is the "touchstone of the constitutionality of a governmental search." *Bd. of Educ. v. Earls*, 536 U.S. 822, 828 (2002). "What is reasonable, of course, depends on all of the circumstances surrounding the search or seizure and the nature of the search or seizure itself." *Skinner v. Railway Labor Exec. Ass'n*, 489 U.S. 602 (1989) (internal quotation marks omitted). As a "general matter," a search is un-reasonable unless supported "by a warrant issued upon probable cause. . . ." *Nat'l Treasury Employees Union v. Von Raab*, 489 U.S. 656, 665 (1989). However, "neither a warrant nor probable cause, nor, indeed, any measure of individualized suspicion, is an indispensable component of reasonableness in every circumstance." *Id.*

In light of those "longstanding" principles, *id.,* we upheld a program employing metal detectors and hand searches of carry-on baggage at airports. *See United States v. Edwards*, 498 F.2d 496, 500-501 (2d Cir. 1974). We determined that the "purpose" of the search program was not to serve "as a general means for enforcing the criminal laws" but rather to "prevent airplane hijacking" by "terrorists[.]" *Id.* at 500. We then dispensed with the traditional warrant and probable cause requirements and instead balanced "the need for a search against the offensiveness of the intrusion." *Id.* We concluded that,

> When the risk is the jeopardy to hundreds of human lives and millions of dollars of property inherent in the pirating or blowing up of a large airplane, the danger alone meets the test of reasonableness, so long as the search is conducted in good faith for the purpose of preventing hijacking or like damage and with reasonable scope and the passenger has been given advance notice of his liability to such a search so that he can avoid it by choosing not to travel by air.

Id. Although at the time we lodged our decision within the broad rubric of reasonableness, *id.* at 498 n.5, our reasoning came to be known as the "special needs exception" roughly one decade later. *See New Jersey v. T.L.O.*, 469 U.S. 325, 351 (1985) (Blackmun, J., concurring) ("Only in those exceptional circumstances in which special needs, beyond the need for normal law enforcement, make the warrant and probable-cause requirement impracticable, is a court entitled to substitute its balancing of interests for that of the Framers."). . . .

The doctrine's central aspects are as follows. First, as a threshold matter, the search must "serve as [its] immediate purpose an objective distinct from the ordinary evidence gathering associated with crime investigation." *Nicholas v. Goord*, 430 F.3d 652, 663 (2d Cir. 2005). Second, once the government satisfies that threshold requirement, the court determines whether the search is reasonable by balancing several competing considerations. These balancing factors include (1) the weight and immediacy of the government interest, *Earls,* 536 U.S. at 834; (2) "the nature of the privacy interest allegedly compromised by" the search, *id.* at 830; (3) "the character of the intrusion imposed" by the search, *id.* at 832; and (4) the efficacy of the search in advancing the government interest.

III. *The Program Is Constitutional . . .*

A. *The special needs doctrine does not require that the subject of the search possess a diminished privacy interest*

Plaintiffs first raise the purely legal contention that, as a threshold matter, the special needs doctrine applies only where the subject of the search possesses a reduced privacy interest. While it is true that in most special needs cases the relevant privacy interest is somewhat "limited," *see Earls,* 536 U.S. at 832 (considering the privacy interest of public schoolchildren), the Supreme Court never has implied – much less actually held – that a reduced privacy expectation is a *sine qua non* of special needs analysis. . . .

Accordingly, to the extent that the principle needs clarification, we expressly hold that the special needs doctrine does not require, as a threshold matter, that the subject of the search possess a reduced privacy interest. Instead, once the government establishes a special need, the nature of the privacy interest is a factor to be weighed in the balance.

B. *The container inspection program serves a special need*

Plaintiffs next maintain that the District Court erred in concluding that the Program serves the special need of preventing a terrorist attack on the subway. . . .

As a factual matter, we agree with the District Court's conclusion that the Program aims to prevent a terrorist attack on the subway. Defendants implemented the Program in response to a string of bombings on commuter trains and subway systems abroad, which indicates that its purpose is to prevent similar occurrences in New York City. In its particulars, the Program seeks out explosives only: officers are trained to recognize different explosives, they search only those containers capable of carrying explosive devices, and they may not intentionally search for other contraband, read written or printed material, or request personal information. Additionally, the Program's voluntary nature illuminates its purpose: that an individual may refuse the search *provided* he leaves the subway establishes that the Program seeks to prevent a terrorist, laden with concealed explosives, from boarding a subway train in the first place.

As a legal matter, courts traditionally have considered special the government's need to "prevent" and "discover . . . latent or hidden" hazards, *Von Raab,* 489 U.S. at 668, in order to ensure the safety of mass transportation mediums, such as trains, airplanes, and highways. We have no doubt that concealed explosives are a hidden hazard, that the Program's purpose is prophylactic, and that the nation's busiest subway system implicates the public's safety. Accordingly, preventing a terrorist from bombing the subways constitutes a special need that is distinct from ordinary post hoc criminal investigation. Further, the fact that an officer incidentally may discover a different kind of contraband and arrest its possessor does not alter the Program's intended purpose.

Relying on dicta in [*City of Indianapolis v. Edmond*, 531 U.S. 32 (2000),] in which the Supreme Court struck down a drug interdiction checkpoint, plaintiffs urge the extraordinarily broad legal principle that a terrorist checkpoint serves a special need only in the face of an imminent attack. The *Edmond* Court merely remarked that under such dire circumstances, "[f]or example," a checkpoint regime "would almost certainly" be constitutional. *Edmond,* 531 U.S. at 44. . . . Where, as here, a search program is designed and implemented to seek out concealed explosives in order to safeguard a means of mass transportation from terrorist attack, it serves a special need.

C. On balance, the Program is constitutional

Having concluded that the Program serves a special need, we next balance the factors set forth above to determine whether the search is reasonable and thus constitutional.

(i) The government interest is immediate and substantial

. . . In light of the thwarted plots to bomb New York City's subway system, its continued desirability as a target, and the recent bombings of public transportation systems in Madrid, Moscow, and London, the risk to public safety is substantial and real. . . .

(ii) A subway rider has a full expectation of privacy in his containers

. . . [A] person carrying items in a closed, opaque bag has manifested his subjective expectation of privacy by keeping his belongings from plain view and indicating "that, for whatever reason, [he] prefer[s] to keep [them] close at hand." [*Bond v. United States*, 529 U.S. 334, 338 (2000).] Further, the Supreme Court has recognized as objectively reasonable a bus rider's expectation that his bag will not be felt "in an exploratory manner" from the outside, *id.* at 338-39, let alone opened and its contents visually inspected or physically manipulated. Accordingly, a subway rider who keeps his bags on his person possesses an undiminished expectation of privacy therein. We therefore weigh this factor in favor of plaintiffs.

(iii) The search is minimally intrusive

Although a subway rider enjoys a full privacy expectation in the contents of his baggage, the kind of search at issue here minimally intrudes upon that interest. Several uncontested facts establish that the Program is narrowly tailored to achieve its purpose: (1) passengers receive notice of the searches and may decline to be searched so long as they leave the subway, (2) police search only those containers capable of concealing explosives, inspect eligible containers only to determine whether they contain explosives, inspect the containers visually unless it is necessary to manipulate their contents, and do not read printed or written material or request personal information, (3) a typical search lasts only a matter of seconds, (4) uniformed personnel conduct the searches out in the open, which reduces the fear and stigma that removal to a hidden area can cause, and (5) police exercise no discretion in selecting whom to search, but rather employ a formula that ensures they do not arbitrarily exercise their authority. Although defendants need not employ "the least intrusive means" to serve the state interest, it appears they have approximated that model. Given the narrow tailoring that the Program achieves, this factor weighs strongly in favor of defendants, as the District Court properly concluded.

(iv) The Program is reasonably effective

In considering the "degree to which the seizure advances the public interest," we must remember not to wrest "from politically accountable officials . . . the decision as to which among reasonable alternative law enforcement techniques should be employed to deal with a serious public danger." *Michigan Dep't of State Police v. Sitz*, 496 U.S. 444, 453-454 (1990) (internal quotation marks omitted). That decision is best left to those with "a unique understanding of, and responsibility for, limited public resources, including a finite number of police officers." *Id.* 22 at 454. Accordingly, we ought not conduct a "searching examination of effectiveness." *Id.* at 454 (internal quotation marks omitted). Instead, we need only determine whether the Program is "a reasonably effective means of addressing" the government interest in deterring and detecting a terrorist attack on the subway system. *Earls,* 536 U.S. at 837. . . .

. . . [T]he expert testimony established that terrorists seek predictable and vulnerable targets, and the Program generates uncertainty that frustrates that goal, which, in turn, deters an attack. . . .

Plaintiffs further claim that the Program is ineffective because police notify passengers of the searches, and passengers are free to walk away and attempt to reenter the subway at another point or time. Yet we always have viewed notice and the opportunity to decline as beneficial aspects of a suspicionless search regime because those features minimize intrusiveness. *Edwards,* 498 F.2d at 500 (upholding suspicionless airport searches as reasonable "so long as . . . the passenger has been given advance notice of his liability to such a search so that he can avoid it by choosing not to travel by air"). Striking a search program as ineffective on account of its narrow tailoring would create a most perverse result: those programs "more pervasive and more invasive of privacy" more likely would satisfy the Fourth Amendment. *Von Raab,* 489 U.S. at 676-677 n.4 (internal quotation marks omitted).

Importantly, if a would-be bomber declines a search, he must leave the subway or be arrested – an outcome that, for the purpose of preventing subway bombings, we consider reasonably effective, especially since the record establishes that terrorists prize predictability. An unexpected change of plans might well stymie the attack, disrupt the synchronicity of multiple bombings, or at least reduce casualties by forcing the terrorist to detonate in a less populated location. . . .

CONCLUSION

In sum, we hold that the Program is reasonable, and therefore constitutional, because (1) preventing a terrorist attack on the subway is a special need; (2) that need is weighty; (3) the Program is a reasonably effective deterrent; and (4) even though the searches intrude on a full privacy interest, they do so to a minimal degree. We thus AFFIRM the judgment of the District Court.

[NSL p. 613, insert after Note 9. CTL p. 238, insert after Note 10.]

Tabbaa v. Chertoff
United States Court of Appeals, Second Circuit, 2007
509 F.3d 89

STRAUB, Circuit Judge: . . .

BACKGROUND . . .

In December 2004, CBP [the U.S. Bureau of Customs and Border Protection] received intelligence information that raised "specific concerns about certain national and international conferences," including the Reviving the Islamic Spirit Conference ("RIS Conference") that was being held from December 24 through December 26, 2004 at the Skydome in Toronto, Canada. Specifically, CBP had "reason to believe that certain individuals who were associated with terrorist organizations or activities and might pose a danger to the United States, or who were associated with organizations that provide financial support to terrorists, *would be* in attendance at the 2004 RIS conference." CBP also had reason to believe that the 2004 RIS Conference "*would serve* as a possible meeting point for terrorists" to "coordinate operations, and raise funds intended for terrorist activities," as well as "exchange ideas and documents," including "travel or identification documents such as passports or driver's licenses."[1]

Based on this intelligence, in late December 2004, CBP prepared an Intelligence Driven Special Operation ("IDSO"), which directed CBP officials at various ports of entry, including the one in Buffalo, where plaintiffs entered the United States, to undertake special enforcement actions. The IDSO instructed the officials to: (a) identify and examine all persons associated with any of the Islamic conferences at issue who sought entry into the United States, (b) contact CBP's National Targeting Center upon encountering conference participants "in order to determine whether individuals seeking to enter the United States posed a particular threat," and (c) question conference attendees about their activities during their trip and examine their documentation and persons and vehicles for "evidence of terrorist-related activities, such as plans, money, or even weapons." The IDSO also permitted, but did not require, border officials to fingerprint and photograph conference attendees. The purpose of these measures – which were designed to process travelers who are suspected terrorists – was to "confirm each individual's identity and verify that they were not on any watch list of suspected terrorists, or seeking to use the conference as a cover for crossing the U.S. border, or otherwise involved in illegal activity, or carrying any illegal weapons, documents, monetary instruments, or any other prohibited items across the border." Attendance at one of the Islamic conferences at issue was the sole factor that triggered the enhanced processing.

Plaintiffs – Sawsaan Tabbaa, Hassan Shibly, Asmaa Elshinawy, Karema Atassi, and Galeb Rizek – are U.S. citizens who were among an estimated 13,000 individuals from across North America who attended the RIS Conference. The conference, which lasted three days, included religious and cultural activities, musical performances, a series of prominent Islamic speakers, and communal prayer three times a day. Plaintiffs viewed participation in the conference as an act of religious observance and as a way to learn more about their religion. Tabbaa and

---

1. . . . [W]e viewed, *ex parte* and *in camera*, the classified intelligence at issue in order to ensure independently that there was a sufficient basis for [the CBP's statement of reasons for its concerns]. (The District Court was given the option of viewing this classified intelligence, but chose not to do so.) These materials confirmed what the record available to both parties already made plain: CBP had reason to believe that known terrorists, or those with terrorist ties, would be attending the RIS Conference.

Atassi viewed their participation as a "hajj," or pilgrimage; Tabbaa considered attendance to be part of her religious obligations.

Following the conference, plaintiffs reached the U.S. border at various times on December 26 and 27, 2004. Plaintiffs had no criminal records, and at no time did CBP have reasonable suspicion that any particular plaintiff had committed a crime or was associated with terrorists. Yet each experienced similar treatment. Plaintiffs were initially asked where they had been in Canada, and after responding that they had attended an Islamic conference at the Skydome, they were ordered to pull their cars into a separate area and enter a nearby building, where they saw several other people who appeared to be Muslims who also had attended the RIS Conference.

Inside this secondary inspection area, plaintiffs were directed to fill out several forms, and then were questioned about, *inter alia,* their past travels, their relationship to other vehicle occupants, what occurred at the RIS Conference, and why they had attended the conference. Plaintiffs were frisked, fingerprinted, and photographed, and their cars were searched. They were not told why they were being fingerprinted and photographed, or why they had been detained and inspected so thoroughly. Four of the plaintiffs at some point questioned part of the processing, but, after being told that he or she would not be released until all of the screening measures had been completed, eventually complied. Rizek and Shibly assert, and we assume for the purposes of this appeal, that CBP officers forcibly kicked their feet open and almost knocked them on the ground in order to effectuate the pat-downs. We also assume for the purposes of this appeal that, as plaintiffs allege, some physical force – i.e., grabbing of hands – was used to take the fingerprints of Tabbaa, Shibly, and Elshinawy. All told, each plaintiff was detained and searched for between four and six hours, after which he or she was released into the United States.

Within seven days of the searches, the government removed from its databases plaintiffs' fingerprints and photographs. However, the government continues to hold some information about plaintiffs in its Treasury Enforcement Communication System ("TECS"), including each plaintiff's name, date of birth, address, and the details of their 2004 detentions. . . .

DISCUSSION . . .

II. Defendants Did Not Violate the Administrative Procedure Act

Plaintiffs' first substantive claim is brought pursuant to the APA. Plaintiffs argue that CBP did not have statutory authority to detain them in order to screen for possible association with terrorist activity, in violation of section 706 of the APA. *See* 5 U.S.C. §706(2)(c) (providing that a reviewing court shall set aside agency action "found to be . . . in excess of statutory jurisdiction, authority, or limitations. . . ."). Plaintiffs do not contest that CBP, as a general matter, can implement any of the screening procedures to which plaintiffs were subject, including detailed questioning, fingerprinting, and photographing. . . .

The customs statutes and regulations, however, do not so confine CBP's authority to detain and search individuals, especially in the wake of the creation of the Department of Homeland Security. A crucial aspect of the new "primary mission" of CBP is to "prevent terrorist attacks within the United States" and "reduce the vulnerability of the United States to terrorism." 6 U.S.C. §111(b)(1). The undersecretary in charge of CBP has specific statutory responsibility for "[p]reventing the entry of terrorists and the instruments of terrorism into the United States." 6 U.S.C. §202(1). Given these provisions, we cannot conclude that it is beyond the power of CBP to search and detain an individual for the limited purpose of determining whether he or she is or has been associated with known terrorists, so long as CBP is not violating the individual's other constitutional or statutory rights. Indeed, the customs laws provide sufficient authority for CBP to conduct the type of searches at issue here. *Cf.* 19 U.S.C. §1582 ("[A]ll persons coming into the United States from foreign countries shall be liable to detention and search by authorized officers or agents of the Government under [CBP regulations]."); 19 U.S.C. §1433(e) (providing that after arriving in the United States, a vehicle may "depart from the . . . place . . . of arrival; or discharge any passenger" only "in accordance with regulations prescribed by the Secretary [of Homeland Security]"); 8 U.S.C. §1225(b) (providing that an alien "shall be detained" unless he or she appears to the examining immigration officer to be "clearly and beyond a doubt entitled" to enter). Accordingly, the District Court was correct to conclude that the searches and detentions of plaintiffs were "entirely consistent with the CBP's statutory mandate. . . ."

III. The Searches and Detention of Plaintiffs Did Not Violate the Fourth Amendment

Plaintiffs' second claim is that CBP's searches were unreasonable in violation of the Fourth Amendment to the U.S. Constitution.

It is well established that the government has broad powers to conduct searches at the border even where, as here, there is no reasonable suspicion that the prospective entrant has committed a crime. *See, e.g., United States v. Flores-Montano*, 541 U.S. 149, 153 (2004) ("Congress, since the beginning of our Government, has granted the Executive plenary authority to conduct routine searches and seizures at the border, without probable cause or a warrant. . . .") (internal quotation marks omitted); *United States v. Montoya de Hernandez*, 473 U.S. 531, 538, (1985) ("Routine searches of the persons and effects of entrants are not subject to any requirement of reasonable suspicion, probable cause, or warrant. . . ."); *United States v. Ramsey*, 431 U.S. 606, 616 (1977) ("[S]earches made at the border, pursuant to the longstanding right of the sovereign to protect itself by stopping and examining persons and property crossing into this country, are reasonable simply by virtue of the fact that they occur at the border. . . ."); *United States v. Nieves*, 609 F.2d 642, 645 (2d Cir. 1979) ("It long has been established that routine border searches, conducted for the purpose of controlling the movement of people and goods across our national boundaries, do not violate the Fourth Amendment's prohibition against unreasonable searches."). Accordingly, a suspicionless search at the border is permissible under the Fourth Amendment so long as it is considered to be "routine." *See, e.g., United States v. Irving*, 452 F.3d 110, 123 (2d Cir. 2006).

The precise line between what is routine and what is not routine, however, has not been clearly delineated. On the one hand, it has been held that "[r]outine searches include those searches of outer clothing, luggage, a purse, wallet, pockets, or shoes which, unlike strip searches, do not substantially infringe on a traveler's privacy rights." *Id.* (citing *United States v. Grotke*, 702 F.2d 49, 51-52 (2d Cir. 1983)). By contrast, "more invasive searches, like strip searches, require reasonable suspicion." *Id.* The Supreme Court has stated that "non-routine" searches include "strip, body cavity, or involuntary x-ray searches." *Montoya de Hernandez*, 473 U.S. at 541 n.4. The determining factor is not how ordinary or commonplace a search is, but rather "the level of intrusion into a person's privacy." *Irving*, 452 F.3d at 123.

There is, of course, a good deal of distance between strip and body cavity searches near one end of the spectrum and a search of pockets or outer clothing near the other, and the searches at issue here fall somewhere in the middle. . . .

Plaintiffs focus on three aspects of the searches in question, which we address in turn. First, plaintiffs urge us to find that their treatment, when considered in its entirety, was not routine because of the combined effect of the various measures employed, including intrusive questioning, photographing, and fingerprinting. We are sympathetic to plaintiffs' argument because there arguably was a stigma associated with being subject to the IDSO procedures. In *MacWade v. Kelly*, 460 F.3d 260, 273 (2d Cir. 2006), we found that police searches of subway passengers' bags were "minimally intrusive" in part because the searches were conducted "out in the open, which reduces the fear and stigma that removal to a hidden area can cause. . . ." Here, plaintiffs were gathered into a separate building along with several other Muslims who had attended the RIS Conference – and all of these attendees were subject to a form of border processing normally reserved for suspected terrorists. As a result, it is not unreasonable for plaintiffs to have felt there was a stigma attached to the searches. *Cf. United States v. Edwards*, 498 F.2d 496, 500 (2d Cir. 1974) ("The search of carry-on baggage, *applied to everyone,* involves not the slightest stigma. More than a million Americans subject themselves to it daily. . . .") (emphasis added and citation omitted).

On the other hand, none of the specific measures taken by CBP was more invasive than the types of searches at the border that courts have regularly held to be routine. Plaintiffs complain that they were required to answer intrusive questions about their activities at the conference, the content of the lectures they attended, and their reasons for attending. But these questions are not materially different than the types of questions border officers typically ask prospective entrants in an effort to determine the places they have visited and the purpose and duration of their trip. Likewise, pat-down searches have repeatedly been found to be routine, even when they were followed by the lifting of an applicant's shirt or the forced removal of shoes. The forcing open of plaintiffs' feet that we assume to have occurred here in at least two instances, while perhaps marginally more invasive than the lifting of a shirt, is not so invasive of plaintiffs' privacy as to be distinguishable from our holdings that pat-down searches are routine.

We also conclude that the fingerprinting and photographing of plaintiffs does not take the searches out of the realm of what is considered routine because, at least in the context of a border search, being fingerprinted (even forcibly) and photographed is not particularly invasive, especially considering that the photographs and fingerprints were used solely to verify plaintiffs' identities and then were discarded from the government's databases. *See Davis v. Mississippi*, 394 U.S. 721, 727 (1969) ("Fingerprinting involves none of the probing into an individual's private life and thoughts that marks an interrogation or search."); *Nicholas v. Goord*, 430 F.3d 652, 658 (2d Cir. 2005) (noting that the Supreme Court has suggested that fingerprinting is not entitled to Fourth Amendment protection and describing fingerprinting as a "non-intrusive means of obtaining physical evidence . . ."); *Montoya de Hernandez*, 473 U.S. at 539-40 ("[N]ot only is the expectation of privacy less at the border than in the interior, the Fourth Amendment balance between the interests of the Government and the privacy right of the individual is also struck much more favorably to the Government at the border.") (internal citation omitted).

Thus, each of the individual elements of the searches was routine. And while we leave open the possibility that in some circumstances the cumulative effect of several routine search methods could render an overall search non-routine, we do not find that to be the case here. While plaintiffs were undoubtedly made uncomfortable and angry by the searches, and they may understandably have felt stigmatized, their personal privacy was not invaded in the same way as it would have been had they been subject to a body cavity or strip search, or involuntary x-ray. Because the decisive factor in the analysis is invasiveness of privacy – not overall inconvenience – we find that CBP's searches of plaintiffs, considered in their entirety, were routine in the border context, albeit near the outer limits of what is permissible absent reasonable suspicion.

Plaintiffs' second argument is that the searches were not routine because CBP agents threatened to detain plaintiffs until they cooperated. We have not previously considered whether a threat of continued detention can turn an otherwise routine search into one requiring reasonable suspicion. However, as noted above, CBP has clear statutory authority to detain persons at the border in order to, *inter alia,* confirm their citizenship or ensure that they are not bringing illicit goods into the country. *See, e.g.,* 19 U.S.C. §1582; 19 U.S.C. §1433(e); 8 U.S.C. §1225(b). Thus, it would no doubt be considered routine for customs officials to continue to detain prospective entrants if, for example, they did not willingly turn over their passports or permit their vehicles to be searched. It is, quite reasonably, not the practice of CBP to allow prospective entrants who fail to comply with inspection to freely leave the checkpoint, as that would enable smugglers, terrorists, and others not

entitled to enter the country to continuously try other checkpoints until
they find one that provides a less rigorous screening. Thus, CBP's
ability to threaten with extended detention those who do not comply with
lawful screening measures is an important aspect of the "longstanding
right of the sovereign to protect itself" at the border, and therefore is
"reasonable simply by virtue of the fact that [it] occur[s] at the border. . . ."
Ramsey, 431 U.S. at 616. In other words, border crossers cannot, by
their own non-compliance, turn an otherwise routine search into a
non-routine one.

Finally, plaintiffs argue that the duration of their detentions –
between four and six hours – cannot be considered routine because U.S.
citizens do not expect to be held at the border for that length of time.
Plaintiffs rely on *United States v. Montoya de Hernandez,* in which the
Supreme Court treated as non-routine the 16-hour detention of a woman
whom customs officials suspected of smuggling drugs via her alimentary
canal. 473 U.S. at 535, 540. Defendants, on the other hand, cite *United
States v. Flores-Montano,* in which the Supreme Court held that a
one-hour delay incident to a border search did not render that search
non-routine because "[w]e think it clear that delays of one to two hours
at international borders are to be expected." 541 U.S. at 155 n.3.

While the searches here fall between these two poles, we believe
they are more akin to the one-hour delay in *Flores-Montano* than the
overnight detention in *Montoya de Hernandez.* The Supreme Court
noted in *Flores-Montano* that "no cases indicat[e] [that] the Fourth
Amendment shields entrants from inconvenience or delay at the
international border." 541 U.S. at 155 n.3. Moreover, the Supreme
Court has "consistently rejected hard-and-fast time limits" in evaluating
the reasonableness of border searches and has stressed that "'common
sense and ordinary human experience must govern over rigid criteria.'"
Montoya de Hernandez, 473 U.S. at 543 (quoting *United States v.
Sharpe,* 470 U.S. 675, 685 (1985). In other words, we must consider
"whether the detention of [the traveler] was reasonably related in scope
to the circumstances which justified it initially." *Id.* at 542.

While a delay of four, five, or six hours is obviously of more serious
magnitude than a delay of "one to two hours," "common sense and
ordinary human experience" suggest that it may take up to six hours for
CBP to complete the various steps at issue here, including vehicle
searches, questioning, and identity verification, all of which we have
already found to be routine. The additional four hours, while certainly
inconvenient, thus cannot be considered an unexpected "level of
intrusion into a person's privacy," *Irving,* 452 F.3d at 123, that by itself

would render the searches non-routine. Accordingly, the searches and detention of plaintiffs were routine in the border context and thus did not violate the Fourth Amendment.

IV. Defendants' Actions Did Not Violate Plaintiffs' Right of Association

Plaintiffs next argue that the searches and detentions violated their First Amendment right of freedom of expressive association. Plaintiffs unquestionably had a protected right to express themselves through association at the RIS Conference. "[I]mplicit in the right to engage in activities protected by the First Amendment [is] a corresponding right to associate with others in pursuit of a wide variety of political, social, economic, educational, religious, and cultural ends." *Roberts v. United States Jaycees*, 468 U.S. 609, 622 (1984). As the Supreme Court observed in *Roberts,* the right of expressive association "is especially important in preserving political and cultural diversity and in shielding dissident expression from suppression by the majority." *Id.* Participation in the RIS Conference – a social, religious, and cultural gathering – falls squarely within the forms of associational activity protected by the First Amendment.

The first question we must answer, then, is whether and to what extent defendants' actions burdened that right. *See Boy Scouts of Am. v. Dale*, 530 U.S. 640, 657-59 (2000); *Fighting Finest, Inc. v. Bratton*, 95 F.3d 224, 228 (2d Cir. 1996). Mere incidental burdens on the right to associate do not violate the First Amendment; rather, "[t]o be cognizable, the interference with [plaintiffs'] associational rights must be "direct and substantial" or "significant." *Fighting Finest, Inc.,* 95 F.3d at 228 (quoting *Lyng v. Int'l Union*, 485 U.S. 360, 366, 367 & n.5 (1988)). . . .

. . . Government action can constitute a direct and substantial interference with associational rights even if there is no prior restraint and no clear chilling of future expressive activity. For example, when government action substantially penalizes members of a group for exercising their First Amendment rights, that penalty in itself can constitute a substantial burden, even if the government did not prevent the group from associating and regardless of any future chilling effect. . . .

Here, plaintiffs suffered a significant penalty, or disability, solely by virtue of associating at the RIS Conference: they were detained for a lengthy period of time, interrogated, fingerprinted, and photographed when others, who had not attended the conference, did not have to endure these measures. Moreover, even though some of the plaintiffs expressed a willingness to attend future RIS conferences, the prospect of being singled out for such extensive processing could reasonably deter others from associating at similar conferences. And contrary to the government's contention, the burden on plaintiffs was no less simply by virtue of the fact that they were not aware of the IDSO prior to going to the conference and therefore were not deterred from attending; First Amendment rights do not turn on whether their potential infringement came as a surprise. Thus, we find that the burden on plaintiffs' associational rights was sufficiently "significant" to implicate the protections of the First Amendment.[4]

Having found a cognizable burden, we must next determine the appropriate level of scrutiny to employ in evaluating defendants' actions. The District Court applied the test established in *Roberts v. United States Jaycees*: an infringement on associational rights is not unconstitutional so long as it "serve[s] compelling state interests, unrelated to the suppression of ideas, that cannot be achieved through means significantly less restrictive of associational freedoms." 468 U.S. at 623. Courts have regularly applied this test when evaluating associational claims, and we believe this test to be appropriate here.[5]

---

4. Our conclusion that the searches constituted a significant or substantial burden on plaintiffs' First Amendment associational rights is unaltered by our holding that the searches were routine under the Fourth Amendment. As is clear from the above discussion, distinguishing between incidental and substantial burdens under the First Amendment requires a different analysis, applying different legal standards, than distinguishing what is and is not routine in the Fourth Amendment border context.

5. The author of this opinion, speaking for himself, does note, however, that because the infringement on association here occurred as part of a border search, a less rigorous form of scrutiny could potentially be warranted. The Supreme Court has pointed out on several occasions that "searches of persons or packages at the national border rest on different considerations and different rules of constitutional law from domestic regulations." *Montoya de Hernandez*, 473 U.S. at 537 (quoting *Ramsey*, 431 U.S. at 618-619); United States v. 12 200-Ft. Reels of Super 8mm. Film, 413 U.S. 123, 125 (1973). As the opinion has already explained, "the Fourth Amendment's balance of reasonableness is qualitatively different at the international border than in the interior" due to the government's "broad" and "comprehensive" powers "to protect the Nation by stopping and examining persons entering this country." *Montoya de Hernandez*, 473 U.S. at 537-38. It may also be true that the First Amendment's balance of interests is qualitatively different where, as here, the action being challenged is

It is undisputed that the government's interest in protecting the nation from terrorism constitutes a compelling state interest unrelated to the suppression of ideas, and that the IDSO was instituted to serve this compelling state interest. The only question, therefore, is whether this interest could have been "achieved through means significantly less restrictive of [plaintiffs'] associational freedoms." *Roberts,* 468 U.S. at 623.

The government has established that it could not have been. As the District Court observed, "[i]nterception and detection at international border crossings is likely the most effective way to protect the United States from terrorists and instruments of terrorism."

Thus, when CBP officials received intelligence that gave them reason to believe that "certain individuals who were associated with terrorist organizations or activities . . . would be in attendance at the 2004 [RIS] conference," and that the conference "would serve as a possible meeting point for terrorists to exchange ideas and documents, coordinate operations, and raise funds intended for terrorist activities," CBP had ample justification to implement the IDSO, which was explicitly designed to detect and intercept potential terrorists from the conference who attempted to enter the United States. Importantly, the IDSO's reach was carefully circumscribed: it applied only to those conferences about which the government had specific intelligence regarding the possible congregation of suspected terrorists, it was limited to routine screening measures, and it was confined to those individuals, regardless of their religion, whom CBP could establish had attended the conferences in question.

Plaintiffs put forth two responses. First, they assert that *no* burden on their associational rights could be justified because "the First Amendment bars the government from penalizing mere participation in an expressive assembly, even if there is reason to believe that others associated with the assembly might be engaged in unlawful activity intended to undermine if not destroy the nation." For this extraordinary proposition, plaintiffs cite *De Jonge v. Oregon,* 299 U.S. 353 (1937), *United States v. Robel,* 389 U.S. 258 (1967), and *Aptheker v. Sec'y of State,* 378 U.S. 500 (1964).

---

the government's attempt to exercise its broad authority to control who and what enters the country. We do not need to reach this issue because defendants' actions easily pass muster under *Roberts.*

These cases, however, are inapposite because they all involve categorical *prohibitions* on forms of association, as opposed to the indirect *burden* on association at issue here. In *De Jonge,* the Supreme Court struck down Oregon's criminal syndicalism statute, which made it a crime to speak at meetings of groups that advocate crime or sabotage. 299 U.S. at 357, 365. The Court emphasized that "[t]he holding of a meeting for peaceable political action cannot be proscribed," and held the statute unconstitutional because it made "mere participation in a peaceable assembly . . . the basis for a criminal charge." *Id.* at 365. Similarly, *Robel* involved a statute that made it unlawful for members of the Communist Party to work in a defense facility, 389 U.S. at 260-61, and *Aptheker* struck down a statute prohibiting members of the Communist Party from applying for or using passports, 378 U.S. at 515-16. Here, the government did not make attendance at or participation in the RIS Conference unlawful, and the purpose of the government's actions was not to prevent people from associating at the conference, but rather to prevent terrorists from entering the country. Defendants' actions are not *per se* unconstitutional simply because innocent U.S. citizens such as plaintiffs were subject to enhanced processing techniques and thus experienced an indirect burden on their right to associate.

Second, plaintiffs contend that CBP could have achieved its interest in preventing terrorists from entering the country in a manner that would have been less restrictive of plaintiffs' associational freedoms. According to plaintiffs, rather than instituting the IDSO, the government could have surveilled the individuals identified in the intelligence as being associated with terrorism, or stopped at the border only those conference attendees whom the government had reason to believe had personally interacted with suspected terrorists. These are plainly not viable alternatives. As defendants point out, the U.S. government cannot freely conduct surveillance on private individuals in Canada, and, given that approximately 13,000 people attended the RIS Conference, it is entirely unrealistic to expect the government to have been able to identify and keep track of all those who personally interacted with suspected terrorists who attended the conference. Indeed, the IDSO was necessary precisely because of the infeasibility of knowing who at the conference may have interacted, and potentially exchanged identification or travel documents, with suspected terrorists.

Plaintiffs also suggest that CBP could have instituted a graduated process of inspection such that only those conference attendees about whom the government had individualized suspicion of a terrorist link or other criminal activity would have been subject to fingerprinting and photographing. Plaintiffs place great emphasis on the fact that in February 2005 – two months after the searches at issue here – CBP modified its fingerprinting policy "to clarify that fingerprint checks should be run if there is at least one articulable fact concerning whether a traveler may lawfully enter the United States. . . ." . . .

Plaintiffs' argument fails for three reasons. First, CBP could have modified its fingerprinting policy for a host of reasons – such as political pressure or fear of litigation – unrelated to the policy's effectiveness in preventing terrorism. Second, even assuming that plaintiffs are correct about how the revised policy would be implemented, that does not mean it was unnecessary for CBP to fingerprint and photograph plaintiffs when they crossed the border in late 2004, especially given the nature of the intelligence the government received in advance of the RIS Conference. That intelligence gave rise to a reasonable concern that terrorists might use the conference to exchange "travel or identification documents such as passports or driver's licenses." In light of this concern, fingerprinting and photographing conference attendees was necessary to "ensure" that they were "who the[y] claim[ed] to be" – an objective that would not have been possible if CBP officials were limited to reviewing passports and other identification documents.

Finally, *Roberts* does not require the government to exhaust every possible means of furthering its interest; rather, the government must show only that its interest "cannot be achieved through means *significantly less restrictive* of associational freedoms." *Roberts,* 468 U.S. at 623 (emphasis added). Plaintiffs' argument supposes that it would have been acceptable for CBP to have segregated conference attendees into the secondary search area, rigorously searched and questioned them, and detained them for a considerable period of time while running their names through various government databases – so long as plaintiffs were not also fingerprinted and photographed absent individualized suspicion. We do not believe the extra hassle of being fingerprinted and photographed – for the sole purpose of having their identities verified – is a "significant[ ]" additional burden that turns an otherwise constitutional policy into one that is unconstitutional.

Thus, we agree with the District Court that the government has a compelling interest in protecting against terrorism, and that it could not have achieved that interest "through means significantly less restrictive of [plaintiffs'] associational freedoms." *Id.* We therefore affirm the District Court's grant of summary judgment on plaintiffs' freedom of association claim.

V. Defendants Did Not Violate Plaintiffs' Free Exercise Rights under RFRA or the First Amendment . . .

[The court held that the same strict scrutiny test applied to the plaintiffs' free exercise and Religious Freedom Restoration Act (RFRA) claims.]

Accordingly, the District Court was correct in finding that plaintiffs' claims under RFRA and the free exercise clause of the First Amendment fail.

CONCLUSION

In sum, we hold that, as a matter of law, defendants, in detaining and searching plaintiffs as they crossed the U.S.-Canada border following the RIS Conference, did not violate the Administrative Procedure Act or plaintiffs' rights under RFRA or the First or Fourth Amendments to the U.S. Constitution. We therefore AFFIRM the judgment of the District Court.

[NSL p. 613, CTL p. 238. Insert after *Tabbaa v. Chertoff.*]

Farag v. United States
United States District Court, Eastern District of New York, 2008
587 F. Supp. 2d 436

BLOCK, Senior District Judge: . . . On August 22, 2004, weeks away from the third anniversary of 9/11, plaintiffs Tarik Farag ("Farag") and Amro Elmasry ("Elmasry"), both Arabs, flew from San Diego to New York's John F. Kennedy Airport ("JFK") on American Airlines Flight 236. [Farag and Elmasry, long-time friends, were flying to JFK after vacationing in California. Both were born in Egypt, but Farag, 36, had moved to the United States in 1971 at age five and later became an American citizen. He was a retired New York City police officer, and was then employed by the United States Bureau of Prisons as a corrections officer. Elmasry, 37, was an Egyptian citizen; he was employed in Egypt by General Electric as an area sales manager for its Africa-East Mediterranean region and had a valid United States visa.] They claim that when they deplaned they were met by at least ten armed police officers in SWAT gear with shotguns and police dogs, ordered to raise their hands, frisked, handcuffed and taken to a police station, where they were placed in jail cells; they were not released until about four hours later, after having been interrogated at length during their imprisonment regarding suspected terrorist surveillance activity aboard the plane. The investigation yielded absolutely no evidence of wrongdoing.

Alleging that they were unlawfully seized and imprisoned, Farag and Elmasry have each brought an action under *Bivens v. Six Unknown Named Agents of Federal Bureau of Narcotics,* 403 U.S. 388 (1971), against defendants FBI Special Agent William Ryan Plunkett ("Plunkett") and New York City Police Department Detective Thomas P. Smith ("Smith"), two counterterrorism agents responsible for plaintiffs' seizures, detentions and interrogations. . . . Plunkett and Smith seek summary judgment as to plaintiffs' *Bivens* claims on the ground of qualified immunity. . . .

The Government's Justification for Its Conduct

The Government lists the following actions of Farag and Elmasry on the aircraft, which, they argue, supported the agents' "concern that [plaintiffs] may [have been] conducting [terrorist] surveillance or probing operations," Gov't Br. at 5,[20] and justified the agents' seizures, detentions, and interrogations of plaintiffs:

> • At the beginning of the flight, despite sitting on opposite sides of the aisle, plaintiffs spoke to each other over the heads of other passengers in a mixture of Arabic and English;
> • Elmasry made an allegedly "unusual" initial seat change "from a window seat . . . to a middle seat . . . between two other male passengers";
> • After Elmasry changed seats, he and Farag talked to each other "loudly" over the heads of other passengers in a mixture of Arabic and English;
> • Elmasry looked at his watch when the plane took off, when the plane landed, and at other points during the flight;
> • After the meal service, Elmasry "got out of his seat . . ., went into the aisle, leaned over to Farag, and spoke a 'very short sentence' to Farag in a mixture of Arabic and English";

---

20. In particular, the Government argues that "there was probable cause to believe that Plaintiffs were violating the Destruction of Aircraft Act, 18 U.S.C. §32, and the federal conspiracy statute, 18 U.S.C. §371, both of which have been upheld by the Second Circuit as providing legitimate grounds for prosecuting potential terrorist plots against United States-flag aircraft." Gov't Br. at 25 (citing *United States v. Yousef,* 327 F.3d 56, 86-88 (2d Cir. 2003)).

• Immediately thereafter, plaintiffs moved together to the back of the plane, and did not take their carry-on luggage with them;
• Plaintiffs got up to return to the front of the cabin at the very end of the flight, after the "fasten seatbelt" indicator was lit;
• Upon returning to the front of the plane, Farag did not sit in his original seat (17E), but rather, in Elmasry's original seat (18A), which was located directly behind Smith;
• After the plane landed, Elmasry took out his cellular phone and deleted five or six numbers;
• While the plane was taxiing to the gate, Elmasry told Smith that "he is from Egypt, that he works for GE, and that '[his] work is always traveling.'"

See Gov't Br. at 14-16.

The Government lists the following events that took place in the terminal at JFK, after plaintiffs were first detained, as further support for the agents' actions:

• Farag told Smith that "after 9/11, when the CIA had c[o]me into the Federal Bureau of Prisons, my supervisors had asked me to translate documents, to translate tapes, [and] in fact I did translate tapes";
• Farag told Smith that "I had guns pointed at me as a police officer";
• While Farag was telling these things to Smith, Farag was "jittery" and "shaking" and "[his] speech was not calm." He appeared "nervous" and seemed "jumpy and agitated," and he raised his voice.

See Gov't Br. at 25-26. . . .

II. Analysis

A. *Were Plaintiffs Arrested?*

. . . There is no question but that plaintiffs were subjected to a "seizure" cognizable under the Fourth Amendment, since Smith, Plunkett and the Port Authority officers (acting under Smith and Plunkett's authorization) "by means of physical force or show of authority . . . restrained the liberty" of plaintiffs, *Florida v. Bostick,* 501 U.S. 429, 434 (1991) (quoting *Terry v. United States,* 392 U.S. 1, 19 n.16 (1968)), and because under these circumstances, "a reasonable person would [not] feel free to decline the officers' requests or otherwise terminate the encounter. . . ." *Id.* at 436.

Nor can there be a serious question but that the plaintiffs were subject to a *de facto* arrest, notwith-standing the Government's contention that the entire episode was nothing more than a *Terry* stop. Each of three sets of factors standing alone – not to mention collectively – sufficed to convert the seizures into *de facto* arrests: (1) the officers' show of force and restraint of plaintiffs' movement at the terminal; (2) the transportation of plaintiffs to the police station, the confinement of plaintiffs in jail cells, and the custodial interrogation of plaintiffs; and (3) the duration of plaintiffs' confinements and interrogations. . . .

. . . The question, then, is whether, viewing the facts in the light most favorable to the plaintiffs, the Government is entitled to summary judgment that there was probable cause for the arrests.

B. *Was There Probable Cause for the Arrests?*

Probable cause to arrest exists "where the arresting officer has 'knowledge or reasonably trustworthy information of facts and circumstances that are sufficient to warrant a person of reasonable caution in the belief that the person to be arrested has committed or is committing a crime.'" [*United States v. Delossantos*, 536 F.3d 155, 158 (2d Cir. 2008) (quoting *Walczyk v. Rio*, 496 F.3d 139, 156 (2d Cir. 2007))]. Only "those facts available to the officer at the time of the arrest and immediately before it" may be considered. *Lowth v. Town of Cheektowaga*, 82 F.3d 563, 569 (2d Cir. 1996) (citation omitted). Moreover, "[p]robable cause is to be assessed on an objective basis[,]" *Zellner v. Summerlin*, 494 F.3d 344, 369 (2d Cir. 2007); thus, "[a]n arresting officer's state of mind (*except for the facts that he knows*) is irrelevant. . . ." *Id.* The standard is a "fluid and contextual" one, requiring "examin[ation of] the totality of the circumstances of a given arrest." *Delossantos*, 536 F.3d at 159 (citations omitted). . . .

1. Was There Probable Cause Based on Non-Ethnic Factors Alone?

The Government contends that even if the Court does not consider that plaintiffs were Arabs and that they were at times conversing in Arabic, the other factors relied upon by the Government constitute probable cause. The Court disagrees. The Government tacks together a number of benign circumstances in the apparent belief that their numerosity will carry the day. The Court acknowledges that the Second Circuit has cautioned district courts not to "engage[ ] in erroneous 'divide-and-conquer analysis'" by "declining to give weight to [individual] observation[s] 'that [were] by [themselves] readily susceptible to . . . innocent explanation[s.]'" *Id.* at 161 (quoting *United*

States v. Arvizu, 534 U.S. 266, 274 (2002)); *accord [United States v. Sokolow,* 490 U.S. 1, 9 (1989)] ("Any one of these factors is . . . quite consistent with innocent travel. But we think taken together they amount to reasonable suspicion."). Yet, even viewing all of these circumstances as a whole, it cannot rationally be held that if, hypothetically, the plaintiffs were two Caucasian traveling companions speaking French, or another non-Arabic language which the agents did not understand, "a person of reasonable caution" would have believed that they were engaged in terrorist surveillance. *Delossantos,* 536 F.3d at 158.

Principally, the Government relies on the agents' observations of plaintiffs' seat-changing and Elmasry's "timing" events with his watch. But the agents acknowledged in their incident report that they knew the plaintiffs were friends; quite logically, friends would want to sit as close to each other as possible, and they would also logically return to the vicinity of their original seats when the plane was landing to retrieve their carry-on luggage. As for Elmasry looking at his watch upon takeoff, landing, and at various other times during the flight, the proportion of airline passengers who do this is probably higher than the proportion who do not. *See United States v. Jones,* 149 F.3d 364, 369 (5th Cir. 1998) ("A factual condition which is consistent with [criminal activity] will not predicate reasonable suspicion, if that factual condition occurs even more frequently among the law abiding public. . . .").

The Government also argues that Elmasry's deletion of five or six telephone numbers from his cellular phone while he waited for the plane to reach the gate "could have been interpreted as destroying evidence[,]" Gov't Br. at 16. This conclusion, however, is utter speculation; the Government's Rule 56.1 Statement does not assert that *Elmasry* made any telephone calls during or after the flight, and the record gives no indication that Elmasry suspected he was about to be caught sufficient to imbue his acts with a suggestion of guilt. *Cf. United States v. Gomez,* 633 F.2d 999, 1002, 1008 (2d Cir. 1980) (holding that "sounds indicating destruction of evidence" *after* officers announced themselves and began to kick and bang on apartment door helped generate probable cause).

Most troubling, the heavy reliance which the Government places on the plaintiffs' speaking "loudly" to each other over the heads of other passengers and otherwise drawing attention to themselves is counterintuitive: it simply makes no sense that if Elmasry were a terrorist on a surveillance mission, he would speak "loudly" across the aisle to his companion before takeoff, seek out and converse with the flight attendant, relocate to a seat "between two large men," or volunteer to one of those "large men" that he was from Egypt. What terrorist engaged in surveillance activity would behave so conspicuously? One would expect that such activity would be characterized by secrecy. *See Bigford v. Taylor,* 834 F.2d 1213, 1218 (5th Cir. 1988) ("As a corollary . . . of the rule that the police may rely on the totality of facts available to them in establishing probable cause, they also may not disregard facts tending to dissipate probable cause."); *cf. United States v. Lopez,* 482 F.3d 1067, 1075 (9th Cir. 2007) ("[W]e find that attendant facts gathered by the police tended to dissipate, rather than support, probable cause to believe [defendant] was the attempted shooter.").

Nor could plaintiffs' conduct in the terminal be reasonably viewed as an escalation of events that would then have given rise to probable cause. *See United States v. Romain,* 393 F.3d 63, 71 (1st Cir. 2004) ("The propriety of an officer's actions after an initial stop depends on . . . how events unfold."); *cf. [United States v. Hooper,* 935 F.2d 484 (2d Cir. 1991)] at 494-95 (noting that investigation conducted pursuant to a valid *Terry* stop had yielded probable cause to arrest). The Court fails to grasp the significance of Farag telling Smith that because he spoke Arabic he had been asked by the Bureau of Prisons to translate tapes, and that guns had been pointed at him as a police officer – both logical consequences of his past and present employments.

Reliance on Farag's nervousness and raised voice is also problematic. *See, e.g., United States v. Ten Thousand Seven Hundred Dollars and No Cents in U.S. Currency,* 258 F.3d 215, 226-27 (3d Cir. 2001) ("[C]laimants' apparent nervousness is of minimal probative value, given that many, if not most, individuals can become nervous or agitated when detained by police officers." (citation omitted)); *United States v. Salzano,* 158 F.3d 1107, 1113 (10th Cir. 1998) ("[I]t is common for most people to exhibit signs of nervousness when confronted by a law enforcement officer whether or not the person is currently engaged in criminal activity.") (internal quotation marks and citation omitted); *United States v. Crump,* 62 F. Supp. 2d 560, 565 (D. Conn. 1999) ("The fact that the defendant was acting 'a little nervous' has limited significance since most citizens, whether innocent or guilty, are likely to exhibit some signs of nervousness when confronted by the police." (citation omitted)). Moreover, Farag's "nervous" response to an unlawful show of force could not retroactively justify plaintiffs' arrests. *See, e.g., United States v. Alvarez-Manzo,* No. 8:07CR432, 2008 WL 2704163, at *8 (D. Neb. July 3, 2008) ("While the government argues that the arrest was supported by the defendant's nervous behavior, this behavior occurred after he was illegally seized. . . .").

In sum, viewed in the light most favorable to plaintiffs, the non-ethnic factors cited by the Government do not constitute probable cause.

2. Would Consideration of Plaintiffs' Ethnicity Warrant a Finding of Probable Cause?

Allowing consideration of the plaintiffs' ethnicity and their use of Arabic would still not warrant a finding, in the context of the defendants' summary-judgment motion, that there was probable cause to arrest them. In other words, if the plaintiffs' view of events holds up at trial, their conduct was so benign that the ethnicity factor – even if it could be considered – would not change the outcome.

Nonetheless, the Court will address the ethnicity issue since the Government, given the importance it ascribes to the issue, would otherwise undoubtedly raise it at trial; moreover, the issue would probably surface if Smith and Plunkett were to take an interlocutory appeal from the Court's denial of that aspect of their motion seeking qualified immunity.

3. Can Plaintiffs' Arab Ethnicity Serve as a Probable Cause Factor?

The Government argues that plaintiffs' Arab ethnicity and use of the Arabic language are relevant factors in the probable-cause, as well as the reasonable-suspicion, calculus because "all of the persons who participated in the 9/11 terrorist attacks were Middle Eastern males[,]" Tr. of Oral Argument, July 18, 2008, at 18, and "the United States continues to face a very real threat of domestic terrorism from Islamic terrorists." Gov't Br. at 17.

The Government's position has some superficial appeal. After all, probable cause, and undoubtedly reasonable suspicion as well, is, once again, "a practical, nontechnical conception that deals with the factual and practical considerations of everyday life[,]' " *Delossantos,* 536 F.3d at 159 (internal quotation marks and citation omitted), and what American would not acknowledge that everyday life has changed in myriad ways, both great and small, since 9/11? Indeed, earlier this fall, the Second Circuit upheld a government program "that singled out male immigrants from two dozen predominantly Arab and Muslim countries for accelerated deportation after the Sept. 11, 2001, terrorist attacks[,]" Mark Hamblett, *Circuit Upholds Post-9/11 Effort That Singled Out Muslim Men,* N.Y.L.J., Sept. 25, 2008 at 1, finding it a "plainly rational attempt to enhance national security." *Rajah v. Mukasey,* 544 F.3d 427, 2008 WL 4350021, at *5 (2d Cir. Sept. 24, 2008).

Rajah, however, did not deal with ethnicity in the context of probable cause or reasonable suspicion. Indeed, the Government recognizes that "[t]here is no single precedent that resolves this case," Tr. of Oral Argument, July 18, 2008, at 17, which presumably accounts for its view of the case as one of first impression. Nevertheless, the interplay between race[33] and the Fourth Amendment is not a recent phenomenon; courts and commentators have long struggled with the issue of whether and to what extent race can be a relevant consideration in the decision to detain an individual. *See, e.g.,* Samuel R. Gross & Katherine Y. Barnes, *Road Work: Racial Profiling and Drug Interdiction on the Highway,* 101 Mich. L. Rev. 651 (2002); Anthony C. Thompson, *Stopping the Usual Suspects: Race and the Fourth Amendment,* 74 N.Y.U. L. Rev. 956 (1999); Tracey Maclin, *Race and the Fourth Amendment,* 51 Vanderbilt L. Rev. 333 (1998); Sheri Lynn Johnson, *Race and the Decision to Detain a Suspect,* 93 Yale L.J. 214, 237 (1983). That legal backdrop obviously bears on the Court's analysis here.

At the outset, it should be understood that the Fourth Amendment – unlike the Equal Protection Clause – imposes no *a priori* restriction on race-based governmental action. As the Supreme Court noted in *Whren v. United States,* 517 U.S. 806 (1996):

> [T]he Constitution prohibits selective enforcement of the law based on considerations such as race. But the constitutional basis for objecting to intentionally discriminatory application of laws is the Equal Protection Clause, not the Fourth Amendment. Subjective intentions play no role in ordinary, probable-cause Fourth Amendment analysis.

Id. at 813; *see also United States v. Scopo,* 19 F.3d 777, 786 (2d Cir. 1994) (Newman, J., concurring) ("Though the Fourth Amendment permits a pretext arrest, if otherwise supported by probable cause, the

---

33. For present purposes, the Court treats the "technically" distinct concepts of race and ethnicity as legal equivalents. *Iqbal v. Hasty,* 490 F.3d 143, 148 n.2 (2d Cir. 2007), *cert. granted sub nom. Ashcroft v. Iqbal,* --- U.S. ----, 128 S. Ct. 2931 (2008). Moreover, the Court considers the fact that the plaintiffs spoke their native tongue, Arabic – as opposed to some other language equally unfamiliar to the agents – as inextricably related to, and legally indistinguishable from, plaintiffs' ethnicity per se.

Equal Protection Clause still imposes restraint on impermissibly class-based discriminations."). *But see* Thompson, 75 N.Y.U. L. Rev. at 991-98 (arguing that the Framers intended the Fourth Amendment to protect political minorities from selective governmental scrutiny).

In *Whren,* the existence of probable cause based on non-racial factors was conceded. *See* 517 U.S. at 810 ("Petitioners accept that Officer Soto had probable cause to believe that various provisions of the District of Columbia traffic code had been violated."). Thus, the Court opined only that an officer's subjective, potentially race-based motivations were irrelevant to the Fourth Amendment *once probable cause is established*; it was not called upon to address whether race might be relevant to the probable-cause analysis itself.

Although the Fourth Amendment does not single out race as a matter of special concern, it does impose a general requirement that *any* factor considered in a decision to detain must contribute to "a particularized and objective basis for suspecting the particular person stopped of criminal activity." *United States v. Cortez,* 449 U.S. 411, 417-18 (1981). Thus, as one commentator has observed, "race cannot affect probable cause or reasonable suspicion calculations unless it is statistically related to suspected criminal activity." Johnson, 93 Yale L.J. at 237. Whether such a relationship exists in a given case is necessarily a fact-specific inquiry; nevertheless, the case law reveals some recurring themes.

Perhaps the least controversial use of race in the context of the Fourth Amendment is its use as an *identifying* factor. If the victim of, or witness to, a crime describes the perpetrator as a young white male wearing a white shirt and black pants, there can be little doubt that law enforcement officials may consider that description in deciding whom to detain, even though the description is based, in part, on race.

Courts have also confronted the so-called "racial incongruity" argument – i.e., that race is indicative of criminality when members of a particular race seem "out of place" in a particular location. Some courts – including the Second Circuit – have sidestepped the issue by finding probable cause or reasonable suspicion based on other, non-racial factors. For example, in *United States v. Magda,* 409 F. Supp. 734 (S.D.N.Y. 1976), the district court found reasonable suspicion lacking where "[t]he reason for the stop was primarily because of an observed exchange . . . between a young black man and a young white man in an area of the city defined as 'narcotics prone.'" *Id.* at 740. The Second Circuit reversed, concluding that the circumstances and location of the transaction were sufficient to create reasonable suspicion; the circuit court made no mention of the race of the participants. *See United States v. Magda*, 547 F.2d 756, 758-59 (2d Cir. 1976); *see also United States v. Richard*, 535 F.2d 246, 248-249 (3d Cir. 1976) (noting that "the presence of two black males cruising in a car in a predominately white neighborhood is, by itself, insufficient cause for a belief that those persons have participated in a recent crime in the neighborhood," but reversing suppression order based on other factors); *State v. Wilson*, 775 So. 2d 1051, 1052 (La. 2000) ("[T]he officer made clear . . . that while racial incongruity 'did factor in,' he considered other circumstances more important in his decision to make an investigatory stop.").

Those courts that have squarely addressed the incongruity argument have uniformly rejected it. *See People v. Bower*, 24 Cal. 3d 638 (1979) ("[T]he presence of an individual of one race in an area inhabited primarily by members of another race is not a sufficient basis to suggest that crime is afoot."); *State v. Barber*, 118 Wash. 2d 335 (1992) ("It is the law that racial incongruity, i.e., a person of any race being allegedly 'out of place' in a particular geographic area, should never constitute a finding of reasonable suspicion of criminal activity."); *Phillips v. State*, 781 So. 2d 477, 479 (Fla. Dist. Ct. App. 2001) ("Clearly, the fact that a black person is merely walking in a predominantly white neighborhood does not indicate that he has committed, is committing, or is about to commit a crime."). . . .

But this case involves neither identification nor racial incongruity. Rather, defendants' argument that plaintiffs' Arab ethnicity is a relevant consideration is premised on the notion that Arabs have a greater *propensity* than non-Arabs toward criminal activity – namely, terrorism.

In support of this argument, defendants rely principally on language from the Supreme Court's opinion in *United States v. Brignoni-Ponce*, 422 U.S. 873 (1975). There, a roving border patrol agent had made a traffic stop based on nothing more than "the apparent Mexican ancestry" of the car's occupants. *Id.* at 885. The Supreme Court held that "this factor alone would [not] justify . . . a reasonable [suspicion]" of an immigration violation. *Id.* at 886. But it stated – in dictum – that "[t]he likelihood that any given person of Mexican ancestry is an alien is high enough to make Mexican appearance *a relevant factor* " in the Fourth Amendment calculus, if it were not *the only* basis for suspicion. *Id.* at 886-87 (emphasis added).[34]

---

34. A year after *Brignoni-Ponce*, the Supreme Court held that officials at a border-control checkpoint could constitutionally single out motorists for inspection "even if it be assumed that such referrals are made largely on the basis of apparent Mexican ancestry." *United States v. Martinez-Fuerte*, 428 U.S.

Brignoni-Ponce's dictum was predicated on 1970 census figures establishing that in the border states between 8.5% and 20.4% of the ethnic-Mexican population self-registered as aliens. *Id.* at 886-87 & n.12. To the Court's knowledge, no court has ever marshaled statistics to conclude that racial or ethnic appearance is correlated with, and thus probative of, any type of criminal conduct *other than* immigration violations. *See, e.g., United States v. Avery,* 137 F.3d 343, 354 (6th Cir. 1997) ("[A]lthough the Court in *Brignoni-Ponce* stated 'the likelihood that any given person of Mexican ancestry is an alien is high enough to make Mexican appearance a relevant factor,' we refuse to adopt, by analogy, the concept that 'the likelihood that any given person of African ancestry is involved in drug trafficking is high enough to make African ancestry a relevant fact' in investigating drug trafficking . . . ." (citation omitted)).

Moreover, the statistical rationale behind the *Brignoni-Ponce* dictum does not translate to the present case: Even granting that all of the participants in the 9/11 attacks were Arabs, and even assuming *arguendo* that a large proportion of would-be anti-American terrorists are Arabs, the likelihood that *any given airline passenger* of Arab ethnicity is a terrorist is so negligible that Arab ethnicity has no probative value in a particularized reasonable-suspicion or probable-cause determination. *Accord United States v. Ramos,* Cr. No. 04-10198-MLW, 2008 WL 4117184, at *9 (D. Mass. Aug. 29, 2008) (considering, in dicta, the applicability of *Brignoni-Ponce* to Arabs suspected of terrorist activity post-9/11, and noting that "[a]mong other things, the type of statistics relied upon in *Brignoni-Ponce* . . . have not been presented here."); *United States v. Nevitt,* 409 F. Supp. 1075, 1079 (D. Mich. 1976) ("In *Brignoni-Ponce,* . . . the Court held that apparent Mexican ancestry could be used as a relevant factor. . . . There, however, the Court specifically found, on the basis of statistical evidence, that 'the likelihood that any given person of Mexican ancestry is an alien is high enough' to justify its use as a factor. In our case, the United States has presented no [statistical] evidence . . . ." (internal citation omitted)).

543, 563 (1976). The Court recognized that such a criterion "would not sustain a roving-patrol stop," *id.*, but concluded that border-control checkpoints were exempt from the usual Fourth Amendment requirement of individualized suspicion. *See id.* at 562 ("[W]e hold that the stops and questioning at issue may be made in the absence of any individualized suspicion at reasonably located checkpoints."). Since there is obviously no contention that a traditional arrest or *Terry* stop is similarly exempt from that requirement, *Martinez-Fuerte* cannot support plaintiffs' detention.

Indeed, the Ninth Circuit, whose judgment the Supreme Court upheld in *Brignoni-Ponce,* revisited *Brignoni-Ponce*'s dictum 25 years later and held, albeit also in dicta, that the statistical inference on which it was based was no longer valid, even in its original illegal-immigration context:

> *Brignoni-Ponce* was handed down in 1975, some twenty-five years ago. Current demographic data demonstrate that the statistical premises on which its dictum relies are no longer applicable. The Hispanic population of this nation, and of the Southwest and Far West in particular, has grown enormously. . . . Accordingly, Hispanic appearance is of little or no use in determining which particular individuals among the vast Hispanic populace should be stopped by law enforcement officials on the lookout for illegal aliens. Reasonable suspicion requires *particularized* suspicion, and in an area in which a large number of people share a specific characteristic, that characteristic casts too wide a net to play any part in a particularized reasonable suspicion determination.

[*United States v. Montero-Camargo,* 208 F.3d 1122 (9th Cir. 2000)] at 1133-34 (emphasis in original). Notably, the Supreme Court has never revisited its dictum in *Brignoni-Ponce,* nor has it ever addressed whether, *absent* compelling statistical evidence, race or ethnicity may be used as a factor in the Fourth Amendment calculus to indicate criminal propensity. Accordingly, the Court finds that *Brignoni-Ponce* offers no support for the Government's position. . . .

There is no doubt that the specter of 9/11 looms large over this case. Although this is the first post-9/11 case to address whether race may be used to establish criminal propensity under the Fourth Amendment, the Court cannot subscribe to the notion that in the wake of 9/11 this may now be permissible. As the Second Circuit recently admonished, "the strength of our system of constitutional rights derives from the steadfast protection of those rights in both normal and unusual times." *Iqbal v. Hasty,* 490 F.3d 143, 159 (2d Cir. 2007), *cert. granted sub nom. Ashcroft v. Iqbal,* --- U.S. ----, 128 S. Ct. 2931 (2008).

History teaches much the same lesson: The Supreme Court's approval of the internment of large numbers of Japanese-Americans during World War II, *see Korematsu v. United States,* 323 U.S. 214 (1945), is now widely regarded as a black mark on our constitutional jurisprudence. The daughter of two such internees – Kiyo Matsumoto – recently became the third Asian-American woman to be elevated to the federal bench. At her induction ceremony, Judge Matsumoto recalled the closing words of Justice Murphy's dissent in *Korematsu*; they are equally apt here:

All residents of this nation are kin in some way by blood or culture to a foreign land. Yet they are primarily and necessarily a part of the new and distinct civilization of the United States. They must accordingly be treated at all times as the heirs of the American experiment and as entitled to all the rights and freedoms guaranteed by the Constitution.

323 U.S. at 206.

The Court "fully recognize[s] the gravity of the situation that confront[s] investigative officials of the United States as a consequence of the 9/11 attack[,]" *Iqbal,* 490 F.3d at 159 (2d Cir. 2007), and that the mindset of airline travelers has understandably been altered by 9/11. This justifiable apprehension must be assuaged by ensuring that security is strictly enforced, and by the passage of time without, hopefully, other episodic affronts to our country; but fear cannot be a factor to allow for the evisceration of the bedrock principle of our Constitution that no one can be arrested without probable cause that a crime has been committed.

C. Are Smith and Plunkett Entitled to Qualified Immunity?

[The court held that there were genuine disputes of material fact precluding summary judgment for defendants on the defense of qualified immunity.] . . .

On a concluding note, nothing that the Court has written should be construed as suggesting that law enforcement officials should be anything but vigilant in policing suspicious conduct on domestic airline flights. Moreover, "individuals consent to substantial intrusions on their Fourth Amendment interests at airports and onboard commercial aircraft." *Shqeirat v. U.S. Airways Group, Inc.,* 515 F. Supp. 2d 984, 993 (D. Minn. 2007) (citing *Cassidy v. Chertoff,* 471 F.3d 67, 76 (2d Cir. 2006) ("[S]ociety has long accepted a heightened level of security and privacy intrusion with regard to air travel.")).

Certainly, the agents could have engaged the plaintiffs in consensual conversation. See [*Florida v. Royer,* 460 U.S. 491, 497-98 (1983)] ("[L]aw enforcement officers do not violate the Fourth Amendment by merely approaching an individual . . . in [a] public place, by asking him if he is willing to answer some questions, by putting questions to him if the person is willing to listen, or by offering in evidence in a criminal prosecution his voluntary answers to such questions."); *United States v. Lee,* 916 F.2d 814, 816-19 (2d Cir. 1990) (holding that, where officers approached a suspicious person in an airport terminal "and, with credentials displayed, asked if they could speak with him"; the individual consented; the officers told him "that he was suspected of carrying contraband"; and he consequently allowed them to search his person; the encounter did not implicate the Fourth Amendment).[40] For aught that appears on the present record, the plaintiffs were more than willing to answer any questions put to them and give the agents whatever information they may have required. And if the plaintiffs had fully cooperated by telling the agents where they worked and, in Farag's case, giving his federal employee tax identification number, the agents should have been able to quickly confirm whether plaintiffs were being truthful.

The trial will flush all this out, as well as whether there was ever any danger to the safety of any of the passengers or to the officers, and whether there was any justification to believe that an act of terrorism was in progress. . . .

CONCLUSION

For the reasons described above, the Court grants summary judgment in the Government's favor with respect to plaintiffs' conspiracy claims, plaintiffs' common-law claims against Smith, and plaintiffs' § 1981 claims. The Court denies summary judgment with respect to plaintiffs' *Bivens* claims against Smith and Plunkett, plaintiffs' FTCA claims against the United States, and Smith and Plunkett's qualified-immunity defense.

So ordered.

---

40. Although such a consensual encounter would not have qualified as a "seizure," and therefore would not trigger Fourth Amendment scrutiny, the Court notes that even consensual questioning may violate the constitution where race or ethnicity is the sole reason for the officer's approach. *See* [*United States v. Avery*, 137 F.3d 343, 354 (6th Cir. 1997)] ("[Airport] surveillance could not be challenged under the Fourth Amendment because it does not involve a seizure. The Fourteenth Amendment, however, prohibits agents from engaging in investigative surveillance of an individual based solely on impermissible factors such as race."); *United States v. Travis*, 62 F.3d 170, 173 (6th Cir. 1995) ("[C]onsensual searches may violate the Equal Protection Clause when they are initiated solely based on racial considerations . . . even though they are permissible under the Fourth Amendment.").

[NSL Chapter 22 – Organization and Coordination of Counterterrorism Investigations, CTL Chapter 8 – Organizing and Coordinating Counter-terrorism Investigations. Replace the entire text of the chapter with material found on the "Professor Materials" section of each casebook's website.]

[NSL p. 650, CTL p. 278. Substitute the following decision for *United States v. Bin Laden*.]

In re Terrorist Bombings of U.S. Embassies in East Africa (Fourth Amendment Challenges)
United States Court of Appeals for the Second Circuit, 2008
552 F.3d 157

[Two other opinions in the same case were filed the same day, dealing with, respectively, the admissibility, sufficiency, and alleged withholding of evidence, and sentencing, 552 F.3d 93; and Fifth and Sixth Amendment challenges, 552 F.3d 177.]

JOSÉ A. CABRANES, Circuit Judge. Defendant-appellant Wadih El-Hage, a citizen of the United States, challenges his conviction in the United States District Court for the Southern District of New York (Leonard B. Sand, Judge) on numerous charges arising from his involvement in the August 7, 1998 bombings of the American Embassies in Nairobi, Kenya and Dar es Salaam, Tanzania (the "August 7 bombings"). . . .

El-Hage contends that the District Court erred by (1) recognizing a foreign intelligence exception to the Fourth Amendment's warrant requirement, (2) concluding that the search of El-Hage's home and surveillance of his telephone lines qualified for inclusion in that exception, and (3) resolving El-Hage's motion on the basis of an *ex parte* review of classified materials, without affording El-Hage's counsel access to those materials or holding a suppression hearing. Because we hold that the Fourth Amendment's requirement of reasonableness – and not the Warrant Clause – governs extraterritorial searches of U.S. citizens and that the searches challenged on this appeal were reasonable, we find no error in the District Court's denial of El-Hage's suppression motion. In addition, the District Court's *ex parte, in camera* evaluation of evidence submitted by the government in opposition to El-Hage's suppression motion was appropriate in light of national security considerations that argued in favor of maintaining the confidentiality of that evidence. El-Hage's challenge to his conviction is therefore without merit.

I. BACKGROUND

A. Factual Overview

American intelligence became aware of al Qaeda's presence in Kenya by mid-1996 and identified five telephone numbers used by suspected al Qaeda associates. *United States v. Bin Laden*, 126 F. Supp. 2d 264, 269 (S.D.N.Y. 2000). From August 1996 through August 1997, American intelligence officials monitored these telephone lines, including two El-Hage used: a phone line in the building where El-Hage lived and his cell phone. *See id.* The Attorney General of the United States then authorized intelligence operatives to target El-Hage in particular. *Id.* This authorization, first issued on April 4, 1997, was renewed in July 1997. *Id.* Working with Kenyan authorities, U.S. officials searched El-Hage's home in Nairobi on August 21, 1997, pursuant to a document shown to El-Hage's wife that was "identified as a Kenyan warrant authorizing a search for 'stolen property.'" *Id.* At the completion of the search, one of the Kenyan officers gave El-Hage's wife an inventory listing the items seized during the search. *Id.* El-Hage was not present during the search of his home. *Id.* It is uncontested that the agents did not apply for or obtain a warrant from a U.S. court. . . .

II. DISCUSSION

A. *In Camera, Ex Parte* Review of Evidence

As a preliminary matter, we address El-Hage's objection to the District Court's resolution of his suppression motion on the basis of an *in camera, ex parte* review of evidence submitted by the government. . . . The District Court's failure to hold a hearing, El-Hage urges, cast aside the integral role of the adversarial process in determining the primary purpose of the surveillance and whether the government acted in good faith. We disagree. . . .

. . . [T]he suppression motion at issue here involved a "limited" factual inquiry into the purpose and scope of the contested surveillance based on evidence relating to national security. . . . [T]he District Court observed that "the issues raised by El-Hage's motion were predominantly legal questions and the fact-based inquiry [into whether the surveillance was conducted for foreign intelligence purposes or law enforcement purposes] was limited." *Bin Laden,* 126 F. Supp. 2d at 287. In addition, the District Court found "persuasive [the government's] arguments about [an] ongoing threat posed by al Qaeda and the potentially damaging impact of disclosure [of the surveillance records] on existing foreign intelligence operations." *Id.* Our own review of the record persuades us of the correctness of the conclusions of the District Court with respect to the limited nature of the inquiry into the purpose of the surveillance and the need, at the time, to keep the government's submissions confidential.

In reaching this conclusion, we do not minimize El-Hage's valid interest in examining the government's evidence and challenging the government's assertions. Nor do we doubt the utility of the adversary process to determine facts or ventilate legal arguments in the normal course. Nevertheless, the imperatives of national security and the capacity of *"in camera* procedures [to] adequately safeguard [El-Hage's] Fourth Amendment rights," [*United States v. Ajlouny*, 629 F.2d 830, 839 (2d Cir. 1980)], weighed against holding an evidentiary hearing under these circumstances. *See* [*United States v. Belfield*, 692 F.2d 141, 149 (D.C. Cir. 1982)] ("[I]n a field as delicate and sensitive as foreign intelligence gathering, as opposed to domestic, criminal surveillance, there is every reason why the court should proceed *in camera* and without disclosure to determine the legality of a surveillance." (internal citation and quotation marks omitted)). Accordingly, we conclude that the District Court's decision to resolve El-Hage's suppression motion without a hearing does not constitute error, much less an abuse of discretion.

B. The District Court's Denial of El-Hage's Motion to Suppress Evidence

1. Standard of Review

We review *de novo* the legal issues raised on a motion to suppress evidence. We review a district court's factual findings for clear error, viewing the evidence in the light most favorable to the government.

2. Extraterritorial Application of the Fourth Amendment

In order to determine whether El-Hage's suppression motion was properly denied by the District Court, we must first determine whether and to what extent the Fourth Amendment's safeguards apply to overseas searches involving U.S. citizens. In *United States v. Toscanino*, a case involving a Fourth Amendment challenge to overseas wiretapping of a non-U.S. citizen, we observed that it was "well settled" that "the Bill of Rights has extraterritorial application to the conduct abroad of federal agents directed against United States citizens." 500 F.2d 267, 280-81 (2d Cir. 1974); *see also United States v. Verdugo-Urquidez*, 494 U.S. 259, 283 n.7 (1990) (Brennan, J., dissenting) (recognizing "the rule, accepted by every Court of Appeals to have considered the question, that the Fourth Amendment applies to searches conducted by the United States Government against United States citizens abroad").

Nevertheless, we have not yet determined the specific question of the applicability of the Fourth Amendment's Warrant Clause to overseas searches. Faced with that question now, we hold that the Fourth Amendment's warrant requirement does not govern searches conducted abroad by U.S. agents; such searches of U.S. citizens need only satisfy the Fourth Amendment's requirement of reasonableness. . . .

. . . While never addressing the question directly, the Supreme Court provided some guidance on the issue in *United States v. Verdugo-Urquidez* . . . . [That guidance] and the following reasons weigh against imposing a warrant requirement on overseas searches.

First, there is nothing in our history or our precedents suggesting that U.S. officials must first obtain a warrant before conducting an overseas search. El-Hage has pointed to no authority — and we are aware of none — directly supporting the proposition that warrants are necessary for searches conducted abroad by U.S. law enforcement officers or local agents acting in collaboration with them; nor has El-Hage identified any instances in our history where a foreign search was conducted pursuant to an American search warrant. This dearth of authority is not surprising in light of the history of the Fourth Amendment and its Warrant Clause as well as the history of international affairs. As the *Verdugo-Urquidez* Court explained, "[w]hat we know of the history of the drafting of the Fourth Amendment . . . suggests that its purpose was to restrict searches and seizures which might be conducted by the United States in domestic matters." 494 U.S. at 266. In addition, the Warrant Clause appears to have been invested with a meaning at the time of the drafting that differs significantly from our modern view of the requirement. Justice White observed that "at the time of the Bill of Rights, the warrant functioned as a powerful tool of law enforcement rather than as a protection for the rights of criminal suspects," and "it was the abusive use of the warrant power, rather than any excessive zeal in the discharge of peace officers' inherent authority, that precipitated the Fourth Amendment." *Payton v. New York*, 445 U.S. 573, 604-14 (1980) (White, J., dissenting) (documenting the history of the Fourth Amendment's warrant requirement). Accordingly, we agree with the Ninth Circuit's observation that "foreign searches have neither been historically subject to the warrant procedure, nor could they be as a practical matter." *United States v. Barona*, 56 F.3d 1087, 1092 n.1 (9th Cir. 1995).[7]

Second, nothing in the history of the foreign relations of the United States would require that U.S. officials obtain warrants from foreign magistrates before conducting searches overseas or, indeed, to suppose that all other states have search and investigation rules akin to our own. As the Supreme Court explained in *Verdugo-Urquidez:*

> For better or for worse, we live in a world of nation-states in which our Government must be able to function effectively in the company of sovereign nations. Some who violate our laws may live outside our borders under a regime quite different from that which obtains in this country. Situations threatening to important American interests may arise halfway around the globe, situations which in the view of the political branches of our Government require an American response with armed force. If there are to be restrictions on searches and seizures which occur incident to such American action, they must be imposed by the political branches through diplomatic understanding, treaty, or legislation.

---

7. A U.S. citizen who is a target of a search by our government executed in a foreign country is not without constitutional protection – namely, the Fourth Amendment's guarantee of reasonableness which protects a citizen from unwarranted government intrusions. Indeed, in many instances, as appears to have been the case here, searches targeting U.S. citizens on foreign soil will be supported by probable cause.

The interest served by the warrant requirement in having a "neutral and detached magistrate" evaluate the reasonableness of a search is, in part, based on separation of powers concerns – namely, the need to interpose a judicial officer between the zealous police officer ferreting out crime and the subject of the search. These interests are lessened in the circumstances presented here for two reasons. First, a domestic judicial officer's ability to determine the reasonableness of a search is diminished where the search occurs on foreign soil. Second, the acknowledged wide discretion afforded the executive branch in foreign affairs ought to be respected in these circumstances.

A warrant serves a further purpose in limiting the scope of the search to places described with particularity or "the persons or things to be seized" in the warrant. U.S. Const. amend. IV. In the instant case, we are satisfied that the scope of the searches at issue was not unreasonable. *See* Parts II.B.3, *post.*

494 U.S. at 275 (internal citation, quotation marks and brackets omitted). The American procedure of issuing search warrants on a showing of probable cause simply does not extend throughout the globe and, pursuant to the Supreme Court's instructions, the Constitution does not condition our government's investigative powers on the practices of foreign legal regimes "quite different from that which obtains in this country." *Id.*

Third, if U.S. judicial officers were to issue search warrants intended to have extraterritorial effect, such warrants would have dubious legal significance, if any, in a foreign nation. *Cf. The Schooner Exchange v. M'Faddon,* 7 Cranch 116, 11 U.S. 116, 135 (1812) ("The jurisdiction of the nation within its own territory is necessarily exclusive and absolute. It is susceptible of no limitation not imposed by itself."). As a District Court in this Circuit recently observed, "it takes little to imagine the diplomatic and legal complications that would arise if American government officials traveled to another sovereign country and attempted to carry out a search of any kind, professing the authority to do so based on an American-issued search warrant." *United States v. Vilar,* No. 05-CR-621, 2007 WL 1075041, at *52 (S.D.N.Y. Apr. 4, 2007). We agree with that observation. A warrant issued by a U.S. court would neither empower a U.S. agent to conduct a search nor would it necessarily compel the intended target to comply.[8] It would be a nullity, or in the words of the Supreme Court, "a dead letter." *Verdugo-Urquidez,* 494 U.S. at 274.

Fourth and finally, it is by no means clear that U.S. judicial officers could be authorized to issue warrants for overseas searches, *cf. Weinberg v. United States,* 126 F.2d 1004, 1006 (2d Cir. 1942) (statute authorizing district court to issue search warrants construed to limit authority to the court's territorial jurisdiction), although we need not resolve that issue here.

For these reasons, we hold that the Fourth Amendment's Warrant Clause has no extraterritorial application and that foreign searches of U.S. citizens conducted by U.S. agents are subject only to the Fourth Amendment's requirement of reasonableness.

---

8. A warrant represents the delegation of the authority of the government to its agent to execute a search on the property identified therein. The subject of a validly issued search warrant has no right to resist the search. *See, e.g.,* Bumper v. North Carolina, 391 U.S. 543, 550 (1968) ("When a law enforcement officer claims authority to search a home under a warrant, he announces in effect that the occupant has no right to resist the search.") . . . .

The District Court's recognition of an exception to the warrant requirement for foreign intelligence searches finds support in the pre-FISA law of other circuits. *See United States v. Truong Dinh Hung,* 629 F.2d 908, 913 (4th Cir. 1980); *United States v. Buck,* 548 F.2d 871, 875 (9th Cir. 1977); *United States v. Butenko,* 494 F.2d 593, 605 (3d Cir. 1974); *United States v. Brown,* 484 F.2d 418, 426 (5th Cir. 1973). We decline to adopt this view, however, because the exception requires an inquiry into whether the "primary purpose" of the search is foreign intelligence collection. *See Bin Laden,* 126 F. Supp. 2d at 277. This distinction between a "primary purpose" and other purposes is inapt. As the U.S. Foreign Intelligence Surveillance Court of Review has explained:

> [The primary purpose] analysis, in our view, rested on a false premise and the line the court sought to draw was inherently unstable, unrealistic, and confusing. The false premise was the assertion that once the government moves to criminal prosecution, its "foreign policy concerns" recede. . . . [T]hat is simply not true as it relates to counterintelligence. In that field the government's primary purpose is to halt the espionage or terrorism efforts, and criminal prosecutions can be, and usually are, interrelated with other techniques used to frustrate a foreign power's efforts.

In re Sealed Case No. 02-001, 310 F.3d 717, 743 (Foreign Int. Surv. Ct. Rev. 2002).

In addition, the purpose of the search has no bearing on the factors making a warrant requirement inapplicable to foreign searches – namely, (1) the complete absence of any precedent in our history for doing so, (2) the inadvisability of conditioning our government's surveillance on the practices of foreign states, (3) a U.S. warrant's lack of authority overseas, and (4) the absence of a mechanism for obtaining a U.S. warrant. Accordingly, we cannot endorse the view that the normal course is to obtain a warrant for overseas searches involving U.S. citizens unless the search is "primarily" targeting foreign powers.

3. The Kenyan Searches Were Reasonable and Therefore Did Not Violate the Fourth Amendment.

. . . First, El-Hage insists that his Nairobi home deserves special consideration in light of the home's status as "the most fundamental bastion of privacy protected by the Fourth Amendment." Second, he contends that the electronic surveillance was far broader than necessary because it encompassed "[m]any calls, if not the predominant amount,

[that] were related solely to legitimate commercial purposes, and/or purely family and social matters."

To determine whether a search is reasonable under the Fourth Amendment, we examine the "totality of the circumstances" to balance "on the one hand, the degree to which it intrudes upon an individual's privacy and, on the other, the degree to which it is needed for the promotion of legitimate governmental interests." *Samson v. California*, 547 U.S. 843, 848 (2006) (quoting *United States v. Knights*, 534 U.S. 112, 118-19 (2001)) (internal quotation marks omitted). . . .

a. The Search of El-Hage's Home in Nairobi Was Reasonable . . . .

Applying that test to the facts of this case, we first examine the extent to which the search of El-Hage's Nairobi home intruded upon his privacy. The intrusion was minimized by the fact that the search was not covert; indeed, U.S. agents searched El-Hage's home with the assistance of Kenyan authorities, pursuant to what was identified as a "Kenyan warrant authorizing [a search]." *Bin Laden*, 126 F. Supp. 2d at 269. The search occurred during the daytime, *id.* at 285, and in the presence of El-Hage's wife, *id.* at 269. At the conclusion of the search, an inventory listing the items seized during the search was prepared and given to El-Hage's wife. *Id.* at 269. In addition, the District Court found that "[t]he scope of the search was limited to those items which were believed to have foreign intelligence value[,] and retention and dissemination of the evidence acquired during the search were minimized." *Id.* at 285.

As described above, U.S. intelligence officers became aware of al Qaeda's presence in Kenya in the spring of 1996. *Id.* at 268-69. At about that time, they identified five telephone lines used by suspected al Qaeda associates, one of which was located in the same building as El-Hage's Nairobi home; another was a cellular phone used by El-Hage. *Id.* After these telephone lines had been monitored for several months, the Attorney General of the United States authorized surveillance specifically targeting El-Hage. *Id.* That authorization was renewed four months later, and, one month after that, U.S. agents searched El-Hage's home in Nairobi. *Id.* This sequence of events is indicative of a disciplined approach to gathering indisputably vital intelligence on the activities of a foreign terrorist organization. U.S. agents did not breach the privacy of El-Hage's home on a whim or on the basis of an unsubstantiated tip; rather, they monitored telephonic communications involving him for nearly a year and conducted surveillance of his activities for five months before concluding that it was necessary to search his home. In light of these findings of fact, which El-Hage has not contested as clearly erroneous, we conclude that the search, while undoubtedly intrusive on El-Hage's privacy, was restrained in execution and narrow in focus.

Balanced against this restrained and limited intrusion on El-Hage's privacy, we have the government's manifest need to investigate possible threats to national security. As the District Court noted, al Qaeda "declared a war of terrorism against all members of the United States military worldwide" in 1996 and later against American civilians. *Id.* at 269. The government had evidence establishing that El-Hage was working with al Qaeda in Kenya. *Id.* On the basis of these findings of fact, we agree with the District Court that, at the time of the search of El-Hage's home, the government had a powerful need to gather additional intelligence on al Qaeda's activities in Kenya, which it had linked to El-Hage.

Balancing the search's limited intrusion on El-Hage's privacy against the manifest need of the government to monitor the activities of al Qaeda, which had been connected to El-Hage through a year of surveillance, we hold that the search of El-Hage's Nairobi residence was reasonable under the Fourth Amendment.

b. The Surveillance of El-Hage's Kenyan Telephone Lines Was Also Reasonable.

El-Hage appears to challenge the reasonableness of the electronic surveillance of the Kenyan telephone lines on the grounds that (1) they were overbroad, encompassing calls made for commercial, family or social purposes and (2) the government failed to follow procedures to "minimize" surveillance. Indeed, pursuant to defense counsel's analysis, "as many as 25 percent of the calls were either made by, or to" a Nairobi businessman not alleged to have been associated with al Qaeda. El-Hage also criticizes the government for retaining transcripts of irrelevant calls – such as conversations between El-Hage and his wife about their children – despite the government's assurance to the District Court that the surveillance had been properly "minimized." *See United States v. Ruggiero*, 928 F.2d 1289, 1302 (2d Cir. 1991) ("[A]ny [electronic] interception 'shall be conducted in such a way as to minimize the interception of communications not otherwise subject to interception.'" (quoting 18 U.S.C. §2518(5))).

It cannot be denied that El-Hage suffered, while abroad, a significant invasion of privacy by virtue of the government's year-long surveillance of his telephonic communications. The Supreme Court has recognized that, like a physical search, electronic monitoring intrudes on "the innermost secrets of one's home or office" and that "[f]ew threats to liberty exist which are greater than that posed by the use of eavesdropping devices." *Berger v. New York*, 388 U.S. 41, 63 (1967); *cf. Katz v. United States*, 389 U.S. 347, 352-54 (1967). For its part, the government does not contradict El-Hage's claims that the surveillance was broad and loosely "minimized." Instead, the government sets forth a variety of reasons justifying the breadth of the surveillance. These justifications, regardless of their merit, do not lessen the intrusion El-Hage suffered while abroad, and we accord this intrusion substantial weight in our balancing analysis.

Turning to the government's interest, we encounter again the self-evident need to investigate threats to national security presented by foreign terrorist organizations. When U.S. intelligence learned that five telephone lines were being used by suspected al Qaeda operatives, the need to monitor communications traveling on those lines was paramount, and we are loath to discount – much less disparage – the government's decision to do so.

Our balancing of these compelling, and competing, interests turns on whether the scope of the intrusion here was justified by the government's surveillance needs. We conclude that it was, for at least the following four reasons.

First, complex, wide-ranging, and decentralized organizations, such as al Qaeda, warrant sustained and intense monitoring in order to understand their features and identify their members. *See In re Sealed Case No. 02-001*, 310 F.3d 717, 740-41 (Foreign Int. Surv. Ct. Rev. 2002) ("Less minimization in the acquisition stage may well be justified to the extent . . . 'the investigation is focusing on what is thought to be a widespread conspiracy[,] [where] more extensive surveillance may be justified in an attempt to determine the precise scope of the enterprise.'" (quoting *Scott v. United States*, 436 U.S. 128, 140 (1978) (alteration in original))).

Second, foreign intelligence gathering of the sort considered here must delve into the superficially mundane because it is not always readily apparent what information is relevant. *Cf. United States v. Rahman*, 861 F. Supp. 2d 247, 252-53 (S.D.N.Y. 1994) (recognizing the "argument that when the purpose of surveillance is to gather intelligence about international terrorism, greater flexibility in acquiring and storing information is necessary, because innocent-sounding conversations may later prove to be highly significant, and because individual items of information, not apparently significant when taken in isolation, may become highly significant when considered together over time").

Third, members of covert terrorist organizations, as with other sophisticated criminal enterprises, often communicate in code, or at least through ambiguous language. *See, e.g., United States v. Salameh*, 152 F.3d 88, 108 (2d Cir. 1998) ("Because Ajaj was in jail and his telephone calls were monitored, Ajaj and Yousef spoke in code when discussing the bomb plot."). Hence, more extensive and careful monitoring of these communications may be necessary.

Fourth, because the monitored conversations were conducted in foreign languages, the task of determining relevance and identifying coded language was further complicated.

Because the surveillance of suspected al Qaeda operatives must be sustained and thorough in order to be effective, we cannot conclude that the scope of the government's electronic surveillance was overbroad. While the intrusion on El-Hage's privacy was great, the need for the government to so intrude was even greater. Accordingly, the electronic surveillance, like the search of El-Hage's Nairobi residence, was reasonable under the Fourth Amendment.

In sum, because the searches at issue on this appeal were reasonable, they comport with the applicable requirement of the Fourth Amendment and, therefore, El-Hage's motion to suppress the evidence resulting from those searches was properly denied by the District Court.

III. CONCLUSION . . .

For these reasons, and for those set forth in *In re Terrorist Bombings of U.S. Embassies in East Africa*, [552 F.3d 177] (2d Cir. 2008), the judgment of conviction entered by the District Court against El-Hage is **AFFIRMED** in all respects except that the sentence is **VACATED**, and the case is **REMANDED** to the District Court for the sole purpose of resentencing El-Hage as directed in *In re Terrorist Bombings of U.S. Embassies in East Africa*, [552 F.3d 93] (2d Cir. 2008).

[NSL p. 675, CTL p. 307. Insert at the end of Note 4.]

Al-Kidd v. Ashcroft
United States Court of Appeals, 9th Circuit, 2009
580 F.3d 949

MILAN D. SMITH, JR., Circuit Judge: . . .

FACTS AND PROCEDURAL BACKGROUND

A. al-Kidd

Plaintiff-Appellee al-Kidd was born Lavoni T. Kidd in Wichita, Kansas. While attending college at the University of Idaho, where he was a highly regarded running back on the University's football team, he converted to Islam and changed his name. In the spring and summer of 2002, he and his then-wife were the target of a Federal Bureau of Investigation (FBI) surveillance as part of a broad anti-terrorism investigation allegedly aimed at Arab and Muslim men.[2] No evidence of criminal activity by al-Kidd was ever discovered. Al-Kidd planned to fly to Saudi Arabia in the spring of 2003 to study Arabic and Islamic law on a scholarship at a Saudi university.

On February 13, 2003, a federal grand jury in Idaho indicted Sami Omar Al-Hussayen for visa fraud and making false statements to U.S. officials. On March 14, the Idaho U.S. Attorney's Office submitted an application to a magistrate judge of the District of Idaho, seeking al-Kidd's arrest as a material witness in the Al-Hussayen trial. Appended to the application was an affidavit by Scott Mace, a Special Agent of the FBI in Boise (the Mace Affidavit). The Mace Affidavit described two contacts al-Kidd had with Al-Hussayen: al-Kidd had received "in excess of $20,000" from Al-Hussayen (though the Mace Affidavit does not indicate what this payment was for), and al-Kidd had "met with Al-Hussayen's associates" after returning from a trip to Yemen. It also contained evidence of al-Kidd's contacts with officials of the Islamic Assembly of North America (IANA, an organization with which Al-Hussayen was affiliated), including one official "who was recently arrested in New York." It ended with the statement, "[d]ue to Al-Kidd's demonstrated involvement with the defendant . . . he is believed to be in

---

2. Al-Kidd is Muslim, but is African-American and not of Arab descent.

possession of information germane to this matter which will be crucial to the prosecution." The Mace Affidavit did not elaborate on what "information" al-Kidd might have had, nor how his testimony might be "germane" – let alone "crucial" – to the prosecution of Al-Hussayen. The affidavit further stated:

> Kidd is scheduled to take a one-way, first class flight (costing approximately $5,000) to Saudi Arabia on Sunday, March 16, 2003, at approximately 6:00 EST. He is scheduled to fly from Dulles International Airport to JFK International Airport in New York and then to Saudi Arabia. . . . It is believed that if Al-Kidd travels to Saudi Arabia, the United States Government will be unable to secure his presence at trial via subpoena.

In fact, al-Kidd had a round-trip, coach class ticket, costing approximately $1,700. The Mace Affidavit omitted the facts that al-Kidd was a U.S. resident and citizen; that his parents, wife, and two children were likewise U.S. residents and citizens; and that he had previously cooperated with the FBI on several occasions when FBI agents asked to interview him. The magistrate judge issued the warrant the same day.

Pursuant to the material witness warrant, al-Kidd was arrested two days later at the ticket counter at Dulles International Airport. He was handcuffed and taken to the airport's police substation, where he was interrogated. Thereafter, he was detained for an aggregate of sixteen days at the Alexandria Detention Center in Virginia, the Oklahoma Federal Transfer Center, and the Ada County, Idaho, Jail. He was strip searched on multiple occasions and confined in the high-security unit of each facility. During transfer between facilities, al-Kidd was handcuffed and shackled about his wrists, legs, and waist. He was allowed out of his cell only one to two hours each day, and his cell was kept lit twenty-four hours a day, unlike other cells in the high-security wing.

On March 31, after petitioning the court, al-Kidd was ordered released, on the conditions that he live with his wife at his in-laws' home in Nevada, limit his travel to Nevada and three other states, report regularly to a probation officer and consent to home visits throughout the period of supervision, and surrender his passport. After almost a year under these conditions, the court permitted al-Kidd to secure his own residence in Las Vegas, Nevada, as al-Kidd and his wife were separating. He lived under these conditions for three more months before being released at the end of Al-Hussayen's trial, more than fifteen months after being arrested.[4] In July 2004, al-Kidd was fired from his job. He alleges he was terminated when he was denied a security clearance because of his arrest. He is now separated from his wife, and has been unable to find steady employment. He was also deprived of his chance to study in Saudi Arabia on scholarship.

Al-Kidd was never called as a witness in the Al-Hussayen trial or in any other criminal proceeding.

B. Ashcroft

Defendant-Appellant Ashcroft was Attorney General of the United States during the relevant time period. According to al-Kidd's complaint, following the September 11, 2001 terrorist attacks, Ashcroft developed and promulgated a policy by which the FBI and DOJ would use the federal material witness statute as a pretext "to arrest and detain terrorism *suspects* about whom they did not have sufficient evidence to arrest on criminal charges but wished to hold preventatively or to investigate further." (Cited in, and emphasis added to, al-Kidd's complaint.)

To support this allegation, the complaint first quotes Ashcroft's own statement at a press briefing:

> Today, I am announcing several steps that we are taking to enhance our ability to protect the United States from the threat of terrorist aliens. These measures form one part of the department's strategy to prevent terrorist attacks by taking *suspected terrorists* off the street . . . . Aggressive *detention* of lawbreakers and *material witnesses* is vital to preventing, disrupting or delaying new attacks.

John Ashcroft, Attorney General, *Attorney General Ashcroft Outlines Foreign Terrorist Tracking Task Force* (Oct. 31, 2001), *available at* http://www.usdoj.gov/archive/ag/speeches/2001/agcrisisremarks10_31. htm (emphasis added in complaint). . . .

[The complaint contained other allegations in support of its claim that Attorney General developed and promulgated the policy of using the

---

4. Al-Hussayen was not convicted of any of the charges brought against him. His trial ended in acquittal on the most serious charges, including conspiracy to provide material support to terrorists, 18 U.S.C. §§2339A, 2339B. After the jury failed to reach a verdict on the remaining lesser charges, the district court declared a mistrial. The government agreed not to retry Al-Hussayen and deported him to Saudi Arabia for visa violations.

material witness statute pretextually for preventive detention. The complaint also alleged that material witnesses were routinely held in high security detention facilities and subjected to unreasonable conditions of confinement.]

DISCUSSION

Al-Kidd asserts three independent claims against Ashcroft. First, he alleges that Ashcroft is responsible for a policy or practice under which the FBI and the DOJ sought material witness orders without sufficient evidence that the witness's testimony was material to another proceeding, or that it was impracticable to secure the witness's testimony – in other words, in violation of the express terms of §3144 itself – and that al-Kidd was arrested as a result of this policy (the §3144 Claim). Second, al-Kidd alleges that Ashcroft designed and implemented a policy under which the FBI and DOJ would arrest individuals who may have met the facial statutory requirements of §3144, but with the ulterior and allegedly unconstitutional purpose of investigating or preemptively detaining them, in violation of the Fourth Amendment (the Fourth Amendment Claim). Finally, al-Kidd alleges that Ashcroft designed and implemented policies, or was aware of policies and practices that he failed to correct, under which material witnesses were subjected to unreasonably punitive conditions of confinement, in violation of the Fifth Amendment (the Conditions of Confinement Claim).

Ashcroft argues that he is entitled to absolute prosecutorial immunity as to the §3144 and Fourth Amendment Claims. He concedes that no absolute immunity attaches with respect to the Conditions of Confinement Claim. He also argues that he is entitled to qualified immunity from liability for all three claims.

A. Absolute Immunity . . .

We hold . . . that when a prosecutor seeks a material witness warrant in order to investigate or preemptively detain a suspect, rather than to secure his testimony at another's trial, the prosecutor is entitled at most to qualified, rather than absolute, immunity. We emphasize that our holding here does not rest upon an unadorned assertion of secret, unprovable motive, as the dissent seems to imply. Even before the Supreme Court's decision in *Bell Atlantic v. Twombly* and *Ashcroft v. Iqbal,* it was likely that conclusory allegations of motive, without more, would not have been enough to survive a motion to dismiss. *Twombly's* general requirement that" [f]actual allegations must be enough to raise a right to relief above the speculative level," 550 U.S. 555, applies with equal force to allegations that a prosecutor's actions served an investigatory function. In this case, however, al-Kidd has averred ample facts to render plausible the allegation of an investigatory function:

> • Al-Kidd's arrest was sought a month *after* Al-Hussayen was indicted, and more than a year *before* trial began, temporally distant from the time any testimony would have been needed.

> • The FBI had previously investigated and interviewed al-Kidd, but had never suggested, let alone demanded, that he appear as a witness.

> • The FBI conducted lengthy interrogations with al-Kidd while in custody, including about matters apparently unrelated to Al-Hussayen's alleged visa violations.

> • Al-Kidd *never actually testified* for the prosecution in Al-Hussayen's or any other case, despite his assurances that he would be willing to do so.

All of these are objective indicia . . . that al-Kidd's arrest functioned as an investigatory arrest or national security-related preemptive detention, rather than as one to secure a witness's testimony for trial. Finally:

> • Ashcroft's immediate subordinate, FBI Director Mueller, testified before Congress that al-Kidd's *arrest* (rather than, say, the obtaining of the evidence he was supposedly going to provide against Al-Hussayen) constituted a "major success[ ]" in "identifying and dismantling terrorist networks."

We conclude that the practice of detaining a material witness in order to investigate him, on the facts alleged by al-Kidd, fulfills an investigative function.

B. Qualified Immunity

The Attorney General may still be entitled to qualified immunity for acts taken in furtherance of an investigatory or national security function. . . .

3. The Fourth Amendment Claim

Al-Kidd's complaint principally alleges that Ashcroft "developed, implemented and set into motion a policy and/or practice under which the FBI and DOJ would use the material witness statute to arrest and detain terrorism *suspects* about whom they did not have sufficient evidence to arrest on criminal charges but wished to hold preventively or to investigate further." Al-Kidd argues that using §3144 to detain suspects to investigate them violates the Fourth Amendment's guarantee against unreasonable seizure.

a. Al-Kidd's Fourth Amendment Rights Were Violated

. . . We have previously held that material witness arrests are "seizures" within the meaning of the Fourth Amendment and are therefore subject to its reasonableness requirement. *Bacon v. United States,* 449 F.2d 933, 942 (9th Cir. 1971).

The Supreme Court has never held that detention of innocent persons as material witnesses is permissible under the Fourth Amendment, and this circuit, in one of the few circuit-level cases to examine the validity of material witness detentions under the Fourth Amendment, declined to reach the facial constitutionality of the predecessor of §3144. *Id.* at 941. Al-Kidd does not contend that §3144 is facially unconstitutional. Rather, he contends that it is intended to be a "limited exception" to the ordinary rule that arrests may only be made upon probable cause of criminal wrongdoing. He further claims that its use for any purpose other than obtaining testimony, and specifically to investigate or preemptively detain terrorism suspects, without probable cause, is unconstitutional. Ashcroft contends that this position is inconsistent with *Whren v. United States's* rule that "[s]ubjective intentions play no role in ordinary, probable-cause Fourth Amendment analysis." 517 U.S. 806, 813 (1996). But arrests of material witnesses are neither "ordinary,"[16] nor involve "probable cause" as that term has historically been understood.

Whren rejected only the proposition that "ulterior motives can invalidate police conduct that is justifiable on the basis of probable cause

---

16. In 2003, the year of al-Kidd's arrest, material witness arrests made up only 3.6% of all arrests by federal law enforcement agents. Of those, 92.3% were made by the former Immigration and Naturalization Service, typically to detain illegally smuggled aliens for testimony against their smugglers before removal. *See, e.g., Aguilar-Ayala v. Ruiz,* 973 F.2d 411 (5th Cir. 1992). Less than 0.3% of arrests by non-immigration federal law enforcement agents were material witness arrests. *See* Bureau of Justice Statistics, U.S. Dep't of Justice, *Compendium of Federal Justice Statistics, 2003,* NCJ No. 210299 (2005), *available at* http://www.ojp.usdoj.gov/bjs/pub/pdf/cfjs0301.pdf, at 18.

to believe that a violation of law has occurred." Id. at 811 (emphasis added). Indeed, *probable cause,* since before the founding, has always been a term of art of criminal procedure. . . .

> This Court repeatedly has explained that "probable cause" to justify an arrest means facts and circumstances within the officer's knowledge that are sufficient to warrant a prudent person, or one of reasonable caution, in believing, in the circumstances shown, that the suspect has committed, is committing, or is about to commit an offense. . . .

Michigan v. DeFillippo, 443 U.S. 31, 37 (1979). . . .

Because material witness arrests are seizures without suspicion of wrongdoing, the *Whren* rule, that subjective motivation is irrelevant in the presence of probable cause, does not apply to our Fourth Amendment analysis in this case. In *City of Indianapolis v. Edmond,* the Supreme Court struck down motor vehicle checkpoints set up "to interdict unlawful drugs" carried by those stopped. 531 U.S. 32, 35 (2000). The Court explained that "programmatic purposes may be relevant to the validity of Fourth Amendment intrusions undertaken pursuant to a general scheme without individualized suspicion. Accordingly, *Whren* does not preclude an inquiry into programmatic purpose in such contexts." *Id.* at 45-46. The Court went on to clarify:

> our cases dealing with intrusions that occur pursuant to a general scheme absent individualized suspicion have often required an inquiry into purpose at the programmatic level.
> . . . [W]e examine the available evidence to determine the primary purpose of the checkpoint program. While we recognize the challenges inherent in a purpose inquiry, courts routinely engage in this enterprise in many areas of constitutional jurisprudence as a means of sifting abusive governmental conduct from that which is lawful. As a result, a program driven by an impermissible purpose may be proscribed while a program impelled by licit purposes is permitted, even though the challenged conduct may be outwardly similar. While reasonableness under the Fourth Amendment is predominantly an objective inquiry, our special needs and administrative search cases demonstrate that purpose is often relevant when suspicionless intrusions pursuant to a general scheme are at issue.

Id. at 46-47 (citation omitted).

Edmond, therefore, establishes that "programmatic purpose" is relevant to Fourth Amendment analysis of programs of seizures without probable cause. It further establishes that if that programmatic purpose is criminal investigation, it is fatal to the program's constitutionality: "the constitutional defect of the program is that its primary purpose is to advance the general interest in crime control." *Id.* at 44. The following year's *Ferguson v. City of Charleston* held unconstitutional a program of mandatory drug testing of maternity patients because "the immediate objective of the searches was to generate evidence *for law enforcement purposes* " against the women tested. 532 U.S. 67, 83 (2001). By contrast, in *Illinois v. Lidster,* the Court *upheld* seizures at a motor vehicle checkpoint set up by the police a week after a hit-and-run accident, "at about the same time of night and at about the same place" as the accident, where the checkpoint was "designed to obtain more information about the accident from the motoring public." 540 U.S. 419, 422 (2004). The Court in *Lidster* distinguished the seizure in *Edmond* on the basis that, in *Lidster:*

> the stop's primary law enforcement purpose was *not* to determine whether a vehicle's occupants were committing a crime, but to ask vehicle occupants, as members of the public, for their help in providing information about a crime in all likelihood committed by others. The police expected the information elicited to help them apprehend, not the vehicle's occupants, but other individuals.

Id. at 423. As Justice Stevens wrote in concurrence, "[t]here is a valid and important distinction between seizing a person to determine whether she has committed a crime and seizing a person to ask whether she has any information about an unknown person who committed a crime a week earlier." *Id.* at 428 (Stevens, J., concurring in part, dissenting in part).[19]

---

19. We are mindful of the difference between a traffic stop and a material witness arrest. The material witness is subject to a seizure an order of magnitude greater than that at issue in *Lidster*, where the stops were "brief," and were of drivers in their cars. (As the Court noted, the "Fourth Amendment does not treat a motorist's car as his castle." 540 U.S. at 424.) An individual seized as a material witness is taken from her home and daily affairs and confined to a small space for a period of time measured not in minutes or even hours, but ranging from days to months. Al-Kidd disclaims any attack on material witness detention generally, and we are in any event bound by *Bacon's* determination that the material witness statute, backed by a "probable cause" requirement to guarantee particularity, has struck a "reasonable" balance between the witness's interest in liberty and the government's need for testimony. But the severity of the deprivation of liberty in material witness arrests only militates for correspondingly more severe judicial scrutiny of its application.

That is precisely the distinction at work here, and the reason we hold that Ashcroft's policy as alleged was unconstitutional.

Al-Kidd alleges that he was arrested without probable cause pursuant to a general policy, designed and implemented by Ashcroft, whose programmatic purpose was not to secure testimony, but to investigate those detained. Assuming that allegation to be true, he has alleged a constitutional violation. Contrary to the dissent's alarmist claims, we are not probing into the minds of individual officers at the scene; instead, we are inquiring into the programmatic purpose of a general policy as contemplated by *Edmond*, 531 U.S. at 457, and finding that the purpose of the policy alleged in al-Kidd's first amended complaint impermissible under the Fourth Amendment.

Further, the dissent's assertion that we are suggesting "the only governmental interest of sufficient weight to justify an arrest is a reasonable belief that the arrestee has committed a crime" grossly mischaracterizes our holding. Dissent at 12336. To the contrary, we recognize that when the material witness statute is genuinely used to secure "testimony of a person . . . material in a criminal proceeding" because "it is shown that it may become impracticable to secure the presence of the person by subpoena," 18 U.S.C. §3144, a showing of probable cause is not required. Our holding does nothing to curb the use of the material witness statute for its stated purpose. *What we do hold is that probable cause – including individualized suspicion of criminal wrongdoing – is required when 18 U.S.C. §3144 is not being used for its stated purpose, but instead for the purpose of criminal investigation.* We thus do not render the material witness statute "entirely superfluous," dissent at 12339; it is only the *misuse* of the statute, resulting in the detention of a person without probable cause for purposes of criminal investigation, that is repugnant to the Fourth Amendment.

All seizures of criminal suspects require probable cause of criminal activity. To use a material witness statute pretextually, in order to investigate or preemptively detain suspects without probable cause, is to violate the Fourth Amendment. *Accord Awadallah II,* 349 F.3d at 59 ("[I]t would be improper for the government to use §3144 for other ends, such as the detention of persons suspected of criminal activity for which probable cause has not yet been established.").

b. *Al-Kidd's Right Was "Clearly Established"*

Ashcroft alternatively contends that if we conclude that the use of material witness orders for investigatory purposes violates the

Constitution, we should still grant him qualified immunity because that constitutional right was not "clearly established" in March 2003, when al-Kidd was arrested. We disagree.

... [T]he Supreme Court has stated:

> For a constitutional right to be clearly established, its contours "must be sufficiently clear that a reasonable official would understand that what he is doing violates that right. This is not to say that an official action is protected by qualified immunity unless the very action in question has previously been held unlawful; but it is to say that in the light of preexisting law the unlawfulness must be apparent."

[*Hope v. Pelzer*, 536 U.S. 730 (2002),] at 739 (quoting *Anderson v. Creighton,* 483 U.S. 635, 640 (1987)) (internal citations omitted)." "[O]fficials can still be on notice that their conduct violates established law even in novel factual circumstances." *Id.* at 741.

What *was* clearly established in March 2003? No federal appellate court had yet squarely held that the federal material witness statute satisfied the requirements of the Fourth Amendment. Even our decision in *Bacon* held only that it was unconstitutional as applied to the petitioner. 449 F.2d at 943. What *obiter dicta* existed on material witness detention, however, clearly linked its justification only to the state's overriding need to compel testimony in criminal cases. Even dicta, if sufficiently clear, can suffice to "clearly establish" a constitutional right. *See Hope,* 536 U.S. at 740-41. But there is more.

The definition of probable cause, as set forth in *Beck v. Ohio,* was certainly clearly established. While the Supreme Court's decision *permitting* suspicionless seizures in some circumstances in *Lidster* had not yet been decided, its decision in *Edmond,* stating that an investigatory programmatic purpose renders a program of seizures without probable cause unconstitutional, had been decided two and a half years earlier. 531 U.S. at 47. That holding was reaffirmed the following year in *Ferguson,* 532 U.S. at 81-83, which highlighted the close connection between the investigative "programmatic purpose" and the search scheme that was ruled unconstitutional. Those decisions, which emphasized that an investigatory programmatic purpose would invalidate a scheme of searches and seizures without probable cause, should have been sufficient to put Ashcroft on notice that the material witness detentions – involving a far more severe seizure than a mere traffic stop – would be similarly subject to an inquiry into programmatic purpose.

Moreover, the history and purposes of the Fourth Amendment were known well before 2003:

The central importance of the probable-cause requirement to the protection of a citizen's privacy afforded by the Fourth Amendment's guarantees cannot be compromised in this fashion. "The requirement of probable cause has roots that are deep in our history." Hostility to seizures based on mere suspicion was a prime motivation for the adoption of the Fourth Amendment, and decisions immediately after its adoption affirmed that "common rumor or report, suspicion, or even 'strong reason to suspect' was not adequate to support a warrant for arrest."

Dunaway v. New York, 442 U.S. 200, 213 (1979) (quoting *Henry v. United States,* 361 U.S. 98, 100-01 (1959)) (internal citation omitted). The Fourth Amendment "reflect[s] the determination of those who wrote the Bill of Rights that the people of this new Nation should forever 'be secure in their persons, houses, papers, and effects' from intrusion and seizure by officers acting under the unbridled authority of a general warrant." *Stanford v. Texas,* 379 U.S. 476, 481 (1965).

The facts alleged of al-Kidd's arrest, that he was arrested because he was associated with the webmaster of an allegedly jihadist website, demonstrate the continued relevance of the Founders' concerns. The Fourth Amendment was, in large measure, a direct response to the so-called "Wilkes cases." As summarized by the Supreme Court:

> The *Wilkes* case arose out of the Crown's attempt to stifle a publication called The North Briton, anonymously published by John Wilkes, then a member of Parliament-particularly issue No. 45 of that journal. Lord Halifax, as Secretary of State, issued a warrant ordering four of the King's messengers "to make strict and diligent search for the authors, printers, and publishers of a seditious and treasonable paper, entitled, The North Briton, No. 45, * * * and them, or any of them, having found, to apprehend and seize, together with their papers." "Armed with their roving commission, they set forth in quest of unknown offenders; and unable to take evidence, listened to rumors, idle tales, and curious guesses. They held in their hands the liberty of every man whom they were pleased to suspect." Holding that this was "a ridiculous warrant against the whole English nation," the Court of Common Pleas awarded Wilkes damages against the Secretary of State.

Id. at 483 (alteration in original) (footnotes omitted). Within three days of the issuance of Halifax's general warrants, forty-nine people had been arrested, none of whom was named in the warrant, but all of whom were alleged associates of the allegedly seditious pamphleteer. Nelson B. Lasson, *The Fourth Amendment to the Constitution* 43-44 (1937). The warrant authorizing al-Kidd named him in particular, and so was not a general warrant in that sense. But the result was the same: gutting the substantive protections of the Fourth Amendment's "probable cause" requirement and giving the state the power to arrest upon the executive's mere suspicion.

Finally, months before al-Kidd's arrest, one district court in a high-profile case had already indicated, in the spring of 2002, that *§3144 itself* should not be abused as an investigatory anti-terrorism tool, calling out Ashcroft by name:

> Other reasons may motivate prosecutors and law enforcement officers to rely upon the material witness statute. Attorney General John Ashcroft has been reported as saying: "Aggressive detention of lawbreakers and material witnesses is vital to preventing, disrupting or delaying new attacks." *Relying on the material witness statute to detain people who are presumed innocent under our Constitution in order to prevent potential crimes is an illegitimate use of the statute.* If there is probable cause to believe an individual has committed a crime or is conspiring to commit a crime, then the government may lawfully arrest that person, but only upon *such* a showing.

Awadallah I, 202 F. Supp. 2d at 77 n.28 (citation omitted, first emphasis added). The statement was dicta in a footnote of a district court opinion. But it was categorical, and it addressed *exactly* what al-Kidd alleges happened ten months after the opinion was first issued. It is difficult to imagine what, in early 2003, might have given John Ashcroft "fair[er] warning" that he could be haled into court for his alleged material witness policies. *Hope,* 536 U.S. at 741.

We therefore hold that al-Kidd's right not to be arrested as a material witness in order to be investigated or preemptively detained was clearly established in 2003. Although Ashcroft has raised in this appeal neither a national security nor an exigency defense to al-Kidd's action, we note that we are mindful of the pressures under which the Attorney General must operate. We do not intend to "dampen the ardor of all but the most resolute, or the most irresponsible, in the unflinching discharge of their duties." *Gregoire v. Biddle,* 177 F.2d 579, 581 (2d Cir. 1949). But, as the Supreme Court has aptly noted, qualified immunity must

> not allow the Attorney General to carry out his national security functions wholly free from concern for his personal liability; he may on occasion have to pause to consider whether a proposed course of action can be squared with the Constitution and laws of the United States. But this is precisely the point of the *Harlow* standard: "Where an official could be expected to know that his conduct would violate statutory or constitutional rights, he *should* be made to hesitate. . . ." This is as true in matters of national security as in other fields of governmental action. We do not believe that the security of

the Republic will be threatened if its Attorney General is given incentives to abide by clearly established law.

[*Mitchell v. Forsyth*, 472 U.S. 511, 524 (1985)] at 524 (quoting [*Harlow v. Fitzgerald*, 457 U.S. 800 (1982)] at 819) (internal citations omitted).

4. The §3144 Claim

[The Court holds that the complaint plausibly pled facts sufficient to state a claim for supervisory liability for the §3314 claim that the Mace Affidavit failed to demonstrate probable cause for either the materiality of al-Kidd's testimony or the reasons it would be impracticable to secure that testimony by subpoena.] . . .

CONCLUSION

Almost two and a half centuries ago, William Blackstone, considered by many to be the preeminent pre-Revolutionary War authority on the common law, wrote:

> To bereave a man of life, or by violence to confiscate his estate, without accusation or trial, would be so gross and notorious an act of despotism, as must at once convey the alarm of tyranny throughout the whole kingdom. But confinement of the person, by secretly hurrying him to gaol, where his sufferings are unknown or forgotten; is a less public, a less striking, and therefore a more dangerous engine of arbitrary government.

1 WILLIAM BLACKSTONE, COMMENTARIES ON THE LAWS OF ENGLAND 131-32 (1765). The Fourth Amendment was written and ratified, in part, to deny the government of our then-new nation such an engine of potential tyranny. And yet, if the facts alleged in al-Kidd's complaint are actually true, the government has recently exercised such a "dangerous engine of arbitrary government" against a significant number of its citizens, and given good reason for disfavored minorities (whoever they may be from time to time) to fear the application of such arbitrary power to them.

We are confident that, in light of the experience of the American colonists with the abuses of the British Crown, the Framers of our Constitution would have disapproved of the arrest, detention, and harsh confinement of a United States citizen as a "material witness" under the circumstances, and for the immediate purpose alleged, in al-Kidd's complaint. Sadly, however, even now, more than 217 years after the ratification of the Fourth Amendment to the Constitution, some confidently assert that the government has the power to arrest and detain or restrict American citizens for months on end, in sometimes primitive conditions, not because there is evidence that they have committed a crime, but merely because the government wishes to investigate them for possible wrongdoing, or to prevent them from having contact with others in the outside world. We find this to be repugnant to the Constitution, and a painful reminder of some of the most ignominious chapters of our national history.

For the reasons indicated in this opinion, we AFFIRM in part and REVERSE in part the decision of the district court. Each party shall bear its own costs on appeal.

BEA, Circuit Judge, concurring in part and dissenting in part: This case raises the question whether a person whom a prosecutor can *rightly* arrest under a statute becomes *wrongly* arrested if the prosecutor's purpose in arresting him had nothing to do with the statute. . . .

II. Qualified Immunity . . .

Al-Kidd bases his claims of liberty from arrest on the Fourth Amendment. The Supreme Court has repeatedly stated that under the Fourth Amendment, an officer's subjective intentions are irrelevant so long as the officer's conduct is objectively justified.

Whren v. United States, 517 U.S. 806 (1996), cited by the majority, is but one example of the general rule that pretextual searches and seizures do not violate the Fourth Amendment. In *Whren,* the Supreme Court held the stop of a vehicle for a minor traffic violation did not violate the Fourth Amendment even though the officer was using the stop "as pretext[ ] for pursuing other investigatory agendas." *Id.* at 811. The Court stated:

> We [have] flatly dismissed the idea that an ulterior motive might serve to strip the agents of their legal justification. . . . [S]ubjective intent alone . . . does not make otherwise lawful conduct illegal or unconstitutional. We described [*United States v. Robinson,* 414 U.S. 218 (1973), at 236] as having established that "the fact that the officer does not have the state of mind which is hypothecated by the reasons which provide the legal justification for the officer's action does not invalidate the action taken as long as the circumstances, viewed objectively, justify that action."

Id. at 812-13 (internal citations omitted). It is really quite simple. If you are engaged in conduct that justifies your detention, you must put up with that detention, even if the officer who detained you did so out of some secret-and constitutionally insufficient-motive.

There is good reason to eschew inquiry into the subjective motivations of individual officers. First, such an approach provides "arbitrarily variable" protection to individual rights. *Devenpeck v. Alford,* 543 U.S. 146, 154 (2004). If the subjective intentions of the arresting officers are the touchstone of constitutional analysis, courts may reach divergent results about searches and seizures that are utterly indistinguishable in the eyes of the person whose rights are at stake. *See id.* at 154. Second, the inquiry into subjective intentions is impossibly difficult, expensive, and prone to error. As the Supreme Court explained in *Harlow v. Fitzgerald,*

> [t]here are special costs to subjective inquiries of this kind. . . . Judicial inquiry into subjective motivation therefore may entail broad-ranging discovery and the deposing of numerous persons, including an official's professional colleagues. Inquiries of this kind can be peculiarly disruptive of effective government.

457 U.S. 800, 816-817 (1982) (footnotes and internal quotation marks omitted). *Whren,* along with *Harlow, Robinson,* [*Scott v. United States,* 436 U.S. 128 (1978)], and [*Maryland v. Macon,* 472 U.S. 463 (1985)], makes clear that al-Kidd's arrest on an objectively valid warrant supported by probable cause violated none of al-Kidd's constitutional rights. At a minimum, these cases would have given a reasonable officer good reason to believe that al-Kidd's arrest was constitutionally permissible.

The majority's efforts to distinguish *Whren* are unpersuasive. The majority contends that *Whren* and like cases are inapplicable whenever the government acts without probable cause to believe that the *subject* of the arrest is guilty of some criminal wrongdoing. Maj. Op. at 12296-97. To reach this result, the majority imports the "programmatic purpose" test ordinarily reserved for administrative or "special needs" search cases. The programmatic purpose test, of course, tests the constitutional validity of *warrantless* searches and seizures, such as drunk driving roadblocks, by requiring the government to prove its program serves governmental interests other than the routine collection of evidence for criminal prosecution. *See, e.g., Ferguson v. City of Charleston,* 532 U.S. 67, 78 (2001); *City of Indianapolis v. Edmond,* 531 U.S. 32, 45 (2000).

The special needs cases are the sole exception to the general principle that, in testing compliance with the Fourth Amendment, courts are limited to an examination of the objective circumstances which justify the search or seizure, and may not inquire into official purpose. *Whren,* 517 U.S. at 812 ("Not only have we *never* held, outside the context of inventory search or administrative inspection[,] . . . that an officer's motive invalidates objectively justifiable behavior[,] . . . we have repeatedly held and asserted the contrary."). The programmatic purpose test applies here, the majority says, because in *Edmonds,* the Supreme Court said that *Whren* did not apply whenever the government conducted a search or seizure without "probable cause," and because "probable cause" means only probable cause to believe the subject of the arrest committed some wrongdoing. The cases the majority cites offer no support whatsoever for the majority's approach.

First, the special needs cases have no bearing on the inquiry into al-Kidd's arrest for the simple reason that al-Kidd was arrested pursuant to a warrant issued by a neutral magistrate. The "programmatic purpose" inquiry is necessary to test the validity of a special needs search precisely because such searches occur without the procedural protections of the warrant requirement and the magisterial supervision it entails. As the Supreme Court explained in *New York v. Burger,* a statute authorizing a warrantless administrative or special needs search must provide

> a constitutionally adequate *substitute for a warrant.* In other words, the regulatory statute must perform the two basic functions of a warrant: it must advise the owner of the commercial premises that the search is being made pursuant to the law and has a properly defined scope, and it must limit the discretion of the inspecting officers.

482 U.S. 691, 710-11 (1987) (emphasis added) (quotations omitted). Material witness warrants, though not based on individualized suspicion of wrongdoing are, of course, warrants: they are based on an individualized determination that the subject of the warrant is in possession of information material in a criminal proceeding and is likely to flee; they are approved by a neutral magistrate; they are subject to continuing oversight; and they issue only upon a showing of probable cause. *Bacon v. United States,* 449 F.2d 933, 942 (9th Cir. 1971); 18 U.S.C. §§3144; Fed. R. Civ. P. 46. The "special needs" cases bear little resemblance to the highly supervised process of obtaining a material witness warrant. Given the protections in §3144, there is simply no need to inquire into the government's "programmatic purpose," and no case has ever so required.

Second, the majority's "traditional" definition of "probable cause," which limits probable cause to mean only probable cause to believe that the arrestee is guilty of wrongdoing, Maj. Op. at 12297-98, reflects a fundamental misunderstanding of the Fourth Amendment. The validity of a police action under the Fourth Amendment turns not on the guilt or innocence of the arrestee, but on whether the government's reasons for arresting the individual are weighty enough, and probably factually likely enough, to justify the intrusion into some individual's rights. *See United States v. Knights,* 534 U.S. 112, 118-19 (2001) ("The touchstone of the Fourth Amendment is reasonableness, and the reasonableness of a search is determined by assessing, on the one hand, the degree to which it intrudes upon an individual's privacy and, on the other, the degree to which it is needed for the promotion of legitimate governmental interests.") (internal quotation marks omitted). The "probable cause" requirement assures that there is sufficient evidence to believe that the facts that justify the issuance of the warrant exist – that there is a sufficient "probability" the government will find what it is looking for when it intrudes. *Id.* at 121.

Until today, no case has suggested that the only governmental interest of sufficient weight to justify an arrest is a reasonable belief that the arrestee has committed a crime. Most importantly, the Supreme Court has stated that the government's interest in the integrity of the justice system is important enough to justify the arrest of a wholly innocent person to secure that witness's appearance at trial. *See Stein v. New York,* 346 U.S. 156, 184 (1953) ("The duty to disclose knowledge of crime rests upon all citizens. It is so vital that one known to be innocent may be detained, in the absence of bail, as a material witness."), *rev'd on other grounds by Jackson v. Denno,* 378 U.S. 368 (1964); *Barry v. United States ex rel. Cunningham,* 279 U.S. 597, 616-17 (1929) ("The constitutionality of [the material witness statute] apparently has never been doubted."). Our own jurisprudence, too, has recognized that "probable cause" for an arrest may exist even in the absence of a reasonable belief that the arrestee has committed wrongdoing. For example, police officers may arrest individuals innocent of any crime if the officer has reason to believe that the individual is a danger to himself. *Maag v. Wessler,* 960 F.2d 773, 776 (9th Cir. 1992). To be sure, in the great run of arrest cases, the relevant inquiry will be whether officers had probable cause to believe the subject committed wrongdoing. But none of the cases the majority claims defines probable cause had occasion to consider whether such belief was the *only* belief that could justify an arrest. . . .

In short, our cases, and those of the Supreme Court, have routinely recognized that "probable cause," within the meaning of the Fourth Amendment, may be satisfied by proof of something other than wrongdoing by the subject of the search or seizure.

Of course, taken to its logical conclusion, the majority opinion renders the material witness statute entirely superfluous. To arrest and confine an individual pursuant to the material witness statute, the government must establish "probable cause." *Bacon*, 449 F.2d at 941-43. If "probable cause" exists only when the *subject* of an arrest is suspected of a crime, then a material witness can be arrested as a suspect, and the material witness statute adds nothing. This result is risible.

Once the government demonstrated to a neutral magistrate that it had probable cause to believe al-Kidd had information material to a criminal proceeding and was likely to run off to Saudi Arabia, the *Whren* rule applied with full force, and nothing in *Edmond* or any case the majority cites suggests otherwise. . . .

Finally, [*United States v. Villamonte-Marquez*, 462 U.S. 579 (1983)] also underlines the point that, even assuming we must consider the "programmatic purpose" behind al-Kidd's detention, the relevant inquiry is not into the motivations of individual officers who obtained and executed the particular warrant on which al-Kidd was detained, but into the "programmatic purpose" that provides the constitutional justification for the material witness statute. *See Edmond*, 531 U.S. at 457 ("[W]e caution that the purpose inquiry in this context is to be conducted only at the programmatic level and is not an invitation to probe the minds of individual officers acting at the scene."). The justification for the use of material witness warrants is the need to assure the proper functioning of the judicial system; this interest is divorced from the government's general interest in crime control and is sufficient, al-Kidd concedes, to justify an arrest. Because this governmental interest justifies this intrusion into al-Kidd's liberty, and because the intrusion is subject to a warrant requirement, inquiry into the minds of individual officers is neither necessary nor desirable. *See Villamonte-Marquez*, 462 U.S. at 584 n.3.

But even if al-Kidd's arrest on a pretextual material witness warrant violated his Fourth Amendment constitutional right not to be subjected to an unreasonable seizure, any such right was certainly not "clearly established" in March 2003. As the majority notes, for a right to be clearly established there need not be a case on point, but the violation must be "apparent" to a reasonable official. *Hope v. Pelzer*, 536 U.S. 730, 739 (2002). In March 2003, when al-Kidd was arrested on a material witness warrant, it would hardly have been "apparent" to a reasonable official that using a valid material witness warrant as a pretext to accomplish other law-enforcement objectives was constitutionally impermissible, especially if the official had read *Whren, Robinson, Scott,* or *Macon.*

No court had ever questioned the constitutional validity of the material witness statute. No court had ever held that the "programmatic purpose" test applied to searches or seizures conducted pursuant to a warrant. No court had held that "probable cause" in the Fourth Amendment meant *only* probable cause to believe the subject of the search or seizure had committed criminal wrongdoing. Every pronouncement by the Supreme Court would have suggested that the pretextual use of a valid warrant was perfectly legal. . . .

V. Conclusion

The majority opinion closes with a quote from Blackstone. What Blackstone describes and condemns therein-the indefinite and secret detention of individuals accused of no crime in harsh conditions-is simply not a description of this case. Even the majority agrees that the harsh conditions of al-Kidd's confinement are not before us because al-Kidd has not adequately pleaded John Ashcroft's personal responsibility for such conditions. Al-Kidd's confinement was neither indefinite nor in secret. He was detained on a warrant issued by a neutral magistrate. The duration of that confinement was subject to continuing judicial supervision. There is no allegation that al-Kidd was held incommunicado. Nor is there any allegation al-Kidd was somehow denied the right to petition for a writ of habeas corpus, a right that has long secured individuals' freedom from the horrors Blackstone envisioned. We are not called upon to judge the constitutionality of the material witness statute. And we are not called upon to judge whether al-Kidd should be released, only whether he is entitled to proceed in his suit to recover money damages from the pocket of a cabinet-level official. Were we presented with the Blackstonian case the majority envisions, I would surely agree.[21] But we are not, and for the reasons explained above, I dissent in part and concur in part.

---

21. Although I would distance myself from a certain measure of bristling righteousness in its remarks that al-Kidd was a U.S. citizen, married and with children at the time of his arrest. Maj. Op. at 12270. For all of that, his rights under the Constitution against unlawful arrest were no greater than those of an illegally entered, Mexican, childless spinster.

[NSL p. 679, CTL p. 310. Insert after Notes and Questions.]

Iqbal v. Hasty

United States Court of Appeals, Second Circuit, 2007
490 F.3d 143
rev'd and remanded, 129 S. Ct. 1937 (2009)

JON O. NEWMAN, Circuit Judge. These interlocutory appeals present several issues concerning the defense of qualified immunity in the aftermath of the events of 9/11. . . .

[Javaid Iqbal is a Muslim Pakistani who was arrested by agents of the FBI and the Immigration and Naturalization Service on November 2, 2001, and charged with conspiracy to defraud and identity fraud. Following his arrest, he was detained in the MDC's (Metropolitan Detention Center in Brooklyn) general prison population until January 8, 2002, when he was removed from the general prison population and assigned to a special section of the MDC known as the Administrative Maximum Special Housing Unit ("ADMAX SHU"), where he remained until he was reassigned to the general prison population at the end of July 2002. He alleged that he was arrested in the PENTTBOM investigation and detained as a person "of high interest" solely because of his race, religion, and national origin, and not because of any involvement in terrorism. The complaint further alleges that Attorney General John Ashcroft and FBI Director Robert Mueller approved a policy of holding detainees "of high interest" in highly restrictive conditions until they were "cleared" by the FBI. Iqbal further alleges that he was kept in solitary confinement.]

. . . Until March, [Iqbal alleges,] the lights in his cell were left on almost 24 hours a day, and MDC staff deliberately turned on air conditioning during the winter and heating during the summer. MDC staff left the Plaintiff in the open-air recreation area for hours when it was raining and then turned on the air conditioner when he returned to his cell. Whenever the Plaintiff was removed from his cell, he was handcuffed and shackled. The Plaintiff was not provided with adequate food and lost 40 pounds while in custody. MDC staff called him, among other things, a "terrorist" and a "Muslim killer."

The complaint further alleges that the Plaintiff was brutally beaten by MDC guards on two occasions: upon his transfer to the ADMAX SHU in January 2002 and again in March. Following the March beating, the Plaintiff was denied medical care for two weeks even though he was in excruciating pain. He was also subjected to daily strip and body-cavity searches. The March beating was prompted by the Plaintiff's protestations to a fourth consecutive strip and body-cavity search in the same room. MDC staff interfered with the Plaintiff's prayers, routinely confiscated his Koran, and refused to permit him to participate in Friday prayer services. They also interfered with the Plaintiff's communications with his defense attorney, for example, by disconnecting the phone if the Plaintiff complained about his conditions of confinement and delaying his receipt of legal mail for up to two months. . . .

[Iqbal pled guilty to non-terrorism charges, was sentenced, and eventually was removed to Pakistan. He brought this suit against his jailers, the Director of the FBI, and the Attorney General for damages based on violations of his constitutional and statutory rights as a result of the conditions of his confinement. Defendants moved to dismiss on grounds of qualified immunity. The lower court denied the motion, and this interlocutory appeal followed.] . . .

I. General Principles of Qualified Immunity . . .

. . . A defendant will be entitled to qualified immunity if either (1) his actions did not violate clearly established law or (2) it was objectively reasonable for him to believe that his actions did not violate clearly established law. . . .

. . . Several Defendants contend that even if the Plaintiff's complaint would survive a motion to dismiss in the face of a qualified immunity defense under normal circumstances, the post-9/11 context requires a different outcome. This argument is advanced on three fronts. First, some Defendants contend that the Government was entitled to take certain actions that might not have been lawful before 9/11 because the Government's interests assumed special weight in the post-9/11 context. Second, some Defendants contend that, even if the law was clearly established as to the existence of a right claimed to have been violated, it was not clearly established in the extraordinary circumstances of the 9/11 attack and its aftermath. Third, some Defendants contend that the post-9/11 context renders their actions objectively reasonable, an argument we do not reach in view of our disposition of their second contention.

We fully recognize the gravity of the situation that confronted investigative officials of the United States as a consequence of the 9/11 attack. We also recognize that some forms of governmental action are permitted in emergency situations that would exceed constitutional limits in normal times. *See Home Building & Loan Association v. Blaisdell,*

290 U.S. 398, 425-26 (1934) ("While emergency does not create power, emergency may furnish the occasion for the exercise of power."). But most of the rights that the Plaintiff contends were violated do not vary with surrounding circumstances, such as the right not to be subjected to needlessly harsh conditions of confinement, the right to be free from the use of excessive force, and the right not to be subjected to ethnic or religious discrimination. The strength of our system of constitutional rights derives from the steadfast protection of those rights in both normal and unusual times.

With some rights, for example, the right to be free from unreasonable searches, the existence of exigent circumstances might justify governmental action that would not otherwise be permitted. But, as we discuss below, the exigent circumstances of the post-9/11 context do not diminish the Plaintiff's right not to be needlessly harassed and mistreated in the confines of a prison cell by repeated strip and body-cavity searches. This and other rights, such as the right to be free from use of excessive force and not to be subjected to ethnic or religious discrimination, were all clearly established prior to 9/11, and they remained clearly established even in the aftermath of that horrific event. To whatever extent exigent circumstances might affect the lawfulness of the Defendants' actions or might have justified an objectively reasonable belief that their actions did not violate clearly established law, we consider the argument in connection with a particular claim.

With these general principles in mind, we turn to the Plaintiff's specific claims.

II. Procedural Due Process

The Plaintiff alleges that Ashcroft and Mueller, the FBI Defendants, the BOP [Bureau of Prisons] Defendants, and [former MDC Warden Dennis] Hasty adopted a policy under which he was deprived of a liberty interest without any of the procedural protections required by due process of law. . . .

(a) Has a Violation of a Procedural Due Process Right Been Adequately Pleaded? . . .

(i) *The Plaintiff's procedural due process right.*

. . . Under this Court's case law, the Plaintiff's confinement of more than six months fell in the intermediate range, thereby requiring inquiry

into the conditions of his confinement, which he sufficiently alleges to
have been severe. . . . [T]he conditions under which the Plaintiff alleges
that he was confined – solitary confinement, repeated strip and
body-cavity searches, beatings, exposure to excessive heat and cold, very
limited exercise, and almost constant lighting – as well as the initially
indefinite duration of confinement could be found to constitute atypical
and significant hardships. The Plaintiff has alleged a protected liberty
interest in avoiding more than six months' detention in the ADMAX
SHU, especially in light of his status as a pretrial detainee. . . .

We recognize that in the post-9/11 context the third *Mathews* factor[*] –
the gravity of the Government's interest – is appropriately accorded more
weight than would otherwise be warranted. It might be that the
combination of (1) the Plaintiff's interest in avoiding confinement under
harsh conditions, (2) the risk of an erroneous determination of the need
for such confinement, and (3) the Government's interest, accorded added
weight in the post-9/11 context, would, on balance, lead to the
conclusion that the Government need not have given the Plaintiff notice
and a chance for rebuttal *before* placing him in the ADMAX SHU.
However, once it became clear that the Plaintiff was going to be confined
in the ADMAX SHU for an extended period of time, some process was
required. We cannot say in the absence of a developed factual record
whether the FBI's clearance procedure comported with the requirements
of the Due Process Clause as interpreted in *Mathews* and subsequent
cases. The sparse record thus far developed provides no indication as to
what security-related steps the Defendants were taking that might justify
prolonged confinement. Nor does that record indicate in what respect
providing the Plaintiff with some notice of the basis for his separation in
the ADMAX SHU and affording some opportunity for rebuttal would
have impaired national security interests or legitimate penological
interests of the Government. The Government has not as yet had an
opportunity to refute the Plaintiff's allegation that there was no evidence
connecting him to terrorism. Accordingly, we cannot say whether the
Government's national security interests rendered the clearance
procedure sufficient to satisfy procedural due process requirements or
whether more traditional procedural protections were required.
Nevertheless, because we are required at this stage of the litigation to

---

[* The reference is to *Mathews v. Eldridge*, 424 U.S. 319 (1976). *See* NSL
pp. 725, 850 n.4; CTL pp. 364, 611 n.3, summarizing the *Mathews* balancing
test. – Eds.]

accept all of the Plaintiff's allegations as true and draw all reasonable inferences in his favor, we cannot say that the Plaintiff has failed to plead a viable claim under the procedural component of the Due Process Clause. . . .

(b) Was the Plaintiff's Right to Procedural Due Process Clearly Established?

Although we conclude that the Plaintiff has adequately pleaded a violation of a procedural due process right, we also conclude that in this case "officers of reasonable competence could [have] disagree[d]," *Malley v. Briggs,* 475 U.S. 335, 341 (1986), whether their conduct violated a clearly established procedural due process right. Accordingly, the Plaintiff's right to additional procedures was not clearly established with the level of specificity that is required to defeat a qualified immunity defense.

Several factors combine to create this lack of clarity in prior case law. First, some uncertainty exists in determining when administrative segregation procedures are required even in the ordinary criminal context. Our case law would require an officer in the Defendants' situation to consider various factors, including the length of the Plaintiff's confinement, the extent to which the conditions of confinement were atypical, the text of relevant BOP regulations, and the Plaintiff's status as a pretrial detainee. As noted above, no single factor is dispositive in this case, which concerns administrative segregation of approximately six months. Although the harshness of the conditions alleged weigh in favor of requiring procedural protections, an officer could reasonably note that the Plaintiff's six-month continued confinement was comparable to the duration of confinements in cases that we [have] characterized . . . as involving "relatively brief periods of confinement."

Second, uncertainty in existing case law is heightened by the fact that, even on the facts alleged in the complaint, which specified that the "of high interest" designation pertained to the Government's post-9/11 terrorism investigation, the investigation leading to the Plaintiff's separation from the general prison population could be reasonably understood by all of the Defendants to relate to matters of national security, rather than an ordinary criminal investigation. Prior to the instant case, neither the Supreme Court nor our Court had considered whether the Due Process Clause requires officials to provide ordinary administrative segregation hearings to persons detained under special conditions of confinement until cleared of connection with activities threatening national security.

Third, the BOP regulation on which the Plaintiff relies itself contains potentially relevant exceptions that undermine certainty as to established requirements of law. "Administrative detention is to be used only for short periods of time except . . . where there are exceptional circumstances, *ordinarily tied to security or complex investigative concerns,*" 28 C.F.R. §541.22(c)(1) (emphasis added), and inmates are entitled to "an administrative detention order detailing the reasons for placing an inmate in administrative detention . . . *provided institutional security is not compromised thereby,*" *id.* §541.22(b) (emphasis added).

In sum, these factors, taken together, would suffice to raise "a legitimate question" among Government officials as to whether the Due Process Clause required administrative segregation hearings or any procedures other than the FBI's clearance system. Accordingly, we will direct dismissal of the portions of the Plaintiff's complaint alleging violations of procedural due process rights.

III. Conditions of Confinement

[Defendant] Hasty contends that [District Court] Judge Gleeson should have dismissed the Plaintiff's conditions of confinement claims against him on the ground of qualified immunity because (1) the Plaintiff did not allege conditions amounting to a violation of substantive due process rights, (2) the Plaintiff failed to allege Hasty's deliberate indifference to the maintenance of the conditions of confinement, and (3) Hasty's actions were objectively reasonable under the circumstances.

Because the Plaintiff was a pretrial detainee during his detention in the ADMAX SHU, his challenge to the conditions of his confinement arises from the substantive component of the Due Process Clause of the Fifth Amendment and not from the cruel and unusual punishment standards of the Eighth Amendment. *See Benjamin v. Fraser*, 343 F.3d 35, 49 (2d Cir. 2003) ("*Benjamin II* "). Pretrial detainees have not been convicted of a crime and thus "may not be punished in any manner – neither cruelly and unusually nor otherwise." *Id.* at 49-50. Courts considering challenges to confinement brought by pretrial detainees must first consider whether the circumstances of the particular confinement render the confinement punitive; since some restraint is necessary to confine a pretrial detainee, not all uncomfortable conditions or restrictions are necessarily punitive. *Id.* at 50. In *Bell v. Wolfish*, [441 U.S. 520 (1979)], the seminal case on the substantive due process claims of pretrial detainees, the Supreme Court recognized the following factors as relevant to the determination of whether a condition of confinement is punitive:

> "Whether the sanction involves an affirmative disability or restraint, whether it has historically been regarded as a punishment, whether it comes into play only on a finding of *scienter,* whether its operation will promote the traditional aims of punishment – retribution and deterrence, whether the behavior to which it applies is already a crime, whether an alternative purpose to which it may rationally be connected is assignable for it, and whether it appears excessive in relation to the alternative purpose assigned. . . ."

441 U.S. at 537-38 (quoting [*Kennedy v. Mendoza-Martinez*, 372 U.S. 144, 168-169 (1963)]). A court may infer that a condition of confinement is intended as punishment if it is not reasonably related to a legitimate government objective.

The complaint alleges, among other things, that MDC staff placed the Plaintiff in solitary confinement, deliberately subjected him to extreme hot and cold temperatures, shackled him every time he left his cell, and repeatedly subjected him to strip and body-cavity searches, and that these conditions were intended to be, and were in fact, punitive. Applying *Wolfish,* Judge Gleeson found these allegations sufficient to state a substantive due process claim, observing that whether the conditions were reasonably related to legitimate government objectives could not be determined on a motion to dismiss. . . .

The Plaintiff has alleged the purposeful infliction of restraints that were punitive in nature. Accordingly, the District Court need not have considered whether a Defendant was "deliberately indifferent" in inflicting the restraints or whether the restraints constituted cruel and unusual punishment. The right of pretrial detainees to be free from punitive restraints was clearly established at the time of the events in question, and no reasonable officer could have thought that he could punish a pretrial detainee by subjecting him to the practices and conditions alleged by the Plaintiff. . . .

VII. Interference with Religious Practices

Hasty also argues that Judge Gleeson should have dismissed the Plaintiff's First Amendment claim against him on qualified immunity grounds because . . . the Plaintiff did not allege a violation of his First Amendment rights. . . .

Hasty's . . . argument is that Plaintiff has not alleged a violation of his First Amendment rights. He relies on *O'Lone v. Estate of Shabazz,* 482 U.S. 342 (1987), which applied *Turner*'s [*Turner v. Safley,* 482 U.S. 78 (1987)] "legitimate penological interests" test to First Amendment claims, *see id.* at 348-49. Though recognizing that a prison regulation precluded some Muslim prisoners from attending Friday prayers, the Supreme Court found the regulation justified under *Turner,* focusing on the officials' legitimate security objectives and the availability of other channels by which prisoners could exercise their religious rights. In the pending case, however, the Plaintiff alleges that he was not allowed to attend Friday prayers, that prison guards banged on his door when he tried to pray, and that his Koran was routinely confiscated. These allegations suffice to preclude a qualified immunity defense at this stage of the litigation. . . .

VIII. Racial and Religious Discrimination

The Defendants argue that they are entitled to qualified immunity on the Plaintiff's First Amendment claim of religious discrimination and Fifth Amendment claim of racial or ethnic discrimination on three grounds: (1) the Plaintiff has failed to state a violation of clearly established rights, (2) the Plaintiff's allegations of discriminatory intent are too conclusory, and (3) the Plaintiff has not alleged the personal involvement of Ashcroft and Mueller.

The arguments of Ashcroft and Mueller challenging the sufficiency of the Plaintiff's race, ethnic, and religious discrimination claims misunderstand his complaint. They contend that his "complaint amounts to an objection that most of those persons determined to be of high interest to the 9/11 investigation were Muslim or from certain Arab countries," which they justify by pointing out that the 9/11 hijackers were Muslims from Arab countries. However, what the Plaintiff is alleging is that he was deemed to be "of high interest," and accordingly was kept in the ADMAX SHU under harsh conditions, solely because of his race, ethnicity, and religion. The Plaintiff also alleges that "Defendants specifically targeted [him] for mistreatment because of [his] race, religion, and national origin." These allegations are sufficient to state a claim of animus-based discrimination that any "reasonably competent officer" would understand to have been illegal under prior case law. *See Malley,* 475 U.S. at 341. Accordingly, the Plaintiff's racial, ethnic, and religious discrimination claims cannot be dismissed on qualified immunity grounds at this stage of the litigation.

Hasty also argues that the Plaintiff has failed to state a claim of discrimination. Citing *Reno v. American-Arab Anti-Discrimination Committee*, 525 U.S. 471 (1999) ("*AAADC*"), he argues that the Equal Protection Clause does not apply in the context of proceedings to remove illegal aliens and that the Government can permissibly deem nationals of a particular country to be a special threat. In *AAADC*, the Supreme Court concluded that a provision of the Illegal Immigration Reform and Immigrant Responsibility Act of 1996, 8 U.S.C. §1252(g), deprived the federal courts of jurisdiction to consider an illegal alien's selective enforcement challenge to deportation. *See* 525 U.S. at 487. The Court rejected the argument that it nevertheless had jurisdiction to consider an alien's constitutional arguments, holding that "an alien unlawfully in this country has no constitutional right to assert selective enforcement as a defense against his deportation," *see id.* at 488, even when the Government deports the alien "for the additional reason that it believes him to be a member of an organization that supports terrorist activity," *id.* at 492. *AAADC* affords the Defendants no relief. The Plaintiff is not challenging his deportation or even his arrest on criminal charges. Moreover, *AAADC* does not stand for the proposition that the Government may subject members of a particular race, ethnicity, or religion to more restrictive conditions of confinement than members of other races, ethnic backgrounds, or religions. . . .

The Plaintiff's allegations suffice to state claims of racial, ethnic, and religious discrimination. He alleges in particular that the FBI Defendants classified him "of high interest" solely because of his race, ethnic background, and religion and not because of any evidence of involvement in terrorism. He offers additional factual support for this allegation, stating that "within the New York area, all Arab Muslim men arrested on criminal or immigration charges while the FBI was following an investigative lead into the September 11th attacks – however unrelated the arrestee was to the investigation – were immediately classified as 'of interest' to the post-September 11th investigation." We need not consider at this stage of the litigation whether these allegations are alone sufficient to state a clearly established constitutional violation under the circumstances presented because they are sufficient to state a violation when combined with the Plaintiff's allegation that, under the policy created and implemented by the Defendants, he was singled out for unnecessarily punitive conditions of confinement based on his racial, ethnic, and religious characteristics. . . .

Conclusion . . .

In sum, the serious allegations of gross mistreatment set forth in the complaint suffice, except as noted in this opinion, to defeat the Defendants' attempt to terminate the lawsuit at a preliminary stage, but, consistent with the important policies that justify the defense of qualified immunity, the defense may be reasserted in advance of trial after the carefully controlled and limited discovery that the District Court expects to supervise.

Affirmed in part, reversed in part, and remanded.

[Concurring opinion of JOSÉ A. CABRANES, J., omitted.]

[NSL p. 679, CTL p. 310. Insert after *Iqbal v. Hasty.*]

Ashcroft v. Iqbal
United States Supreme Court, 2009
129 S. Ct. 1937

Justice KENNEDY delivered the opinion of the Court. . . . Respondent's account of his prison ordeal could, if proved, demonstrate unconstitutional misconduct by some governmental actors. But the allegations and pleadings with respect to these actors are not before us here. This case instead turns on a narrower question: Did respondent, as the plaintiff in the District Court, plead factual matter that, if taken as true, states a claim that petitioners deprived him of his clearly established constitutional rights. We hold respondent's pleadings are insufficient. . . .

III. . . .

. . . Based on the rules our precedents establish, respondent correctly concedes that Government officials may not be held liable for the unconstitutional conduct of their subordinates under a theory of *respondeat superior.* Because vicarious liability is inapplicable to *Bivens* [*Bivens v. Six Unknown Fed. Narcotics Agents,* 403 U.S. 388 (1971)] and §1983 suits, a plaintiff must plead that each Government-official defendant, through the official's own individual actions, has violated the Constitution.

The factors necessary to establish a *Bivens* violation will vary with the constitutional provision at issue. Where the claim is invidious discrimination in contravention of the First and Fifth Amendments, our decisions make clear that the plaintiff must plead and prove that the defendant acted with discriminatory purpose. . . . It follows that, to state a claim based on a violation of a clearly established right, respondent must plead sufficient factual matter to show that petitioners adopted and implemented the detention policies at issue not for a neutral, investigative reason but for the purpose of discriminating on account of race, religion, or national origin.

Respondent disagrees. He argues that, under a theory of "supervisory liability," petitioners can be liable for "knowledge and acquiescence in their subordinates' use of discriminatory criteria to make classification decisions among detainees." That is to say, respondent believes a supervisor's mere knowledge of his subordinate's discriminatory purpose amounts to the supervisor's violating the Constitution. We reject this argument. Respondent's conception of "supervisory liability" is inconsistent with his accurate stipulation that petitioners may not be held accountable for the misdeeds of their agents. In a § 1983 suit or a *Bivens* action – where masters do not answer for the torts of their servants – the term "supervisory liability" is a misnomer. Absent vicarious liability, each Government official, his or her title notwithstanding, is only liable for his or her own misconduct. In the context of determining whether there is a violation of clearly established right to overcome qualified immunity, purpose rather than knowledge is required to impose *Bivens* liability on the subordinate for unconstitutional discrimination; the same holds true for an official charged with violations arising from his or her superintendent responsibilities.

IV. . . .

Under [the] construction of Rule 8 in [*Bell Atlantic Corp. v. Twombly*, 550 U.S. 544 (2007)], we conclude that respondent's complaint has not "nudged [his] claims" of invidious discrimination "across the line from conceivable to plausible." [*Id.* at 555.]

We begin our analysis by identifying the allegations in the complaint that are not entitled to the assumption of truth. Respondent pleads that petitioners "knew of, condoned, and willfully and maliciously agreed to subject [him]" to harsh conditions of confinement "as a matter of policy, solely on account of [his] religion, race, and/or national origin and for no legitimate penological interest." The complaint alleges that Ashcroft was the "principal architect" of this invidious policy, and that Mueller was "instrumental" in adopting and executing it. These bare assertions, much like the pleading of conspiracy in *Twombly,* amount to nothing more than a "formulaic recitation of the elements" of a constitutional discrimination claim, namely, that petitioners adopted a policy "'because of,' not merely 'in spite of,' its adverse effects upon an identifiable group." As such, the allegations are conclusory and not entitled to be assumed true. To be clear, we do not reject these bald allegations on the ground that they are unrealistic or nonsensical. We do not so characterize them any more than the Court in *Twombly* rejected the plaintiffs' express allegation of a "'contract, combination or conspiracy to prevent competitive entry,'" because it thought that claim too chimerical to be maintained. It is the conclusory nature of respondent's allegations, rather than their extravagantly fanciful nature, that disentitles them to the presumption of truth.

We next consider the factual allegations in respondent's complaint to determine if they plausibly suggest an entitlement to relief. The complaint alleges that "the [FBI], under the direction of Defendant Mueller, arrested and detained thousands of Arab Muslim men . . . as part of its investigation of the events of September 11." It further claims that "[t]he policy of holding post-September-11th detainees in highly restrictive conditions of confinement until they were 'cleared' by the FBI was approved by Defendants Ashcroft and Mueller in discussions in the weeks after September 11, 2001." Taken as true, these allegations are consistent with petitioners' purposefully designating detainees "of high interest" because of their race, religion, or national origin. But given more likely explanations, they do not plausibly establish this purpose.

The September 11 attacks were perpetrated by 19 Arab Muslim hijackers who counted themselves members in good standing of al Qaeda, an Islamic fundamentalist group. Al Qaeda was headed by another Arab Muslim – Osama bin Laden – and composed in large part of his Arab Muslim disciples. It should come as no surprise that a legitimate policy directing law enforcement to arrest and detain individuals because of their suspected link to the attacks would produce a disparate, incidental impact on Arab Muslims, even though the purpose of the policy was to target neither Arabs nor Muslims. On the facts respondent alleges the arrests Mueller oversaw were likely lawful and justified by his nondiscriminatory intent to detain aliens who were illegally present in the United States and who had potential connections to those who committed terrorist acts. As between that "obvious alternative explanation" for the arrests, and the purposeful, invidious discrimination respondent asks us to infer, discrimination is not a plausible conclusion.

But even if the complaint's well-pleaded facts give rise to a plausible inference that respondent's arrest was the result of unconstitutional discrimination, that inference alone would not entitle respondent to relief. It is important to recall that respondent's complaint challenges neither the constitutionality of his arrest nor his initial detention in the MDC. Respondent's constitutional claims against petitioners rest solely on their ostensible "policy of holding post-September-11th detainees" in the ADMAX SHU once they were categorized as "of high interest." To prevail on that theory, the complaint must contain facts plausibly showing that petitioners purposefully adopted a policy of classifying post-September-11 detainees as "of high interest" because of their race, religion, or national origin.

This the complaint fails to do. Though respondent alleges that various other defendants, who are not before us, may have labeled him a person of "of high interest" for impermissible reasons, his only factual allegation against petitioners accuses them of adopting a policy approving "restrictive conditions of confinement" for post-September-11 detainees until they were "'cleared' by the FBI." Accepting the truth of that allegation, the complaint does not show, or even intimate, that petitioners purposefully housed detainees in the ADMAX SHU due to their race, religion, or national origin. All it plausibly suggests is that the Nation's top law enforcement officers, in the aftermath of a devastating terrorist attack, sought to keep suspected terrorists in the most secure conditions available until the suspects could be cleared of terrorist activity. Respondent does not argue, nor can he, that such a motive would violate petitioners' constitutional obligations. He would need to allege more by way of factual content to "nudg[e]" his claim of purposeful discrimination "across the line from conceivable to plausible." *Twombly*, 550 U.S. at 570. . . .

It is important to note, however, that we express no opinion concerning the sufficiency of respondent's complaint against the defendants who are not before us. Respondent's account of his prison ordeal alleges serious official misconduct that we need not address here. Our decision is limited to the determination that respondent's complaint does not entitle him to relief from petitioners. . . .

V

We hold that respondent's complaint fails to plead sufficient facts to state a claim for purposeful and unlawful discrimination against petitioners. The Court of Appeals should decide in the first instance whether to remand to the District Court so that respondent can seek leave to amend his deficient complaint.

The judgment of the Court of Appeals is reversed, and the case is remanded for further proceedings consistent with this opinion.

It is so ordered.

Justice SOUTER, with whom Justice STEVENS, Justice GINSBURG, and Justice BREYER join, dissenting. This case is here on the uncontested assumption that *Bivens v. Six Unknown Fed. Narcotics Agents,* 403 U.S. 388 (1971), allows personal liability based on a federal officer's violation of an individual's rights under the First and Fifth Amendments, and it comes to us with the explicit concession of petitioners Ashcroft and Mueller that an officer may be subject to *Bivens* liability as a supervisor on grounds other than *respondeat superior.* The Court apparently rejects this concession and, although it has no bearing on the majority's resolution of this case, does away with supervisory liability under *Bivens.* The majority then misapplies the pleading standard under *Bell Atlantic Corp. v. Twombly,* 550 U.S. 544 (2007), to conclude that the complaint fails to state a claim. I respectfully dissent from both the rejection of supervisory liability as a cognizable claim in the face of petitioners' concession, and from the holding that the complaint fails to satisfy Rule 8(a)(2) of the Federal Rules of Civil Procedure. . . .

[The dissenting opinion of Justice BREYER is omitted.]

[NSL p. 690. Insert after heading "C".]

Johnson v. Eisentrager
United States Supreme Court, 1950
339 U.S. 763

Mr. Justice JACKSON delivered the opinion of the Court. The ultimate question in this case is one of jurisdiction of civil courts of the United States *vis-à-vis* military authorities in dealing with enemy aliens overseas. . . .

[U.S. armed forces captured 21 German nationals in service of German armed forces in China. A U.S. military commission sitting in China tried and convicted them of violating laws of war, namely, engaging in, permitting, or ordering continued military activity against the United States after the surrender of Germany and before the surrender of Japan. After conviction, their sentences were reviewed and approved by military reviewing authority. They were then repatriated to the U.S.-run Landsberg Prison in Germany to serve their sentences.

They filed a petition for a writ of habeas corpus in the District of Columbia, naming the Secretary of Defense, among others, and asserting that their trial, conviction, and imprisonment violated Articles I and III of the Constitution, the Fifth Amendment, and provisions of the Geneva Convention governing the treatment of prisoners of war.]

We are cited to no instance where a court, in this or any other country where the writ is known, has issued it on behalf of an alien enemy who, at no relevant time and in no stage of his captivity, has been within its territorial jurisdiction. Nothing in the text of the Constitution extends such a right, nor does anything in our statutes. . . .

I.

Modern American law has come a long way since the time when outbreak of war made every enemy national an outlaw, subject to both public and private slaughter, cruelty and plunder. But even by the most magnanimous view, our law does not abolish inherent distinctions recognized throughout the civilized world between citizens and aliens, nor between aliens of friendly and of enemy allegiance, nor between resident enemy aliens who have submitted themselves to our laws and nonresident enemy aliens who at all times have remained with, and adhered to, enemy governments.

With the citizen we are now little concerned, except to set his case apart as untouched by this decision and to take measure of the difference between his status and that of all categories of aliens. . . .

The alien, to whom the United States has been traditionally hospitable, has been accorded a generous and ascending scale of rights as he increases his identity with our society. Mere lawful presence in the country creates an implied assurance of safe conduct and gives him certain rights . . . .

But, in extending constitutional protections beyond the citizenry, the Court has been at pains to point out that it was the alien's presence within its territorial jurisdiction that gave the Judiciary power to act. In the pioneer case of *Yick Wo v. Hopkins*, the Court said of the Fourteenth Amendment, "These provisions are universal in their application, to all persons within the territorial jurisdiction, without regard to any differences of race, of color, or of nationality; * * *." 118 U.S. 356, 369. . . .

Since most cases involving aliens afford this ground of jurisdiction, and the civil and property rights of immigrants or transients of foreign nationality so nearly approach equivalence to those of citizens, courts in peace time have little occasion to inquire whether litigants before them are alien or citizen.

It is war that exposes the relative vulnerability of the alien's status. The security and protection enjoyed while the nation of his allegiance remains in amity with the United States are greatly impaired when his nation takes up arms against us. While his lot is far more humane and endurable than the experience of our citizens in some enemy lands, it is still not a happy one. But disabilities this country lays upon the alien who becomes also an enemy are imposed temporarily as an incident of war and not as an incident of alienage. . . .

. . . [T]he nonresident enemy alien, especially one who has remained in the service of the enemy, does not have even this qualified access to our courts, for he neither has comparable claims upon our institutions nor could his use of them fail to be helpful to the enemy. Our law on this subject first emerged about 1813 when the Supreme Court of the State of New York had occasion, in a series of cases, to examine the foremost authorities of the Continent and of England. It concluded the rule of the common law and the law of nations to be that alien enemies resident in the country of the enemy could not maintain an action in its courts during the period of hostilities. This Court has recognized that rule, and it continues to be the law throughout this country and in England.

II.

The foregoing demonstrates how much further we must go if we are to invest these enemy aliens, resident, captured and imprisoned abroad, with standing to demand access to our courts.

We are here confronted with a decision whose basic premise is that these prisoners are entitled, as a constitutional right, to sue in some court of the United States for a writ of *habeas corpus*. To support that assumption we must hold that a prisoner of our military authorities is constitutionally entitled to the writ, even though he (a) is an enemy alien; (b) has never been or resided in the United States; (c) was captured outside of our territory and there held in military custody as a prisoner of war; (d) was tried and convicted by a Military Commission sitting outside the United States; (e) for offenses against laws of war committed outside the United States; (f) and is at all times imprisoned outside the United States.

We have pointed out that the privilege of litigation has been extended to aliens, whether friendly or enemy, only because permitting their presence in the country implied protection. No such basis can be invoked here, for these prisoners at no relevant time were within any territory over which the United States is sovereign, and the scenes of their offense, their capture, their trial and their punishment were all beyond the territorial jurisdiction of any court of the United States.

Another reason for a limited opening of our courts to resident aliens is that among them are many of friendly personal disposition to whom the status of enemy is only one imputed by law. But these prisoners were actual enemies, active in the hostile service of an enemy power. . . .

A basic consideration in *habeas corpus* practice is that the prisoner will be produced before the court. This is the crux of the statutory scheme established by the Congress; indeed, it is inherent in the very term *"habeas corpus."* . . . To grant the writ to these prisoners might mean that our army must transport them across the seas for hearing. This would require allocation of shipping space, guarding personnel, billeting and rations. It might also require transportation for whatever witnesses the prisoners desired to call as well as transportation for those necessary to defend legality of the sentence. The writ, since it is held to be a matter of right, would be equally available to enemies during active hostilities as in the present twilight between war and peace. Such trials would hamper the war effort and bring aid and comfort to the enemy. They would diminish the prestige of our commanders, not only with enemies but with wavering neutrals. It would be difficult to devise more effective fettering of a field commander than to allow the very enemies he is ordered to reduce to submission to call him to account in his own civil courts and divert his efforts and attention from the military offensive abroad to the legal defensive at home. Nor is it unlikely that the result of such enemy litigiousness would be a conflict between judicial and military opinion highly comforting to enemies of the United States. . . .

III.

The Court of Appeals dispensed with all requirement of territorial jurisdiction based on place of residence, captivity, trial, offense, or confinement. It could not predicate relief upon any intraterritorial contact of these prisoners with our laws or institutions. Instead, it gave our Constitution an extraterritorial application to embrace our enemies in arms. Right to the writ, it reasoned, is a subsidiary procedural right that follows from possession of substantive constitutional rights. These prisoners, it considered, are invested with a right of personal liberty by our Constitution and therefore must have the right to the remedial writ. The court stated the steps in its own reasoning as follows: "*First.* The Fifth Amendment, by its terms, applies to 'any person.' *Second.* Action of Government officials in violation of the Constitution is void. This is the ultimate essence of the present controversy. *Third.* A basic and inherent function of the judicial branch of a government built upon a constitution is to set aside void action by government officials, and so to restrict executive action to the confines of the constitution. In our jurisprudence, no Government action which is void under the Constitution is exempt from judicial power. *Fourth.* The writ of habeas corpus is the established, time-honored process in our law for testing the authority of one who deprives another of his liberty, – 'the best and only sufficient defense of personal freedom.' * * *" 174 F.2d 961, 963-964. . . .

When we analyze the claim prisoners are asserting and the court below sustained, it amounts to a right not to be tried at all for an offense against our armed forces. If the Fifth Amendment protects them from military trial, the Sixth Amendment as clearly prohibits their trial by civil courts. The latter requires in all criminal prosecutions that "the accused" be tried "by an impartial jury of the State and district wherein the crime shall have been committed, which district shall have been previously ascertained by law." And if the Fifth be held to embrace these prisoners because it uses the inclusive term "no person," the Sixth must, for it applies to all "accused." No suggestion is advanced by the court below or by prisoners of any constitutional method by which any violations of the laws of war endangering the United States forces could be reached or punished, if it were not by a Military Commission in the theatre where the offense was committed. . . .

If this Amendment invests enemy aliens in unlawful hostile action against us with immunity from military trial, it puts them in a more protected position than our own soldiers. American citizens conscripted into the military service are thereby stripped of their Fifth Amendment rights and as members of the military establishment are subject to its discipline, including military trials for offenses against aliens or Americans. . . .

If the Fifth Amendment confers its rights on all the world except Americans engaged in defending it, the same must be true of the companion civil-rights Amendments, for none of them is limited by its express terms, territorially or as to persons. Such a construction would mean that during military occupation irreconcilable enemy elements, guerrilla fighters, and "were-wolves" [German nationals trained to

conduct terrorist activities in postwar Germany] could require the
American Judiciary to assure them freedoms of speech, press, and
assembly as in the First Amendment, right to bear arms as in the Second,
security against "unreasonable" searches and seizures as in the Fourth, as
well as rights to jury trial as in the Fifth and Sixth Amendments.

Such extraterritorial application of organic law would have been so
significant an innovation in the practice of governments that, if intended
or apprehended, it could scarcely have failed to excite contemporary
comment. Not one word can be cited. No decision of this Court
supports such a view. None of the learned commentators on our
Constitution has ever hinted at it. The practice of every modern
government is opposed to it.

We hold that the Constitution does not confer a right of personal
security or an immunity from military trial and punishment upon an alien
enemy engaged in the hostile service of a government at war with the
United States. . . .

V. . . .

Since in the present application we find no basis for invoking federal
judicial power in any district, we need not debate as to where, if the case
were otherwise, the petition should be filed.

For reasons stated, the judgment of the Court of Appeals is reversed
and the judgment of the District Court dismissing the petition is affirmed.

Reversed.

Mr. Justice BLACK, with whom Mr. Justice DOUGLAS and Mr.
Justice BURTON concur, dissenting. . . . In Parts I, II, and III of its
opinion, the Court apparently holds that no American court can even
consider the jurisdiction of the military tribunal to convict and sentence
these prisoners for the alleged crime. . . . [T]his holding . . . is based on
the facts that (1) they were enemy aliens who were belligerents when
captured, and (2) they were captured, tried, and imprisoned outside our
realm, never having been in the United States.

The contention that enemy alien belligerents have no standing
whatever to contest conviction for war crimes by habeas corpus
proceedings has twice been emphatically rejected by a unanimous Court
[citing *Ex parte Quirin* and *In re Yamashita*]. . . . That we went on to
deny the requested writ [in both cases] in no way detracts from the clear
holding that habeas corpus jurisdiction is available even to belligerent

aliens convicted by a military tribunal for an offense committed in actual acts of warfare.

. . . Does a prisoner's right to test legality of a sentence then depend on where the Government chooses to imprison him? Certainly the *Quirin* and *Yamashita* opinions lend no support to that conclusion, for in upholding jurisdiction they place no reliance whatever on territorial location. The Court is fashioning wholly indefensible doctrine if it permits the executive branch, by deciding where its prisoners will be tried and imprisoned, to deprive all federal courts of their power to protect against a federal executive's illegal incarcerations.

If the opinion thus means, and it apparently does, that these petitioners are deprived of the privilege of habeas corpus solely because they were convicted and imprisoned overseas, the Court is adopting a broad and dangerous principle. . . .

. . . It has always been recognized that actual warfare can be conducted successfully only if those in command are left the most ample independence in the theatre of operations. Our Constitution is not so impractical or inflexible that it unduly restricts such necessary independence. It would be fantastic to suggest that alien enemies could hail our military leaders into judicial tribunals to account for their day to day activities on the battlefront. Active fighting forces must be free to fight while hostilities are in progress. But that undisputable axiom has no bearing on this case or the general problem from which it arises. . . .

The question here involves a far narrower issue. Springing from recognition that our government is composed of three separate and independent branches, it is whether the judiciary has power in habeas corpus proceedings to test the legality of criminal sentences imposed by the executive through military tribunals in a country which we have occupied for years. . . .

Though the scope of habeas corpus review of military tribunal sentences is narrow, I think it should not be denied to these petitioners and others like them. We control that part of Germany we occupy. These prisoners were convicted by our own military tribunals under our own Articles of War, years after hostilities had ceased. However illegal their sentences might be, they can expect no relief from German courts or any other branch of the German Government we permit to function. Only our own courts can inquire into the legality of their imprisonment. Perhaps, as some nations believe, there is merit in leaving the administration of criminal laws to executive and military agencies completely free from judicial scrutiny. Our Constitution has emphatically expressed a contrary policy. . . .

. . . Our nation proclaims a belief in the dignity of human beings as such, no matter what their nationality or where they happen to live. Habeas corpus, as an instrument to protect against illegal imprisonment, is written into the Constitution. Its use by courts cannot in my judgment be constitutionally abridged by Executive or by Congress. I would hold that our courts can exercise it whenever any United States official illegally imprisons any person in any land we govern. . . .

[NSL p. 702, insert after Note 8. CTL pp. 336-348, substitute for D.C. Circuit opinion, 2007 Supreme Court opinion, and Notes and Questions.]

Boumediene v. Bush
United States Supreme Court, 2008
128 S. Ct. 2229

Justice KENNEDY delivered the opinion of the Court. Petitioners are aliens designated as enemy combatants and detained at the United States Naval Station at Guantanamo Bay, Cuba. There are others detained there, also aliens, who are not parties to this suit.

Petitioners present a question not resolved by our earlier cases relating to the detention of aliens at Guantanamo: whether they have the constitutional privilege of habeas corpus, a privilege not to be withdrawn except in conformance with the Suspension Clause, Art. I, §9, cl. 2. We hold these petitioners do have the habeas corpus privilege. Congress has enacted a statute, the Detainee Treatment Act of 2005 (DTA), 119 Stat. 2739, that provides certain procedures for review of the detainees' status. We hold that those procedures are not an adequate and effective substitute for habeas corpus. Therefore, §7 of the Military Commissions Act of 2006 (MCA), 28 U.S.C.A. §2241(e) (Supp. 2007), operates as an unconstitutional suspension of the writ. We do not address whether the President has authority to detain these petitioners nor do we hold that the writ must issue. These and other questions regarding the legality of the detention are to be resolved in the first instance by the District Court.

I . . .

Interpreting the AUMF [Authorization for Use of Military Force, Pub. L. No. 107-40 (2001), NSL p. 100, CTL p. 59], the Department of Defense ordered the detention of these petitioners, and they were transferred to Guantanamo. Some of these individuals were apprehended on the battlefield in Afghanistan, others in places as far away from there as Bosnia and Gambia. All are foreign nationals, but none is a citizen of a nation now at war with the United States. Each denies he is a member of the al Qaeda terrorist network that carried out the September 11 attacks or of the Taliban regime that provided sanctuary for al Qaeda. Each petitioner appeared before a separate CSRT [Combatant Status Review Tribunal, *see* NSL p. 700, Note 3; CTL p. 334, Note 3]; was determined to be an enemy combatant; and has sought a writ of habeas corpus in the United States District Court for the District of Columbia.

[These initial petitions culminated in the Supreme Court's decision in *Rasul v. Bush*, 524 U.S. 466 (2004), extending *statutory* habeas corpus jurisdiction to Guantanamo. The Court there did not reach the question of *constitutional* habeas corpus jurisdiction, which is presented in the instant cases.] . . .

II

As a threshold matter, we must decide whether MCA §7 denies the federal courts jurisdiction to hear habeas corpus actions pending at the time of its enactment. We hold the statute does deny that jurisdiction, so that, if the statute is valid, petitioners' cases must be dismissed.

As amended by the terms of the MCA, §2241(e) now provides:

(1) No court, justice, or judge shall have jurisdiction to hear or consider an application for a writ of habeas corpus filed by or on behalf of an alien detained by the United States who has been determined by the United States to have been properly detained as an enemy combatant or is awaiting such determination.

(2) Except as provided in [§1005(e)(2) and (e)(3) of the DTA] no court, justice, or judge shall have jurisdiction to hear or consider any other action against the United States or its agents relating to any aspect of the detention, transfer, treatment, trial, or conditions of confinement of an alien who is or was detained by the United States and has been determined by the United States to have been properly detained as an enemy combatant or is awaiting such determination. . . .

III

In deciding the constitutional questions now presented we must determine whether petitioners are barred from seeking the writ or invoking the protections of the Suspension Clause either because of their status, *i.e.,* petitioners' designation by the Executive Branch as enemy combatants, or their physical location, *i.e.,* their presence at Guantanamo

Bay. The Government contends that noncitizens designated as enemy combatants and detained in territory located outside our Nation's borders have no constitutional rights and no privilege of habeas corpus. Petitioners contend they do have cognizable constitutional rights and that Congress, in seeking to eliminate recourse to habeas corpus as a means to assert those rights, acted in violation of the Suspension Clause.

We begin with a brief account of the history and origins of the writ. Our account proceeds from two propositions. First, protection for the privilege of habeas corpus was one of the few safeguards of liberty specified in a Constitution that, at the outset, had no Bill of Rights. In the system conceived by the Framers the writ had a centrality that must inform proper interpretation of the Suspension Clause. Second, to the extent there were settled precedents or legal commentaries in 1789 regarding the extraterritorial scope of the writ or its application to enemy aliens, those authorities can be instructive for the present cases.

A

The Framers viewed freedom from unlawful restraint as a fundamental precept of liberty, and they understood the writ of habeas corpus as a vital instrument to secure that freedom. Experience taught, however, that the common-law writ all too often had been insufficient to guard against the abuse of monarchial power. That history counseled the necessity for specific language in the Constitution to secure the writ and ensure its place in our legal system. . . .

This history was known to the Framers. It no doubt confirmed their view that pendular swings to and away from individual liberty were endemic to undivided, uncontrolled power. The Framers' inherent distrust of governmental power was the driving force behind the constitutional plan that allocated powers among three independent branches. This design serves not only to make Government accountable but also to secure individual liberty. Because the Constitution's separation-of-powers structure, like the substantive guarantees of the Fifth and Fourteenth Amendments, *see Yick Wo v. Hopkins*, 118 U.S. 356, 374 (1886), protects persons as well as citizens, foreign nationals who have the privilege of litigating in our courts can seek to enforce separation-of-powers principles, see, *e.g., INS v. Chadha*, 462 U.S. 919, 958-959 (1983).

That the Framers considered the writ a vital instrument for the protection of individual liberty is evident from the care taken to specify the limited grounds for its suspension: "The Privilege of the Writ of

Habeas Corpus shall not be suspended, unless when in Cases of Rebellion or Invasion the public Safety may require it." Art. I, §9, cl. 2; see Amar, *Of Sovereignty and Federalism*, 96 Yale L.J. 1425, 1509 n.329 (1987) ("[T]he non-suspension clause is the original Constitution's most explicit reference to remedies"). . . .

In our own system the Suspension Clause is designed to protect against these cyclical abuses. The Clause protects the rights of the detained by a means consistent with the essential design of the Constitution. It ensures that, except during periods of formal suspension, the Judiciary will have a time-tested device, the writ, to maintain the "delicate balance of governance" that is itself the surest safeguard of liberty. See Hamdi [v. Rumsfeld, 542 U.S. 507 (2004)], at 536 (plurality opinion). The Clause protects the rights of the detained by affirming the duty and authority of the Judiciary to call the jailer to account. The separation-of-powers doctrine, and the history that influenced its design, therefore must inform the reach and purpose of the Suspension Clause.

B

The broad historical narrative of the writ and its function is central to our analysis, but we seek guidance as well from founding-era authorities addressing the specific question before us: whether foreign nationals, apprehended and detained in distant countries during a time of serious threats to our Nation's security, may assert the privilege of the writ and seek its protection. The Court has been careful not to foreclose the possibility that the protections of the Suspension Clause have expanded along with post-1789 developments that define the present scope of the writ. See INS v. St. Cyr, 533 U.S. 289, 300-301 (2001). But the analysis may begin with precedents as of 1789, for the Court has said that "at the absolute minimum" the Clause protects the writ as it existed when the Constitution was drafted and ratified. Id., at 301.

To support their arguments, the parties in these cases have examined historical sources to construct a view of the common-law writ as it existed in 1789 – as have amici whose expertise in legal history the Court has relied upon in the past. The Government argues the common-law writ ran only to those territories over which the Crown was sovereign. Petitioners argue that jurisdiction followed the King's officers. Diligent search by all parties reveals no certain conclusions. In none of the cases cited do we find that a common-law court would or would not have granted, or refused to hear for lack of jurisdiction, a petition for a writ of habeas corpus brought by a prisoner deemed an

enemy combatant, under a standard like the one the Department of
Defense has used in these cases, and when held in a territory, like
Guantanamo, over which the Government has total military and civil
control. . . .

. . . Recent scholarship points to the inherent shortcomings in the
historical record. And given the unique status of Guantanamo Bay and
the particular dangers of terrorism in the modern age, the common-law
courts simply may not have confronted cases with close parallels to this
one. We decline, therefore, to infer too much, one way or the other, from
the lack of historical evidence on point.

IV

Drawing from its position that at common law the writ ran only to
territories over which the Crown was sovereign, the Government says the
Suspension Clause affords petitioners no rights because the United States
does not claim sovereignty over the place of detention.

Guantanamo Bay is not formally part of the United States. *See* DTA
§1005(g), 119 Stat. 2743. And under the terms of the lease between the
United States and Cuba, Cuba retains "ultimate sovereignty" over the
territory while the United States exercises "complete jurisdiction and
control." *See* Lease of Lands for Coaling and Naval Stations, Feb. 23,
1903, U.S.-Cuba, Art. III, T.S. No. 418 (hereinafter 1903 Lease
Agreement); *Rasul,* 542 U.S., at 471. Under the terms of the 1934
Treaty, however, Cuba effectively has no rights as a sovereign until the
parties agree to modification of the 1903 Lease Agreement or the United
States abandons the base. *See* Treaty Defining Relations with Cuba,
May 29, 1934, U.S.-Cuba, Art. III, 48 Stat. 1683, T.S. No. 866.

The United States contends, nevertheless, that Guantanamo is not
within its sovereign control. This was the Government's position well
before the events of September 11, 2001. And in other contexts the
Court has held that questions of sovereignty are for the political branches
to decide. Even if this were a treaty interpretation case that did not
involve a political question, the President's construction of the lease
agreement would be entitled to great respect.

We therefore do not question the Government's position that Cuba,
not the United States, maintains sovereignty, in the legal and technical
sense of the term, over Guantanamo Bay. But this does not end the
analysis. Our cases do not hold it is improper for us to inquire into the
objective degree of control the Nation asserts over foreign territory. . . .

A

The Court has discussed the issue of the Constitution's extraterritorial application on many occasions. These decisions undermine the Government's argument that, at least as applied to noncitizens, the Constitution necessarily stops where *de jure* sovereignty ends.

[The Court reviewed cases, including the *Insular Cases* and *Reid v. Covert*, 345 U.S. 1 (1957), as standing for the proposition that "whether a constitutional provision has extraterritorial effect depends upon the 'particular circumstances, the practical necessities, and the possible alternatives which Congress had before it' and, in particular, whether judicial enforcement of the provision would be 'impracticable and anomalous.'" (quoting Justice Harlan in *Reid*).] . . .

Practical considerations weighed heavily as well in *Johnson v. Eisentrager*, 339 U.S. 763 (1950), where the Court addressed whether habeas corpus jurisdiction extended to enemy aliens who had been convicted of violating the laws of war. The prisoners were detained at Landsberg Prison in Germany during the Allied Powers' postwar occupation. The Court stressed the difficulties of ordering the Government to produce the prisoners in a habeas corpus proceeding. It "would require allocation of shipping space, guarding personnel, billeting and rations" and would damage the prestige of military commanders at a sensitive time. *Id.*, at 779. In considering these factors the Court sought to balance the constraints of military occupation with constitutional necessities. *Id.*, at 769-779; *see Rasul*, 542 U.S., at 475-476 (discussing the factors relevant to *Eisentrager*'s constitutional holding); 542 U.S., at 486 (KENNEDY, J., concurring in judgment) (same).

True, the Court in *Eisentrager* denied access to the writ, and it noted the prisoners "at no relevant time were within any territory over which the United States is sovereign, and [that] the scenes of their offense, their capture, their trial and their punishment were all beyond the territorial jurisdiction of any court of the United States." 339 U.S., at 778. The Government seizes upon this language as proof positive that the *Eisentrager* Court adopted a formalistic, sovereignty-based test for determining the reach of the Suspension Clause. We reject this reading for three reasons.

First, we do not accept the idea that the above-quoted passage from *Eisentrager* is the only authoritative language in the opinion and that all the rest is dicta. The Court's further determinations, based on practical considerations, were integral to Part II of its opinion and came before the decision announced its holding. *See* 339 U.S., at 781.

. . . Even if we assume the *Eisentrager* Court considered the United States' lack of formal legal sovereignty over Landsberg Prison as the decisive factor in that case, its holding is not inconsistent with a functional approach to questions of extraterritoriality. The formal legal status of a given territory affects, at least to some extent, the political branches' control over that territory. *De jure* sovereignty is a factor that bears upon which constitutional guarantees apply there.

Third, if the Government's reading of *Eisentrager* were correct, the opinion would have marked not only a change in, but a complete repudiation of, the *Insular Cases'* (and later *Reid*'s) functional approach to questions of extraterritoriality. We cannot accept the Government's view. Nothing in *Eisentrager* says that *de jure* sovereignty is or has ever been the only relevant consideration in determining the geographic reach of the Constitution or of habeas corpus. Were that the case, there would be considerable tension between *Eisentrager,* on the one hand, and the *Insular Cases* and *Reid,* on the other. Our cases need not be read to conflict in this manner. A constricted reading of *Eisentrager* overlooks what we see as a common thread uniting the *Insular Cases, Eisentrager,* and *Reid:* the idea that questions of extraterritoriality turn on objective factors and practical concerns, not formalism.

B

The Government's formal sovereignty-based test raises troubling separation-of-powers concerns as well. The political history of Guantanamo illustrates the deficiencies of this approach. The United States has maintained complete and uninterrupted control of the bay for over 100 years. . . . The necessary implication of the argument is that by surrendering formal sovereignty over any unincorporated territory to a third party, while at the same time entering into a lease that grants total control over the territory back to the United States, it would be possible for the political branches to govern without legal constraint.

Our basic charter cannot be contracted away like this. The Constitution grants Congress and the President the power to acquire, dispose of, and govern territory, not the power to decide when and where its terms apply. Even when the United States acts outside its borders, its powers are not "absolute and unlimited" but are subject "to such restrictions as are expressed in the Constitution." *Murphy v. Ramsey,* 114 U.S. 15, 44 (1885). Abstaining from questions involving formal sovereignty and territorial governance is one thing. To hold the political branches have the power to switch the Constitution on or off at will is quite another. The former position reflects this Court's recognition that certain matters requiring political judgments are best left to the political branches. The latter would permit a striking anomaly in our tripartite system of government, leading to a regime in which Congress and the President, not this Court, say "what the law is." *Marbury v. Madison*, 1 Cranch 137, 177 (1803).

These concerns have particular bearing upon the Suspension Clause question in the cases now before us, for the writ of habeas corpus is itself an indispensable mechanism for monitoring the separation of powers. The test for determining the scope of this provision must not be subject to manipulation by those whose power it is designed to restrain.

C

As we recognized in *Rasul*, 542 U.S., at 476; *id.*, at 487 (KENNEDY, J., concurring in judgment), the outlines of a framework for determining the reach of the Suspension Clause are suggested by the factors the Court relied upon in *Eisentrager*. In addition to the practical concerns discussed above, the *Eisentrager* Court found relevant that each petitioner:

> "(a) is an enemy alien; (b) has never been or resided in the United States; (c) was captured outside of our territory and there held in military custody as a prisoner of war; (d) was tried and convicted by a Military Commission sitting outside the United States; (e) for offenses against laws of war committed outside the United States; (f) and is at all times imprisoned outside the United States." 339 U.S., at 777.

Based on this language from *Eisentrager,* and the reasoning in our other extraterritoriality opinions, we conclude that at least three factors are relevant in determining the reach of the Suspension Clause: (1) the citizenship and status of the detainee and the adequacy of the process through which that status determination was made; (2) the nature of the sites where apprehension and then detention took place; and (3) the practical obstacles inherent in resolving the prisoner's entitlement to the writ.

Applying this framework, we note at the onset that the status of these detainees is a matter of dispute. The petitioners, like those in *Eisentrager,* are not American citizens. But the petitioners in *Eisentrager* did not contest, it seems, the Court's assertion that they were "enemy alien[s]." In the instant cases, by contrast, the detainees deny they are enemy combatants. They have been afforded some process in

CSRT proceedings to determine their status; but, unlike in *Eisentrager,* there has been no trial by military commission for violations of the laws of war. The difference is not trivial. The records from the *Eisentrager* trials suggest that, well before the petitioners brought their case to this Court, there had been a rigorous adversarial process to test the legality of their detention. The *Eisentrager* petitioners were charged by a bill of particulars that made detailed factual allegations against them. To rebut the accusations, they were entitled to representation by counsel, allowed to introduce evidence on their own behalf, and permitted to cross-examine the prosecution's witnesses.

In comparison, the procedural protections afforded to the detainees in the CSRT hearings are far more limited, and, we conclude, fall well short of the procedures and adversarial mechanisms that would eliminate the need for habeas corpus review. Although the detainee is assigned a "Personal Representative" to assist him during CSRT proceedings, the Secretary of the Navy's memorandum makes clear that person is not the detainee's lawyer or even his "advocate." The Government's evidence is accorded a presumption of validity. The detainee is allowed to present "reasonably available" evidence, but his ability to rebut the Government's evidence against him is limited by the circumstances of his confinement and his lack of counsel at this stage. And although the detainee can seek review of his status determination in the Court of Appeals, that review process cannot cure all defects in the earlier proceedings. *See* Part V, *infra.*

As to the second factor relevant to this analysis, the detainees here are similarly situated to the *Eisentrager* petitioners in that the sites of their apprehension and detention are technically outside the sovereign territory of the United States. As noted earlier, this is a factor that weighs against finding they have rights under the Suspension Clause. But there are critical differences between Landsberg Prison, circa 1950, and the United States Naval Station at Guantanamo Bay in 2008. Unlike its present control over the naval station, the United States' control over the prison in Germany was neither absolute nor indefinite. Like all parts of occupied Germany, the prison was under the jurisdiction of the combined Allied Forces. The United States was therefore answerable to its Allies for all activities occurring there. The Court's holding in *Eisentrager* was thus consistent with the *Insular Cases,* where it had held there was no need to extend full constitutional protections to territories the United States did not intend to govern indefinitely. Guantanamo Bay, on the other hand, is no transient possession. In every practical sense Guantanamo is not abroad; it is within the constant jurisdiction of the United States.

As to the third factor, we recognize, as the Court did in *Eisentrager*, that there are costs to holding the Suspension Clause applicable in a case of military detention abroad. Habeas corpus proceedings may require expenditure of funds by the Government and may divert the attention of military personnel from other pressing tasks. While we are sensitive to these concerns, we do not find them dispositive. Compliance with any judicial process requires some incremental expenditure of resources. Yet civilian courts and the Armed Forces have functioned along side each other at various points in our history. *See, e.g., Duncan v. Kahanamoku*, 327 U.S. 304 (1946); *Ex parte Milligan*, 4 Wall. 2 (1866). The Government presents no credible arguments that the military mission at Guantanamo would be compromised if habeas corpus courts had jurisdiction to hear the detainees' claims. And in light of the plenary control the United States asserts over the base, none are apparent to us.

The situation in *Eisentrager* was far different, given the historical context and nature of the military's mission in post-War Germany. When hostilities in the European Theater came to an end, the United States became responsible for an occupation zone encompassing over 57,000 square miles with a population of 18 million. In addition to supervising massive reconstruction and aid efforts the American forces stationed in Germany faced potential security threats from a defeated enemy. In retrospect the post-War occupation may seem uneventful. But at the time *Eisentrager* was decided, the Court was right to be concerned about judicial interference with the military's efforts to contain "enemy elements, guerilla fighters, and 'were-wolves.'" 339 U.S., at 784.

Similar threats are not apparent here; nor does the Government argue that they are. The United States Naval Station at Guantanamo Bay consists of 45 square miles of land and water. The base has been used, at various points, to house migrants and refugees temporarily. At present, however, other than the detainees themselves, the only long-term residents are American military personnel, their families, and a small number of workers. The detainees have been deemed enemies of the United States. At present, dangerous as they may be if released, they are contained in a secure prison facility located on an isolated and heavily fortified military base.

There is no indication, furthermore, that adjudicating a habeas corpus petition would cause friction with the host government. No Cuban court has jurisdiction over American military personnel at Guantanamo or the enemy combatants detained there. While obligated to abide by the terms of the lease, the United States is, for all practical purposes, answerable to no other sovereign for its acts on the base. Were that not the case, or if the detention facility were located in an active theater of war, arguments that issuing the writ would be "impracticable or anomalous" would have more weight. *See Reid,* 354 U.S., at 74 (HARLAN, J., concurring in result). Under the facts presented here, however, there are few practical barriers to the running of the writ. To the extent barriers arise, habeas corpus procedures likely can be modified to address them.

It is true that before today the Court has never held that noncitizens detained by our Government in territory over which another country maintains *de jure* sovereignty have any rights under our Constitution. But the cases before us lack any precise historical parallel. They involve individuals detained by executive order for the duration of a conflict that, if measured from September 11, 2001, to the present, is already among the longest wars in American history. The detainees, moreover, are held in a territory that, while technically not part of the United States, is under the complete and total control of our Government. Under these circumstances the lack of a precedent on point is no barrier to our holding.

We hold that Art. I, §9, cl. 2, of the Constitution has full effect at Guantanamo Bay. If the privilege of habeas corpus is to be denied to the detainees now before us, Congress must act in accordance with the requirements of the Suspension Clause. *Cf. Hamdi,* 542 U.S., at 564 (SCALIA, J., dissenting) ("[I]ndefinite imprisonment on reasonable suspicion is not an available option of treatment for those accused of aiding the enemy, absent a suspension of the writ"). This Court may not impose a *de facto* suspension by abstaining from these controversies. The MCA does not purport to be a formal suspension of the writ; and the Government, in its submissions to us, has not argued that it is. Petitioners, therefore, are entitled to the privilege of habeas corpus to challenge the legality of their detention.

V

In light of this holding the question becomes whether the statute stripping jurisdiction to issue the writ avoids the Suspension Clause mandate because Congress has provided adequate substitute procedures for habeas corpus. The Government submits there has been compliance with the Suspension Clause because the DTA review process in the Court of Appeals, *see* DTA §1005(e), provides an adequate substitute. Congress has granted that court jurisdiction to consider "(i) whether the status determination of the [CSRT] . . . was consistent with the standards and procedures specified by the Secretary of Defense . . . and (ii) to the extent the Constitution and laws of the United States are applicable, whether the use of such standards and procedures to make the determination is consistent with the Constitution and laws of the United States." §1005(e)(2)(C), 119 Stat. 2742. . . .

A

Our case law does not contain extensive discussion of standards defining suspension of the writ or of circumstances under which suspension has occurred. This simply confirms the care Congress has taken throughout our Nation's history to preserve the writ and its function. Indeed, most of the major legislative enactments pertaining to habeas corpus have acted not to contract the writ's protection but to expand it or to hasten resolution of prisoners' claims. . . .

. . . [Unlike those statutes], here we confront statutes, the DTA and the MCA, that were intended to circumscribe habeas review. Congress' purpose is evident not only from the unequivocal nature of MCA §7's jurisdiction-stripping language, 28 U.S.C.A. §2241(e)(1) (Supp. 2007) ("No court, justice, or judge shall have jurisdiction to hear or consider an application for a writ of habeas corpus . . ."), but also from a comparison of the DTA to the statutes at issue in [cases construing habeas-strengthening statutes]. . . . When Congress has intended to replace traditional habeas corpus with habeas-like substitutes, . . . it has granted to the courts broad remedial powers to secure the historic office of the writ. . . .

In contrast, the DTA's jurisdictional grant is quite limited. The Court of Appeals has jurisdiction not to inquire into the legality of the detention generally but only to assess whether the CSRT complied with the "standards and procedures specified by the Secretary of Defense" and whether those standards and procedures are lawful. DTA §1005(e)(2)(C), 119 Stat. 2742. If Congress had envisioned DTA review as coextensive with traditional habeas corpus, it would not have drafted the statute in this manner. . . . [M]oreover, there has been no effort to preserve habeas corpus review as an avenue of last resort. No saving clause exists in either the MCA or the DTA. And MCA §7 eliminates habeas review for these petitioners. . . .

To the extent any doubt remains about Congress' intent, the legislative history confirms what the plain text strongly suggests: In passing the DTA Congress did not intend to create a process that differs from traditional habeas corpus process in name only. It intended to create a more limited procedure. *See, e.g.,*151 Cong. Rec. S14263 (Dec. 21, 2005) (statement of Sen. Graham) (noting that the DTA "extinguish[es] these habeas and other actions in order to effect a transfer of jurisdiction over these cases to the DC Circuit Court" and agreeing that the bill "create[s] in their place a very limited judicial review of certain military administrative decisions"); *id.,* at S14268 (statement of Sen. Kyl) ("It is important to note that the limited judicial review authorized by paragraphs 2 and 3 of subsection (e) [of DTA §1005] are not habeas-corpus review. It is a limited judicial review of its own nature").

It is against this background that we must interpret the DTA and assess its adequacy as a substitute for habeas corpus. . . .

B

We do not endeavor to offer a comprehensive summary of the requisites for an adequate substitute for habeas corpus. We do consider it uncontroversial, however, that the privilege of habeas corpus entitles the prisoner to a meaningful opportunity to demonstrate that he is being held pursuant to "the erroneous application or interpretation" of relevant law. *St. Cyr,* 533 U.S. at 302. And the habeas court must have the power to order the conditional release of an individual unlawfully detained – though release need not be the exclusive remedy and is not the appropriate one in every case in which the writ is granted. These are the easily identified attributes of any constitutionally adequate habeas corpus proceeding. But, depending on the circumstances, more may be required.

Indeed, common-law habeas corpus was, above all, an adaptable remedy. Its precise application and scope changed depending upon the circumstances. It appears the common-law habeas court's role was most extensive in cases of pretrial and noncriminal detention, where there had been little or no previous judicial review of the cause for detention. Notably, the black-letter rule that prisoners could not controvert facts in the jailer's return was not followed (or at least not with consistency) in such cases.

There is evidence from 19th-century American sources indicating that, even in States that accorded strong res judicata effect to prior adjudications, habeas courts in this country routinely allowed prisoners to introduce exculpatory evidence that was either unknown or previously unavailable to the prisoner. . . .

The idea that the necessary scope of habeas review in part depends upon the rigor of any earlier proceedings accords with our test for procedural adequacy in the due process context. *See Mathews v. Eldridge*, 424 U.S. 319, 335 (1976) (noting that the Due Process Clause requires an assessment of, *inter alia,* "the risk of an erroneous deprivation of [a liberty interest;] and the probable value, if any, of additional or substitute procedural safeguards"). . . .

Accordingly, where relief is sought from a sentence that resulted from the judgment of a court of record, . . . considerable deference is owed to the court that ordered confinement. Likewise in those cases the prisoner should exhaust adequate alternative remedies before filing for the writ in federal court. Both aspects of federal habeas corpus review are justified because it can be assumed that, in the usual course, a court of record provides defendants with a fair, adversary proceeding. . . . The present cases fall outside these categories, however; for here the detention is by executive order.

Where a person is detained by executive order, rather than, say, after being tried and convicted in a court, the need for collateral review is most pressing. A criminal conviction in the usual course occurs after a judicial hearing before a tribunal disinterested in the outcome and committed to procedures designed to ensure its own independence. These dynamics are not inherent in executive detention orders or executive review procedures. In this context the need for habeas corpus is more urgent. The intended duration of the detention and the reasons for it bear upon the precise scope of the inquiry. Habeas corpus proceedings need not resemble a criminal trial, even when the detention is by executive order. But the writ must be effective. The habeas court must have sufficient authority to conduct a meaningful review of both the cause for detention and the Executive's power to detain.

To determine the necessary scope of habeas corpus review, therefore, we must assess the CSRT process, the mechanism through which petitioners' designation as enemy combatants became final. Whether one characterizes the CSRT process as direct review of the Executive's battlefield determination that the detainee is an enemy combatant – as the parties have and as we do – or as the first step in the collateral review of a battlefield determination makes no difference in a proper analysis of whether the procedures Congress put in place are an adequate substitute for habeas corpus. What matters is the sum total of procedural protections afforded to the detainee at all stages, direct and collateral.

Petitioners identify what they see as myriad deficiencies in the CSRTs. The most relevant for our purposes are the constraints upon the detainee's ability to rebut the factual basis for the Government's assertion that he is an enemy combatant. As already noted, at the CSRT stage the detainee has limited means to find or present evidence to challenge the Government's case against him. He does not have the assistance of counsel and may not be aware of the most critical allegations that the Government relied upon to order his detention. *See* App. to Pet. for Cert. in No. 06-1196, at 156, ¶F(8) (noting that the detainee can access only the "unclassified portion of the Government Information"). The detainee can confront witnesses that testify during the CSRT proceedings. *Id.,* at 144, ¶g(8). But given that there are in effect no limits on the admission of hearsay evidence – the only requirement is that the tribunal deem the evidence "relevant and helpful," *ibid.,* ¶g(9) – the detainee's opportunity to question witnesses is likely to be more theoretical than real. . . .

Even if we were to assume that the CSRTs satisfy due process standards, it would not end our inquiry. Habeas corpus is a collateral process that exists, in Justice Holmes' words, to "cu[t] through all forms and g[o] to the very tissue of the structure. It comes in from the outside, not in subordination to the proceedings, and although every form may have been preserved opens the inquiry whether they have been more than an empty shell." *Frank v. Mangum,* 237 U.S. 309, 346 (1915) (dissenting opinion). Even when the procedures authorizing detention are structurally sound, the Suspension Clause remains applicable and the writ relevant. *See* 2 Chambers, Course of Lectures on English Law 1767-1773, at 6 ("Liberty may be violated either by arbitrary *imprisonment* without law or the appearance of law, or by a lawful magistrate for an unlawful reason"). . . .

Although we make no judgment as to whether the CSRTs, as currently constituted, satisfy due process standards, we agree with petitioners that, even when all the parties involved in this process act with diligence and in good faith, there is considerable risk of error in the tribunal's findings of fact. This is a risk inherent in any process that, in the words of the former Chief Judge of the Court of Appeals, is "closed and accusatorial." *See [Bismullah v. Gates,* 514 F.3d 1291, 1296 (D.C. Cir. 2008)] (Ginsburg, C.J., concurring in denial of rehearing en banc). And given that the consequence of error may be detention of persons for the duration of hostilities that may last a generation or more, this is a risk too significant to ignore.

For the writ of habeas corpus, or its substitute, to function as an effective and proper remedy in this context, the court that conducts the habeas proceeding must have the means to correct errors that occurred during the CSRT proceedings. This includes some authority to assess the sufficiency of the Government's evidence against the detainee. It also must have the authority to admit and consider relevant exculpatory evidence that was not introduced during the earlier proceeding. . . .

The extent of the showing required of the Government in these cases is a matter to be determined. We need not explore it further at this stage. We do hold that when the judicial power to issue habeas corpus properly is invoked the judicial officer must have adequate authority to make a determination in light of the relevant law and facts and to formulate and issue appropriate orders for relief, including, if necessary, an order directing the prisoner's release.

C

We now consider whether the DTA allows the Court of Appeals to conduct a proceeding meeting these standards. "[W]e are obligated to construe the statute to avoid [constitutional] problems" if it is "'fairly possible'" to do so. *St. Cyr*, 533 U.S., at 299-300 (quoting *Crowell v. Benson*, 285 U.S. 22, 62 (1932)). There are limits to this principle, however. The canon of constitutional avoidance does not supplant traditional modes of statutory interpretation. *See Clark v. Martinez*, 543 U.S. 371, 385 (2005) ("The canon of constitutional avoidance comes into play only when, after the application of ordinary textual analysis, the statute is found to be susceptible of more than one construction; and the canon functions as *a means of choosing between them*"). We cannot ignore the text and purpose of a statute in order to save it.

The DTA does not explicitly empower the Court of Appeals to order the applicant in a DTA review proceeding released should the court find that the standards and procedures used at his CSRT hearing were insufficient to justify detention. This is troubling. Yet, for present purposes, we can assume congressional silence permits a constitutionally required remedy. . . .

The absence of a release remedy and specific language allowing AUMF challenges are not the only constitutional infirmities from which the statute potentially suffers, however. The more difficult question is whether the DTA permits the Court of Appeals to make requisite findings of fact. The DTA enables petitioners to request "review" of their CSRT determination in the Court of Appeals, DTA §1005(e)(2)(B)(i), 119 Stat. 2742; but the "Scope of Review" provision confines the Court of Appeals' role to reviewing whether the CSRT followed the "standards and procedures" issued by the Department of Defense and assessing whether those "standards and procedures" are lawful. §1005(e)(C), *ibid*. Among these standards is "the requirement that the conclusion of the

Tribunal be supported by a preponderance of the evidence . . . allowing a rebuttable presumption in favor of the Government's evidence." §1005(e)(C)(i), *ibid.*

Assuming the DTA can be construed to allow the Court of Appeals to review or correct the CSRT's factual determinations, as opposed to merely certifying that the tribunal applied the correct standard of proof, we see no way to construe the statute to allow what is also constitutionally required in this context: an opportunity for the detainee to present relevant exculpatory evidence that was not made part of the record in the earlier proceedings.

On its face the statute allows the Court of Appeals to consider no evidence outside the CSRT record. . . .

By foreclosing consideration of evidence not presented or reasonably available to the detainee at the CSRT proceedings, the DTA disadvantages the detainee by limiting the scope of collateral review to a record that may not be accurate or complete. In other contexts, *e.g.,* in post-trial habeas cases where the prisoner already has had a full and fair opportunity to develop the factual predicate of his claims, similar limitations on the scope of habeas review may be appropriate. In this context, however, where the underlying detention proceedings lack the necessary adversarial character, the detainee cannot be held responsible for all deficiencies in the record. . . .

We do not imply DTA review would be a constitutionally sufficient replacement for habeas corpus but for these limitations on the detainee's ability to present exculpatory evidence. For even if it were possible, as a textual matter, to read into the statute each of the necessary procedures we have identified, we could not overlook the cumulative effect of our doing so. To hold that the detainees at Guantanamo may, under the DTA, challenge the President's legal authority to detain them, contest the CSRT's findings of fact, supplement the record on review with exculpatory evidence, and request an order of release would come close to reinstating the §2241 habeas corpus process Congress sought to deny them. The language of the statute, read in light of Congress' reasons for enacting it, cannot bear this interpretation. Petitioners have met their burden of establishing that the DTA review process is, on its face, an inadequate substitute for habeas corpus.

Although we do not hold that an adequate substitute must duplicate §2241 in all respects, it suffices that the Government has not established that the detainees' access to the statutory review provisions at issue is an adequate substitute for the writ of habeas corpus. MCA §7 thus effects an unconstitutional suspension of the writ. In view of our holding we need not discuss the reach of the writ with respect to claims of unlawful conditions of treatment or confinement.

VI

A

In light of our conclusion that there is no jurisdictional bar to the District Court's entertaining petitioners' claims the question remains whether there are prudential barriers to habeas corpus review under these circumstances.

The Government argues petitioners must seek review of their CSRT determinations in the Court of Appeals before they can proceed with their habeas corpus actions in the District Court. . . .

The real risks, the real threats, of terrorist attacks are constant and not likely soon to abate. The ways to disrupt our life and laws are so many and unforeseen that the Court should not attempt even some general catalogue of crises that might occur. Certain principles are apparent, however. Practical considerations and exigent circumstances inform the definition and reach of the law's writs, including habeas corpus. The cases and our tradition reflect this precept.

In cases involving foreign citizens detained abroad by the Executive, it likely would be both an impractical and unprecedented extension of judicial power to assume that habeas corpus would be available at the moment the prisoner is taken into custody. If and when habeas corpus jurisdiction applies, as it does in these cases, then proper deference can be accorded to reasonable procedures for screening and initial detention under lawful and proper conditions of confinement and treatment for a reasonable period of time. Domestic exigencies, furthermore, might also impose such onerous burdens on the Government that here, too, the Judicial Branch would be required to devise sensible rules for staying habeas corpus proceedings until the Government can comply with its requirements in a responsible way. *Cf. Ex parte Milligan*, 4 Wall., at 127 ("If, in foreign invasion or civil war, the courts are actually closed, and it is impossible to administer criminal justice according to law, *then,* on the theatre of active military operations, where war really prevails, there is a necessity to furnish a substitute for the civil authority, thus overthrown, to preserve the safety of the army and society; and as no power is left but the military, it is allowed to govern by martial rule until the laws can have their free course"). Here, as is true with detainees apprehended abroad, a relevant consideration in determining the courts' role is whether there are suitable alternative processes in place to protect against the arbitrary exercise of governmental power.

The cases before us, however, do not involve detainees who have been held for a short period of time while awaiting their CSRT determinations. Were that the case, or were it probable that the Court of Appeals could complete a prompt review of their applications, the case for requiring temporary abstention or exhaustion of alternative remedies would be much stronger. These qualifications no longer pertain here. In some of these cases six years have elapsed without the judicial oversight that habeas corpus or an adequate substitute demands. And there has been no showing that the Executive faces such onerous burdens that it cannot respond to habeas corpus actions. To require these detainees to complete DTA review before proceeding with their habeas corpus actions would be to require additional months, if not years, of delay. The first DTA review applications were filed over a year ago, but no decisions on the merits have been issued. While some delay in fashioning new procedures is unavoidable, the costs of delay can no longer be borne by those who are held in custody. The detainees in these cases are entitled to a prompt habeas corpus hearing.

Our decision today holds only that the petitioners before us are entitled to seek the writ; that the DTA review procedures are an inadequate substitute for habeas corpus; and that the petitioners in these cases need not exhaust the review procedures in the Court of Appeals before proceeding with their habeas actions in the District Court. The only law we identify as unconstitutional is MCA §7, 28 U.S.C.A. §2241(e) (Supp. 2007). Accordingly, both the DTA and the CSRT process remain intact. Our holding with regard to exhaustion should not be read to imply that a habeas court should intervene the moment an enemy combatant steps foot in a territory where the writ runs. The Executive is entitled to a reasonable period of time to determine a detainee's status before a court entertains that detainee's habeas corpus petition. The CSRT process is the mechanism Congress and the President set up to deal with these issues. Except in cases of undue delay, federal courts should refrain from entertaining an enemy combatant's habeas corpus petition at least until after the Department, acting via the CSRT, has had a chance to review his status.

B

Although we hold that the DTA is not an adequate and effective substitute for habeas corpus, it does not follow that a habeas corpus court may disregard the dangers the detention in these cases was intended to prevent. . . . [T]he Suspension Clause does not resist innovation in the field of habeas corpus. Certain accommodations can be made to reduce the burden habeas corpus proceedings will place on the military without impermissibly diluting the protections of the writ.

In the DTA Congress sought to consolidate review of petitioners' claims in the Court of Appeals. Channeling future cases to one district court would no doubt reduce administrative burdens on the Government. This is a legitimate objective that might be advanced even without an amendment to §2241. If, in a future case, a detainee files a habeas petition in another judicial district in which a proper respondent can be served, see *Rumsfeld v. Padilla*, 542 U.S. 426, 435-436 (2004), the Government can move for change of venue to the court that will hear these petitioners' cases, the United States District Court for the District of Columbia.

Another of Congress' reasons for vesting exclusive jurisdiction in the Court of Appeals, perhaps, was to avoid the widespread dissemination of classified information. The Government has raised similar concerns here and elsewhere. We make no attempt to anticipate all of the evidentiary and access-to-counsel issues that will arise during the course of the detainees' habeas corpus proceedings. We recognize, however, that the Government has a legitimate interest in protecting sources and methods of intelligence gathering; and we expect that the District Court will use its discretion to accommodate this interest to the greatest extent possible. *Cf. United States v. Reynolds*, 345 U.S. 1, 10 (1953) (recognizing an evidentiary privilege in a civil damages case where "there is a reasonable danger that compulsion of the evidence will expose military matters which, in the interest of national security, should not be divulged").

These and the other remaining questions are within the expertise and competence of the District Court to address in the first instance.

* * *

In considering both the procedural and substantive standards used to impose detention to prevent acts of terrorism, proper deference must be accorded to the political branches. *See United States v. Curtiss-Wright Export Corp., 299 U.S. 304, 320 (1936). Unlike the President and some designated Members of Congress, neither the Members of this Court nor most federal judges begin the day with briefings that may describe new and serious threats to our Nation and its people. The law must accord the

Executive substantial authority to apprehend and detain those who pose a real danger to our security.

Officials charged with daily operational responsibility for our security may consider a judicial discourse on the history of the Habeas Corpus Act of 1679 and like matters to be far removed from the Nation's present, urgent concerns. Established legal doctrine, however, must be consulted for its teaching. Remote in time it may be; irrelevant to the present it is not. Security depends upon a sophisticated intelligence apparatus and the ability of our Armed Forces to act and to interdict. There are further considerations, however. Security subsists, too, in fidelity to freedom's first principles. Chief among these are freedom from arbitrary and unlawful restraint and the personal liberty that is secured by adherence to the separation of powers. It is from these principles that the judicial authority to consider petitions for habeas corpus relief derives.

Our opinion does not undermine the Executive's powers as Commander in Chief. On the contrary, the exercise of those powers is vindicated, not eroded, when confirmed by the Judicial Branch. Within the Constitution's separation-of-powers structure, few exercises of judicial power are as legitimate or as necessary as the responsibility to hear challenges to the authority of the Executive to imprison a person. Some of these petitioners have been in custody for six years with no definitive judicial determination as to the legality of their detention. Their access to the writ is a necessity to determine the lawfulness of their status, even if, in the end, they do not obtain the relief they seek.

Because our Nation's past military conflicts have been of limited duration, it has been possible to leave the outer boundaries of war powers undefined. If, as some fear, terrorism continues to pose dangerous threats to us for years to come, the Court might not have this luxury. This result is not inevitable, however. The political branches, consistent with their independent obligations to interpret and uphold the Constitution, can engage in a genuine debate about how best to preserve constitutional values while protecting the Nation from terrorism. *Cf. Hamdan* [*v. Rumsfeld*, 548 U.S. 557 (2006)], at 636 (BREYER, J., concurring) ("[J]udicial insistence upon that consultation does not weaken our Nation's ability to deal with danger. To the contrary, that insistence strengthens the Nation's ability to determine – through democratic means – how best to do so").

It bears repeating that our opinion does not address the content of the law that governs petitioners' detention. That is a matter yet to be determined. We hold that petitioners may invoke the fundamental procedural protections of habeas corpus. The laws and Constitution are designed to survive, and remain in force, in extraordinary times. Liberty and security can be reconciled; and in our system they are reconciled within the framework of the law. The Framers decided that habeas corpus, a right of first importance, must be a part of that framework, a part of that law.

The determination by the Court of Appeals that the Suspension Clause and its protections are inapplicable to petitioners was in error. The judgment of the Court of Appeals is reversed. The cases are remanded to the Court of Appeals with instructions that it remand the cases to the District Court for proceedings consistent with this opinion.

It is so ordered.

Justice SOUTER, with whom Justice GINSBURG and Justice BREYER join, concurring. . . . A . . . fact insufficiently appreciated by the dissents is the length of the disputed imprisonments, some of the prisoners represented here today having been locked up for six years. Hence the hollow ring when the dissenters suggest that the Court is somehow precipitating the judiciary into reviewing claims that the military (subject to appeal to the Court of Appeals for the District of Columbia Circuit) could handle within some reasonable period of time. These suggestions of judicial haste are all the more out of place given the Court's realistic acknowledgment that in periods of exigency the tempo of any habeas review must reflect the immediate peril facing the country.

It is in fact the very lapse of four years from the time *Rasul* put everyone on notice that habeas process was available to Guantanamo prisoners, and the lapse of six years since some of these prisoners were captured and incarcerated, that stand at odds with the repeated suggestions of the dissenters that these cases should be seen as a judicial victory in a contest for power between the Court and the political branches. The several answers to the charge of triumphalism might start with a basic fact of Anglo-American constitutional history: that the power, first of the Crown and now of the Executive Branch of the United States, is necessarily limited by habeas corpus jurisdiction to enquire into the legality of executive detention. And one could explain that in this Court's exercise of responsibility to preserve habeas corpus something much more significant is involved than pulling and hauling between the judicial and political branches. Instead, though, it is enough to repeat that some of these petitioners have spent six years behind bars. After six years of sustained executive detentions in Guantanamo, subject to habeas jurisdiction but without any actual habeas scrutiny, today's decision is no judicial victory, but an act of perseverance in trying to make habeas review, and the obligation of the courts to provide it, mean something of value both to prisoners and to the Nation.

Chief Justice ROBERTS, with whom Justice SCALIA, Justice THOMAS, and Justice ALITO join, dissenting. Today the Court strikes down as inadequate the most generous set of procedural protections ever afforded aliens detained by this country as enemy combatants. The political branches crafted these procedures amidst an ongoing military conflict, after much careful investigation and thorough debate. The Court rejects them today out of hand, without bothering to say what due process rights the detainees possess, without explaining how the statute fails to vindicate those rights, and before a single petitioner has even attempted to avail himself of the law's operation. And to what effect? The majority merely replaces a review system designed by the people's representatives with a set of shapeless procedures to be defined by federal courts at some future date. One cannot help but think, after surveying the modest practical results of the majority's ambitious opinion, that this decision is not really about the detainees at all, but about control of federal policy regarding enemy combatants. . . .

. . . The important point for me, however, is that the Court should have resolved these cases on other grounds. Habeas is most fundamentally a procedural right, a mechanism for contesting the legality of executive detention. The critical threshold question in these cases, prior to any inquiry about the writ's scope, is whether the system the political branches designed protects whatever rights the detainees may possess. If so, there is no need for any additional process, whether called "habeas" or something else. . . .

I . . .

The political branches created a two-part, collateral review procedure for testing the legality of the prisoners' detention: It begins with a hearing before a Combatant Status Review Tribunal (CSRT) followed by review in the D.C. Circuit. As part of that review, Congress authorized the D.C. Circuit to decide whether the CSRT proceedings are consistent with "the Constitution and laws of the United States." DTA §1005(e)(2)(C), 119 Stat. 2742. No petitioner, however, has invoked the D.C. Circuit review the statute specifies. As a consequence, that court has had no occasion to decide whether the CSRT hearings, followed by review in the Court of Appeals, vindicate whatever constitutional and statutory rights petitioners may possess.

Remarkably, this Court does not require petitioners to exhaust their remedies under the statute; it does not wait to see whether those remedies will prove sufficient to protect petitioners' rights. Instead, it not only denies the D.C. Circuit the opportunity to assess the statute's remedies, it refuses to do so itself: the majority expressly declines to decide whether the CSRT procedures, coupled with Article III review, satisfy due process. . . .

. . . If the majority were truly concerned about delay, it would have required petitioners to use the DTA process that has been available to them for 2 1/2 years, with its Article III review in the D.C. Circuit. That system might well have provided petitioners all the relief to which they are entitled long before the Court's newly installed habeas review could hope to do so.[10] . . .

II . . .

. . . After much hemming and hawing, the majority appears to concede that the DTA provides an Article III court competent to order release. The only issue in dispute is the process the Guantanamo prisoners are entitled to use to test the legality of their detention. . . .

A . . .

. . . [T]he *Hamdi* plurality concluded that [two-layered] . . . review would be enough to satisfy due process, even for citizens. Congress followed the Court's lead, only to find itself the victim of a constitutional bait and switch.

---

10. In light of the foregoing, the concurrence is wrong to suggest that I "insufficiently appreciat[e]" the issue of delay in these cases. This Court issued its decisions in *Rasul v. Bush*, 542 U.S. 466, and *Hamdi v. Rumsfeld*, 542 U.S. 507, in 2004. The concurrence makes it sound as if the political branches have done nothing in the interim. In fact, Congress responded 18 months later by enacting the DTA. Congress cannot be faulted for taking that time to consider how best to accommodate both the detainees' interests and the need to keep the American people safe. Since the DTA became law, petitioners have steadfastly refused to avail themselves of the statute's review mechanisms. It is unfair to complain that the DTA system involves too much delay when petitioners have consistently refused to use it, preferring to litigate instead. Today's decision obligating district courts to craft new procedures to replace those in the DTA will only prolong the process – and delay relief.

Hamdi merits scant attention from the Court – a remarkable omission, as *Hamdi* bears directly on the issues before us. The majority attempts to dismiss *Hamdi*'s relevance by arguing that because the availability of §2241 federal habeas was never in doubt in that case, "the Court had no occasion to define the necessary scope of habeas review . . . in the context of enemy combatant detentions." Hardly. *Hamdi* was all about the scope of habeas review in the context of enemy combatant detentions. The petitioner, an American citizen held within the United States as an enemy combatant, invoked the writ to challenge his detention. After "a careful examination both of the writ . . . and of the Due Process Clause," this Court enunciated the "basic process" the Constitution entitled Hamdi to expect from a habeas court under §2241. That process consisted of the right to "receive notice of the factual basis for his classification, and a fair opportunity to rebut the Government's factual assertions before a neutral decisionmaker." In light of the Government's national security responsibilities, the plurality found the process could be "tailored to alleviate [the] uncommon potential to burden the Executive at a time of ongoing military conflict." For example, the Government could rely on hearsay and could claim a presumption in favor of its own evidence.

Hamdi further suggested that this "basic process" on collateral review could be provided by a military tribunal. It pointed to prisoner-of-war tribunals as a model that would satisfy the Constitution's requirements. Only "[i]n the *absence* of such process" before a military tribunal, the Court held, would Article III courts need to conduct full-dress habeas proceedings to "ensure that the minimum requirements of due process are achieved." *Ibid.* (emphasis added). And even then, the petitioner would be entitled to no more process than he would have received from a properly constituted military review panel, given his limited due process rights and the Government's weighty interests.

Contrary to the majority, *Hamdi* is of pressing relevance because it establishes the procedures American *citizens* detained as enemy combatants can expect from a habeas court proceeding under §2241. The DTA system of military tribunal hearings followed by Article III review looks a lot like the procedure *Hamdi* blessed. If nothing else, it is plain from the design of the DTA that Congress, the President, and this Nation's military leaders have made a good-faith effort to follow our precedent.

The Court, however, will not take "yes" for an answer. . . .

B . . .

By virtue of its refusal to allow the D.C. Circuit to assess petitioners' statutory remedies, and by virtue of its own refusal to consider, at the outset, the fit between those remedies and due process, the majority now finds itself in the position of evaluating whether the DTA system is an adequate substitute for habeas review without knowing what rights either habeas or the DTA is supposed to protect. . . .

For my part, I will assume that any due process rights petitioners may possess are no greater than those of American citizens detained as enemy combatants. It is worth noting again that the *Hamdi* controlling opinion said the Constitution guarantees citizen detainees only "basic" procedural rights, and that the process for securing those rights can "be tailored to alleviate [the] uncommon potential to burden the Executive at a time of ongoing military conflict." The majority, however, objects that "the procedural protections afforded to the detainees in the CSRT hearings are . . . limited." But the evidentiary and other limitations the Court complains of reflect the nature of the issue in contest, namely, the status of aliens captured by our Armed Forces abroad and alleged to be enemy combatants. Contrary to the repeated suggestions of the majority, DTA review need not parallel the habeas privileges enjoyed by noncombatant American citizens, as set out in 28 U.S.C. §2241 (2000 ed. and Supp. V). It need only provide process adequate for noncitizens detained as alleged combatants. . . .

III . . .

The majority rests its decision on abstract and hypothetical concerns. Step back and consider what, in the real world, Congress and the Executive have actually granted aliens captured by our Armed Forces overseas and found to be enemy combatants:

• The right to hear the bases of the charges against them, including a summary of any classified evidence.

• The ability to challenge the bases of their detention before military tribunals modeled after Geneva Convention procedures. Some 38 detainees have been released as a result of this process.

• The right, before the CSRT, to testify, introduce evidence, call witnesses, question those the Government calls, and secure release, if and when appropriate.

• The right to the aid of a personal representative in arranging and presenting their cases before a CSRT.
• Before the D.C. Circuit, the right to employ counsel, challenge the factual record, contest the lower tribunal's legal determinations, ensure compliance with the Constitution and laws, and secure release, if any errors below establish their entitlement to such relief.

In sum, the DTA satisfies the majority's own criteria for assessing adequacy. This statutory scheme provides the combatants held at Guantanamo greater procedural protections than have ever been afforded alleged enemy detainees – whether citizens or aliens – in our national history. . . .
I respectfully dissent.

Justice SCALIA, with whom THE CHIEF JUSTICE, Justice THOMAS, and Justice ALITO join, dissenting. . . . Contrary to my usual practice, . . . I think it appropriate to begin with a description of the disastrous consequences of what the Court has done today.

I

America is at war with radical Islamists. . . .
The game of bait-and-switch that today's opinion plays upon the Nation's Commander in Chief will make the war harder on us. It will almost certainly cause more Americans to be killed. That consequence would be tolerable if necessary to preserve a time-honored legal principle vital to our constitutional Republic. But it is this Court's blatant *abandonment* of such a principle that produces the decision today. The President relied on our settled precedent in *Johnson v. Eisentrager*, 339 U.S. 763 (1950), when he established the prison at Guantanamo Bay for enemy aliens. Citing that case, the President's Office of Legal Counsel advised him "that the great weight of legal authority indicates that a federal district court could not properly exercise habeas jurisdiction over an alien detained at [Guantanamo Bay]." Memorandum from Patrick F. Philbin and John C. Yoo, Deputy Assistant Attorneys General, Office of Legal Counsel, to William J. Haynes II, General Counsel, Dept. of Defense (Dec. 28, 2001). Had the law been otherwise, the military surely would not have transported prisoners there, but would have kept them in Afghanistan, transferred them to another of our foreign military bases, or turned them over to allies for detention. Those other facilities might well have been worse for the detainees themselves.

In the long term, then, the Court's decision today accomplishes little, except perhaps to reduce the well-being of enemy combatants that the Court ostensibly seeks to protect. In the short term, however, the decision is devastating. At least 30 of those prisoners hitherto released from Guantanamo Bay have returned to the battlefield. Some have been captured or killed. But others have succeeded in carrying on their atrocities against innocent civilians. . . .

These, mind you, were detainees whom *the military* had concluded were not enemy combatants. Their return to the kill illustrates the incredible difficulty of assessing who is and who is not an enemy combatant in a foreign theater of operations where the environment does not lend itself to rigorous evidence collection. Astoundingly, the Court today raises the bar, requiring military officials to appear before civilian courts and defend their decisions under procedural and evidentiary rules that go beyond what Congress has specified. As THE CHIEF JUSTICE's dissent makes clear, we have no idea what those procedural and evidentiary rules are, but they will be determined by civil courts and (in the Court's contemplation at least) will be more detainee-friendly than those now applied, since otherwise there would no reason to hold the congressionally prescribed procedures unconstitutional. If they impose a higher standard of proof (from foreign battlefields) than the current procedures require, the number of the enemy returned to combat will obviously increase.

But even when the military has evidence that it can bring forward, it is often foolhardy to release that evidence to the attorneys representing our enemies. And one escalation of procedures that the Court *is* clear about is affording the detainees increased access to witnesses (perhaps troops serving in Afghanistan?) and to classified information. During the 1995 prosecution of Omar Abdel Rahman, federal prosecutors gave the names of 200 unindicted co-conspirators to the "Blind Sheik's" defense lawyers; that information was in the hands of Osama Bin Laden within two weeks. In another case, trial testimony revealed to the enemy that the United States had been monitoring their cellular network, whereupon they promptly stopped using it, enabling more of them to evade capture and continue their atrocities. . . .

. . . The Court today decrees that no good reason to accept the judgment of the other two branches is "apparent." "The Government," it declares, "presents no credible arguments that the military mission at Guantanamo would be compromised if habeas corpus courts had jurisdiction to hear the detainees' claims." What competence does the Court have to second-guess the judgment of Congress and the President on such a point? None whatever. But the Court blunders in nonetheless. Henceforth, as today's opinion makes unnervingly clear, how to handle enemy prisoners in this war will ultimately lie with the branch that knows least about the national security concerns that the subject entails.

II

A . . .

. . . The Court admits that it cannot determine whether the writ historically extended to aliens held abroad, and it concedes (necessarily) that Guantanamo Bay lies outside the sovereign territory of the United States. Together, these two concessions establish that it is (in the Court's view) perfectly ambiguous whether the common-law writ would have provided a remedy for these petitioners. If that is so, the Court has no basis to strike down the Military Commissions Act, and must leave undisturbed the considered judgment of the coequal branches.

How, then, does the Court weave a clear constitutional prohibition out of pure interpretive equipoise? The Court resorts to "fundamental separation-of-powers principles" to interpret the Suspension Clause. According to the Court, because "the writ of habeas corpus is itself an indispensable mechanism for monitoring the separation of powers," the test of its extraterritorial reach "must not be subject to manipulation by those whose power it is designed to restrain."

That approach distorts the nature of the separation of powers and its role in the constitutional structure. The "fundamental separation-of-powers principles" that the Constitution embodies are to be derived not from some judicially imagined matrix, but from the sum total of the individual separation-of-powers provisions that the Constitution sets forth. Only by considering them one-by-one does the full shape of the *Constitution's* separation-of-powers principles emerge. It is nonsensical to interpret those provisions themselves in light of some general "separation-of-powers principles" dreamed up by the Court. Rather, they must be interpreted to mean what they were understood to mean when the people ratified them. And if the understood scope of the writ of habeas corpus was "designed to restrain" (as the Court says) the actions of the Executive, the understood *limits* upon that scope were (as the Court seems not to grasp) just as much "designed to restrain" the incursions of the Third Branch. "Manipulation" of the territorial reach of the writ by the Judiciary poses just as much a threat to the proper separation of powers as "manipulation" by the Executive. As I will show below, manipulation is what is afoot here. The understood limits upon the writ deny our jurisdiction over the habeas petitions brought by these enemy aliens, and entrust the President with the crucial wartime determinations about their status and continued confinement.

B

The Court purports to derive from our precedents a "functional" test for the extraterritorial reach of the writ, which shows that the Military Commissions Act unconstitutionally restricts the scope of habeas. That is remarkable because the most pertinent of those precedents, *Johnson v. Eisentrager*, 339 U.S. 763, conclusively establishes the opposite. . . .

The Court would have us believe that *Eisentrager* rested on "[p]ractical considerations," such as the "difficulties of ordering the Government to produce the prisoners in a habeas corpus proceeding." Formal sovereignty, says the Court, is merely one consideration "that bears upon which constitutional guarantees apply" in a given location. This is a sheer rewriting of the case. *Eisentrager* mentioned practical concerns, to be sure – but not for the purpose of determining *under what circumstances* American courts could issue writs of habeas corpus for aliens abroad. It cited them to support *its holding* that the Constitution does not empower courts to issue writs of habeas corpus to aliens abroad *in any circumstances*. . . .

. . . *Eisentrager* nowhere mentions a "functional" test, and the notion that it is based upon such a principle is patently false. . . .

The category of prisoner comparable to these detainees are not the *Eisentrager* criminal defendants, but the more than 400,000 prisoners of war detained in the United States alone during World War II. Not a single one was accorded the right to have his detention validated by a habeas corpus action in federal court – and that despite the fact that they were present on U.S. soil. The Court's analysis produces a crazy result: Whereas those convicted and sentenced to death for war crimes are without judicial remedy, all enemy combatants detained during a war, at least insofar as they are confined in an area away from the battlefield over which the United States exercises "absolute and indefinite" control, may seek a writ of habeas corpus in federal court. And, as an even more bizarre implication from the Court's reasoning, those prisoners whom the military plans to try by full-dress Commission at a future date may file habeas petitions and secure release before their trials take place. . . .

III

Putting aside the conclusive precedent of *Eisentrager,* it is clear that the original understanding of the Suspension Clause was that habeas corpus was not available to aliens abroad, as Judge Randolph's thorough opinion for the court below detailed. . . .

. . . [*A*]*ll* available historical evidence points to the conclusion that the writ would not have been available at common law for aliens captured and held outside the sovereign territory of the Crown. Despite three opening briefs, three reply briefs, and support from a legion of *amici,* petitioners have failed to identify a single case in the history of Anglo-American law that supports their claim to jurisdiction. The Court finds it significant that there is no recorded case *denying* jurisdiction to such prisoners either. But a case standing for the remarkable proposition that the writ could issue to a foreign land would surely have been reported, whereas a case denying such a writ for lack of jurisdiction would likely not. At a minimum, the absence of a reported case either way leaves unrefuted the voluminous commentary stating that habeas was confined to the dominions of the Crown.

What history teaches is confirmed by the nature of the limitations that the Constitution places upon suspension of the common-law writ. It can be suspended only "in Cases of Rebellion or Invasion." Art. I, §9, cl. 2. The latter case (invasion) is plainly limited to the territory of the United States; and while it is conceivable that a rebellion could be mounted by American citizens abroad, surely the overwhelming majority of its occurrences would be domestic. If the extraterritorial scope of habeas turned on flexible, "functional" considerations, as the Court holds, why would the Constitution limit its suspension almost entirely to instances of domestic crisis? Surely there is an even greater justification for suspension in foreign lands where the United States might hold prisoners of war during an ongoing conflict. And correspondingly, there is less threat to liberty when the Government suspends the writ's (supposed) application in foreign lands, where even on the most extreme view prisoners are entitled to fewer constitutional rights. It makes no sense, therefore, for the Constitution generally to forbid suspension of the writ abroad if indeed the writ has application there. . . .

The Nation will live to regret what the Court has done today. I dissent.

[NSL p. 702, CTL p. 336. Insert following the Supreme Court decision in *Boumediene v. Bush*.]

Al Maqaleh v. Gates

United States Court of Appeals, District of Columbia Circuit, 2010

605 F.3d 84

SENTELLE, Chief Judge: Three detainees at Bagram Air Force Base in Afghanistan petitioned the district court for habeas corpus relief from their confinement by the United States military. Appellants (collectively "the United States" or "the government") moved to dismiss for lack of jurisdiction based on §7(a) of the Military Commissions Act of 2006, Pub. L. No. 109-366, 120 Stat. 2600 (2006) ("MCA"). The district court agreed with the United States that §7(a) of the MCA purported to deprive the court of jurisdiction, but held that this section could not constitutionally be applied to deprive the court of jurisdiction under the Supreme Court's test articulated in *Boumediene v. Bush*, 553 U.S. 723, 128 S. Ct. 2229 (2008). The court therefore denied the motion to dismiss but certified the three habeas cases for interlocutory appeal under 28 U.S.C. §1292(b). Pursuant to that certification, the government filed a petition to this court for interlocutory appeal. We granted the petition and now consider the jurisdictional question. Upon review, and applying the Supreme Court decision in *Boumediene*, we determine that the district court did not have jurisdiction to consider the petitions for habeas corpus. We therefore reverse the order of the district court and order that the petitions be dismissed.

I. Background

A. *The Petitioners*

All three petitioners are being held as unlawful enemy combatants at the Bagram Theater Internment Facility on the Bagram Airfield Military Base in Afghanistan. Petitioner Fadi Al-Maqaleh is a Yemeni citizen who alleges he was taken into custody in 2003. While Al-Maqaleh's petition asserts "on information and belief" that he was captured beyond Afghan borders, a sworn declaration from Colonel James W. Gray, Commander of Detention Operations, states that Al-Maqaleh was captured in Zabul, Afghanistan. Redha Al-Najar is a Tunisian citizen who alleges he was captured in Pakistan in 2002. Amin Al-Bakri is a Yemeni citizen who alleges he was captured in Thailand in 2002. Both

Al-Najar and Al-Bakri allege they were first held in some other unknown location before being moved to Bagram.

B. *The Place of Confinement*

Bagram Airfield Military Base is the largest military facility in Afghanistan occupied by United States and coalition forces. The United States entered into an "Accommodation Consignment Agreement for Lands and Facilities at Bagram Airfield" with the Islamic Republic of Afghanistan in 2006, which "consigns all facilities and land located at Bagram Airfield . . . owned by [Afghanistan,] or Parwan Province, or private individuals, or others, for use by the United States and coalition forces for military purposes." The Agreement refers to Afghanistan as the "host nation" and the United States "as the lessee." The leasehold created by the agreement is to continue "until the United States or its successors determine that the premises are no longer required for its use." *Id.*

Afghanistan remains a theater of active military combat. The United States and coalition forces conduct "an ongoing military campaign against al Qaeda, the Taliban regime, and their affiliates and supporters in Afghanistan." These operations are conducted in part from Bagram Airfield. Bagram has been subject to repeated attacks from the Taliban and al Qaeda, including a March 2009 suicide bombing striking the gates of the facility, and Taliban rocket attacks in June of 2009 resulting in death and injury to United States service members and other personnel.

While the United States provides overall security to Bagram, numerous other nations have compounds on the base. Some of the other nations control access to their respective compounds. The troops of the other nations are present at Bagram both as part of the American-led military coalition in Afghanistan and as members of the International Security Assistance Force (ISAF) of the North Atlantic Treaty Organization. The mission of the ISAF is to support the Afghan government in the maintenance of security in Afghanistan. According to the United States, as of February 1, 2010, approximately 38,000 non-United States troops were serving in Afghanistan as part of the ISAF, representing 42 other countries. . . .

II. Analysis

A. *The Legal Framework* . . .

B. *Application to the Bagram Petitioners* . . .

At the outset, we note that each of the parties has asserted both an extreme understanding of the law after *Boumediene* and a more nuanced set of arguments upon which each relies in anticipation of the possible rejection of the bright-line arguments. The United States would like us to hold that the *Boumediene* analysis has no application beyond territories that are, like Guantanamo, outside the *de jure* sovereignty of the United States but are subject to its *de facto* sovereignty. As the government puts it in its reply brief, "[t]he real question before this Court, therefore, is whether Bagram may be considered effectively part of the United States in light of the nature and history of the U.S. presence there." We disagree.

Relying upon three independent reasons, the Court in *Boumediene* expressly repudiated the argument of the United States in that case to the effect "that the *Eisentrager* Court [*Johnson v. Eisentrager*, 339 U.S. 763 (1950)] adopted a formalistic, sovereignty-based test for determining the reach of the Suspension Clause." 128 S. Ct. at 2257. Briefly put, the High Court rejected that argument first on the basis that the *Eisentrager* Court's further analysis beyond recitations concerning sovereignty would not have been undertaken by the Court if the sovereignty question were determinative. The *Boumediene* Court explicitly did "not accept the idea that . . . the [sovereignty discussion] from *Eisentrager* is the only authoritative language in the opinion and that all the rest is dicta. The Court's further determinations, based on practical considerations, were integral to Part II of its opinion and came before the decision announced its holding." *Id.* Second, the Court rejected the Government's reading of *Eisentrager* because the meaning of the word "sovereignty" in the *Eisentrager* opinion was not limited to the "narrow technical sense" of the word and could be read "to connote the degree of control the military asserted over the facility." *Id.* The third reason is . . . that the Court concluded that such a reading of *Eisentrager* as proposed by the United States "would have marked not only a change in, but a complete repudiation of, the *Insular Cases'* (and later *Reid's* [*Reid v. Covert*, 354 U.S. 1 (1957)]) functional approach to questions of extraterritoriality." *Id.* at 2258.

True, the second factor articulated in *Boumediene* for rejecting the government's reading of *Eisentrager* might apply differently in this case because of differences in the levels of control over the military facilities. But we must keep in mind that the second factor is only one of the three reasons offered by the *Boumediene* Court for the rejection of "a formalistic, sovereignty-based test for determining the reach of the Suspension Clause." *Id.* at 2257. Whatever the force of the second reason offered by the Court in *Boumediene*, the first and third reasons make it plain that the Court's understanding of *Eisentrager*, and therefore of the reach of the Suspension Clause, was based not on a formalistic attachment to sovereignty, but on a consideration of practical factors as well. . . .

For similar reasons, we reject the most extreme position offered by the petitioners. At various points, the petitioners seem to be arguing that the fact of United States control of Bagram under the lease of the military base is sufficient to trigger the extraterritorial application of the Suspension Clause, or at least satisfy the second factor of the three set forth in *Boumediene*. Again, we reject this extreme understanding. Such an interpretation would seem to create the potential for the extraterritorial extension of the Suspension Clause to noncitizens held in any United States military facility in the world, and perhaps to an undeterminable number of other United States-leased facilities as well. Significantly, the court engaged in an extended dialog with counsel for the petitioners in which we repeatedly sought some limiting principle that would distinguish Bagram from any other military installation. Counsel was able to produce no such distinction. Again, such an extended application is not a tenable interpretation of *Boumediene*. If it were the Supreme Court's intention to declare such a sweeping application, it would surely have said so. Just as we reject the extreme argument of the United States that would render most of the decision in *Boumediene* dicta, we reject the first line of argument offered by petitioners. Having rejected the bright-line arguments of both parties, we must proceed to their more nuanced arguments, and reach a conclusion based on the application of the Supreme Court's enumerated factors to the case before us.

The first of the enumerated factors is "the citizenship and status of the detainee and the adequacy of the process through which that status determination was made." Citizenship is, of course, an important factor in determining the constitutional rights of persons before the court. It is well established that there are "constitutional decisions of [the Supreme] Court expressly according differing protection to aliens than to citizens." *United States v. Verdugo-Urquidez*, 494 U.S. [259, 273 (1990)]. However, clearly the alien citizenship of the petitioners in this case does not weigh against their claim to protection of the right of habeas corpus under the Suspension Clause. So far as citizenship is concerned, they differ in no material respect from the petitioners at Guantanamo who prevailed in *Boumediene*. As to status, the petitioners before us are held as enemy aliens. . . . This question is governed by *Boumediene* and the status of the petitioners before us again is the same as the Guantanamo detainees, so this factor supports their argument for the extension of the availability of the writ.

So far as the adequacy of the process through which that status determination was made, the petitioners are in a stronger position for the availability of the writ than were either the *Eisentrager* or *Boumediene* petitioners. As the Supreme Court noted, the *Boumediene* petitioners were in a very different posture than those in *Eisentrager* in that "there ha[d] been no trial by military commission for violations of the laws of war." 128 S. Ct. at 2259. Unlike the *Boumediene* petitioners or those before us, "[t]he *Eisentrager* petitioners were charged by a bill of particulars that made detailed factual allegations against them." *Id.* at 2260. The *Eisentrager* detainees were "entitled to representation by counsel, allowed to introduce evidence on their own behalf, and permitted to cross-examine the prosecution's witnesses" in an adversarial proceeding. *Id.* The status of the *Boumediene* petitioners was determined by Combatant Status Review Tribunals (CSRTs) affording far less protection. Under the CSRT proceeding, the detainee, rather than being represented by an attorney, was advised by a "Personal Representative" who was "not the detainee's lawyer or even his 'advocate.'" *Id.* The CSRT proceeding was less protective than the military tribunal procedures in *Eisentrager* in other particulars as well, and the Supreme Court clearly stated that "[t]he difference is not trivial." *Id.* at 2259.

The status of the Bagram detainees is determined not by a Combatant Status Review Tribunal but by an "Unlawful Enemy Combatant Review Board" (UECRB). As the district court correctly noted, proceedings before the UECRB afford even less protection to the rights of detainees in the determination of status than was the case with the CSRT. Therefore, as the district court noted, "while the important adequacy of process factor strongly supported the extension of the Suspension Clause and habeas rights in *Boumediene*, it even more strongly favors petitioners here." *Al Maqaleh*, 604 F. Supp. 2d [205, 227 (2009)]. Therefore, examining only the first of the Supreme Court's three enumerated factors, petitioners have made a strong argument that the right to habeas relief and the Suspension Clause apply in Bagram as in Guantanamo. However, we do not stop with the first factor.

The second factor, "the nature of the sites where apprehension and then detention took place," weighs heavily in favor of the United States. Like all petitioners in both *Eisentrager* and *Boumediene*, the petitioners here were apprehended abroad. While this in itself would appear to weigh against the extension of the writ, it obviously would not be sufficient, otherwise *Boumediene* would not have been decided as it was. However, the nature of the place where the detention takes place weighs more strongly in favor of the position argued by the United States and against the extension of habeas jurisdiction than was the case in either *Boumediene* or *Eisentrager*. In the first place, while *de facto* sovereignty is not determinative, for the reasons discussed above, the very fact that it was the subject of much discussion in *Boumediene* makes it obvious that it is not without relevance. As the Supreme Court set forth, Guantanamo Bay is "a territory that, while technically not part of the United States, is under the complete and total control of our Government." 128 S. Ct. at 2262. While it is true that the United States holds a leasehold interest in Bagram, and held a leasehold interest in Guantanamo, the surrounding circumstances are hardly the same. The United States has maintained its total control of Guantanamo Bay for over a century, even in the face of a hostile government maintaining *de jure* sovereignty over the property. In Bagram, while the United States has options as to duration of the lease agreement, there is no indication of any intent to occupy the base with permanence, nor is there hostility on the part of the "host" country. Therefore, the notion that *de facto* sovereignty extends to Bagram is no more real than would have been the same claim with respect to Landsberg in the *Eisentrager* case. While it is certainly realistic to assert that the United States has *de facto* sovereignty over Guantanamo, the same simply is not true with respect to Bagram. Though the site of detention analysis weighs in favor of the United States and against the petitioners, it is not determinative.

But we hold that the third factor, that is "the practical obstacles inherent in resolving the prisoner's entitlement to the writ," particularly when considered along with the second factor, weighs overwhelmingly in favor of the position of the United States. It is undisputed that Bagram, indeed the entire nation of Afghanistan, remains a theater of war. Not only does this suggest that the detention at Bagram is more like the detention at Landsberg than Guantanamo, the position of the United States is even stronger in this case than it was in *Eisentrager*. As the Supreme Court recognized in *Boumediene*, even though the active hostilities in the European theater had "c[o]me to an end," at the time of the *Eisentrager* decision, many of the problems of a theater of war remained:

> In addition to supervising massive reconstruction and aid efforts the American forces stationed in Germany faced potential security threats from a defeated enemy. In retrospect the post-War occupation may seem uneventful. But at the time *Eisentrager* was decided, the Court was right to be concerned about judicial interference with the military's efforts to contain "enemy elements, guerilla fighters, and 'were-wolves.'"

128 S. Ct. at 2261 (quoting *Eisentrager*, 339 U.S. at 784).

In ruling for the extension of the writ to Guantanamo, the Supreme Court expressly noted that "[s]imilar threats are not apparent here." 128 S. Ct. at 2261. In the case before us, similar, if not greater, threats are indeed apparent. The United States asserts, and petitioners cannot credibly dispute, that all of the attributes of a facility exposed to the vagaries of war are present in Bagram. The Supreme Court expressly stated in *Boumediene* that at Guantanamo, "[w]hile obligated to abide by the terms of the lease, the United States is, for all practical purposes, answerable to no other sovereign for its acts on the base. Were that not the case, *or if the detention facility were located in an active theater of war*, arguments that issuing the writ would be 'impractical or anomalous' would have more weight." *Id.* at 2261-62 (emphasis added). Indeed, the Supreme Court supported this proposition with reference to the separate opinion of Justice Harlan in *Reid*, where the Justice expressed his doubts that "every provision of the Constitution must always be deemed automatically applicable to United States citizens in every part of the world." *See* 354 U.S. at 74 (Harlan, J., concurring in the result). We therefore conclude that under both *Eisentrager* and *Boumediene*, the writ does not extend to the Bagram confinement in an active theater of war in a territory under neither the *de facto* nor *de jure* sovereignty of the United States and within the territory of another *de jure* sovereign.

We are supported in this conclusion by the rationale of *Eisentrager*, which was not only not overruled, but reinforced by the language and reasoning just referenced from *Boumediene*. As we referenced in the background discussion of this opinion, we set forth more fully now concerns expressed by the Supreme Court in reaching its decision in *Eisentrager*:

> Such trials would hamper the war effort and bring aid and comfort to the enemy. They would diminish the prestige of our commanders, not only with enemies but with wavering neutrals. It would be difficult to devise more

effective fettering of a field commander than to allow the very enemies he is
ordered to reduce to submission to call him to account in his own civil
courts and divert his efforts and attention from the military offensive abroad
to the legal defensive at home. Nor is it unlikely that the result of such
enemy litigiousness would be a conflict between judicial and military
opinion highly comforting to enemies of the United States.

Eisentrager, 339 U.S. at 779. Those factors are more relevant to the
situation at Bagram than they were at Landsberg. While it is true, as the
Supreme Court noted in *Boumediene,* that the United States forces in
Germany in 1950 faced the possibility of unrest and guerilla warfare,
operations in the European theater had ended with the surrender of
Germany and Italy years earlier. Bagram remains in a theater of war. We
cannot, consistent with *Eisentrager* as elucidated by *Boumediene*, hold
that the right to the writ of habeas corpus and the constitutional
protections of the Suspension Clause extend to Bagram detention facility
in Afghanistan, and we therefore must reverse the decision of the district
court denying the motion of the United States to dismiss the petitions.

We do not ignore the arguments of the detainees that the United
States chose the place of detention and might be able "to evade judicial
review of Executive detention decisions by transferring detainees into
active conflict zones, thereby granting the Executive the power to switch
the Constitution on or off at will." However, that is not what happened
here. Indeed, without dismissing the legitimacy or sincerity of appellees'
concerns, we doubt that this fact goes to either the second or third of the
Supreme Court's enumerated factors. We need make no determination on
the importance of this possibility, given that it remains only a possibility;
its resolution can await a case in which the claim is a reality rather than a
speculation. In so stating, we note that the Supreme Court did not dictate
that the three enumerated factors are exhaustive. It only told us that "*at
least* three factors" are relevant. *Boumediene*, 128 S. Ct. at 2259
(emphasis added). Perhaps such manipulation by the Executive might
constitute an additional factor in some case in which it is in fact present.
However, the notion that the United States deliberately confined the
detainees in the theater of war rather than at, for example, Guantanamo,
is not only unsupported by the evidence, it is not supported by reason. To
have made such a deliberate decision to "turn off the Constitution"
would have required the military commanders or other Executive
officials making the situs determination to anticipate the complex
litigation history set forth above and predict the *Boumediene* decision
long before it came down.

Also supportive of our decision that the third factor weighs heavily in favor of the United States, as the district court recognized, is the fact that the detention is within the sovereign territory of another nation, which itself creates practical difficulties. Indeed, it was on this factor that the district court relied in dismissing the fourth petition, which was filed by an Afghan citizen detainee. *Al Maqaleh*, 604 F. Supp. 2d at 229-30, 235. While that factor certainly weighed more heavily with respect to an Afghan citizen, it is not without force with respect to detainees who are alien to both the United States and Afghanistan. The United States holds the detainees pursuant to a cooperative arrangement with Afghanistan on territory as to which Afghanistan is sovereign. While we cannot say that extending our constitutional protections to the detainees would be in any way disruptive of that relationship, neither can we say with certainty what the reaction of the Afghan government would be.

In sum, taken together, the second and especially the third factors compel us to hold that the petitions should have been dismissed.

CONCLUSION

For the reasons set forth above, we hold that the jurisdiction of the courts to afford the right to habeas relief and the protection of the Suspension Clause does not extend to aliens held in Executive detention in the Bagram detention facility in the Afghan theater of war. We therefore reverse the order of the district court denying the motion for dismissal of the United States and order that the petitions be dismissed for lack of jurisdiction.

So ordered.

[NSL p. 758, CTL p. 398. Insert after Note 5.]

Al-Marri v. Pucciarelli

United States Court of Appeals, Fourth Circuit (en banc), 2008
534 F.3d 213
vacated and remanded sub nom. Al-Marri v. Spagone,
129 S. Ct. 1545 (2009)

PER CURIAM: Ali Saleh Kahlah al-Marri filed a petition for a writ of habeas corpus challenging his military detention as an enemy combatant. After the district court denied all relief, al-Marri noted this appeal. A divided panel of this court reversed the judgment of the district court and ordered that al-Marri's military detention cease. *See Al-Marri v. Wright,* 487 F.3d 160 (4th Cir. 2007).

Subsequently, this court vacated that judgment and considered the case *en banc.* The parties present two principal issues for our consideration: (1) assuming the Government's allegations about al-Marri are true, whether Congress has empowered the President to detain al-Marri as an enemy combatant; and (2) assuming Congress has empowered the President to detain al-Marri as an enemy combatant provided the Government's allegations against him are true, whether al-Marri has been afforded sufficient process to challenge his designation as an enemy combatant.

Having considered the briefs and arguments of the parties, the *en banc* court now holds: (1) by a 5 to 4 vote (Chief Judge Williams and Judges Wilkinson, Niemeyer, Traxler, and Duncan voting in the affirmative; Judges Michael, Motz, King, and Gregory voting in the negative), that, if the Government's allegations about al-Marri are true, Congress has empowered the President to detain him as an enemy combatant; and (2) by a 5 to 4 vote (Judges Michael, Motz, Traxler, King, and Gregory voting in the affirmative; Chief Judge Williams and Judges Wilkinson, Niemeyer, and Duncan voting in the negative), that, assuming Congress has empowered the President to detain al-Marri as an enemy combatant provided the Government's allegations against him are true, al-Marri has not been afforded sufficient process to challenge his designation as an enemy combatant.[*]

Accordingly, the judgment of the district court is reversed and remanded for further proceedings consistent with the opinions that follow.

[* The badly fractured en banc court produced concurring and dissenting opinions that are a nightmare to read and reconcile. Judge Motz first opined that the executive lacked authority for the military detention of al-Marri, although only three other judges joined her on this. Thus, a bare majority of the court *upheld* the military detention authority. Judge Traxler then abandoned *that* majority to form a different majority for the proposition that the process afforded al-Marri to challenge his designation did not meet due process standards. These five votes sufficed to send the case back to the district court. Along the way, several judges provided noteworthy explanations of their individual reasoning, some of which are excerpted here. – Eds.]

DIANA GRIBBON MOTZ, Circuit Judge, concurring in the judgment: . . .

I.

Al-Marri, a citizen of Qatar, lawfully entered the United States with his wife and children on September 10, 2001, to pursue a master's degree at Bradley University in Peoria, Illinois, where he had obtained a bachelor's degree in 1991. The following day, terrorists hijacked four commercial airliners and used them to kill and inflict grievous injury on thousands of Americans. Three months later, on December 12, 2001, FBI agents arrested al-Marri at his home in Peoria as a material witness in the Government's investigation of the September 11th attacks. Al-Marri was imprisoned in civilian jails in Peoria and then New York City.

In February 2002, al-Marri was charged in the Southern District of New York with the possession of unauthorized or counterfeit credit card numbers with the intent to defraud. A year later, in January 2003, he was charged in a second, six-count indictment with two counts of making a false statement to the FBI, three counts of making a false statement on a bank application, and one count of using another person's identification for the purpose of influencing the action of a federally insured financial institution. Al-Marri pleaded not guilty to all of these charges. In May 2003, a federal district court in New York dismissed the charges against al-Marri for lack of venue.

The Government then returned al-Marri to Peoria, and he was re-indicted in the Central District of Illinois on the same seven counts, to which he again pleaded not guilty. The district court set a July 21, 2003, trial date. On Friday, June 20, 2003, the court scheduled a hearing on pre-trial motions, including a motion to suppress evidence against al-Marri assertedly obtained by torture. On the following Monday, June 23, before that hearing could be held, the Government moved *ex parte* to dismiss the indictment based on an order signed that morning by the President.

In the order, President George W. Bush stated that he "DETER-MINE[D] for the United States of America that" al-Marri: (1) is an enemy combatant; (2) is closely associated with al Qaeda; (3) "engaged in conduct that constituted hostile and war-like acts, including conduct in preparation for acts of international terrorism"; (4) "possesses intelligence . . . that . . . would aid U.S. efforts to prevent attacks by al Qaeda"; and (5) "represents a continuing, present, and grave danger to the national security of the United States." The President determined that al-Marri's detention by the military was "necessary to prevent him from aiding al Qaeda" and thus ordered the Attorney General to surrender al-Marri to the Secretary of Defense and further directed the Secretary of Defense to "detain him as an enemy combatant."

The federal district court in Illinois granted the Government's motion to dismiss the criminal indictment against al-Marri. In accordance with the President's order, al-Marri was then transferred to military custody and brought to the Naval Consolidated Brig in South Carolina.

Since that time (that is, for five years) the military has held al-Marri as an enemy combatant, without charge and without any indication when this confinement will end. For the first sixteen months of his military confinement, the Government did not permit al-Marri any communication with the outside world, including his attorneys, his wife, and his children. . . .

[Al-Marri's lawyer filed a petition for a writ of habeas corpus on his behalf. The government responded with a declaration of Jeffrey N. Rapp, Director of the Joint Intelligence Task Force for Combating Terrorism, as support for the President's order for military detention.] . . .

The Rapp Declaration asserts that al-Marri: (1) is "closely associated with al Qaeda, an international terrorist organization with which the United States is at war"; (2) trained at an al Qaeda terrorist training camp in Afghanistan sometime between 1996 and 1998; (3) in the summer of 2001, was introduced to Osama Bin Laden by Khalid Shaykh Muhammed; (4) at that time, volunteered for a "martyr mission" on behalf of al Qaeda; (5) was ordered to enter the United States sometime before September 11, 2001, to serve as a "sleeper agent" to facilitate terrorist activities and explore disrupting this country's financial system through computer hacking; (6) in the summer of 2001, met with terrorist financier Mustafa Ahmed al-Hawsawi, who gave al-Marri money, including funds to buy a laptop; (7) gathered technical information about poisonous chemicals on his laptop; (8) undertook efforts to obtain false identification, credit cards, and banking information, including stolen credit card numbers; (9) communicated with known terrorists, including Khalid Shaykh Muhammed and al-Hawsawi, by phone and e-mail; and (10) saved information about jihad, the September 11th attacks, and Bin Laden on his laptop computer.

The Rapp Declaration does *not* assert that al-Marri: (1) is a citizen, or affiliate of the armed forces, of any nation at war with the United States; (2) was seized on, near, or having escaped from a battlefield on which the armed forces of the United States or its allies were engaged in combat; (3) was ever in Afghanistan during the armed conflict between the United States and the Taliban there; or (4) directly participated in any hostilities against United States or allied armed forces. . . .

II. . . .

A. . . .

[Judge Motz found that as a lawfully admitted alien with a substantial connection to the United States, al-Marri was entitled to due process before he could be deprived of his liberty. But she also acknowledged that in *Hamdi v. Rumsfeld*, 542 U.S. 507 (2004), the Supreme Court found that Congress had constitutionally authorized the President to order the military detention, without the criminal process ordinarily required by the Due Process Clause, of persons who qualify as "enemy combatants."]

B.

The Government's primary argument is that the AUMF, as construed by precedent and considered against "the legal background against which [it] was enacted," i.e., constitutional and law-of-war principles, empowers the President to order the military to seize and detain al-Marri as an enemy combatant. The AUMF provides:

> . . . the President is authorized to use all necessary and appropriate force against those nations, organizations, or persons he determines planned, authorized, committed, or aided the terrorist attacks that occurred on September 11, 2001, or harbored such organizations or persons, in order to prevent any future acts of international terrorism against the United States by such nations, organizations or persons.

§2(a), 115 Stat. 224. . . .

1.

Tellingly, the Deputy Solicitor General conceded at oral argument before the *en banc* court that the AUMF only authorizes detention of enemy combatants. Thus, the Government does *not* argue that the broad language of the AUMF authorizes the President to subject to indefinite military detention anyone he believes to have aided any "nation[ ], organization [ ], or person[ ]" related to the September 11th attacks. *See*

§2(a), 115 Stat. 224. Such an interpretation would lead to absurd results that Congress could not have intended.

Under that reading of the AUMF, the President would be able to subject to indefinite military detention anyone, including an American citizen, whom the President believed was associated with any organization that the President believed in some way "planned, authorized, committed, or aided" the September 11th attacks, so long as the President believed this to be "necessary and appropriate" to prevent future acts of terrorism.

Under such an interpretation of the AUMF, if some money from a nonprofit charity that feeds Afghan orphans made its way to al Qaeda, the President could subject to indefinite military detention any donor to that charity. Similarly, this interpretation of the AUMF would allow the President to detain indefinitely any employee or shareholder of an American corporation that built equipment used by the September 11th terrorists; or allow the President to order the military seizure and detention of an American-citizen physician who treated a member of al Qaeda. . . .

2.

. . . [T]he Government wisely limits its argument. It relies only on the scope of the AUMF as construed by precedent and considered in light of "the legal background against which [it] was enacted." Specifically, the Government contends that "[t]he Supreme Court's and this Court's prior construction of the AUMF govern[s] this case and compel[s] the conclusion that the President is authorized to detain al-Marri as an enemy combatant."

i.

The precedent interpreting the AUMF on which the Government relies for this argument consists of two cases: the Supreme Court's opinion in *Hamdi*, 542 U.S. 507, and our opinion in *Padilla v. Hanft*, 423 F.3d 386 (4th Cir. 2005). The "legal background" for the AUMF, which the Government cites, consists of two cases from earlier conflicts, *Ex Parte Quirin*, 317 U.S. 1 (1942) (World War II), and *Ex Parte Milligan*, 71 U.S. (4 Wall.) 2 (1866) (U.S. Civil War), as well as constitutional and law-of-war principles.

With respect to the latter, we note that American courts have often been reluctant to follow international law in resolving domestic disputes.

In the present context, however, they, like the Government here, have relied on the law of war-treaty obligations including the Hague and Geneva Conventions and customary principles developed alongside them. The law of war provides clear rules for determining an individual's status during an international armed conflict, distinguishing between "combatants" (members of a nation's military, militia, or other armed forces, and those who fight alongside them) and "civilians" (all other persons).[11] *See, e.g.,* Geneva Convention Relative to the Treatment of Prisoners of War (Third Geneva Convention) arts. 2, 4, 5, Aug. 12, 1949, 6 U.S.T. 3316, 75 U.N.T.S. 135; Geneva Convention Relative to the Protection of Civilian Persons in Time of War (Fourth Geneva Convention) art. 4, Aug. 12, 1949, 6 U.S.T. 3516, 75 U.N.T.S. 287. American courts have repeatedly looked to these careful distinctions made in the law of war in identifying which individuals fit within the "legal category" of "enemy combatant" under our Constitution. *See, e.g., Hamdi,* 542 U.S. at 518; *Quirin,* 317 U.S. at 30-31 & n.7; *Milligan,* 71 U.S. at 121-22; *Padilla,* 423 F.3d at 391. . . .

    Quirin, Hamdi, and *Padilla* all emphasize that *Milligan's* teaching – that our Constitution does not permit the Government to subject *civilians* within the United States to military jurisdiction – remains good law. The *Quirin* Court explained that while the petitioners before it were affiliated with the armed forces of an enemy nation and so were enemy belligerents, Milligan was a "non-belligerent" and so "not subject to the law of war." 317 U.S. at 45. The *Hamdi* plurality similarly took care to note that *Milligan* "turned in large part on the fact that Milligan was not a

---

    11. Thus, "civilian" is a term of art in the law of war, not signifying an innocent person, but rather someone in a certain legal category who is *not* subject to *military* seizure or detention. So, too, a "combatant" is by no means always a wrongdoer, but rather a member of a different "legal category" who *is* subject to *military* seizure and detention. *Hamdi,* 542 U.S. at 522 n.1. For example, our brave soldiers fighting in Germany during World War II were "combatants" under the law of war, and viewed from Germany's perspective they were "enemy combatants." While civilians are subject to trial and punishment in civilian courts for all crimes committed during wartime in the country in which they are captured and held, combatant status protects an individual from trial and punishment by the capturing nation, unless the combatant has violated the law of war. *See id.* at 518; *Quirin,* 317 U.S. at 28-31. Nations in international conflicts can summarily remove the adversary's "combatants," i.e., the "enemy combatants," from the battlefield and detain them for the duration of such conflicts, but no such provision is made for "civilians." *Hamdi,* 542 U.S. at 518; *Quirin,* 317 U.S. at 28-31.

prisoner of war" (i.e., combatant) and suggested that "[h]ad Milligan been captured while he was assisting Confederate soldiers by carrying a rifle against Union troops on a Confederate battlefield, the holding of the Court might well have been different." 542 U.S. at 522. And in *Padilla*, we reaffirmed that "*Milligan* does not extend to enemy combatants" and so "is inapposite here because Padilla, unlike Milligan, associated with, and has taken up arms against the forces of the United States on behalf of, an enemy of the United States." 423 F.3d at 396-97. Thus, although *Hamdi, Quirin,* and *Padilla* distinguish *Milligan,* they recognize that its core holding remains the law of the land. That is, civilians within this country (even "dangerous enemies" like Milligan who perpetrate "enormous crime[s]" on behalf of "secret" enemy organizations bent on "overthrowing the Government" of this country) may not be subjected to military control and deprived of constitutional rights.

In sum, the holdings of *Hamdi* and *Padilla* share two characteristics: (1) they look to law-of-war principles to determine who fits within the "legal category" of enemy combatant; and (2) following the law of war, they rest enemy combatant status on affiliation with the military arm of an enemy nation.

ii.

In view of the holdings in *Hamdi* and *Padilla,* we find it remarkable that the Government contends that they "compel the conclusion" that the President may detain al-Marri as an enemy combatant. For unlike Hamdi and Padilla, al-Marri is not alleged to have been part of a Taliban unit, not alleged to have stood alongside the Taliban or the armed forces of any other enemy nation, not alleged to have been on the battlefield during the war in Afghanistan, not alleged to have even been in Afghanistan during the armed conflict there, and not alleged to have engaged in combat with United States forces anywhere in the world. *See* Rapp Declaration (alleging none of these facts, but instead that "[a]l-Marri engaged in conduct in preparation for acts of international terrorism intended to cause injury or adverse effects on the United States"). Indeed, unlike Hamdi and Padilla, al-Marri had been imprisoned in the United States by civil authorities on criminal charges for more than a year before being seized by the military and indefinitely confined in a Navy brig as an enemy combatant.

In place of the "classic wartime detention" that the Government argued justified Hamdi's detention as an enemy combatant, or the "classic battlefield" detention it maintained justified Padilla's, here the

Government argues that al-Marri's seizure and indefinite detention by the military in this country are justified "because he engaged in, and continues to pose a very real threat of carrying out, . . . acts of international terrorism." And instead of seeking judicial deference to decisions of "military officers who are engaged in the serious work of waging battle," *Hamdi,* 542 U.S. at 531-32, the Government asks us to defer to the "multi-agency evaluation process" of government bureaucrats in Washington made eighteen months after al-Marri was taken into custody. Neither the holding in *Hamdi* nor that in *Padilla* supports the Government's contentions here. . . .

. . . Instead, the *Hamdi* plurality emphasized the narrowness of its holding, 542 U.S. at 509, 516-19, and the "limited category" of individuals controlled by that holding, *id.* at 518. In *Padilla,* we similarly saw no need to embrace a broader construction of the AUMF than that adopted by the Supreme Court in *Hamdi.* Indeed, the Government itself *principally* argued that Padilla was an enemy combatant because he, like Hamdi, "engaged in armed conflict" alongside the Taliban "against our forces in Afghanistan."

Thus, the Government is mistaken in its representation that *Hamdi* and *Padilla* "recognized" "[t]he President's authority to detain 'enemy combatants' during the current conflict with al Qaeda." *Hamdi* and *Padilla* evidence no sympathy for the view that the AUMF permits indefinite military detention beyond the "limited category" of people covered by the "narrow circumstances" of those cases. Therefore the Government's argument – that *Hamdi* and *Padilla* "compels the conclusion" that the AUMF authorizes the President "to detain al-Marri as an enemy combatant" – fails.

3. . . .

i.

. . . [T]he Supreme Court's most recent terrorism cases – *Hamdan* [v. Rumsfeld, 548 U.S. 557, 126 S. Ct. 2749 (2006)] and *Boumediene* – provide no support for the dissenters' position. In *Hamdan,* the Court held that because the conflict between the United States and al Qaeda in Afghanistan is not "between nations," it is a "'conflict not of an international character'" – and so is governed by Common Article 3 of the Geneva Conventions.

Common Article 3 and other Geneva Convention provisions applying to non-international conflicts (in contrast to those applying to international conflicts) simply do *not* recognize the "legal category" of enemy combatant. *See* Third Geneva Convention, art. 3, 6 U.S.T. at 3318. As the International Committee of the Red Cross – the official codifier of the Geneva Conventions – explains, "an 'enemy combatant' is a person who, either lawfully or unlawfully, engages in hostilities for the opposing side in an *international* armed conflict"; in contrast, "[i]n non-international armed conflict combatant status *does not exist.*" Int'l Comm. of the Red Cross, Official Statement: The Relevance of IHL in the Context of Terrorism, at 1, 3 (Feb. 21, 2005), http://www.icrc.org/ Web/Eng/siteeng0.nsf/htmlall/terrorismihl-210705 (emphasis added).

Perhaps for this reason, our dissenting colleagues and the Government ignore *Hamdan's* holding that the conflict with al Qaeda in Afghanistan is a non-international conflict and ignore the fact that, in such conflicts, the legal category of enemy combatant does not exist. . . .

. . . Furthermore, in *Boumediene,* the Court demonstrated no more sympathy for the Government's position than it had in any of the other recent terrorism cases. Rather, the Court expressly held that persons designated by the Executive "as enemy combatants" and held by United States forces at Guantanamo Bay must be afforded "the fundamental procedural protections of habeas corpus" guaranteed by our Constitution, even though they were foreign nationals who had been seized in foreign lands. The Court explained that "[t]he laws and Constitution are designed to survive, and remain in force, in extraordinary times."

Moreover, even were the Supreme Court ultimately to approve the detention of Boumediene, Hamdan, and those like them, that would not bolster the view that the Government can militarily detain al-Marri as an enemy combatant. Because the legal status of enemy combatant does not exist in non-international conflicts, the law of war leaves the detention of persons in such conflicts to the applicable law of the detaining country. In al-Marri's case, the applicable law is our Constitution. Under our Constitution, even if the Supreme Court should hold that the Government may detain indefinitely Boumediene, Hamdan, and others like them, who were captured *outside* the United States and lack substantial and voluntary connections to this country, that holding would provide no support for approving al-Marri's military detention. For not only was al-Marri seized and detained *within* the United States, he also has substantial connections to the United States and so plainly is protected by the Due Process Clause.

ii. . . .

We recognize the understandable instincts of those who wish to treat domestic terrorists as "combatants" in a "global war on terror." Allegations of criminal activity in association with a terrorist organization, however, do not permit the Government to transform a civilian into an enemy combatant subject to indefinite military detention, just as allegations of murder in association with others while in military service do not permit the Government to transform a civilian into a soldier subject to trial by court martial. *See United States ex rel. Toth v. Quarles,* 350 U.S. 11, 23 (1955) (holding that ex-servicemen, "like other civilians, are entitled to have the benefit of safeguards afforded those tried in the regular courts authorized by Article III of the Constitution").

To be sure, enemy combatants may commit crimes just as civilians may. When an enemy combatant violates the law of war, that conduct will render the person an "unlawful" enemy combatant, subject not only to detention but also to military trial and punishment. *Quirin,* 317 U.S. at 31. But merely engaging in unlawful behavior does not make one an enemy combatant. *Quirin* illustrates these distinctions well. The *Quirin* petitioners were first enemy combatants – associating themselves with the military arm of the German government with which the United States was at war. They became *unlawful* enemy combatants when they violated the law of war by "without uniform com[ing] secretly through the lines for the purpose of waging war." *Id.* By doing so, in addition to being subject to military detention for the duration of the conflict as enemy combatants, they also became "subject to trial and punishment by military tribunals for acts which render their belligerency illegal." *Id.* Had the *Quirin* petitioners never "secretly and without uniform" passed our "military lines," *id.*, they still would have been enemy combatants, subject to military detention, but would not have been *unlawful* enemy combatants subject to military trial and punishment.

Neither *Quirin* nor any other precedent even suggests, as our dissenting colleagues seem to believe, that individuals with constitutional rights, unaffiliated with the military arm of any enemy government, can be subjected to military jurisdiction and deprived of those rights solely on the basis of their conduct on behalf of a terrorist organization. In fact, *Milligan* rejected the Government's attempt to do just this. There, the Court acknowledged that Milligan's conduct – "joining and aiding" a "secret political organization, armed to oppose the laws, and seek[ing] by stealthy means to introduce the enemies of the country into peaceful communities, there to . . . overthrow the power of the United States" –

made him and his co-conspirators "dangerous enemies to their country."
71 U.S. at 6, 130. But the Government did not allege that Milligan took
orders from any enemy government or took up arms against this country
on the battlefield. And so the Court held that the Government could not
subject Milligan to trial by military tribunal or treat him as an enemy
combatant subject to military detention as a prisoner of war. Milligan
was an "enem[y] of the country" and associated with an organization
seeking to "overthrow[ ] the Government" of this country, but he was
still a civilian and had to be treated as one. *Id.* . . .

iii. . . .

. . . [B]ecause the AUMF contains only a broad grant of war powers
and lacks any specific language authorizing detention, the *Hamdi*
plurality explained that its opinion "only finds legislative authority to
detain under the AUMF once it is sufficiently clear that the individual *is,*
in fact, an enemy combatant." 542 U.S. at 523 (emphasis added).
Although the military detention of enemy combatants like Hamdi is
certainly "a fundamental incident of waging war," *id.* at 519, the military
detention of civilians like al-Marri just as certainly is not.

Even assuming the Constitution permitted Congress to grant the
President such an awesome and unprecedented power, if Congress
intended to grant this authority, it could and would have said so
explicitly. The AUMF lacks the particularly clear statement from
Congress that would, at a minimum, be necessary to authorize the
indefinite military detention of *civilians* as enemy combatants. *See, e.g.,*
Greene v. McElroy, 360 U.S. 474, 508 (1959) (rejecting Government
argument that executive orders and statutes permitted deprivation of
liberty rights absent "explicit authorization"); *Duncan v. Kahanamoku,*
327 U.S. 304, 324 (1946) (rejecting Government argument that statute
authorized trial of civilians by military tribunals because Congress could
not have intended "to exceed the boundaries between military and
civilian power, in which our people have always believed"); *Ex Parte*
Endo, 323 U.S. 283, 300 (1944) (rejecting Government argument that a
"wartime" executive order and statute permitted detention of citizen of
Japanese heritage when neither "use[d] the language of detention");
Brown v. United States, 12 U.S. (8 Cranch) 110, 128-29 (1814) (rejecting
Government argument that declaration of war authorized confiscation of
enemy property because it did not clearly "declare[ ]" the legislature's
"will"). We are exceedingly reluctant to infer a grant of authority that is
so far afield from anything recognized by precedent or law-of-war

principles, especially given the serious constitutional concerns it would raise. . . .

C.

Thus, we turn to the Government's final contention. The Government summarily argues that even if the AUMF does not authorize al-Marri's seizure and indefinite detention as an enemy combatant, the President has "inherent constitutional authority" to order the military to seize and detain al-Marri. According to the Government, the President's "war-making powers" afford him "inherent" authority to subject persons legally residing in this country and protected by our Constitution to military arrest and detention, without the benefit of any criminal process, if the President believes these individuals have "engaged in conduct in preparation for acts of international terrorism." *See* Rapp Declaration. Given that the Government has now acknowledged that aliens lawfully residing in the United States have the same due process rights as United States citizens, this is a breathtaking claim – and one that no member of the court embraces. . . .

1.

In contrast to the AUMF, which is silent on the detention of asserted alien terrorists captured and held within the United States, in the Patriot Act, enacted shortly after the AUMF, Congress carefully stated how it wished the Government to handle aliens believed to be terrorists who were seized and held within the United States. The Patriot Act provides the Executive with broad powers to deal with "terrorist aliens," but it *explicitly prohibits* their indefinite detention.

Section 412 of the Patriot Act, entitled "Mandatory Detention of Suspected Terrorists," permits the short-term "[d]etention of [t]errorist [a]liens." Patriot Act §412(a). The statute authorizes the Attorney General to detain any alien whom he "has reasonable grounds to believe": (1) "seeks to enter the United States" to "violate any law of the United States relating to espionage or sabotage" or to use "force, violence, or other unlawful means" in opposition to the government of the United States; (2) "has engaged in a terrorist activity"; or (3) is "likely to engage after entry in any terrorist activity," has "incited terrorist activity," is a "representative" or "member" of a "terrorist organization," is a "representative" of a "group that endorses or espouses terrorist activity," or "has received military-type training" from a terrorist organization. *Id.*; 8 U.S.C.A. §1182(a)(3)(A)-(B) (West 2007); *see also* 8 U.S.C.A. §1227(a)(4)(A)(i), (a)(4)(A)(iii), (a)(4)(B) (West 2007). In addition, the Patriot Act authorizes the Attorney General to detain any other alien who "is engaged in any other activity that endangers the national security of the United States." Patriot Act §412(a). In particular, the Patriot Act permits the Attorney General to "take into custody" any "terrorist aliens" based only on the Attorney General's "belie[fs]" as to the aliens' threat, with *no* process or evidentiary hearing, and judicial review available only through petition for habeas corpus. *Id.*

Recognizing the breadth of this grant of power, however, Congress also imposed strict limits in the Patriot Act on the duration of the detention of such "terrorist aliens" within the United States. Thus, the Patriot Act expressly prohibits unlimited "indefinite detention"; instead it requires the Attorney General either to begin "removal proceedings" or to "charge the alien with a criminal offense" "not later than 7 days after the commencement of such detention." *Id.* If a terrorist alien's removal "is unlikely for the reasonably foreseeable future," he "may be detained for additional periods of up to six months" if his release "will threaten the national security of the United States." *Id.* But no provision of the Patriot Act allows for unlimited indefinite detention. Moreover, the Attorney General must provide the legislature with reports on the use of this detention authority every six months, which must include the number of aliens detained, the grounds for their detention, and the length of the detention. *Id.* §412(c).

Therefore, the Patriot Act establishes a specific method for the Government to detain aliens affiliated with terrorist organizations who the Government believes have come to the United States to endanger our national security, conduct espionage and sabotage, use force and violence to overthrow the government, engage in terrorist activity, or are likely to engage in any terrorist activity. Congress could not have better described the Government's allegations against al-Marri – *and* Congress decreed that individuals so described are *not* to be detained indefinitely, but only for a limited time, and only by civilian authorities, prior to deportation or criminal prosecution.

In sum, Congress has carefully prescribed the process by which it wishes to permit detention of "terrorist aliens" within the United States, and it has expressly prohibited the indefinite detention the President seeks here. The Government's argument that the President may indefinitely detain al-Marri is thus contrary to Congress's expressed will. "When the President takes measures incompatible with the expressed or implied will of Congress, his power is at its lowest ebb, for then he can rely only upon his own constitutional powers minus any constitutional powers of Congress over the matter." *Youngstown [Sheet & Tube Co. v. Sawyer,* 343 U.S. 579 (1952),] at 637 (Jackson, J., concurring). As the Supreme Court has recently explained, "[w]hether or not the President has independent power . . . he may not disregard limitations that Congress has, in proper exercise of its own war powers, placed on his powers." *Hamdan,* 126 S. Ct. at 2774 n.23 (citing *Youngstown,* 343 U.S. at 637 (Jackson, J., concurring)). In such cases, "Presidential claim[s]" to power "must be scrutinized with caution, for what is at stake is the equilibrium established by our constitutional system." *Youngstown,* 343 U.S. at 638 (Jackson, J., concurring). . . .

3.

In light of al-Marri's due process rights under our Constitution and Congress's express prohibition in the Patriot Act on the indefinite detention of those civilians arrested as "terrorist aliens" within this country, we can only conclude that, in the case at hand, the President claims power that far exceeds that granted him by the Constitution.

We do not question the President's wartime authority over enemy combatants, but absent suspension of the writ of habeas corpus, the Constitution simply does not provide the President the power to exercise military authority over civilians within the United States. *See Toth,* 350 U.S. at 14 ("[A]ssertion of military authority over civilians cannot rest on the President's power as commander-in-chief."). The President cannot eliminate constitutional protections with the stroke of a pen by proclaiming a civilian, even a criminal civilian, an enemy combatant subject to indefinite military detention. Put simply, the Constitution does not empower the President to order the military to seize civilians residing within the United States and detain them indefinitely without criminal process, and this is so even if he calls them "enemy combatants."

A "well-established purpose of the Founders" was "to keep the military strictly within its proper sphere, subordinate to civil authority." *Reid* [v. Covert, 354 U.S. 1, 30 (1957)]. In the Declaration of Independence, our forefathers lodged the complaint that the King of Great Britain had "affected to render the Military independent of and superior to the Civil power" and objected that the King had "depriv[ed] us in many cases, of the benefits of Trial by Jury." *The Declaration of Independence* paras. 14, 20 (U.S. 1776). Thus, a resolute conviction that civilian authority should govern the military animated the framing of the Constitution. As Alexander Hamilton, no foe of executive power, observed, the President's Commander-in-Chief powers "amount to nothing more than the supreme command and direction of the military and naval forces." The Federalist No. 69, at 386 (Alexander Hamilton) (Clinton Rossiter ed., 1961). "That military powers of the Commander in Chief were not to supersede representative government of *internal affairs* seems obvious from the Constitution and from elementary American history." *Youngstown,* 343 U.S. at 644 (Jackson, J., concurring) (emphasis added). For this reason, in *Youngstown,* the Supreme Court rejected the President's claim to "inherent power" to use the military even to seize property within the United States, despite the Government's argument that the refusal would "endanger the well-being and safety of the Nation." *Id.* at 584 (majority opinion). . . .

To sanction such presidential authority to order the military to seize and indefinitely detain civilians, even if the President calls them "enemy combatants," would have disastrous consequences for the Constitution – and the country. For a court to uphold a claim to such extraordinary power would do more than render lifeless the Suspension Clause, the Due Process Clause, and the rights to criminal process in the Fourth, Fifth, Sixth, and Eighth Amendments; it would effectively undermine all of the freedoms guaranteed by the Constitution. It is that power – were a court to recognize it – that could lead all our laws "to go unexecuted, and the government itself to go to pieces." We refuse to recognize a claim to power that would so alter the constitutional foundations of our Republic.

III. . . .

. . . We believe that it is unnecessary to litigate whether al-Marri is an enemy combatant, but joining in remand for the evidentiary proceedings outlined by Judge Traxler will at least place the burden on the Government to make an initial showing that normal due process protections are unduly burdensome and that the Rapp declaration is "the most reliable available evidence," supporting the Government's allegations before it may order al-Marri's military detention. Therefore, we concur in the per curiam opinion reversing and remanding for evidentiary proceedings to determine whether al-Marri actually is an enemy combatant subject to military detention.

Judges Michael, King, and Gregory have authorized me to indicate that they join in this opinion.

TRAXLER, Circuit Judge, concurring in the judgment: . . . I agree with my colleagues who hold that the AUMF . . . grants the President the power to detain enemy combatants in the war against al Qaeda, including belligerents who enter our country for the purpose of committing hostile and war-like acts such as those carried out by the al Qaeda operatives on 9/11. And, I agree that the allegations made by the government against al-Marri, if true, would place him within this category and permit the President to militarily detain him.

However, I depart from my dissenting colleagues on the issue of whether al-Marri has been afforded a fair opportunity to challenge the factual basis for his designation as an enemy combatant. Because the process afforded al-Marri by the district court to challenge the factual basis for his designation as an enemy combatant did not meet the minimal requirements of due process guaranteed by the Fifth Amendment, I would reverse the district court's dismissal of al-Marri's habeas petition and remand for further evidentiary proceedings on the issue of whether al-Marri is, in fact, an enemy combatant subject to military detention . . . .

II. The Authority to Detain. . . .

B.

Like my colleagues, I agree that neither *Hamdi* nor *Padilla* compels the conclusion that the AUMF authorized the President to detain al-Marri as an enemy combatant, although they do provide guidance. I disagree, however, that *Ex Parte Milligan,* 71 U.S. (4 Wall.) 2 (1866), compels the opposite conclusion. Having carefully considered these cases, as well as the Supreme Court's decision in *Quirin,* I am of the opinion that the AUMF also grants the President the authority to detain enemy combatants who associate themselves "with al Qaeda, an entity with which the United States is at war," and "travel[ ] to the United States for the avowed purpose of further prosecuting that war on American soil, against American citizens and targets," even though the government cannot establish that the combatant also "took up arms on behalf of that enemy and against our country in a *foreign* combat zone of that war." *Padilla,* 423 F.3d at 389 (emphasis added).

1. . . .

In my opinion . . . there is no doubt that individuals who are dispatched here by al Qaeda, the organization known to have carried out the 9/11 attacks upon our country, as sleeper agents and terrorist operatives charged with the task of committing additional attacks upon our homeland "are [also] individuals Congress sought to target in passing the AUMF." *Hamdi,* 542 U.S. at 518. Citing the right of the United States "to protect United States citizens *both at home and abroad,*" the AUMF authorized the President's use of "all necessary and appropriate force against" the nations *and organizations* that "planned, authorized, committed, or aided" the 9/11 attacks, "or harbored such organizations or persons, in order to prevent any future acts of international terrorism against the United States." 115 Stat. 224. Clearly, Congress was not merely authorizing military retaliation against a reigning foreign government known to have *supported* the enemy force that attacked us in our homeland, but was also authorizing military action against al Qaeda operatives who, like the 9/11 hijackers, were sent by the al Qaeda organization to the United States to conduct additional terror operations here.

As persuasively pointed out by the government, it was the 9/11 attacks which triggered the passage of the AUMF. The al Qaeda operatives who successfully carried out those attacks entered this country under false pretenses for the purpose of carrying out al Qaeda orders and, while finalizing the preparations for these attacks, maintained a facade of peaceful residence until the very moment they boarded the commercial airliners that they used as weapons. The hijackers never engaged in combat operations against our forces on a foreign battlefield. Yet al-Marri would have us rule that when Congress authorized the President to deal militarily with those responsible for the 9/11 attacks upon our country, it did not intend to authorize the President to deal militarily with al Qaeda operatives identically situated to the 9/11 hijackers. There is nothing in the language of the AUMF that suggests that Congress intended to limit the military response or the presidential authorization to acts occurring in foreign territories, and it strains reason to believe that Congress, in enacting the AUMF in the wake of those attacks, did *not* intend for it to encompass al Qaeda operatives standing in the exact position as the attackers who brought about its enactment. Furthermore, Congress has not revised or revoked the AUMF since its enactment or since the Supreme Court decided *Hamdi.*

I am also unpersuaded by the claim that because al Qaeda itself is an international terrorist organization instead of a "nation state" or "enemy government," the AUMF cannot apply, consistent with the laws of war and our constitutional guarantees, to such persons. The premise of that claim seems to be that because al Qaeda is not technically in control of an enemy nation or its government, it cannot be considered as anything other than a criminal organization whose members are entitled to all the protections and procedures granted by our constitution. I disagree.

In my view, al Qaeda is much more and much worse than a criminal organization. And while it may be an unconventional enemy force in a historical context, it is an enemy force nonetheless. The fact that it allied itself with an enemy government of a foreign nation only underscores this point, rendering attempts to distinguish its soldiers or operatives as something meaningfully different from military soldiers in service to the Taliban government (or al Qaeda operatives such as Hamdi and Padilla, who fought beside them) equally strained. The President attacked the Taliban in Afghanistan as *retaliation* for al Qaeda's strike upon our nation *because* al Qaeda was centralized there and allied with the Taliban, and it also strains credulity to assert that while we are legitimately at war with the Taliban government, we cannot be at war with al Qaeda. . . .

2.

If the allegations of the Rapp Declaration are true, I am also of the view that al-Marri would fall within the category of persons who may be lawfully detained pursuant to the authority granted by the AUMF. . . .

III. Due Process

While I agree with my colleagues who would hold that the President has the legal authority under the AUMF to detain al-Marri as an enemy combatant for the duration of the hostilities, we part company on the issue of whether the process afforded al-Marri to challenge his detention was sufficient to meet the minimum requirements of due process of law. In my opinion, due process demands more procedural safeguards than those provided to al-Marri in the habeas proceedings below. . . .

C. . . .

. . . [I]n my opinion, the district court erred in the initial step of accepting the hearsay affidavit of Rapp "as the most reliable available evidence from the [g]overnment," *id.* at 534, without any inquiry into whether the provision of nonhearsay evidence would unduly burden the government, and erred in failing to then weigh the competing interests of the litigants in light of the factual allegations and burdens placed before it for consideration.

1. . . .

Although I do not rule out the possibility that hearsay evidence might ultimately prove to be the most reliable available evidence from the government in this case, *Hamdi* does not support such a categorical relaxation of the protections due persons who are detained within our borders. . . . The *Hamdi* plurality's acceptance of hearsay evidence from the government in such settings . . . clearly arose from the context of a battlefield detainee, the "exigencies of [such] circumstances," and the "uncommon potential to burden the Executive at a time of ongoing military conflict." *Id.* at 533. The relaxed evidentiary standard was accepted in the balance as appropriate in light of the facts of that case – a person initially detained abroad by our allies on a battlefield in Afghanistan. The plurality rejected an outright disapproval of such hearsay declarations, and described lesser procedures it believed might be sufficient to satisfy the due process rights of such detainees, noting that the normal evidentiary requirements *might* need to be relaxed to account for the governmental interest in military matters. *See id.* at 533-34 (explaining that hearsay "*may* need to be accepted as the most reliable available evidence from the [g]overnment" and "a presumption in favor of the [g]overnment's evidence" would not "offend[ ]" the Constitution in battlefield detainee proceedings). But while the plurality refused to categorically prohibit hearsay declarations, neither did it categorically approve the use of such hearsay declarations in all enemy-combatant proceedings.[13] Hearsay declarations *may* be accepted upon a weighing of the burdens in time of warfare of "providing greater process" against the detainee's liberty interests. *Id.* at 529. But to decide

---

13. Thus, I do not believe *Hamdi* recognized that the government's burden in enemy-combatant proceedings could always be satisfied by a knowledgeable affiant who summarizes the evidence on which the detention was based. That is not what *Hamdi* said at all. Instead, the plurality merely noted that, in the context of the case before it, the Government had made it clear "that documentation regarding *battlefield detainees* already is kept in the ordinary court of military affairs" and that "[a]ny factfinding imposition created by requiring a knowledgeable affiant to summarize *these* records to an independent tribunal is a minimal one." *Hamdi,* 542 U.S. at 534 (emphasis added). For this reason, the *Hamdi* plurality was unpersuaded by the government's claim that "this basic process [would] have [a] dire impact on the central functions of warmaking." *Id.* I cannot read this language divorced from the context in which it was written and would demand no more than the same benefits/burdens analysis given to Hamdi.

whether a hearsay declaration is acceptable, the court must first take into account "the risk of erroneous deprivation" of the detainee's liberty interest, "the probable value, if any, of any additional or substitute procedural safeguards," and the availability of additional or substitute evidence which might serve the interests of both litigants. . . .

2.

In this case al-Marri's "private interest affected by the official action" is the same as that of Hamdi, *i.e.,* the liberty interest in being free from unlawful seizure and detention. *Hamdi,* 542 U.S. at 529. The risk of an erroneous deprivation of al-Marri's liberty interest, however, is not identical to the risk that was present in *Hamdi.* Al-Marri was not captured on the battlefields of Afghanistan or Iraq, nor even apprehended in a neighboring country where al Qaeda trains its soldiers. He was arrested by civilian federal authorities while residing in Illinois. I am acutely aware of the dangers of detention and imprisonment without compliance with criminal process safeguards, dangers that are even greater when the military detains persons inside the borders of the United States. In my view, the risk of erroneously detaining a civilian or citizen in this country as an enemy combatant is much greater inside the United States than in the very different context addressed by the Supreme Court in *Hamdi, i.e.,* a conventional battlefield within the borders of a foreign country in which we are fighting our enemies.

On the other hand, we must consider the government's interest "in detaining those who actually pose an immediate threat to the national security of the United States during ongoing international conflict," *Hamdi,* 542 U.S. at 530, and in "ensuring that those who have in fact fought with the enemy during a war do not return to battle against the United States," *id.* at 531, as well as "the burdens the [g]overnment would face in providing greater process," *id.* at 529.

Here, the government asserts that the Rapp Declaration, which summarizes the intelligence gathered on al-Marri's activities as an al Qaeda operative, is sufficient to meet its initial burden of proving that al-Marri was properly designated an enemy combatant. However, unlike in *Hamdi,* the government has presented *only* the Rapp Declaration. It has made no attempt to show that this hearsay evidence "need[s] to be accepted as the most reliable available evidence from the [g]overnment," *id.* at 533-34, or that additional protections to ensure that the innocent are not detained by our military would be "unworkable and inappropriate in th[is] enemy-combatant setting," *id.* at 535. Nor has there been any consideration of the "probable value, if any, of additional or substitute procedural safeguards" or the availability of more reliable evidence that might be presented by substitute methods which account for the government's weighty interests. *Id*. at 529.

. . . [A]l-Marri argued below that he believed the discovery [he] sought would be primarily from civilian agencies that could produce it without interfering with the war powers and war operations of this government. At a minimum, I believe the government should be required to demonstrate to the district court why this is not the case and why, in balancing the liberty interest of the detainee and the heightened risk of erroneous deprivation, the Rapp Declaration should be accepted as the most reliable available evidence the government can produce without undue burden or serious jeopardy to either its war efforts or its efforts to ensure the national security of this nation. . . .

GREGORY, Circuit Judge, concurring in the judgment [omitted].

WILLIAMS, Chief Judge, concurring in part and dissenting in part: . . .

I.

A. . . .

A distillation of [the *Milligan*, *Quirin*, and *Hamdi*] precedents, I believe, yields a definition of an enemy combatant subject to detention pursuant to Congressional authorizations as an individual who meets two criteria: (1) he attempts or engages in belligerent acts against the United States, either domestically or in a foreign combat zone; (2) on behalf of an enemy force.

Given the specific allegations against al-Marri, I have little difficulty concluding that he satisfies the first criterion. First, the allegations set forth in the Rapp Declaration, if true, clearly show that al-Marri was on United States soil to commit acts of belligerency against the United States. *See Quirin*, 317 U.S. at 31 (stating that unlawful combatants include those who commit "hostile acts involving destruction of life or property" on United States soil).

According to the Rapp Declaration, al-Marri also meets what I view as the second requirement of an enemy combatant: that the belligerent acts be carried out on behalf of an enemy force. Unlike the plurality, I cannot accept al-Marri's contention that because he allegedly has ties only to al Qaeda, a terrorist organization that does not control any nation, he does not meet this portion of the definition of enemy combatant.

The plurality opinion may very well be correct that, under the traditional "law of war," persons not affiliated with the military of a *nation-state* may not be considered enemy combatants. And I recognize the respect domestic courts have long afforded the "law of nations." *See Murray v. Schooner Charming Betsy*, 6 U.S. (2 Cranch) 64, 118 (1804) ("[A]n act of Congress ought never to be construed to violate the law of nations if any other possible construction remains."). Here, however, Congress has, through the AUMF, addressed precisely this question by clearly authorizing the President to use force against "organizations," as well as against nation-states. *See Padilla v. Hanft*, 423 F.3d 386, 395-96 (4th Cir. 2005) (noting "the AUMF constitutes . . . a clear statement" in favor of detention). As a specific and targeted congressional directive, the AUMF controls the question of who may be detained, for purposes of domestic law – at least with respect to those individuals that fall within its scope. . . .

I wish to emphasize that by permitting the President to militarily detain al-Marri pursuant to the AUMF I am not being expansive; in al-Marri we are dealing with someone *squarely* within the purposes of the AUMF, which was passed to target organizations, like al Qaeda, responsible for the September 11 attacks and to prevent future terrorist attacks. This case does not present what to me are more difficult issues regarding enemy combatants and the scope of AUMF, such as the status of an individual who joined al Qaeda after September 11, 2001, or an individual who is part of a designated foreign terrorist organization, that played no role in the September 11 attacks. Instead, al-Marri is clearly an "individual[ ] Congress sought to target in passing the AUMF." *Hamdi*, 542 U.S. at 518. In addition, while "indefinite detention" of enemy combatants is not permitted, *see generally Hamdi*, 542 U.S. at 519-20, we remain engaged against the forces of al Qaeda in the border regions of Afghanistan to this day. . . .

B. . . .

. . . I view section 412 of the Patriot Act to refer to the President's power, under Article II §3, to "take Care that the Laws be faithfully executed." U.S. Const., art. II, §3. The statute refers to the Attorney General, the President's agent in implementing the Take Care Clause, and it is found nestled within the immigration code. Fairly read, the Patriot Act does not therefore purport to limit the President's separate Commander-in-Chief power. But the authorization granted in the

AUMF, with its explicit reference to military force, relates to the Commander-in-Chief power. Whatever limitations are present in the Patriot Act, therefore, do not restrict the separate and distinct grant of power effected by the AUMF.

C.

I am left with a simple set of facts: the AUMF grants the President, who already has some inherent Article II power to wage war, *see, e.g., Chicago & S. Air Lines, Inc. v. Waterman S.S. Corp.,* 333 U.S. 103, 109 (1948) ("The President . . . possesses in his own right certain powers conferred by the Constitution on him as Commander-in-Chief and as the Nation's organ in foreign affairs."), the power to use necessary and appropriate force against organizations and persons with a role in the September 11 attacks; the Supreme Court has stated that military detention is a "fundamental incident of waging war," *Hamdi,* 542 U.S. at 519; and, the Government alleges that al-Marri has been a member of al Qaeda since at least 1996. I think it clear under these circumstances that al-Marri can be detained as an enemy combatant and agree with the separate opinions of Judge Traxler, Judge Wilkinson, and Judge Niemeyer that so hold. . . .

II.

I do not agree, however, with Judge Traxler's separate concurrence, which concludes that a remand is necessary to permit al-Marri to further challenge his detention. . . .

B. . . .

. . . I see nothing in *Hamdi* that forbids a sworn statement – like the Rapp Declaration – from providing sufficient "notice" of the allegations against al-Marri. Moreover. . . the magistrate judge required the Government to provide al-Marri the declaration in response to his request.

With respect to the Supreme Court's guidance that the process resemble customary habeas review, the procedures the magistrate judge proposed for handling the initial stage of the proceedings – which the district court later adopted in substantial part – in many ways mirrored traditional habeas practice under 28 U.S.C.A. §2254 and §2255 by requiring both parties to put forth affidavits and other materials for an initial determination of which party's presentation was more persuasive. . . .

Finally, and most importantly, *Hamdi* stressed the need for a "prudent" and "incremental" process. The magistrate judge proposed just that, outlining an iterative process in which al-Marri failed to participate "in any meaningful way." Indeed, as the magistrate judge noted, al-Marri refused to deny allegations in the Rapp Declaration that were peculiarly within al-Marri's knowledge. He failed to dispute even the assertion that he was performing poorly in school. It is simply beyond the pale for al-Marri to contend that he was unable, without further discovery from the Government, to put forth evidence that he did or did not attend class. By failing to participate, Al-Marri simply short-circuited the entire "incremental" process. . . .

Judge Duncan has authorized me to indicate that she joins in this opinion.

WILKINSON, Circuit Judge, concurring in part and dissenting in part: . . . There exists not only the obvious need to immobilize enemy combatants, particularly suspected terrorists; there are also often serious barriers to their criminal prosecution. To begin, the arrest of terror suspects will sometimes necessarily be based on evidence that does not meet the constitutional and statutory requirements of a traditional criminal proceeding. The "fog of war" creates confusion, and, in active combat zones such as Afghanistan and Iraq, it is often difficult to respect the evidentiary standards, such as an unbroken chain of custody, that are the hallmarks of criminal trials. In addition, it will often be implausible to allow a terror suspect to confront the witnesses against him because of the difficulties in having American combat personnel leave the front lines to testify. . . .

. . . [P]retrial protections afforded criminal defendants, such as a right to a speedy trial and the immediate assistance of counsel, may hinder the government's need to gather information that could save hundreds, if not thousands, of lives. While all agree that "indefinite detention for the purpose of interrogation" is not allowed, and torture must not be tolerated under any circumstance, this does not negate the fact that terror suspects are likely the "best source of information" on how to prevent future terrorist attacks. Obviously, this information will often be accessible only after interrogation. And interrogation, particularly effective non-torturesome interrogation, typically takes time and may necessitate "[h]olding a terrorist suspect incommunicado." Thus, even if the government has no plans to interrogate a terror suspect indefinitely, the criminal justice system may impede the ability to gather critical information, even in the short term, because of a criminal suspect's pretrial rights.

The problems presented by the criminal prosecution of terrorists are even more pronounced at trial . . . .

First, while a showcase of American values, an open and public criminal trial may also serve as a platform for suspected terrorists. Terror suspects may use the bully pulpit of a criminal trial in an attempt to recruit others to their cause. Likewise, terror suspects may take advantage of the opportunity to interact with others during trial to pass critical intelligence to their allies. For instance, before his appointment as Attorney General, former federal Judge Michael B. Mukasey recounted the story of how, "in the course of prosecuting Omar Abdel Rahman (the so-called 'blind sheik') and others for their role in the 1993 World Trade Center bombing and other crimes, the government was compelled . . . to turn over a list of unindicted coconspirators to the defendants." Michael B. Mukasey, *Jose Padilla Makes Bad Law*, WALL ST. J., Aug. 22, 2007, at A15. One of those coconspirators, it turns out, was Osama bin Laden. Within ten days, a copy of the list was in bin Laden's hands, "letting him know that his connection to that case had been discovered." *Id.*

Second, and relatedly, the prosecution of some terrorists could present security concerns of a different sort: witnesses and jurors may be subjected to threats of violence or become the targets of attack. . . .

Third, and finally, the plurality also neglects to discuss another serious concern: traditional criminal proceedings, especially public trials, may not be responsive to the executive's legitimate need to protect sensitive information. . . .

If such highly classified intelligence were disclosed to suspected terrorists, the consequences would be devastating. Any further use of that intelligence to either prevent future attacks or capture other suspected terrorists would be jeopardized, if not lost. Moreover, the loss of secrecy would place the sources of sensitive information in danger of reprisal. It is for these reasons that the Court has recognized that the "[g]overnment has a compelling interest in protecting . . . the secrecy of information important to our national security." *CIA v. Sims*, 471 U.S. 159, 175 (1985) (quoting *Snepp v. United States*, 444 U.S. 507(1980)).

However, the government's desire to protect such sensitive intelligence may conflict with a defendant's confrontation and compulsory process rights. By employing those rights, a terror suspect like al-Marri may, in a tactic commonly referred to as "graymail," request highly sensitive materials. Such a request leaves the government facing a Hobson's Choice. The government can withdraw all or part of its case to protect its information, or proceed and surrender its sensitive intelligence and possibly its source. And even if the government is able to suppress the defendant's request, defense counsel will be able to insinuate that the government is hiding information that is favorable to the defendant. . . .

. . . Congress may certainly take [such concerns] into account in deciding that the criminal justice system is not the sole permissible means of dealing with suspected terrorists. . . .

III . . .

[Judge Wilkinson here sets out three criteria for determining whom the government may detain within the United States as a suspected terrorist: The person must (1) be a member of (2) an organization or nation against whom Congress has declared war or authorized the use of military force, and (3) knowingly plans or engages in conduct that harms or aims to harm persons or property for the purpose of furthering the military goals of the enemy nation or organization.]

I first address the criterion of membership. While the traditional requirement of residency or other affiliation with an enemy nation still applies, the advent of enemy organizations requires a functional equivalent to residency for this new stateless actor. This is achieved by the requirement of membership in the enemy organization. Because membership may be considered more amorphous than residency or citizenship, it is important that there be identifiable facts that indicate such affiliation with the enemy organization. Such indicia of membership may include: self-identification with the organization through verbal or written statements; participation in the group's hierarchy or command structure; or knowingly taking overt steps to aid or participate in the organization's activities. Thus, for example, someone who sends money to "a nonprofit charity that feeds Afghan orphans" that unknowingly makes "its way to al Qaeda" would not be a member of the al Qaeda organization, and it is beyond hyperbole for the plurality to suggest otherwise. Furthermore, the membership requirement is important because it aids in distinguishing those who are the enemy from those who merely sympathize with the enemy.

The second criterion – congressional authorization – recognizes that Congress may authorize the use of military force against non-state actors, such as terrorist organizations, as it has already with the AUMF. By contemplating such authorization, this second criterion appropriately excludes from the category of "enemy" those persons or groups against whom Congress has not authorized the use of military force. Thus, the notion that any individual affiliated with an organization engaged in purported terrorist activities – such as the "environmental group" mentioned by the plurality – could be considered an enemy combatant is completely unfounded. For certain, there are many individuals and organizations engaged in unlawful conduct, and even terrorism. But most of these individuals and organizations have nothing to do with al Qaeda, its affiliates, or the September 11 attacks. Under this criterion, such persons would not be eligible for military detention under the AUMF. This is both consistent with our traditional conception of who should and should not be eligible for detention and appropriate in light of the constitutional imperative that military detention be the exception and not the rule. Indeed, not to require congressional authorization for such detentions in this country splits the ground beneath the war powers right in two.

If the first two criteria address who in modern warfare is the enemy, the third criterion addresses who is the combatant. Historically, this distinction has separated those with military aims from those who do not present a threat to opposing forces. Though yesterday's soldier has been replaced, at least in part, by those who eschew the conventions of lawful warfare, the purpose underlying this distinction remains unchanged. In light of today's realities, a "combatant" is a person who knowingly plans or engages in conduct that harms or aims to harm persons or property for the purpose of furthering the military goals of an enemy nation or organization. Like the first two criteria, this requirement closely tracks the relevant traditional law of war rules.

Under this criterion, those who use military-like force against American soldiers or civilians obviously qualify as combatants. Similarly, members of an enemy sleeper terrorist cell that have taken steps, even if preliminary in nature, toward an act of destruction are also considered combatants. Conversely, persons traditionally considered civilians, such as members of the enemy organization who do not possess hostile or military designs, are non-combatants and may not be detained by the military. This includes persons who would clearly be non-combatants, such as a "physician who treated a member of al Qaeda," because they intend no harm to persons or property. Such persons would not be subject to military detention.

Two further examples may help illustrate the scope of this framework. First is a person who joins a terrorist organization after Congress has authorized the use of military force against the respective group. In the present conflict, this would include new recruits to al Qaeda or its affiliates after 9/11. Under the above criteria, such persons are clearly part of the "enemy," even if they were not members of the targeted organization at the time Congress initially acted. This is because it was the organization and its affiliates, and not just the then-members of such groups, against whom Congress authorized the use of force. *See* AUMF, 115 Stat. 224 (authorizing the use of "all necessary and appropriate force against those . . . organizations [that] . . . committed" the 9/11 attacks, "in order to prevent any future acts of international terrorism"). Thus, in the current conflict, any "individual can become part of a covered 'organization' by joining it after the September 11 attacks." As a result, such a person, if also a combatant, would be eligible for military detention.

Second is a person who commits, or plans to commit, a terrorist act but is not otherwise affiliated with an organization or country covered by a congressional proclamation. Timothy McVeigh is one example that comes to mind. Because such a person is not a member of an enemy organization, he may not be detained as an enemy combatant under the above criteria. Indeed, Congress has never declared war against a single individual or even a discrete conspiracy (unless the Barbary pirates qualify), and it is difficult to envision a scenario in which it would. This is unsurprising, in part because prosecutions of individual terrorists do not ordinarily present the same sort of logistical, informational, and evidentiary problems as large scale terrorist networks or nations. . . .

. . . [U]nder these criteria, there are at least three significant limitations on the executive's ability to militarily detain persons lawfully residing in the United States.

First, there is the significant political check of congressional authorization. Specifically, absent some limited inherent authority needed during times of emergency, the executive may only detain those persons against whom Congress has authorized the use of force. If history is any indicator, Congress does not take such a decision lightly. Indeed, it was the dire events of September 11th that gave rise to the use of military force in the present instance, and it is likely that only emergencies of similar magnitude will trigger a similar response.

Second, even if Congress were to authorize the use of military force against a particular group, it would not be authorizing the executive to make a sweep on the basis of mere membership. This is because membership, without more, is not enough to qualify as an enemy combatant under my proposed criteria. Rather, the person in question must have taken steps to further the military goals of the organization.

Thus, McCarthy-like accusations of mere group membership would not suffice as a basis for detention.

Third, persons subject to military detention are afforded the opportunity to challenge the accuracy of their detention before a neutral decisionmaker in accordance with the framework articulated in *Hamdi*. This ensures that the government possesses sufficient evidence to justify a measure as serious as military detention. . . .

[The opinion of NIEMEYER, Circuit Judge, concurring in the judgment in part and dissenting in part, is omitted].

[The opinion of DUNCAN, Circuit Judge, concurring in part and dissenting in part, is omitted].

[NSL p. 758, CTL p. 398. Insert after *Al-Marri v. Pucciarelli.*]

Al-Marri v. Spagone
United States Supreme Court, 2009
129 S. Ct. 1545

Case below, *al-Marri v. Pucciarelli*, 534 F.3d 213.

Application of the Acting Solicitor General respecting the custody and transfer of petitioner, seeking to release petitioner from military custody and transfer him to the custody of the Attorney General granted. Judgment vacated, and case remanded to the United States Court of Appeals for the Fourth Circuit with instructions to dismiss the appeal as moot. *See United States v. Munsingwear, Inc.*, 340 U.S. 36 (1950).

[NSL p. 758, CTL p. 398. Insert after *Al-Marri v. Spagone.*]

Al-Bihani v. Obama
United States Court of Appeals, District of Columbia Circuit, 2010
590 F.3d 866

BROWN, Circuit Judge: Ghaleb Nassar Al-Bihani . . . a Yemeni citizen, has been held at the U.S. naval base detention facility in Guantanamo Bay, Cuba since 2002. He came to Guantanamo by a circuitous route. It began in Saudi Arabia in the first half of 2001 when a local sheikh issued a religious challenge to Al-Bihani. In response, Al-Bihani traveled through Pakistan to Afghanistan eager to defend the Taliban's Islamic state against the Northern Alliance. Along the way, he stayed at what the government alleges were Al Qaeda-affiliated guesthouses; Al-Bihani only concedes they were affiliated with the Taliban. During this transit period, he may also have received instruction at two Al Qaeda terrorist training camps, though Al-Bihani disputes this. What he does not dispute is that he eventually accompanied and served a paramilitary group allied with the Taliban, known as the 55th Arab Brigade, which included Al Qaeda members within its command structure and which fought on the front lines against the Northern Alliance. He worked as the brigade's cook and carried a brigade-issued weapon, but never fired it in combat. Combat, however – in the form of bombing by the U.S.-led Coalition that invaded Afghanistan in response to the attacks of September 11, 2001 – forced the 55th to retreat from the front lines in October 2001. At the end of this protracted retreat, Al-Bihani and the rest of the brigade surrendered, under orders, to Northern Alliance forces, and they kept him in custody until his handover to U.S. Coalition forces in early 2002. The U.S. military sent Al-Bihani to Guantanamo for detention and interrogation.

After the Supreme Court held in *Rasul v. Bush,* 542 U.S. 466, 483-84 (2004), that the statutory habeas jurisdiction of federal courts extended to Guantanamo Bay, Al-Bihani filed a habeas petition with the U.S. District Court for the District of Columbia, challenging his detention under 28 U.S.C. §2241(a). . . . [Then, following the Supreme Court's decision in *Boumediene v. Bush,* 128 S. Ct. 2229 (2008), the district court issued a case management order ruling] that the government had the burden of proving the legality of Al-Bihani's detention by a preponderance of the evidence; it obligated the government to explain the legal basis for Al-Bihani's detention, to share all documents used in its factual return, and to turn over any exculpatory evidence found in preparation of its case. [*Al-Bihani v. Bush* (CMO), 588 F. Supp. 2d 19 (D.D.C. 2008).] . . . The order reserved the district court's discretion, when appropriate, to adopt a rebuttable presumption in favor of the accuracy of the government's evidence and to admit relevant and material hearsay, the credibility and weight of which the opposing party could challenge. . . .

. . . [T]he district court denied Al-Bihani's petition. Adopting a definition that allowed the government to detain anyone "who was part of or supporting Taliban or al Qaeda forces, or associated forces that are engaged in hostilities against the United States or its coalition partners," the district court found Al-Bihani's actions met the standard. *See Al-Bihani v. Obama* (Mem. Op.), 594 F. Supp. 2d 35, 38, 40 (D.D.C. 2009). It cited as sufficiently credible the evidence – primarily drawn from Al-Bihani's own admissions during interrogation – that Al-Bihani

stayed at Al Qaeda-affiliated guesthouses and that he served in and
retreated with the 55th Arab Brigade. The district court declined to rely
on evidence drawn from admissions – later recanted by Al-Bihani – that
he attended Al Qaeda training camps on his way to the front lines. . . .

II

Al-Bihani's many arguments present this court with two overarching
questions regarding the detainees at the Guantanamo Bay naval base.
The first concerns whom the President can lawfully detain pursuant to
statutes passed by Congress. The second asks what procedure is due to
detainees challenging their detention in habeas corpus proceedings. The
Supreme Court has provided scant guidance on these questions,
consciously leaving the contours of the substantive and procedural law of
detention open for lower courts to shape in a common law fashion. *See
Hamdi v. Rumsfeld,* 542 U.S. 507, 522 n.1 (2004) (plurality opinion of
O'Connor, J.) ("The permissible bounds of the [enemy combatant]
category will be defined by the lower courts as subsequent cases are
presented to them."); *Boumediene,* 128 S. Ct. at 2276 ("We make no
attempt to anticipate all of the evidentiary and access-to-counsel issues . . .
and the other remaining questions [that] are within the expertise and
competence of the District Court to address in the first instance."). In this
decision, we aim to narrow the legal uncertainty that clouds military
detention.

A

Al-Bihani challenges the statutory legitimacy of his detention by
advancing a number of arguments based upon the international laws of
war. He first argues that relying on "support," or even "substantial
support" of Al Qaeda or the Taliban as an independent basis for
detention violates international law. As a result, such a standard should
not be read into the ambiguous provisions of the Authorization for Use
of Military Force (AUMF), Pub. L. No. 107-40, §2(a), 115 Stat. 224, 224
(2001), the Act empowering the President to respond to the attacks of
September 11, 2001. Al-Bihani interprets international law to mean
anyone not belonging to an official state military is a civilian, and
civilians, he says, must commit a direct hostile act, such as firing a
weapon in combat, before they can be lawfully detained. Because
Al-Bihani did not commit such an act, he reasons his detention is
unlawful. Next, he argues the members of the 55th Arab Brigade were

not subject to attack or detention by U.S. Coalition forces under the laws of co-belligerency because the 55th, although allied with the Taliban against the Northern Alliance, did not have the required opportunity to declare its neutrality in the fight against the United States. His third argument is that the conflict in which he was detained, an international war between the United States and Taliban-controlled Afghanistan, officially ended when the Taliban lost control of the Afghan government. Thus, absent a determination of future dangerousness, he must be released. *See* Geneva Convention Relative to the Treatment of Prisoners of War (Third Geneva Convention) art. 118, Aug. 12, 1949, 6 U.S.T. 3316, 75 U.N.T.S. 135. Lastly, Al-Bihani posits a type of "clean hands" theory by which any authority the government has to detain him is undermined by its failure to accord him the prisoner-of-war status to which he believes he is entitled by international law.

Before considering these arguments in detail, we note that all of them rely heavily on the premise that the war powers granted by the AUMF and other statutes are limited by the international laws of war. This premise is mistaken. There is no indication in the AUMF, the Detainee Treatment Act of 2005 [DTA], Pub. L. No. 109-148, div. A, tit. X, 119 Stat. 2739, 2741-43, or the MCA of 2006 or 2009 [Military Commissions Act of 2006, Pub. L. No. 109-366, 120 Stat. 2600; Military Commissions Act of 2009, Pub. L. No. 111-84, 123 Stat. 2190], that Congress intended the international laws of war to act as extra-textual limiting principles for the President's war powers under the AUMF. The international laws of war as a whole have not been implemented domestically by Congress and are therefore not a source of authority for U.S. courts. *See* RESTATEMENT (THIRD) OF FOREIGN RELATIONS LAW OF THE UNITED STATES §111(3)-(4) (1987). Even assuming Congress had at some earlier point implemented the laws of war as domestic law through appropriate legislation, Congress had the power to authorize the President in the AUMF and other later statutes to exceed those bounds. *See id.* §115(1)(a). Further weakening their relevance to this case, the international laws of war are not a fixed code. Their dictates and application to actual events are by nature contestable and fluid. *See id.* §102 cmts. b & c (stating there is "no precise formula" to identify a practice as custom and that "[i]t is often difficult to determine when [a custom's] transformation into law has taken place"). Therefore, while the international laws of war are helpful to courts when identifying the general set of war powers to which the AUMF speaks, *see Hamdi,* 542 U.S. at 520, their lack of controlling legal force and firm definition render their use both inapposite and inadvisable when courts seek to determine the limits of the President's war powers.

Therefore, putting aside that we find Al-Bihani's reading of international law to be unpersuasive, we have no occasion here to quibble over the intricate application of vague treaty provisions and amorphous customary principles. The sources we look to for resolution of Al-Bihani's case are the sources courts always look to: the text of relevant statutes and controlling domestic case law.

Under those sources, Al-Bihani is lawfully detained . . . . The statutes authorizing the use of force and detention not only grant the government the power to craft a workable legal standard to identify individuals it can detain, but also cabin the application of these definitions. The AUMF authorizes the President to "use all necessary and appropriate force against those nations, organizations, or persons he determines planned, authorized, committed, or aided the terrorist attacks that occurred on September 11, 2001, or harbored such organizations or persons." AUMF §2(a). The Supreme Court in *Hamdi* ruled that "necessary and appropriate force" includes the power to detain combatants subject to such force. 542 U.S. at 519. Congress, in the 2006 MCA, provided guidance on the class of persons subject to detention under the AUMF by defining "unlawful enemy combatants" who can be tried by military commission. 2006 MCA sec. 3, §948a(1). The 2006 MCA authorized the trial of an individual who "engaged in hostilities or who has purposefully and materially supported hostilities against the United States or its co-belligerents who is not a lawful enemy combatant (including a person who is part of the Taliban, al Qaeda, or associated forces)." *Id.* §948a(1)(A)(i). In 2009, Congress enacted a new version of the MCA with a new definition that authorized the trial of "unprivileged enemy belligerents," a class of persons that includes those who "purposefully and materially supported hostilities against the United States or its coalition partners." Military Commissions Act of 2009 sec. 1802, §§948a(7), 948b(a), 948c, 123 Stat. 2575-76. The provisions of the 2006 and 2009 MCAs are illuminating in this case because the government's detention authority logically covers a category of persons no narrower than is covered by its military commission authority. Detention authority in fact sweeps wider, also extending at least to traditional P.O.W.s, *see id.* §948a(6), and arguably to other categories of persons. But for this case, it is enough to recognize that any person subject to a military commission trial is also subject to detention, and that category of persons includes those who are part of forces associated with Al Qaeda or the

Taliban or those who purposefully and materially support such forces in hostilities against U.S. Coalition partners.

In light of these provisions of the 2006 and 2009 MCAs, the facts that were both found by the district court and offered by Al-Bihani . . . place Al-Bihani within the "part of" and "support" prongs of the relevant statutory definition. . . . His acknowledged actions – accompanying the brigade on the battlefield, carrying a brigade-issued weapon, cooking for the unit, and retreating and surrendering under brigade orders – strongly suggest, in the absence of an official membership card, that he was part of the 55th. Even assuming, as he argues, that he was a civilian "contractor" rendering services, those services render Al-Bihani detainable under the "purposefully and materially supported" language of both versions of the MCA. That language constitutes a standard whose outer bounds are not readily identifiable. But wherever the outer bounds may lie, they clearly include traditional food operations essential to a fighting force and the carrying of arms. Viewed in full, the facts show Al-Bihani was part of and supported a group – prior to and after September 11 – that was affiliated with Al Qaeda and Taliban forces and engaged in hostilities against a U.S. Coalition partner. Al-Bihani, therefore, falls squarely within the scope of the President's statutory detention powers.[2]

The government can also draw statutory authority to detain Al-Bihani directly from the language of the AUMF. The AUMF authorizes force against those who "harbored . . . organizations or persons" the President determines "planned, authorized, committed, or aided the terrorist attacks of September 11, 2001." AUMF §2(a). It is not in dispute that Al Qaeda is the organization responsible for September 11 or that it was harbored by the Taliban in Afghanistan. It is also not in dispute that the 55th Arab Brigade defended the Taliban against the Northern Alliance's efforts to oust the regime from power. Drawing from these facts, it cannot be disputed that the actual and foreseeable result of the 55th's defense of the Taliban was the maintenance of Al Qaeda's safe haven in Afghanistan. This result places the 55th within the AUMF's

---

2. In reaching this conclusion, we need not rely on the evidence suggesting that Al-Bihani attended Al Qaeda training camps in Afghanistan and visited Al Qaeda guesthouses. We do note, however, that evidence supporting the military's reasonable belief of either of those two facts with respect to a non-citizen seized abroad during the ongoing war on terror would seem to overwhelmingly, if not definitively, justify the government's detention of such a non-citizen. *Cf.* NAT'L COMM'N ON TERRORIST ATTACKS UPON THE UNITED STATES, THE 9/11 COMMISSION REPORT 66-67.

wide ambit as an organization that harbored Al Qaeda, making it subject
to U.S. military force and its members and supporters – including
Al-Bihani – eligible for detention. . . .

With the government's detention authority established as an initial
matter, we turn to the argument that Al-Bihani must now be released
according to longstanding law of war principles because the conflict with
the Taliban has allegedly ended. *See Hamdi*, 542 U.S. at 521. Al-Bihani
offers the court a choice of numerous event dates – the day Afghans
established a post-Taliban interim authority, the day the United States
recognized that authority, the day Hamid Karzai was elected President –
to mark the official end of the conflict. No matter which is chosen, each
would dictate the release of Al-Bihani if we follow his reasoning. His
argument fails on factual and practical grounds. First, it is not clear if
Al-Bihani was captured in the conflict with the Taliban or with Al
Qaeda; he does not argue that the conflict with Al Qaeda is over. Second,
there are currently 34,800 U.S. troops and a total of 71,030 Coalition
troops in Afghanistan, with tens of thousands more to be added soon.
The principle Al-Bihani espouses – were it accurate – would make each
successful campaign of a long war but a Pyrrhic prelude to defeat. The
initial success of the United States and its Coalition partners in ousting
the Taliban from the seat of government and establishing a young
democracy would trigger an obligation to release Taliban fighters
captured in earlier clashes. Thus, the victors would be commanded to
constantly refresh the ranks of the fledgling democracy's most likely
saboteurs. . . .

Even so, we do not rest our resolution of this issue on international
law or mere common sense. The determination of when hostilities have
ceased is a political decision, and we defer to the Executive's opinion on
the matter, at least in the absence of an authoritative congressional
declaration purporting to terminate the war. *See Ludecke v. Watkins*, 335
U.S. 160, 168-70 & n.13 (1948) ("[T]ermination [of a state of war] is a
political act."). . . . In the absence of a determination by the political
branches that hostilities in Afghanistan have ceased, Al-Bihani's
continued detention is justified.

Al-Bihani also argues he should be released because the
government's failure to accord him P.O.W. status violated international
law and undermined its otherwise lawful authority to detain him. Even
assuming Al-Bihani is entitled to P.O.W. status, we find no controlling
authority for this "clean hands" theory in statute or in caselaw. The
AUMF, DTA, and MCA of 2006 and 2009 do not hinge the
government's detention authority on proper identification of P.O.W.s or

compliance with international law in general. In fact, the MCA of 2006, in a provision not altered by the MCA of 2009, explicitly precludes detainees from claiming the Geneva conventions – which include criteria to determine who is entitled to P.O.W. status – as a source of rights. *See* 2006 MCA sec. 5(a). . . .

B

We now turn to Al-Bihani's procedural challenge. He claims the habeas process afforded him by the district court fell short of the requirements of the Suspension Clause and that his case should be remanded for rehearing in line with new, more protective procedures. The Supreme Court in *Boumediene* held detainees are entitled to the "fundamental procedural protections of habeas corpus." 128 S. Ct. at 2277. The *Boumediene* Court refrained from identifying the full list of procedures that are fundamental, but it did say that a petitioner is entitled to "a meaningful opportunity to demonstrate that he is being held pursuant to the erroneous application or interpretation of relevant law," and that "the habeas court must have the power to order the conditional release" of the petitioner. *Id.* at 2266. Meaningful review in this context requires that a court have "some authority to assess the sufficiency of the Government's evidence against the detainee" and to "admit and consider relevant exculpatory evidence" that may be added to the record by petitioners during review. *Id.* at 2270.

Drawing upon *Boumediene's* holding, Al-Bihani challenges numerous aspects of the habeas procedure devised by the district court. He claims the district court erred by: (1) adopting a preponderance of the evidence standard of proof; (2) shifting the burden to him to prove the unlawfulness of his detention; (3) neglecting to hold a separate evidentiary hearing; (4) admitting hearsay evidence; (5) presuming the accuracy of the government's evidence; (6) requiring him to explain why his discovery request would not unduly burden the government; and (7) denying all but one of his discovery requests. In support of these claims, Al-Bihani cites statutes prescribing habeas procedure for review of federal and state court convictions and analogizes to a number of cases concerning review of detentions related to criminal prosecutions. By referencing these sources, Al-Bihani traces the district court's supposed errors to its failure to accord him procedural parity with safeguards found in review of criminal proceedings.

Al-Bihani's argument clearly demonstrates error, but that error is his own. Habeas review for Guantanamo detainees need not match the procedures developed by Congress and the courts specifically for habeas challenges to criminal convictions. *Boumediene's* holding explicitly stated that habeas procedures for detainees "need not resemble a criminal trial," 128 S. Ct. at 2269. It instead invited "innovation" of habeas procedure by lower courts, granting leeway for "[c]ertain accommodations [to] be made to reduce the burden habeas corpus proceedings will place on the military." *Id.* at 2276. *Boumediene's* holding therefore places Al-Bihani's procedural argument on shaky ground. The Suspension Clause protects only the fundamental character of habeas proceedings, and any argument equating that fundamental character with all the accoutrements of habeas for domestic criminal defendants is highly suspect.

. . . [I]n the shadow of *Boumediene,* courts are neither bound by the procedural limits created for other detention contexts nor obliged to use them as baselines from which any departures must be justified. Detention of aliens outside the sovereign territory of the United States during wartime is a different and peculiar circumstance, and the appropriate habeas procedures cannot be conceived of as mere extensions of an existing doctrine. Rather, those procedures are a whole new branch of the tree. . . .

. . . Al-Bihani is a non-citizen who was seized in a foreign country. Requiring highly protective procedures at the tail end of the detention process for detainees like Al-Bihani would have systemic effects on the military's entire approach to war. From the moment a shot is fired, to battlefield capture, up to a detainee's day in court, military operations would be compromised as the government strove to satisfy evidentiary standards in anticipation of habeas litigation. . . .

With Al-Bihani's limited procedural entitlement established as a general matter, we turn to the specific procedural claims warranting serious consideration. The question of what standard of proof is due in a habeas proceeding like Al-Bihani's has not been answered by the Supreme Court. *See Boumediene,* 128 S. Ct. at 2271 ("The extent of the showing required of the Government in these cases is a matter to be determined."). Attempting to fill this void, Al-Bihani argues the prospect of indefinite detention in this unconventional war augurs for a reasonable doubt standard or, in the alternative, at least a clear and convincing standard. The government disagrees, arguing that *Hamdi's* plurality opinion indirectly endorsed a preponderance standard when it suggested due process requirements may have been satisfied by a military tribunal, the regulations of which adopt a preponderance standard.

We believe the government's argument stands on more solid ground. In addition to the *Hamdi* plurality's approving treatment of military tribunal procedure, it also described as constitutionally adequate – even for the detention of U.S. citizens – a "burden-shifting scheme" in which the government need only present "credible evidence that the habeas petitioner meets the enemy-combatant criteria" before "the onus could shift to the petitioner to rebut that evidence with more persuasive evidence that he falls outside the criteria." *Hamdi,* 542 U.S. at 533-34. That description mirrors a preponderance standard. . . .

. . . [T]raditional habeas review did not entail review of factual findings, particularly in the military context. *See In re Yamashita,* 327 U.S. 1, 8 (1946) ("If the military tribunals have lawful authority to hear, decide and condemn, their action is not subject to judicial review merely because they have made a wrong decision on disputed facts."). Where factual review has been authorized, the burden in some domestic circumstances has been placed *on the petitioner* to prove his case under a clear and convincing standard. *See* 28 U.S.C. §2254(e)(1) (regulating federal review of state court factual findings). If it is constitutionally permissible to place that higher burden on a citizen petitioner in a routine case, it follows a priori that placing a lower burden on the government defending a wartime detention – where national security interests are at their zenith and the rights of the alien petitioner at their nadir – is also permissible.

We find Al-Bihani's hearsay challenges to be similarly unavailing. Al-Bihani claims that government reports of his interrogation answers – which made up the majority, if not all, of the evidence on which the district court relied – and other informational documents were hearsay improperly admitted absent an examination of reliability and necessity. He contends, in fact, that government reports of his interrogation answers were *"double* hearsay" because his answers were first translated by an interpreter and then written down by an interrogator. We first note that Al-Bihani's interrogation answers themselves were not hearsay; they were instead party-opponent admissions that would have been admitted in any U.S. court. *See* FED. R. EVID. 801(d)(2)(A). That they were translated does not affect their status. *See United States v. Da Silva,* 725 F.2d 828, 831-32 (2d Cir. 1983). However, that the otherwise admissible answers were relayed through an interrogator's account does introduce a level of technical hearsay because the interrogator is a third party unavailable for cross examination. Other information, such as a diagram of Al Qaeda's leadership structure, was also hearsay.

But that such evidence was hearsay does not automatically invalidate its admission – it only begins our inquiry. We observe Al-Bihani cannot make the traditional objection based on the Confrontation Clause of the Sixth Amendment. This is so because the Confrontation Clause applies only in criminal prosecutions, *see* U.S. CONST. amend. VI, and is not directly relevant to the habeas setting, *cf.* 28 U.S.C. §2246 (granting discretion to habeas judge to admit affidavits into evidence). The Confrontation Clause seeks to ensure the reliability of evidence, but it also seeks to eliminate the ephemeral perception of unfairness associated with the use of hearsay evidence. *See Coy v. Iowa,* 487 U.S. 1012, 1017-19 (1988). Al-Bihani, however, does not enjoy a right to the psychic value of excluding hearsay and whatever right he has is not an independent procedural entitlement. Rather, it operates only to the extent that it provides the baseline level of evidentiary reliability necessary for the "meaningful" habeas proceeding *Boumediene* requires under the Suspension Clause. *See* 128 S. Ct. at 2266.

Therefore, the question a habeas court must ask when presented with hearsay is not whether it is admissible – it is always admissible – but what probative weight to ascribe to whatever indicia of reliability it exhibits. This approach is evident in the relevant caselaw. *Boumediene* did not say exactly how a habeas court should treat hearsay, but it broadly required that a court be able to "assess the sufficiency of the Government's evidence." *Id.* at 2270. In *Hamdi,* the Supreme Court said hearsay "may need to be accepted as the most reliable available evidence" as long as the petitioner is given the opportunity to rebut that evidence. *See* 542 U.S. at 533-34. . . .

A procedure that seeks to determine hearsay's reliability instead of its mere admissibility comports not only with the requirements of this novel circumstance, but also with the reality that district judges are experienced and sophisticated fact finders. Their eyes need not be protected from unreliable information in the manner the Federal Rules of Evidence aim to shield the eyes of impressionable juries. Where the touchstone of a proceeding is "meaningfulness," empowering a district court to review and assess all evidence from both sides is a logical process. It is one that bolsters the traditional power of the habeas court to "cut[ ] through all forms and go[ ] to the very tissue of the structure" of a proceeding and "look facts in the face." *Frank v. Mangum,* 237 U.S. 309, 346, 349 (1915) (Holmes, J., dissenting). . . . [I]n a detainee case, the judge acts as a neutral decisionmaker charged with seizing the actual truth of a simple, binary question: is detention lawful? This is why the one constant in the history of habeas has never been a certain set of procedures, but rather the independent power of a judge to assess the actions of the Executive. This primacy of independence over process is at the center of the *Boumediene* opinion, which eschews prescribing a detailed procedural regime in favor of issuing a spare but momentous guarantee that a "judicial officer must have adequate authority to make a determination in light of the relevant law and facts." *Boumediene,* 128 S. Ct. at 2271.

In Al-Bihani's case, the district court clearly reserved that authority in its process and assessed the hearsay evidence's reliability as required by the Supreme Court. First, the district court retained the authority to assess the weight of the evidence. Second, the district court had ample contextual information about evidence in the government's factual return to determine what weight to give various pieces of evidence. Third, the district court afforded Al-Bihani the opportunity . . . to rebut the evidence and to attack its credibility. Further, Al-Bihani did not contest the truth of the majority of his admissions upon which the district court relied, enhancing the reliability of those reports. We therefore find that the district court did not improperly admit hearsay evidence.

The rest of Al-Bihani's procedural claims can be disposed of without extended discussion. His claim that the burden of proof was placed on him is based on a strained reading of the hearing transcript that twists and magnifies questions asked by the judge. This claim has no merit and we need not consider it further. Likewise, Al-Bihani's claim that an evidentiary hearing was denied to him in violation of his right to a hearing is groundless. First, while courts reviewing state or federal court decisions have the discretion to grant fact hearings upon a proper showing by a petitioner, Al-Bihani cites no authority that a petitioner in his position is entitled to such a hearing as of right. Second, it is clear from the CMO and the transcript of the full habeas hearing that the district court did hear the facts of Al-Bihani's case and provided ample opportunity in conference and in a hearing for the parties to air concerns over evidence. To the extent that Al-Bihani possesses any right to a hearing to develop facts or argue evidentiary issues, it was satisfied by the district court's procedure. . . .

III

Al-Bihani's detention is authorized by statute and there was no constitutional defect in the district court's habeas procedure that would have affected the outcome of the proceeding. For these reasons, the order of the district court denying Al-Bihani's petition for a writ of habeas corpus is

Affirmed.

BROWN, Circuit Judge, concurring: The Supreme Court in *Boumediene* and *Hamdi* charged this court and others with the unprecedented task of developing rules to review the propriety of military actions during a time of war, relying on common law tools. We are fortunate this case does not require us to demarcate the law's full substantive and procedural dimensions. But as other more difficult cases arise, it is important to ask whether a court-driven process is best suited to protecting both the rights of petitioners and the safety of our nation. The common law process depends on incrementalism and eventual correction, and it is most effective where there are a significant number of cases brought before a large set of courts, which in turn enjoy the luxury of time to work the doctrine supple. None of those factors exist in the Guantanamo context. The number of Guantanamo detainees is limited and the circumstances of their confinement are unique. The petitions they file, as the *Boumediene* Court counseled, are funneled through one federal district court and one appellate court. And, in the midst of an ongoing war, time to entertain a process of literal trial and error is not a luxury we have.

While the common law process presents these difficulties, it is important to note that the Supreme Court has not foreclosed Congress from establishing new habeas standards in line with its *Boumediene* opinion. . . . [T]he circumstances that frustrate the judicial process are the same ones that make this situation particularly ripe for Congress to intervene pursuant to its policy expertise, democratic legitimacy, and oath to uphold and defend the Constitution. These cases present hard questions and hard choices, ones best faced directly. Judicial review, however, is just that: *re*-view, an indirect and necessarily backward looking process. And looking backward may not be enough in this new war. The saying that generals always fight the last war is familiar, but familiarity does not dull the maxim's sober warning. In identifying the shape of the law in response to the challenge of the current war, it is incumbent on the President, Congress, and the courts to realize that the saying's principle applies to us as well. Both the rule of law and the nation's safety will benefit from an honest assessment of the new challenges we face, one that will produce an appropriately calibrated response.

Absent such action, much of what our Constitution requires for this context remains unsettled. In this case, I remain mindful that the conflict in which Al-Bihani was captured was only one phase of hostilities between the United States and Islamic extremists. The legal issues presented by our nation's fight with this enemy have been numerous, difficult, and to a large extent novel. What drives these issues is the unconventional nature of our enemy: they are neither soldiers nor mere criminals, claim no national affiliation, and adopt long-term strategies and asymmetric tactics that exploit the rules of open societies without respect or reciprocity.

War is a challenge to law, and the law must adjust. It must recognize that the old wineskins of international law, domestic criminal procedure, or other prior frameworks are ill-suited to the bitter wine of this new warfare. We can no longer afford diffidence. This war has placed us not just at, but already past the leading edge of a new and frightening paradigm, one that demands new rules be written. Falling back on the comfort of prior practices supplies only illusory comfort.

WILLIAMS, Senior Circuit Judge, concurring in part and concurring in the judgment: I agree with the majority's decision to affirm the district court's denial of Al Bihani's petition for a writ of habeas corpus. I take a slightly different view of the central substantive issue in this case, and a significantly different view as to the necessity of reaching any of Al Bihani's procedural arguments. For purposes of both my analysis and the majority's, the petitioner has conceded facts that render his detention lawful – thereby obviating any need to discuss the constitutionality of the district court's factfinding process. . . .

The petitioner's detention is legally permissible by virtue of facts that he himself has conceded. . . .

. . . [T]he AUMF clearly authorized the President to attack the 55th Brigade. By its terms, the AUMF allows force against "organizations" that "harbored" those who were responsible for the 9/11 attacks. The 55th Brigade fought to preserve the Taliban regime in Afghanistan even as the Taliban was harboring al Qaeda in Afghanistan. This makes the 55th Brigade, itself, an organization that "harbored" al Qaeda within the meaning of the AUMF. . . .

Because the 55th Brigade was properly the target of U.S. force in Afghanistan pursuant to the AUMF, it follows that members of the 55th Brigade taken into custody on the battlefield in Afghanistan in the fall of 2001 may be detained "for the duration of the particular conflict in which they were captured." *See* [*Boumediene*, 128 S. Ct.] at 2241. . . .

Within the portion of the opinion addressing the petitioner's substantive argument that his activities in Afghanistan do not put him in the class of people whom the President may detain pursuant to the AUMF, the majority unnecessarily addresses a number of other points. Most notable is the paragraph that begins "Before considering these arguments in detail," and that reaches the conclusion that "the premise that the war powers granted by the AUMF and other statutes are limited by the international laws of war . . . is mistaken." The paragraph appears hard to square with the approach that the Supreme Court took in *Hamdi.* See 542 U.S. at 521 (O'Connor, J.) (plurality opinion) ("[W]e understand Congress' grant of authority for the use of 'necessary and appropriate force' to include the authority to detain for the duration of the relevant conflict, and our understanding is based on longstanding law-of-war principles."); *id.* at 548-49 (Souter, J., opinion concurring in part and dissenting in part) (advocating a more substantial role for the laws of war in interpretations of the President's authority under the AUMF). In any event, there is no need for the court's pronouncements, divorced from application to any particular argument. Curiously, the majority's dictum goes well beyond what even the *government* has argued in this case.

Because the petitioner's detention is lawful by virtue of facts that he has conceded – a conclusion that the majority seems not to dispute – the majority's analysis of the constitutionality of the *procedures* the district court used is unnecessary. . . .

[NSL p. 758, CTL p. 398. Insert after *Al-Bihani v. Obama.*]

Remarks by President Barack Obama
Protecting Our Security and Our Values
National Archives, Washington, D.C.
May 21, 2009

. . .

Now let me be clear: we are indeed at war with al Qaeda and its affiliates. We do need to update our institutions to deal with this threat. But we must do so with an abiding confidence in the rule of law and due process; in checks and balances and accountability. For reasons that I will explain, the decisions that were made over the last eight years established an ad hoc legal approach for fighting terrorism that was neither effective nor sustainable – a framework that failed to rely on our legal traditions and time-tested institutions; that failed to use our values as a compass. And that is why I took several steps upon taking office to better protect the American people.

First, I banned the use of so-called enhanced interrogation techniques by the United States of America. . . .

The second decision that I made was to order the closing of the prison camp at Guantanamo Bay.

For over seven years, we have detained hundreds of people at Guantanamo. During that time, the system of Military Commissions at Guantanamo succeeded in convicting a grand total of three suspected terrorists. Let me repeat that: three convictions in over seven years. Instead of bringing terrorists to justice, efforts at prosecution met setbacks, cases lingered on, and in 2006 the Supreme Court invalidated the entire system. Meanwhile, over five hundred and twenty-five detainees were released from Guantanamo under the Bush Administration. Let me repeat that: two-thirds of the detainees were released before I took office and ordered the closure of Guantanamo.

There is also no question that Guantanamo set back the moral authority that is America's strongest currency in the world. Instead of building a durable framework for the struggle against al Qaeda that drew upon our deeply held values and traditions, our government was defending positions that undermined the rule of law. Indeed, part of the rationale for establishing Guantanamo in the first place was the misplaced notion that a prison there would be beyond the law – a proposition that the Supreme Court soundly rejected. Meanwhile, instead of serving as a tool to counter-terrorism, Guantanamo became a symbol that helped al Qaeda recruit terrorists to its cause. Indeed, the existence of Guantanamo likely created more terrorists around the world than it ever detained.

So the record is clear: rather than keep us safer, the prison at Guantanamo has weakened American national security. It is a rallying cry for our enemies. It sets back the willingness of our allies to work with us in fighting an enemy that operates in scores of countries. By any measure, the costs of keeping it open far exceed the complications involved in closing it. That is why I argued that it should be closed throughout my campaign. And that is why I ordered it closed within one year.

The third decision that I made was to order a review of all the pending cases at Guantanamo.

I knew when I ordered Guantanamo closed that it would be difficult and complex. There are 240 people there who have now spent years in legal limbo. In dealing with this situation, we do not have the luxury of starting from scratch. We are cleaning up something that is – quite simply – a mess; a misguided experiment that has left in its wake a flood of legal challenges that my Administration is forced to deal with on a constant basis, and that consumes the time of government officials whose time should be spent on better protecting our country.

Indeed, the legal challenges that have sparked so much debate in recent weeks in Washington would be taking place whether or not I decided to close Guantanamo. For example, the court order to release seventeen Uighur detainees took place last fall – when George Bush was President. The Supreme Court that invalidated the system of prosecution at Guantanamo in 2006 was overwhelmingly appointed by Republican Presidents. In other words, the problem of what to do with Guantanamo detainees was not caused by my decision to close the facility; the problem exists because of the decision to open Guantanamo in the first place. . . .

Let me begin by disposing of one argument as plainly as I can: we are not going to release anyone if it would endanger our national security, nor will we release detainees within the United States who endanger the American people. Where demanded by justice and national security, we will seek to transfer some detainees to the same type of facilities in which we hold all manner of dangerous and violent criminals within our borders – highly secure prisons that ensure the public safety. As we make these decisions, bear in mind the following fact: nobody has ever escaped from one of our federal "supermax" prisons, which hold hundreds of convicted terrorists. As Senator Lindsey Graham said: "The idea that we cannot find a place to securely house 250-plus detainees within the United States is not rational."

We are currently in the process of reviewing each of the detainee cases at Guantanamo to determine the appropriate policy for dealing with them. As we do so, we are acutely aware that under the last Administration, detainees were released only to return to the battlefield. That is why we are doing away with the poorly planned, haphazard approach that let those detainees go in the past. Instead, we are treating these cases with the care and attention that the law requires and our security demands. Going forward, these cases will fall into five distinct categories.

First, when feasible, we will try those who have violated American criminal laws in federal courts – courts provided for by the United States Constitution. Some have derided our federal courts as incapable of handling the trials of terrorists. They are wrong. Our courts and juries of our citizens are tough enough to convict terrorists, and the record makes that clear. Ramzi Yousef tried to blow up the World Trade Center – he was convicted in our courts, and is serving a life sentence in U.S. prison.

Zaccarias Moussaoui has been identified as the 20th 9/11 hijacker – he was convicted in our courts, and he too is serving a life sentence in prison. If we can try those terrorists in our courts and hold them in our prisons, then we can do the same with detainees from Guantanamo.

Recently, we prosecuted and received a guilty plea from a detainee – al-Marri – in federal court after years of legal confusion. We are preparing to transfer another detainee to the Southern District of New York, where he will face trial on charges related to the 1998 bombings of our embassies in Kenya and Tanzania – bombings that killed over 200 people. Preventing this detainee from coming to our shores would prevent his trial and conviction. And after over a decade, it is time to finally see that justice is served, and that is what we intend to do.

The second category of cases involves detainees who violate the laws of war and are best tried through Military Commissions. Military commissions have a history in the United States dating back to George Washington and the Revolutionary War. They are an appropriate venue for trying detainees for violations of the laws of war. They allow for the protection of sensitive sources and methods of intelligence-gathering; for the safety and security of participants; and for the presentation of evidence gathered from the battlefield that cannot be effectively presented in federal Courts.

Now, some have suggested that this represents a reversal on my part. They are wrong. In 2006, I did strongly oppose legislation proposed by the Bush Administration and passed by the Congress because it failed to establish a legitimate legal framework, with the kind of meaningful due process and rights for the accused that could stand up on appeal. I did, however, support the use of military commissions to try detainees, provided there were several reforms. And those are the reforms that we are making.

Instead of using the flawed Commissions of the last seven years, my Administration is bringing our Commissions in line with the rule of law. The rule will no longer permit us to use as evidence statements that have been obtained using cruel, inhuman, or degrading interrogation methods. We will no longer place the burden to prove that hearsay is unreliable on the opponent of the hearsay. And we will give detainees greater latitude in selecting their own counsel, and more protections if they refuse to testify. These reforms – among others – will make our Military Commissions a more credible and effective means of administering justice, and I will work with Congress and legal authorities across the political spectrum on legislation to ensure that these Commissions are fair, legitimate, and effective.

The third category of detainees includes those who we have been ordered released by the courts. Let me repeat what I said earlier: this has absolutely nothing to do with my decision to close Guantanamo. It has to do with the rule of law. The courts have found that there is no legitimate reason to hold twenty-one of the people currently held at Guantanamo. Twenty of these findings took place before I came into office. The United States is a nation of laws, and we must abide by these rulings.

The fourth category of cases involves detainees who we have determined can be transferred safely to another country. So far, our review team has approved fifty detainees for transfer. And my Administration is in ongoing discussions with a number of other countries about the transfer of detainees to their soil for detention and rehabilitation.

Finally, there remains the question of detainees at Guantanamo who cannot be prosecuted yet who pose a clear danger to the American people.

I want to be honest: this is the toughest issue we will face. We are going to exhaust every avenue that we have to prosecute those at Guantanamo who pose a danger to our country. But even when this process is complete, there may be a number of people who cannot be prosecuted for past crimes, but who nonetheless pose a threat to the security of the United States. Examples of that threat include people who have received extensive explosives training at al Qaeda training camps, commanded Taliban troops in battle, expressed their allegiance to Osama bin Laden, or otherwise made it clear that they want to kill Americans. These are people who, in effect, remain at war with the United States.

As I said, I am not going to release individuals who endanger the American people. Al Qaeda terrorists and their affiliates are at war with the United States, and those that we capture – like other prisoners of war – must be prevented from attacking us again. However, we must recognize that these detention policies cannot be unbounded. That is why my Administration has begun to reshape these standards to ensure they are in line with the rule of law. We must have clear, defensible and lawful standards for those who fall in this category. We must have fair procedures so that we don't make mistakes. We must have a thorough process of periodic review, so that any prolonged detention is carefully evaluated and justified.

I know that creating such a system poses unique challenges. Other countries have grappled with this question, and so must we. But I want to be very clear that our goal is to construct a legitimate legal framework for Guantanamo detainees – not to avoid one. In our constitutional system, prolonged detention should not be the decision of any one man. If and when we determine that the United States must hold individuals to keep them from carrying out an act of war, we will do so within a system that involves judicial and congressional oversight. And so going forward, my Administration will work with Congress to develop an appropriate legal regime so that our efforts are consistent with our values and our Constitution. . . .

[NSL p. 758, CTL p. 398. Insert after Remarks by President Obama, *supra* p. 256.]

Final Report: Guantanamo
Review Task Force
January 22, 2010
http://www.justice.gov/ag/guantanamo-review-final-report.pdf

EXECUTIVE SUMMARY

On January 22, 2009, the President issued Executive Order 13492, calling for a prompt and comprehensive interagency review of the status of all individuals currently detained at the Guantanamo Bay Naval Base and requiring the closure of the detention facilities there. The Executive Order was based on the finding that the appropriate disposition of all individuals detained at Guantanamo would further the national security and foreign policy interests of the United States and the interests of justice.

. . . After evaluating all of the detainees, the review participants have decided on the proper disposition – transfer, prosecution, or continued detention – of all 240 detainees subject to the review.

Each of these decisions was reached by the unanimous agreement of the agencies responsible for the review: the Department of Justice, Department of Defense, Department of State, Department of Homeland Security, Office of the Director of National Intelligence, and Joint Chiefs of Staff. . . .

II. Background

Following the terrorist attacks of September 11, 2001, the United States was faced with the question of what to do with individuals captured in connection with military operations in Afghanistan or in other counterterrorism operations overseas. Starting in January 2002, the military began transferring a number of these individuals to the detention facilities at Guantanamo. . . . Since 2002, a total of 779 individuals have been detained at Guantanamo in connection with the war against al-Qaida, the Taliban, and associated forces.

From 2002 through 2008, most of the individuals detained at Guantanamo were transferred or released from U.S. custody, with the vast majority being repatriated to their home countries and others resettled in third countries willing to receive them. Of the 779 individuals detained at Guantanamo, approximately 530 – almost 70 percent – were transferred or released from U.S. custody prior to 2009. The countries to which these detainees were transferred include Afghanistan, Albania, Algeria, Australia, Bahrain, Bangladesh, Belgium, Bosnia, Denmark, Egypt, France, Germany, Iran, Iraq, Jordan, Kazakhstan, Kuwait, Libya, Maldives, Mauritania, Morocco, Pakistan, Qatar, Russia, Saudi Arabia, Somalia (Somaliland), Spain, Sudan, Sweden, Tajikistan, Tunisia, Turkey, Uganda, the United Arab Emirates, the United Kingdom, and Yemen.

By January 20, 2009, the population of detainees at Guantanamo had been reduced to 242. Of the 242 remaining detainees, 59 had been approved for transfer by the prior administration and were awaiting implementation of their transfers. . . .

V. Detainee Review Guidelines

In conducting its reviews, the Task Force followed detainee review guidelines ("Guidelines") developed specifically for the Executive Order review and approved by the Review Panel. The Guidelines set forth standards to apply in considering detainees for transfer, prosecution, or continued detention pursuant to the government's authority under the AUMF [Authorization for Use of Military Force, Pub. L. No. 107-40, 115 Stat. 224 (2001)].

A. Transfer Guidelines

The Guidelines addressed three types of evaluations relevant to determining whether a detainee should be recommended for transfer or release.

The first evaluation required by the Guidelines was a threat evaluation. The Guidelines provided that a detainee should be deemed eligible for transfer if any threat he poses could be sufficiently mitigated through feasible and appropriate security measures.[5] The Guidelines set forth a non-exclusive list of factors to be considered in evaluating the threat posed by a detainee. In applying those factors, the Task Force was instructed to consider the totality of available information regarding the detainee, and to give careful consideration to the credibility and reliability of the available information.

The second evaluation required by the Guidelines was an evaluation of potential destination (*i.e.*, receiving) countries. The Guidelines left the Task Force with discretion whether to recommend a detainee for transfer only to specified countries or under specified conditions. As with the threat evaluation, the Guidelines provided a nonexclusive set of factors by which to evaluate potential receiving countries.

The third evaluation required by the Guidelines was a legal evaluation to ensure that any detainee falling outside the government's lawful detention authority under the AUMF was recommended for transfer or release.

B. Prosecution Guidelines

The Guidelines also required cases to be evaluated by Task Force prosecutors to determine whether a federal court or military commission prosecution should be recommended for any offenses the detainees may have committed.

For the evaluation of whether a detainee should be prosecuted in federal court, the Guidelines set forth standards used by federal prosecutors across the country to determine whether to charge a case, as set forth in the *United States Attorneys' Manual.* Consistent with these standards, the Guidelines provided that a case should be recommended for prosecution if the detainee's conduct constitutes a federal offense and the potentially available admissible evidence will probably be sufficient to obtain and sustain a conviction – unless prosecution should be declined because no substantial federal interest would be served by prosecution. Key factors in making this determination include the nature

---

5. The Guidelines further provided that a detainee should be deemed eligible for release if he does not pose an identifiable threat to the national security of the United States. Other than the 17 Chinese Uighur detainees, who were approved for "transfer or release," no detainees were approved for "release" during the course of the review.

and seriousness of the offense; the detainee's culpability in connection with the offense; the detainee's willingness to cooperate in the investigation or prosecution of others; and the probable sentence or other consequences if the detainee is convicted.

For the evaluation of whether a detainee should be prosecuted in a military commission, Task Force prosecutors examined the potentially available admissible evidence and consulted closely with OMC [Office of Military Commissions-Prosecution] to determine the feasibility of prosecution.

Recognizing the unique nature of these cases, the Guidelines provided that other factors were also significant in determining whether to recommend prosecution, including the need to protect classified information, such as intelligence sources and methods.

C. Detention Guidelines

In accordance with the Executive Order, the Guidelines provided that every effort should be made to ensure that all detainees who could be recommended for transfer, release, or prosecution consistent with national security and foreign policy interests and the interests of justice were recommended for such dispositions. Thus, the Guidelines provided that a detainee should be considered eligible for continued detention under the AUMF only if (1) the detainee poses a national security threat that cannot be sufficiently mitigated through feasible and appropriate security measures; (2) prosecution of the detainee by the federal government is not feasible in any forum; and (3) continued detention without criminal charges is lawful.

The Guidelines required the Task Force to consult with the Department of Justice in conducting a legal evaluation for each detainee considered for continued detention. This legal evaluation addressed both the legal basis for holding the detainee under the AUMF and the government's case for defending the detention in any habeas litigation.[6]

As the Supreme Court has held, inherent within the authorization of the AUMF to "use all necessary and appropriate force" is the power to

---

6. The AUMF authorizes the President to "use all necessary and appropriate force against those nations, organizations, or persons he determines planned, authorized, committed, or aided the terrorist attacks that occurred on September 11, 2001, or harbored such organizations or persons, in order to prevent any future attacks of international terrorism against the United States by such nations, organizations or persons." AUMF §2(a).

detain any individuals who fall within the scope of the statute.[7] As the Court observed, "by universal agreement and practice," the power to wage war necessarily includes the authority to capture and detain combatants in order to prevent them from "returning to the field of battle and taking up arms once again."[8] The scope of the AUMF's detention authority extends to those persons who "planned, authorized or committed or aided" the September 11 attacks, "harbored those responsible for those attacks," or "were part of, or substantially supported, Taliban or al Qaeda forces or associated forces that are engaged in hostilities against the United States or its coalition partners."[9] Accordingly, only detainees who satisfied this standard could be designated for continued detention. . . .

VI. Results of the Review

A. Overview of Decisions

By the one-year mark of January 22, 2010, the review participants reached decisions on the appropriate disposition of all 240 detainees subject to the Executive Order. In sum, 126 detainees were approved for transfer; 36 detainees were referred for prosecution; 48 detainees were approved for continued detention under the AUMF; and 30 detainees from Yemen were approved for "conditional" detention based on present security conditions in Yemen. . . .

B. Overview of the Guantanamo Detainee Population

The following section provides an overview of the 240 Guantanamo detainees reviewed under the Executive Order, including their threat characteristics and more general background information, including country of origin, point of capture, and date of arrival at Guantanamo.

---

7. See *Hamdi v. Rumsfeld,* 542 U.S. 507, 519 (2004) (plurality opinion); *id.* at 587 (Thomas, J.) (dissenting).

8. *Id.* at 518; *see also id* at 587 (Thomas, J.) (dissenting) (same).

9. See Gov't Filing, *In re. Guantanamo Bay Detainee Litigation,* Misc. No. 08-442 (D.D.C. March 13, 2009). The United States Court of Appeals for the District of Columbia recently affirmed that Guantanamo detainees who meet this standard are detainable. *See also Al-Bihani v. Obama,* ___ F.3d ___, 2010 WL 10411 at *3 (D.C. Cir. Jan. 5, 2010).

Threat Characteristics. As reflected in the decisions made in the review, there is a substantial degree of variation among the Guantanamo detainees from a security perspective. Although not all detainees can be neatly characterized, the following groupings provide a rough overview of the recurring threat profiles seen in the population.

- *Leaders, operatives, and facilitators involved in terrorist plots against U.S. targets.* At the high end of the threat spectrum are leaders, planners, operatives, and facilitators within al-Qaida or associated groups who are directly implicated in terrorist plots against U.S. interests. Among the most notorious examples in this group are Khalid Sheikh Mohammed, the alleged mastermind of the September 11 attacks; Ramzi bin al-Shibh, the alleged principal coordinator of the September 11 attacks; Abd al-Rahim al-Nashiri, the alleged mastermind of the attack on the U.S.S. *Cole;* Abu Faraj al-Libi, who allegedly succeeded Khalid Sheikh Mohammed as al-Qaida's chief planner of terrorist operations; Hambali, the alleged leader of an al-Qaida affiliate in Indonesia who directed numerous attacks against Western targets in Southeast Asia; and Ahmed Ghailani, an alleged key participant in the 1998 bombings of the U.S. embassies in Kenya and Tanzania. Roughly 10 percent of the detainees subject to the review appear to have played a direct role in plotting, executing, or facilitating such attacks.
- *Others with significant organizational roles within al-Qaida or associated terrorist organizations.* Other detainees played significant organizational roles within al-Qaida or associated terrorist organizations, even if they may not have been directly involved in terrorist plots against U.S. targets. This group includes, for example, individuals responsible for overseeing or providing logistical support to al-Qaida's training operations in Afghanistan; facilitators who helped move money and personnel for al-Qaida; a cadre of Usama bin Laden's bodyguards, who held a unique position of trust within al-Qaida; and well-trained operatives who were being groomed by al-Qaida leaders for future terrorist operations. Roughly 20 percent of the detainees subject to the review fall within this category.
- *Taliban leaders and members of anti-Coalition militia groups.* The detainee population also includes a small number of Afghan detainees who occupied significant positions within the Taliban regime, and a small number of other Afghan detainees who were involved in local insurgent networks in Afghanistan implicated in

attacks on Coalition forces. Less than 10 percent of the detainees subject to the review fall within this category.

- *Low-level foreign fighters.* A majority of the detainees reviewed appear to have been foreign fighters with varying degrees of connection to al-Qaida, the Taliban, or associated groups, but who lacked a significant leadership or other specialized role. These detainees were typically captured in combat zones during the early stages of U.S. military operations in Afghanistan, often by Northern Alliance troops or other allied forces, without being specifically targeted for capture by (or even known to) the U.S. military in advance. Many were relatively recent recruits to training camps in Afghanistan run by al-Qaida or other groups, where they received limited weapons training, but do not appear to have been among those selected for more advanced training geared toward terrorist operations abroad.
- *Miscellaneous others.* The remaining detainees – roughly 5 percent – do not fit into any of the above categories.

Country of Origin. The Guantanamo detainees reviewed included individuals from a number of different countries, including Yemen, Afghanistan, China, Saudi Arabia, Algeria, Tunisia, Syria, Libya, Kuwait, and Pakistan. Approximately 40 percent – 97 detainees – were Yemeni, while over 10 percent were Afghan.

Point of Capture. The large majority of the detainees in the population reviewed – approximately 60 percent – were captured inside Afghanistan or in the Afghanistan-Pakistan border area. Approximately 30 percent of the detainees were captured inside Pakistan. The remaining 10 percent were captured in countries other than Afghanistan or Pakistan.

Arrival at Guantanamo. Most of the detainees reviewed – approximately 80 percent – arrived at Guantanamo in 2002, having been captured during the early months of operations in Afghanistan. The remaining detainees arrived in small numbers over succeeding years.

VII. Transfer Decisions

A. Background . . .

Prior to the initiation of the review, 59 of the 240 detainees subject to review were approved for transfer or release by the prior administration but remained at Guantanamo by the time the Executive Order was issued. One reason for their continued detention was that more than half of the 59 detainees could not be returned to their home countries consistent with U.S. policy due to post-transfer treatment concerns.[11] Thus, many of the 59 detainees required resettlement in a third country, a process that takes time and requires extensive diplomatic efforts.

In addition, 29 of the detainees subject to review were ordered released by a federal district court as the result of habeas litigation. Of these 29 detainees, 18 were ordered released after the government conceded the case.[12] The remaining 11 detainees were ordered released after a court reached the merits of the case and ruled, based on a preponderance of the evidence, that the detainee was not lawfully held because he was not part of, or did not substantially support, al-Qaida, the Taliban, or associated forces.[13] Of the 29 detainees ordered released, 18 were among the 59 who had been approved by the prior administration for transfer or release. Thus, a total of 70 detainees subject to the review were either approved for transfer during the prior administration or ordered released by a federal court.

---

11. It is the longstanding policy of the United States not to transfer a person to a country if the United States determines that the person is more likely than not to be tortured upon return or, in appropriate cases, that the person has a well-founded fear of persecution and is entitled to persecution protection. This policy is consistent with the approach taken by the United States in implementing the Convention Against Torture and other Cruel, Inhuman or Degrading Treatment or Punishment (CAT) and the Protocol Relating to the Status of Refugees. Accordingly, prior to any transfer, the Department of State works closely with relevant agencies to advise on the likelihood of persecution or torture in the given country and the adequacy and credibility of assurances obtained from the foreign government.

12. Of the 18 cases conceded by the government, 17 were brought by the Uighur detainees and were conceded by the prior administration. Eleven of the 18 detainees have been transferred to date.

13. A total of 14 detainees have won their habeas cases on the merits in district court. The government transferred three of these detainees in December 2008; thus, they were not subject to the review. Of the 11 remaining detainees who were reviewed under the Executive Order, seven have been transferred to date. Of the four who have not been transferred, the United States is appealing the district court's ruling in two of the cases, and is still within the time period to appeal the remaining two cases.

B. Decisions

Based on interagency reviews and case-by-case threat evaluations, 126 of the 240 detainees were approved for transfer by agreement of senior officials from the agencies named in the Executive Order. The 126 detainees unanimously approved for transfer include 44 who have been transferred to date – 24 to their home countries, 18 to third countries for resettlement, and two to Italy for prosecution. Of the 82 detainees who remain at Guantanamo and who have been approved for transfer, 16 may be repatriated to their home countries (other than Yemen) consistent with U.S. policies concerning humane treatment, 38 cannot be repatriated due to humane treatment or related concerns in their home countries (other than Yemen) and thus need to be resettled in a third country, and 29 are from Yemen. Half of all detainees approved for transfer – 63 of the 126 – also had been approved for transfer during the prior administration, ordered released by a federal court, or both. . . .

It is important to emphasize that a decision to approve a detainee for transfer does not reflect a decision that the detainee poses no threat or no risk of recidivism. Rather, the decision reflects the best predictive judgment of senior government officials, based on the available information, that any threat posed by the detainee can be sufficiently mitigated through feasible and appropriate security measures in the receiving country. Indeed, all transfer decisions were made subject to the implementation of appropriate security measures in the receiving country, and extensive discussions are conducted with the receiving country about such security measures before any transfer is implemented. Some detainees were approved for transfer only to specific countries or under specific conditions, and a few were approved for transfer only to countries with pending prosecutions against the detainee (or an interest in pursuing a future prosecution). . . .

VIII. Prosecution Decisions

A. Background

The Executive Order provides that "[i]n accordance with United States law, the cases of individuals detained at Guantanamo not approved for release or transfer shall be evaluated to determine whether the Federal Government should seek to prosecute the detained individuals for any offenses they may have committed, including whether it is feasible to prosecute such individuals before a court established pursuant to Article

III of the United States Constitution [*i.e.,* federal court]." In a speech at the National Archives on May 21, 2009, the President reiterated that "when feasible, we will try those who have violated American criminal laws in federal courts." As the President noted in his speech, federal prosecutors have a long history of successfully prosecuting all manner of terrorism offenses in the federal courts:

> Our courts and juries of our citizens are tough enough to convict terrorists, and the record makes that clear. Ramzi Yousef tried to blow up the World Trade Center—he was convicted in our courts, and is serving a life sentence in U.S. prison. Zacarias Moussaoui has been identified as the 20th 9/11 hijacker—he was convicted in our courts, and he too is serving a life sentence in prison. If we can try those terrorists in our courts and hold them in our prisons, then we can do the same with detainees from Guantanamo.

The President also stressed that military commissions "have a history in the United States dating back to George Washington and the Revolutionary War" and remained "an appropriate venue for trying detainees for violations of the laws of war." Accordingly, the administration proposed, and Congress has since enacted, reforms to the military commissions system to ensure that the commissions are fair, legitimate, and effective. . . .

The Department of Justice and Department of Defense agreed upon a joint protocol to establish a process for determining whether prosecution of a referred case should be pursued in a federal court or before a military commission. Under the protocol – titled *Determination of Guantanamo Cases Referred for Prosecution* – there is a presumption that prosecution will be pursued in a federal court wherever feasible, unless other compelling factors make it more appropriate to pursue prosecution before a military commission. The evaluations called for under the protocol are conducted by teams of both federal and military prosecutors. Among the criteria they apply are: the nature of the offenses to be charged; the identity of the victims; the location of the crime; the context in which the defendant was apprehended; and the manner in which the case was investigated and by which investigative agency. The Attorney General, in consultation with the Secretary of Defense, makes the ultimate decision as to where a prosecution will be pursued.

B. Decisions

As a result of the Task Force's review, the Review Panel referred 44 cases to the Department of Justice for potential prosecution and a decision regarding the forum for any prosecution. Decisions to seek prosecution have been announced in 12 of these cases; 24 remain pending under the protocol; and eight of the detainees initially referred were subsequently designated for other dispositions.

On May 21, 2009, the Department of Justice announced that Ahmed Ghailani, who had previously been indicted in the United States District Court for the Southern District of New York for his alleged role in the 1998 bombings of the U.S. embassies in Kenya and Tanzania, would be prosecuted in federal court. On June 9, 2009, Ghailani was transferred from Guantanamo to the Southern District of New York, where his case is pending.

On November 13, 2009, the Attorney General announced that the government would pursue prosecution in federal court in the Southern District of New York against the five detainees who had previously been charged before a military commission for their roles in the September 11 attacks. They are:

- Khalid Sheikh Mohammed, the alleged mastermind of the September 11 plot;
- Ramzi bin al-Shibh, the alleged coordinator of the September 11 plot who acted as intermediary between Khalid Sheikh Mohammed and the hijackers in the United States;
- Walid Muhammed Salih Mubarak Bin Attash (a.k.a. Khallad Bin Attash), an alleged early member of the September 11 plot who tested airline security on United Airlines flights between Bangkok and Hong Kong;
- Mustafa Ahmed al-Hawsawi, an alleged facilitator of hijackers and money to the United States from his base in Dubai; and
- Ali Abdul Aziz Ali (a.k.a. Ammar Baluchi), a second alleged facilitator of hijackers and money to the United States from his base in Dubai.

On the same day, the Attorney General also announced that the prosecution against Abd al-Rahim al-Nashiri, the alleged mastermind of the bombing of the U.S.S. *Cole*, would be pursued before a military commission. The Attorney General further decided that four other detainees whose cases were pending before military commissions when the Executive Order was issued would remain before the commissions: Ahmed al-Dabi, Noor Uthman, Omar Khadr, and Ibrahim al-Qosi. In January 2010, the Department of Justice announced that Obaidullah, whom OMC had charged but whose case had not yet been referred to a military commission, will remain in the military commission system.

Twenty-four of the referred cases remain pending with the Department of Justice under the protocol. No final decision has been made regarding whether or in what forum these detainees will be prosecuted.

Eight of the referred detainees are no longer under active consideration for prosecution. . . .

C. Detainees Who Cannot Be Prosecuted

The Task Force concluded that for many detainees at Guantanamo, prosecution is not feasible in either federal court or a military commission. There are several reasons for these conclusions.

First, the vast majority of the detainees were captured in active zones of combat in Afghanistan or the Pakistani border regions. The focus at the time of their capture was the gathering of intelligence and their removal from the fight. They were not the subjects of formal criminal investigations, and evidence was neither gathered nor preserved with an eye toward prosecuting them. While the intelligence about them may be accurate and reliable, that intelligence, for various reasons, may not be admissible evidence or sufficient to satisfy a criminal burden of proof in either a military commission or federal court. One common problem is that, for many of the detainees, there are no witnesses who are available to testify in any proceeding against them.

Second, many of the detainees cannot be prosecuted because of jurisdictional limitations. In many cases, even though the Task Force found evidence that a detainee was lawfully detainable as part of al-Qaida – e.g., based on information that he attended a training camp, or played some role in the hierarchy of the organization – the Task Force did not find evidence that the detainee participated in a specific terrorist plot. The lack of such evidence can pose obstacles to pursuing a prosecution in either federal court or a military commission. While the federal material support statutes have been used to convict persons who have merely provided services to a terrorist organization, e.g., by attending a terrorist training camp, there are potential limitations to pursuing such a charge against the detainees.[21]

---

21. Among these limitations: First, the two relevant statutes – 18 U.S.C. §§2339A and 2339B – were not amended to expressly apply extraterritorially to non-U.S. persons until October 2001 and December 2004, respectively. Thus, material support may not be available as a charge in the federal system unless there is sufficient evidence to prove that a detainee was supporting al-Qaida after

Notably, the principal obstacles to prosecution in the cases deemed infeasible by the Task Force typically did not stem from concerns over protecting sensitive sources or methods from disclosure, or concerns that the evidence against the detainee was tainted. While such concerns were present in some cases, most detainees were deemed infeasible for prosecution based on more fundamental evidentiary and jurisdictional limitations tied to the demands of a criminal forum, as described above.

Significantly, the Executive Order does not preclude the government from prosecuting at a later date someone who is presently designated for continued detention. Work on these cases continues. . . .

IX. Detention Decisions . . .

B. Decisions

As the result of this review, 48 detainees were unanimously approved for continued detention under the AUMF.

Although each detainee presented unique issues, all of the detainees ultimately designated for continued detention satisfied three core criteria: First, the totality of available information – including credible information that might not be admissible in a criminal prosecution – indicated that the detainee poses a high level of threat that cannot be mitigated sufficiently except through continued detention; second, prosecution of the detainee in a federal criminal court or a military commission did not appear feasible; and third, notwithstanding the infeasibility of criminal prosecution, there is a lawful basis for the detainee's detention under the AUMF.

Broadly speaking, the detainees designated for continued detention were characterized by one or more of the following factors:

- **Significant organizational role within al-Qaida, the Taliban, or associated forces.** In contrast to the majority of detainees

---

October 2001 at the earliest. Second, the statute of limitations for these offenses is typically eight years (*see* 18 U.S.C. §3286), which may bar prosecution for offenses that occurred well before the detainee's capture. Third, because the statutory maximum sentence for material support is 15 years (where death does not result from the offense), sentencing considerations may weigh against pursuing prosecution in certain cases. Some of these considerations would not apply to material support charges brought in the military commissions; however, the legal viability of material support as a charge in the military commission system has been challenged on appeal in commission proceedings.

held at Guantanamo, many of the detainees approved for detention held a leadership or other specialized role within al-Qaida, the Taliban, or associated forces. Some provided operational, logistical, financial, or fundraising support for al-Qaida. Others were al-Qaida members who were selected to serve as bodyguards for Usama bin Laden based on their loyalty to the organization. Others were Taliban military commanders or senior officials, or played significant roles in insurgent groups in Afghanistan allied with the Taliban . . . .

- **Advanced training or experience.** The detainees approved for detention tended to have more extensive training or combat experience than those approved for transfer. Some of these detainees were veteran *jihadists* with lengthy involvement in the training camps in Afghanistan. Several had expertise in explosives or other tactics geared toward terrorist operations.
- **Expressed recidivist intent.** Some detainees designated for detention have, while at Guantanamo, expressly stated or otherwise exhibited an intent to reengage in extremist activity upon release.
- **History of associations with extremist activity.** Some of the detainees approved for detention have a history of engaging in extremist activities or particularly strong ties (either directly or through family members) to extremist organizations.

Lawful basis for detention. Under the Executive Order, every detainee's disposition must be lawful. Accordingly, the Task Force consulted closely with the Department of Justice regarding every detainee approved for continued detention to ensure that the detainee fell within the bounds of the Government's detention authority under the AUMF, as described above.

Prosecution not currently feasible. Although dangerous and lawfully held, the detainees designated for detention currently cannot be prosecuted in either a federal court or a military commission. While the reasons vary from detainee to detainee, generally these detainees cannot be prosecuted because either there is presently insufficient admissible evidence to establish the detainee's guilt beyond a reasonable doubt in either a federal court or military commission, or the detainee's conduct does not constitute a chargeable offense in either a federal court or military commission. Though prosecution currently is not feasible for these detainees, designating a detainee for detention does not preclude future prosecution in either a federal court or a military commission should new evidence or other developments make a prosecution viable.

Transfer or release not currently feasible. Finally, none of the detainees approved for detention can be safely transferred to a third country at this time. This does not mean that the detainee could never be safely transferred to a third country. Rather, designating the detainee for continued detention at this time indicates only that given the detainee's current threat and the current willingness or ability of potential destination countries to mitigate the threat, the detainee is not currently eligible for transfer or release. Should circumstances change *(e.g.,* should potential receiving countries implement appropriate security measures), transfer might be appropriate in the future.

C. Continued Reviews

Detainees approved for continued detention under the AUMF will be subject to further reviews. First, in accordance with the Supreme Court's decision in *Boumediene v. Bush,*[22] each detainee has the opportunity to seek judicial review of their detention by filing a petition for a writ of habeas corpus in federal court. In such cases, the court reviews whether the detainee falls within the government's lawful detention authority. In cases where courts have concluded that the detainee is not lawfully held, the courts have issued orders requiring the government to take diplomatic steps to achieve the detainee's release. Thus far, federal district courts have ruled on cases brought by four of the 48 detainees approved for continued detention. In each of the four cases, the district court denied the habeas petition and upheld the lawfulness of the detention. Many other cases are pending in district court, and some are pending on appeal.

Second, as the President stated in his speech at the National Archives, "a thorough process of periodic review" is needed to ensure that "any prolonged detention is carefully evaluated and justified." Thus, in addition to the judicial review afforded through habeas litigation, each detainee approved for continued detention will be subject to periodic Executive Branch review. . . .

---

22. 122 S. Ct. 2229 (2008).

[NSL p. 758, CTL p. 398. Insert after the Final Report: Guantanamo
Review Task Force.]

Letter from Attorney General Eric Holder
to Senator Mitch McConnell Regarding
Umar Farouk Abdulmutallab

Feb. 3, 2010

http://www.justice.gov/cjs/docs/ag-letter-2-3-10.pdf

Dear Senator McConnell:

I am writing in reply to your letter of January 26, 2010, inquiring
about the decision to charge Umar Farouk Abdulmutallab with federal
crimes in connection with the attempted bombing of Northwest Airlines
Flight 253 near Detroit on December 25, 2009, rather than detaining him
under the law of war. . . .

The decision to charge Mr. Abdulmutallab in federal court, and the
methods used to interrogate him, are fully consistent with the long-
established and publicly known policies and practices of the Department
of Justice, the FBI, and the United States Government as a whole, as
implemented for many years by Administrations of both parties. Those
policies and practices, which were not criticized when employed by
previous Administrations, have been and remain extremely effective in
protecting national security. They are among the many powerful
weapons this country can and should use to win the war against al-
Qaeda. . . .

1. *Detention.* I made the decision to charge Mr. Abdulmutallab with
federal crimes, and to seek his detention in connection with those
charges, with the knowledge of, and with no objection from, all other
relevant departments of the government. On the evening of December 25
and again on the morning of December 26, the FBI informed its partners
in the Intelligence Community that Abdulmutallab would be charged
criminally, and no agency objected to this course of action. In the days
following December 25 – including during a meeting with the President
and other senior members of his national security team on January 5 –
high-level discussions ensued within the Administration in which the
possibility of detaining Mr. Abdulmutallab under the law of war was
explicitly discussed. No agency supported the use of law of war

detention for Abdulmutallab, and no agency has since advised the Department of Justice that an alternative course of action should have been, or should now be, pursued.

Since the September 11, 2001 attacks, the practice of the U.S. government, followed by prior and current Administrations without a single exception, has been to arrest and detain under federal criminal law all terrorist suspects who are apprehended inside the United States. The prior Administration adopted policies expressly endorsing this approach. Under a policy directive issued by President Bush in 2003, for example, "the Attorney General has lead responsibility for criminal investigations of terrorist acts or terrorist threats by individuals or groups inside the United States, or directed at United States citizens or institutions abroad, where such acts are within the Federal criminal jurisdiction of the United States, as well as for related intelligence collection activities within the United States." Homeland Security Presidential Directive 5 (HSPD-5, February 28, 2003). The directive goes on to provide that "[f]ollowing a terrorist threat or an actual incident that falls within the criminal jurisdiction of the United States, the full capabilities of the United States shall be dedicated, consistent with United States law and with activities of other Federal departments and agencies to protect our national security, to assisting the Attorney General to identify the perpetrators and bring them to justice."

In keeping with this policy, the Bush Administration used the criminal justice system to convict more than 300 individuals on terrorism-related charges. For example, Richard Reid, a British citizen, was arrested in December 2001 for attempting to ignite a shoe bomb while on a flight from Paris to Miami carrying 184 passengers and 14 crewmembers. He was advised of his right to remain silent and to consult with an attorney within five minutes of being removed from the aircraft (and was read or reminded of these rights a total of four times within 48 hours), pled guilty in October 2002, and is now serving a life sentence in federal prison. In 2003, Iyman Faris, a U.S. citizen from Pakistan, pled guilty to conspiracy and providing material support to al-Qaeda for providing the terrorist organization with information about possible U.S. targets for attack. Among other things, he was tasked by al-Qaeda operatives overseas to assess the Brooklyn Bridge in New York City as a possible post-9/11 target of destruction. After initially providing significant information and assistance to law enforcement personnel, he was sentenced to 20 years in prison. In 2002, the "Lackawanna Six" were charged with conspiring, providing, and attempting to provide material support to al-Qaeda based upon their pre-9/11 travel to Afghanistan to train in the Al Farooq camp operated by al-Qaeda. They pled guilty, agreed to cooperate, and were sentenced to terms ranging from seven to ten years in prison. There are many other examples of successful terrorism prosecutions – ranging from Zacarias Moussaoui (convicted in 2006 in connection with the 9/11 attacks and sentenced to life in prison) to Ahmed Omar Abu Ali (convicted in 2005 of conspiracy to assassinate the President and other charges and sentenced to life in prison) to Ahmed Ressam (convicted in 2001 for the Millenium plot to bomb the Los Angeles airport and sentenced to 22 years, a sentence recently reversed as too lenient and remanded for resentencing) – which I am happy to provide upon request.

In fact, two (and only two) persons apprehended in this country in recent times have been held under the law of war. Jose Padilla was arrested on a federal material witness warrant in 2002, and was transferred to law of war custody approximately one month later, after his court-appointed counsel moved to vacate the warrant. Ali Saleh Kahlah Al-Marri was also initially arrested on a material witness warrant in 2001, was indicted on federal criminal charges (unrelated to terrorism) in 2002, and then transferred to law of war custody approximately eighteen months later. In both of these cases, the transfer to law of war custody raised serious statutory and constitutional questions in the courts concerning the lawfulness of the government's actions and spawned lengthy litigation. In Mr. Padilla's case, the United States Court of Appeals for the Second Circuit found that the President did not have the authority to detain him under the law of war. In Mr. Al-Marri's case, the United States Court of Appeals for the Fourth Circuit reversed a prior panel decision and found in a fractured *en banc* opinion that the President did have authority to detain Mr. Al Marri, but that he had not been afforded sufficient process to challenge his designation as an enemy combatant. Ultimately, both Al-Marri (in 2009) and Padilla (in 2006) were returned to law enforcement custody, convicted of terrorism charges and sentenced to prison. . . .

3. *The Criminal Justice System as a National Security Tool.* As President Obama has made clear repeatedly, we are at war against a dangerous, intelligent, and adaptable enemy. Our goal in this war, as in

all others, is to win. Victory means defeating the enemy without damaging the fundamental principles on which our nation was founded. To do that, we must use every weapon at our disposal. Those weapons include direct military action, military justice, intelligence, diplomacy, and civilian law enforcement. Each of these weapons has virtues and strengths, and we use each of them in the appropriate situations.

Over the past year, we have used the criminal justice system to disrupt a number of plots, including one in New York and Colorado that might have been the deadliest attack on our country since September 11, 2001, had it been successful. The backbone of that effort is the combined work of thousands of FBI agents, state and local police officers, career prosecutors, and intelligence officials around the world who go to work every day to help prevent terrorist attacks. I am immensely proud of their efforts. At the same time, we have worked in concert with our partners in the military and the Intelligence Community to support their tremendous work to defeat the terrorists and with our partners overseas who have great faith in our criminal justice system.

The criminal justice system has proven to be one of the most effective weapons available to our government for both incapacitating terrorists and collecting intelligence from them. Removing this highly effective weapon from our arsenal would be as foolish as taking our military and intelligence options off the table against al-Qaeda, and as dangerous. In fact, only by using all of our instruments of national power in concert can we be truly effective. As Attorney General, I am guided not by partisanship or political considerations, but by a commitment to using the most effective course of action in each case, depending on the facts of each case, to protect the American people, defeat our enemies, and ensure the rule of law.

Sincerely,
Eric H. Holder, Jr.

[NSL p. 788, CTL p. 429. Insert after Note 3.]

Senate Armed Services Committee Inquiry into the Treatment of Detainees in U.S. Custody

Dec. 11, 2008

http://levin.senate.gov/newsroom/supporting/2008/Detainees.121108.pdf

Executive Summary

"What sets us apart from our enemies in this fight. . . is how we behave. In everything we do, we must observe the standards and values that dictate that we treat noncombatants and detainees with dignity and respect. While we are warriors, we are also all human beings"

> – *General David Petraeus*
> *May 10, 2007*

(U) The collection of timely and accurate intelligence is critical to the safety of U.S. personnel deployed abroad and to the security of the American people here at home. The methods by which we elicit intelligence information from detainees in our custody affect not only the reliability of that information, but our broader efforts to win hearts and minds and attract allies to our side.

(U) Al Qaeda and Taliban terrorists are taught to expect Americans to abuse them. They are recruited based on false propaganda that says the United States is out to destroy Islam. Treating detainees harshly only reinforces that distorted view, increases resistance to cooperation, and creates new enemies. In fact, the April 2006 National Intelligence Estimate "Trends in Global Terrorism: Implications for the United States" cited "pervasive anti U.S. sentiment among most Muslims" as an underlying factor fueling the spread of the global jihadist movement. Former Navy General Counsel Alberto Mora testified to the Senate Armed Services Committee in June 2008 that "there are serving U.S. flag-rank officers who maintain that the first and second identifiable causes of U.S. combat deaths in Iraq – as judged by their effectiveness in recruiting insurgent fighters into combat – are, respectively the symbols of Abu Ghraib and Guantanamo."

(U) The abuse of detainees in U.S. custody cannot simply be attributed to the actions of "a few bad apples" acting on their own. The fact is that senior officials in the United States government solicited information on how to use aggressive techniques, redefined the law to create the appearance of their legality, and authorized their use against detainees. Those efforts damaged our ability to collect accurate intelligence that could save lives, strengthened the hand of our enemies, and compromised our moral authority. This report is a product of the Committee's inquiry into how those unfortunate results came about. . . .

Senate Armed Services Committee Conclusions

Conclusion 1: On February 7, 2002, President George W. Bush made a written determination that Common Article 3 of the Geneva Conventions, which would have afforded minimum standards for humane treatment, did not apply to al Qaeda or Taliban detainees. Following the President's determination, techniques such as waterboarding, nudity, and stress positions, used in SERE [Survival Evasion Resistance and Escape] training to simulate tactics used by enemies that refuse to follow the Geneva Conventions, were authorized for use in interrogations of detainees in U.S. custody.

Conclusion 2: Members of the President's Cabinet and other senior officials participated in meetings inside the White House in 2002 and 2003 where specific interrogation techniques were discussed. National Security Council Principals reviewed the CIA's interrogation program during that period.

Conclusions on SERE Training Techniques and Interrogations

Conclusion 3: The use of techniques similar to those used in SERE resistance training – such as stripping students of their clothing, placing them in stress positions, putting hoods over their heads, and treating them like animals – was at odds with the commitment to humane treatment of detainees in U.S. custody. Using those techniques for interrogating detainees was also inconsistent with the goal of collecting accurate intelligence information, as the purpose of SERE resistance training is to increase the ability of U.S. personnel to resist abusive interrogations and the techniques used were based, in part, on Chinese

Communist techniques used during the Korean War to elicit false confessions.

Conclusion 4: The use of techniques in interrogations derived from SERE resistance training created a serious risk of physical and psychological harm to detainees. The SERE schools employ strict controls to reduce the risk of physical and psychological harm to students during training. Those controls include medical and psychological screening for students, interventions by trained psychologists during training, and code words to ensure that students can stop the application of a technique at any time should the need arise. Those same controls are not present in real world interrogations.

Conclusions on Senior Official Consideration of SERE Techniques for Interrogations

Conclusion 5: In July 2002, the Office of the Secretary of Defense General Counsel solicited information from the Joint Personnel Recovery Agency (JPRA) [an agency whose expertise was in training U.S. personnel to withstand interrogation techniques considered unlawful under the Geneva Conventions] on SERE techniques for use during interrogations. That solicitation, prompted by requests from Department of Defense General Counsel William J. Haynes II, reflected the view that abusive tactics similar to those used by our enemies should be considered for use against detainees in U.S. custody.

Conclusion 6: The Central Intelligence Agency's (CIA) interrogation program included at least one SERE training technique, waterboarding. Senior Administration lawyers, including Alberto Gonzales, Counsel to the President, and David Addington, Counsel to the Vice President, were consulted on the development of legal analysis of CIA interrogation techniques. Legal opinions subsequently issued by the Department of Justice's Office of Legal Counsel (OLC) interpreted legal obligations under U.S. anti-torture laws and determined the legality of CIA interrogation techniques. Those OLC opinions distorted the meaning and intent of anti-torture laws, rationalized the abuse of detainees in U.S. custody and influenced Department of Defense determinations as to what interrogation techniques were legal for use during interrogations conducted by U.S. military personnel.

Conclusions on JPRA Offensive Activities

Conclusion 7: Joint Personnel Recovery Agency (JPRA) efforts in support of "offensive" interrogation operations went beyond the agency's knowledge and expertise. JPRA's support to U.S. government interrogation efforts contributed to detainee abuse. JPRA's offensive support also influenced the development of policies that authorized abusive interrogation techniques for use against detainees in U.S. custody.

Conclusion 8: Detainee abuse occurred during JPRA's support to Special Mission Unit (SMU) Task Force (TF) interrogation operations in Iraq in September 2003. JPRA Commander Colonel Randy Moulton's authorization of SERE instructors, who had no experience in detainee interrogations, to actively participate in Task Force interrogations using SERE resistance training techniques was a serious failure in judgment. The Special Mission Unit Task Force Commander's failure to order that SERE resistance training techniques not be used in detainee interrogations was a serious failure in leadership that led to the abuse of detainees in Task Force custody. Iraq is a Geneva Convention theater and techniques used in SERE school are inconsistent with the obligations of U.S. personnel under the Geneva Conventions.

Conclusion 9: Combatant Command requests for JPRA "offensive" interrogation support and U.S. Joint Forces Command (JFCOM) authorization of that support led to JPRA operating outside the agency's charter and beyond its expertise. Only when JFCOM's Staff Judge Advocate became aware of and raised concerns about JPRA's support to offensive interrogation operations in late September 2003 did JFCOM leadership begin to take steps to curtail JPRA's "offensive" activities. It was not until September 2004, however, that JFCOM issued a formal policy stating that support to offensive interrogation operations was outside JPRA's charter.

Conclusions on GTMO's Request for Aggressive Techniques

Conclusion 10: Interrogation techniques in Guantanamo Bay's (GTMO) October 11, 2002 request for authority submitted by Major General Michael Dunlavey, were influenced by JPRA training for GTMO interrogation personnel and included techniques similar to those used in SERE training to teach U.S. personnel to resist abusive enemy interrogations. GTMO Staff Judge Advocate Lieutenant Colonel Diane Beaver's legal review justifying the October 11, 2002 GTMO request was profoundly in error and legally insufficient. Leaders at GTMO, including Major General Dunlavey's successor, Major General Geoffrey Miller, ignored warnings from DoD's Criminal Investigative Task Force and the Federal Bureau of Investigation that the techniques were potentially unlawful and that their use would strengthen detainee resistance.

Conclusion 11: Chairman of the Joint Chiefs of Staff General Richard Myers's decision to cut short the legal and policy review of the October 11, 2002 GTMO request initiated by his Legal Counsel, then-Captain Jane Dalton, undermined the military's review process. Subsequent conclusions reached by Chairman Myers and Captain Dalton regarding the legality of interrogation techniques in the request followed a grossly deficient review and were at odds with conclusions previously reached by the Army, Air Force, Marine Corps, and Criminal Investigative Task Force.

Conclusion 12: Department of Defense General Counsel William J. Haynes II's effort to cut short the legal and policy review of the October 11, 2002 GTMO request initiated by then Captain Jane Dalton, Legal Counsel to the Chairman of the Joint Chiefs of Staff, was inappropriate and undermined the military's review process. The General Counsel's subsequent review was grossly deficient. Mr. Haynes's one page recommendation to Secretary of Defense Donald Rumsfeld failed to address the serious legal concerns that had been previously raised by the military services about techniques in the GTMO request. Further, Mr. Haynes's reliance on a legal memo produced by GTMO's Staff Judge Advocate that senior military lawyers called "legally insufficient" and "woefully inadequate" is deeply troubling.

Conclusion 13: Secretary of Defense Donald Rumsfeld's authorization of aggressive interrogation techniques for use at Guantanamo Bay was a direct cause of detainee abuse there. Secretary Rumsfeld's December 2, 2002 approval of Mr. Haynes's recommendation that most of the techniques contained in GTMO's October 11, 2002 request be authorized, influenced and contributed to the use of abusive techniques, including military working dogs, forced nudity, and stress positions, in Afghanistan and Iraq.

Conclusion 14: Department of Defense General Counsel William J. Haynes II's direction to the Department of Defense's Detainee Working Group in early 2003 to consider a legal memo from John Yoo of the Department of Justice's OLC as authoritative, blocked the Working Group from conducting a fair and complete legal analysis and resulted in a report that, in the words of then Department of the Navy General Counsel Alberto Mora contained "profound mistakes in its legal analysis." Reliance on the OLC memo resulted in a final Working Group report that recommended approval of several aggressive techniques, including removal of clothing, sleep deprivation, and slapping, similar to those used in SERE training to teach U.S. personnel to resist abusive interrogations.

Conclusions on Interrogations in Iraq and Afghanistan

Conclusion 15: Special Mission Unit (SMU) Task Force (TF) interrogation policies were influenced by the Secretary of Defense's December 2, 2002 approval of aggressive interrogation techniques for use at GTMO. SMU TF interrogation policies in Iraq included the use of aggressive interrogation techniques such as military working dogs and stress positions. SMU TF policies were a direct cause of detainee abuse and influenced interrogation policies at Abu Ghraib and elsewhere in Iraq.

Conclusion 16: During his assessment visit to Iraq in August and September 2003, GTMO Commander Major General Geoffrey Miller encouraged a view that interrogators should be more aggressive during detainee interrogations.

Conclusion 17: Interrogation policies approved by Lieutenant General Ricardo Sanchez, which included the use of military working dogs and stress positions, were a direct cause of detainee abuse in Iraq. Lieutenant General Sanchez's decision to issue his September 14, 2003 policy with the knowledge that there were ongoing discussions as to the legality of some techniques in it was a serious error in judgment. The September policy was superseded on October 12, 2003 as a result of legal concerns raised by U.S. Central Command. That superseding policy, however, contained ambiguities and contributed to confusion about whether aggressive techniques, such as military working dogs, were authorized for use during interrogations.

Conclusion 18: U.S. Central Command (CENTCOM) failed to conduct proper oversight of Special Mission Unit Task Force interrogation policies. Though aggressive interrogation techniques were removed from Combined Joint Task Force 7 interrogation policies after CENTCOM raised legal concerns about their inclusion in the September 14, 2003 policy issued by Lieutenant General Sanchez, SMU TF interrogation policies authorized some of those same techniques, including stress positions and military working dogs.

Conclusion 19: The abuse of detainees at Abu Ghraib in late 2003 was not simply the result of a few soldiers acting on their own. Interrogation techniques such as stripping detainees of their clothes, placing them in stress positions, and using military working dogs to intimidate them appeared in Iraq only after they had been approved for use in Afghanistan and at GTMO. Secretary of Defense Donald Rumsfeld's December 2, 2002 authorization of aggressive interrogation techniques and subsequent interrogation policies and plans approved by senior military and civilian officials conveyed the message that physical pressures and degradation were appropriate treatment for detainees in U.S. military custody. What followed was an erosion in standards dictating that detainees be treated humanely.

[NSL p. 792, CTL p. 434. Insert at the end of Note 9.]

On April 16, 2009, President Obama authorized the release of four OLC memos describing interrogation techniques used by the CIA between 2002 and 2005. The first memo, written by Jay S. Bybee in 2002, gave the CIA legal approval for waterboarding and other harsh treatment, including forced nudity, slamming detainees into walls, and prolonged sleep deprivation. The three others, signed by Stephen G. Bradbury in May 2005, concluded that the harsh techniques were lawful, even when multiple methods were used in combination. The memos are available at http://www.fas.org/irp/agency/doj/olc/index.html.

[NSL p. 799, insert after Note 1. CTL p. 446, insert after Note 3.]

On July 20, 2007, President Bush signed Executive Order 13,340, *Interpretation of the Geneva Conventions Common Article 3 as Applied to a Program of Detention and Interrogation Operated by the Central*

Intelligence Agency, 72 Fed. Reg. 40,707. The executive order did not authorize the use of any particular interrogation techniques. Instead, it barred the CIA from certain practices, including those forbidden by the Torture Act, the DTA, and the MCA. However, the order did not proscribe techniques expressly prohibited from being used by the military under the most recent Army Field Manual – such as waterboarding, hooding, sleep deprivation, or forced standing for long periods.

Executive Order No. 13,491
Ensuring Lawful Interrogations
74 Fed. Reg. 4893 (Jan. 22, 2009)

By the authority vested in me by the Constitution and the laws of the United States of America, in order to improve the effectiveness of human intelligence-gathering, to promote the safe, lawful, and humane treatment of individuals in United States custody and of United States personnel who are detained in armed conflicts, to ensure compliance with the treaty obligations of the United States, including the Geneva Conventions, and to take care that the laws of the United States are faithfully executed, I hereby order as follows:

Section 1. Revocation.

Executive Order 13440 of July 20, 2007, is revoked. All executive directives, orders, and regulations inconsistent with this order, including but not limited to those issued to or by the Central Intelligence Agency (CIA) from September 11, 2001, to January 20, 2009, concerning detention or the interrogation of detained individuals, are revoked to the extent of their inconsistency with this order. Heads of departments and agencies shall take all necessary steps to ensure that all directives, orders, and regulations of their respective departments or agencies are consistent with this order. Upon request, the Attorney General shall provide guidance about which directives, orders, and regulations are inconsistent with this order.

Sec. 2. Definitions.

As used in this order:

(a) "Army Field Manual 2-22.3" means FM 2-22.3, Human Intelligence Collector Operations, issued by the Department of the Army on September 6, 2006.

(b) "Army Field Manual 34-52" means FM 34-52, Intelligence Interrogation, issued by the Department of the Army on May 8, 1987.

(c) "Common Article 3" means Article 3 of each of the Geneva Conventions.

(d) "Convention Against Torture" means the Convention Against Torture and Other Cruel, Inhuman or Degrading Treatment or Punishment, December 10, 1984, 1465 U.N.T.S. 85, S. Treaty Doc. No. 100-20 (1988).

(e) "Geneva Conventions" means:

(i) the Convention for the Amelioration of the Condition of the Wounded and Sick in Armed Forces in the Field, August 12, 1949 (6 UST 3114);

(ii) the Convention for the Amelioration of the Condition of Wounded, Sick and Shipwrecked Members of Armed Forces at Sea, August 12, 1949 (6 UST 3217);

(iii) the Convention Relative to the Treatment of Prisoners of War, August 12, 1949 (6 UST 3316); and

(iv) the Convention Relative to the Protection of Civilian Persons in Time of War, August 12, 1949 (6 UST 3516).

(f) "Treated humanely," "violence to life and person," "murder of all kinds," "mutilation," "cruel treatment," "torture," "outrages upon personal dignity," and "humiliating and degrading treatment" refer to, and have the same meaning as, those same terms in Common Article 3.

(g) The terms "detention facilities" and "detention facility" in section 4(a) of this order do not refer to facilities used only to hold people on a short-term, transitory basis.

Sec. 3. Standards and Practices for Interrogation of Individuals in the Custody or Control of the United States in Armed Conflicts.

(a) Common Article 3 Standards as a Minimum Baseline. Consistent with the requirements of the Federal torture statute, 18 U.S.C.

2340-2340A, section 1003 of the Detainee Treatment Act of 2005,
42 U.S.C. 2000dd, the Convention Against Torture, Common Article 3,
and other laws regulating the treatment and interrogation of individuals
detained in any armed conflict, such persons shall in all circumstances be
treated humanely and shall not be subjected to violence to life and person
(including murder of all kinds, mutilation, cruel treatment, and torture),
nor to outrages upon personal dignity (including humiliating
and degrading treatment), whenever such individuals are in the custody
or under the effective control of an officer, employee, or other agent of
the United States Government or detained within a facility owned,
operated, or controlled by a department or agency of the United States.

(b) Interrogation Techniques and Interrogation-Related Treatment.
Effective immediately, an individual in the custody or under the effective
control of an officer, employee, or other agent of the United States
Government, or detained within a facility owned, operated, or controlled
by a department or agency of the United States, in any armed conflict,
shall not be subjected to any interrogation technique or approach, or any
treatment related to interrogation, that is not authorized by and listed in
Army Field Manual 2-22.3 (Manual). Interrogation techniques,
approaches, and treatments described in the Manual shall be
implemented strictly in accord with the principles, processes, conditions,
and limitations the Manual prescribes. Where processes required by the
Manual, such as a requirement of approval by specified Department of
Defense officials, are inapposite to a department or an agency other than
the Department of Defense, such a department or agency shall use
processes that are substantially equivalent to the processes the Manual
prescribes for the Department of Defense. Nothing in this section shall
preclude the Federal Bureau of Investigation, or other Federal law
enforcement agencies, from continuing to use authorized, non-coercive
techniques of interrogation that are designed to elicit voluntary
statements and do not involve the use of force, threats, or promises.

(c) Interpretations of Common Article 3 and the Army Field
Manual. From this day forward, unless the Attorney General with
appropriate consultation provides further guidance, officers, employees,
and other agents of the United States Government may, in conducting
interrogations, act in reliance upon Army Field Manual 2-22.3, but may
not, in conducting interrogations, rely upon any interpretation of the law
governing interrogation – including interpretations of Federal criminal

laws, the Convention Against Torture, Common Article 3, Army Field
Manual 2-22.3, and its predecessor document, Army Field
Manual 34-52 – issued by the Department of Justice between
September 11, 2001, and January 20, 2009.

Sec. 4. Prohibition of Certain Detention Facilities, and Red Cross Access to Detained Individuals.

(a) CIA Detention. The CIA shall close as expeditiously as possible
any detention facilities that it currently operates and shall not operate any
such detention facility in the future.

(b) International Committee of the Red Cross Access to Detained
Individuals. All departments and agencies of the Federal Government
shall provide the International Committee of the Red Cross with
notification of, and timely access to, any individual detained in any
armed conflict in the custody or under the effective control of an officer,
employee, or other agent of the United States Government or detained
within a facility owned, operated, or controlled by a department or
agency of the United States Government, consistent with Department of
Defense regulations and policies. . . .

Sec. 6. Construction with Other Laws.

Nothing in this order shall be construed to affect the obligations of
officers, employees, and other agents of the United States Government to
comply with all pertinent laws and treaties of the United States
governing detention and interrogation, including but not limited to: the
Fifth and Eighth Amendments to the United States Constitution; the
Federal torture statute, 18 U.S.C. 2340-2340A; the War Crimes Act,
18 U.S.C. 2441; the Federal assault statute, 18 U.S.C. 113; the Federal
maiming statute, 18 U.S.C. 114; the Federal "stalking" statute, 18 U.S.C.
2261A; articles 93, 124, 128, and 134 of the Uniform Code of Military
Justice, 10 U.S.C. 893, 924, 928, and 934; section 1003 of the Detainee
Treatment Act of 2005, 42 U.S.C. 2000dd; section 6(c) of the Military
Commissions Act of 2006, Public Law 109-366; the Geneva
Conventions; and the Convention Against Torture. Nothing in this order
shall be construed to diminish any rights that any individual may have
under these or other laws and treaties. This order is not intended to, and

does not, create any right or benefit, substantive or procedural, enforceable at law or in equity against the United States, its departments, agencies, or other entities, its officers or employees, or any other person.

[NSL p. 804, CTL p. 453. Substitute for the District Court opinion in *Arar v. Ashcroft* and the Notes and Questions that follow it.]

Arar v. Ashcroft
United States Court of Appeals, Second Circuit (en banc), 2009
585 F.3d 559

DENNIS JACOBS, Chief Judge: Maher Arar appeals from a judgment of the United States District Court for the Eastern District of New York (Trager, J.) dismissing his complaint against the Attorney General of the United States, the Secretary of Homeland Security, the Director of the Federal Bureau of Investigation, and others, including senior immigration officials. Arar alleges that he was detained while changing planes at Kennedy Airport in New York (based on a warning from Canadian authorities that he was a member of Al Qaeda), mistreated for twelve days while in United States custody, and then removed to Syria via Jordan pursuant to an inter-governmental understanding that he would be detained and interrogated under torture by Syrian officials. The complaint alleges a violation of the Torture Victim Protection Act ("TVPA") and of his Fifth Amendment substantive due process rights arising from the conditions of his detention in the United States, the denial of his access to counsel and to the courts while in the United States, and his detention and torture in Syria.

The district court dismissed the complaint (with leave to re-plead only as to the conditions of detention in the United States and his access to counsel and the courts during that period) and Arar timely appealed (without undertaking to amend). *Arar v. Ashcroft,* 414 F. Supp.2d 250 (E.D.N.Y. 2006). A three-judge panel of this Court unanimously held that: (1) the District Court had personal jurisdiction over Thompson, Ashcroft, and Mueller; (2) Arar failed to state a claim under the TVPA; and (3) Arar failed to establish subject matter jurisdiction over his request for a declaratory judgment. *Arar v. Ashcroft,* 532 F.3d 157 (2d Cir. 2008). A majority of the panel also dismissed Arar's *Bivens* claims, with one member of the panel dissenting. *Id.* The Court voted to rehear the appeal *in banc.* We now affirm.

We have no trouble affirming the district court's conclusions that Arar sufficiently alleged personal jurisdiction over the defendants who challenged it, and that Arar lacks standing to seek declaratory relief. We do not reach issues of qualified immunity or the state secrets privilege. As to the TVPA, we agree with the unanimous position of the panel that Arar insufficiently pleaded that the alleged conduct of United States officials was done under color of foreign law. We agree with the district court that Arar insufficiently pleaded his claim regarding detention in the United States, a ruling that has been reinforced by the subsequent authority of *Bell Atlantic Corp. v. Twombly,* 550 U.S. 544, 570 (2007). Our attention is therefore focused on whether Arar's claims for detention and torture in Syria can be asserted under *Bivens v. Six Unknown Named Agents of Federal Bureau of Narcotics,* 403 U.S. 388 (1971) ("*Bivens*").

To decide the *Bivens* issue, we must determine whether Arar's claims invoke *Bivens* in a new context; and, if so, whether an alternative remedial scheme was available to Arar, or whether (in the absence of affirmative action by Congress) "'special factors counsel[ ] hesitation.'" *See Wilkie v. Robbins,* 551 U.S. 537, 550 (2007) (quoting *Bush v. Lucas,* 462 U.S. 367, 378 (1983)). This opinion holds that "extraordinary rendition" is a context new to *Bivens* claims, but avoids any categorical ruling on alternative remedies – because the dominant holding of this opinion is that, in the context of extraordinary rendition, hesitation is warranted by special factors. We therefore affirm. . . .

Our ruling does not preclude judicial review and oversight in this context. But if a civil remedy in damages is to be created for harms suffered in the context of extraordinary rendition, it must be created by Congress, which alone has the institutional competence to set parameters, delineate safe harbors, and specify relief. If Congress chooses to legislate on this subject, then judicial review of such legislation would be available.

Applying our understanding of Supreme Court precedent, we decline to create, on our own, a new cause of action against officers and employees of the federal government. Rather, we conclude that, when a case presents the intractable "special factors" apparent here, it is for the Executive in the first instance to decide how to implement extraordinary rendition, and for the elected members of Congress – and not for us as judges – to decide whether an individual may seek compensation from government officers and employees directly, or from the government, for a constitutional violation. Administrations past and present have reserved the right to employ rendition, *see* David Johnston, *U.S. Says Rendition to Continue, but with More Oversight,* N.Y. Times, Aug. 24, 2009, and not withstanding prolonged public debate, Congress has not prohibited the practice, imposed limits on its use, or created a cause of action for those who allege they have suffered constitutional injury as a consequence.

I

Arar's complaint sets forth the following factual allegations.

Arar is a dual citizen of Syria, where he was born and raised, and of Canada, to which his family immigrated when he was 17.

While on vacation in Tunisia in September 2002, Arar was called back to work in Montreal. His itinerary called for stops in Zurich and New York.

Arar landed at Kennedy Airport around noon on September 26. Between planes, Arar presented his Canadian passport to an immigration official who, after checking Arar's credentials, asked Arar to wait nearby. About two hours later, Arar was fingerprinted and his bags searched. Between 4 p.m. and 9 p.m., Arar was interviewed by an agent from the Federal Bureau of Investigation ("FBI"), who asked (*inter alia*) about his relationships with certain individuals who were suspected of terrorist ties. Arar admitted knowing at least one of them, but denied being a member of a terrorist group. Following the FBI interview, Arar was questioned by an official from the Immigration and Nationalization Service ("INS") for three more hours; he continued to deny terrorist affiliations.

Arar spent the night alone in a room at the airport. The next morning (September 27) he was questioned by FBI agents from approximately 9 a.m. until 2 p.m.; the agents asked him about Osama Bin Laden, Iraq, Palestine, and other things. That evening, Arar was given an opportunity to return voluntarily to Syria. He refused, citing a fear of torture, and asked instead to go to Canada or Switzerland. Later that evening, he was transferred to the Metropolitan Detention Center ("MDC") in Brooklyn, where he remained until October 8.

On October 1, the INS initiated removal proceedings, and served Arar with a document stating that he was inadmissible because he belonged to a terrorist organization. Later that day, he called his mother-in-law in Ottawa – his prior requests to place calls and speak to a lawyer having been denied or ignored. His family retained a lawyer to represent him and contacted the Canadian Consulate in New York.

A Canadian consular official visited Arar on October 3. The next day, immigration officers asked Arar to designate in writing the country to which he would want to be removed. He designated Canada. On the evening of October 5, Arar met with his attorney. The following evening, a Sunday, Arar was again questioned by INS officials. The INS District Director in New York left a voicemail message on the office phone of Arar's attorney that the interview would take place, but the attorney did not receive the message in time to attend. Arar was told that she chose not to attend. In days following, the attorney was given false information about Arar's whereabouts.

On October 8, 2002, Arar learned that the INS had: (1) ordered his removal to Syria, (2) made a (required) finding that such removal would be consistent with Article 3 of the Convention Against Torture ("CAT"), and (3) barred him from re-entering the United States for five years. He was found inadmissible to the United States on the basis of 8 U.S.C. §1182(a)(3)(B)(i)(V), which provides that any alien who "is a member of a terrorist organization" is inadmissible to the United States. The finding was based on Arar's association with a suspected terrorist and other (classified) information. Thereafter, Defendant J. Scott Blackman, an INS Regional Director, made a determination that Arar was clearly and unequivocally a member of Al Qaeda and inadmissible to the United States. A "Final Notice of Inadmissibility," dated October 8, and signed by Defendant Deputy Attorney General Larry Thompson, stated that Arar's removal to Syria would be consistent with the CAT, notwithstanding Arar's articulated fear of torture.

Later that day, Arar was taken to New Jersey, whence he flew in a small jet to Washington, D.C., and then to Amman, Jordan. When he arrived in Amman on October 9, he was handed over to Jordanian authorities who treated him roughly and then delivered him to the custody of Syrian officials, who detained him at a Syrian Military Intelligence facility. Arar was in Syria for a year, the first ten months in an underground cell six feet by three, and seven feet high. He was interrogated for twelve days on his arrival in Syria, and in that period was beaten on his palms, hips, and lower back with a two-inch-thick electric cable and with bare hands. Arar alleges that United States officials conspired to send him to Syria for the purpose of interrogation under torture, and directed the interrogations from abroad by providing Syria with Arar's dossier, dictating questions for the Syrians to ask him, and receiving intelligence learned from the interviews.

On October 20, 2002, Canadian Embassy officials inquired of Syria as to Arar's whereabouts. The next day, Syria confirmed to Canada that Arar was in its custody; that same day, interrogation ceased. Arar remained in Syria, however, receiving visits from Canadian consular officials. On August 14, 2003, Arar defied his captors by telling the Canadians that he had been tortured and was confined to a small underground cell. Five days later, after signing a confession that he had trained as a terrorist in Afghanistan, Arar was moved to various locations. On October 5, 2003, Arar was released to the custody of a Canadian embassy official in Damascus, and was flown to Ottawa the next day.

II

On January 22, 2004, Arar filed a four-count complaint in the Eastern District of New York seeking damages from federal officials for harms suffered as a result of his detention and confinement in the United States and his detention and interrogation in Syria. Count One of Arar's complaint seeks relief under the Torture Victim Protection Act ("TVPA"), 28 U.S.C. §1350 note (a)(1) (the "TVPA claim"). Counts Two and Three seek relief under the Fifth Amendment for Arar's alleged torture in Syria (Count Two) and his detention there (Count Three). Count Four seeks relief under the Fifth Amendment for Arar's detention in the United States prior to his removal to Syria. Arar also seeks a declaratory judgment that defendants' conduct violated his "constitutional, civil, and human rights." . . .

III . . .

At the outset, we conclude (as the panel concluded unanimously) that Arar: (1) sufficiently alleged personal jurisdiction over the defendants, and (2) has no standing to seek declaratory relief; in addition, because we dismiss the action for the reasons set forth below, we need not (and do not) reach the issues of qualified immunity or the state secrets privilege. . . .

IV

The TVPA creates a cause of action for damages against any "individual who, under actual or apparent authority, or color of law, of any foreign nation . . . subjects an individual to torture." 28 U.S.C. § 1350 note (a)(1). Count One of Arar's complaint alleges that the defendants conspired with Jordanian and Syrian officials to have Arar tortured in direct violation of the TVPA.

Any allegation arising under the TVPA requires a demonstration that the defendants acted under color of foreign law, or under its authority. *Kadic v. Karadzic,* 70 F.3d 232, 245 (2d Cir. 1995). "In construing the term[ ] . . . 'color of law,' courts are instructed to look . . . to jurisprudence under 42 U.S.C. § 1983. . . ." *Id.* (citing H.R. Rep. No. 367, 102d Cong., 2d Sess., at 5 (1991) *reprinted in* 1992 U.S.C.C.A.N. 84, 87). Under section 1983, "[t]he traditional definition of acting under color of state law requires that the defendant . . . have exercised power 'possessed by virtue of state law and made possible only because the wrongdoer is clothed with the authority of state law.'" *West v. Atkins,* 487 U.S. 42, 49 (1988) (quoting *United States v. Classic,* 313 U.S. 299, 326 (1941)). The determination as to whether a non-state party acts under color of state law requires an intensely fact-specific judgment unaided by rigid criteria as to whether particular conduct may be fairly attributed to the state. . . .

Accordingly, to state a claim under the TVPA, Arar must adequately allege that the defendants possessed power under Syrian law, and that the offending actions (*i.e.,* Arar's removal to Syria and subsequent torture) derived from an exercise of that power, or that defendants could not have undertaken their culpable actions absent such power. The complaint contains no such allegation. Arar has argued that his allegation of conspiracy cures any deficiency under the TVPA. But the conspiracy allegation is that United States officials encouraged and facilitated the exercise of power by Syrians in Syria, not that the United States officials had or exercised power or authority under Syrian law. The defendants are alleged to have acted under color of federal, not Syrian, law, and to have acted in accordance with alleged federal policies and in pursuit of the aims of the federal government in the international context. At most, it is alleged that the defendants encouraged or solicited certain conduct by foreign officials. Such conduct is insufficient to establish that the defendants were in some way clothed with the authority of Syrian law or that their conduct may otherwise be fairly attributable to Syria. *See, e.g., Harbury v. Hayden,* 444 F. Supp. 2d 19, 42-43 (D.D.C. 2006), *aff'd on other grounds,* 522 F.3d 413 (D.C. Cir. 2008). We therefore agree with the unanimous holding of the panel and affirm the District Court's dismissal of the TVPA claim.

V

Count Four of the complaint alleges that the conditions of confinement in the United States (prior to Arar's removal to Syria), and the denial of access to courts during that detention, violated Arar's substantive due process rights under the Fifth Amendment. The District Court dismissed this claim-without prejudice-as insufficiently pleaded, and invited Arar to re-plead the claim in order to "articulate more precisely the judicial relief he was denied" and to "name those defendants that were personally involved in the alleged unconstitutional treatment." *Arar,* 414 F. Supp. 2d at 286, 287. Arar elected (in his counsel's words) to "stand on the allegations of his original complaint."

On a motion to dismiss, courts require "enough facts to state a claim to relief that is plausible on its face." *Twombly,* 550 U.S. at 570; *see also Ashcroft v. Iqbal,* --- U.S. ----, 129 S. Ct. 1937, 1949-50 (2009). "Factual allegations must be enough to raise a right to relief above the speculative level. . . ." *Twombly,* 550 U.S. at 555. Broad allegations of conspiracy are insufficient; the plaintiff "must provide some factual basis supporting a meeting of the minds, such that defendants entered into an agreement, express or tacit, to achieve the unlawful end." *Webb v. Goord,* 340 F.3d 105, 110 (2d Cir. 2003) (internal quotation marks omitted) (addressing conspiracy claims under 42 U.S.C. §1985). Furthermore, a plaintiff in a *Bivens* action is required to allege facts indicating that the defendants were personally involved in the claimed constitutional violation. *See Ellis v. Blum,* 643 F.2d 68, 85 (2d Cir. 1981).

Arar alleges that "Defendants" – undifferentiated – "denied Mr. Arar effective access to consular assistance, the courts, his lawyers, and family members" in order to effectuate his removal to Syria. But he fails to specify any culpable action taken by any single defendant, and does not allege the "meeting of the minds" that a plausible conspiracy claim requires. He alleges (in passive voice) that his requests to make phone calls "were ignored," and that "he was told" that he was not entitled to a lawyer, but he fails to link these denials to any defendant, named or unnamed. Given this omission, and in view of Arar's rejection of an opportunity to re-plead, we agree with the District Court and the panel majority that this Count of the complaint must be dismissed.

We express no view as to the sufficiency of the pleading otherwise, that is, whether the conduct alleged (if plausibly attributable to defendants) would violate a constitutionally protected interest. To the extent that this claim may be deemed to be a *Bivens*-type action, it may raise some of the special factors considered later in this opinion.

VI

Arar's remaining claims seek relief on the basis of torture and detention in Syria, and are cast as violations of substantive due process. At the outset, Defendants argue that the jurisdictional bar of the INA deprived the District Court of subject-matter jurisdiction over these counts because Arar's removal was conducted pursuant to a decision that was "at the discretion" of the Attorney General. . . .

. . . [W]e need not decide the . . . question of whether the INA bar defeats jurisdiction of Arar's substantive due process claims, because we conclude below that the case must be dismissed at the threshold for other reasons.

VII

In *Bivens*, the Supreme Court "recognized for the first time an implied private action for damages against federal officers alleged to have violated a citizen's constitutional rights." *Corr. Servs. Corp. v. Malesko,* 534 U.S. 61, 66, (2001). The plaintiff in *Bivens* had been subjected to an unlawful, warrantless search which resulted in his arrest. The Supreme Court allowed him to state a cause of action for money damages directly under the Fourth Amendment, thereby giving rise to a judicially-created remedy stemming directly from the Constitution itself.

The purpose of the *Bivens* remedy "is to deter individual federal officers from committing constitutional violations." *Malesko,* 534 U.S. at 70. So a *Bivens* action is brought against individuals, and any damages are payable by the offending officers. *Carlson v. Green,* 446 U.S. 14, 21(1980). Notwithstanding the potential breadth of claims that would serve that objective, the Supreme Court has warned that the *Bivens* remedy is an extraordinary thing that should rarely if ever be applied in "new contexts." *See Malesko,* 534 U.S. at 69 (internal quotation marks omitted). In the 38 years since *Bivens,* the Supreme Court has extended it twice only: in the context of an employment discrimination claim in violation of the Due Process Clause, *Davis v. Passman,* 442 U.S. 228 (1979); and in the context of an Eighth Amendment violation by prison officials, *Carlson,* 446 U.S. 14. Since *Carlson* in 1980, the Supreme Court has declined to extend the *Bivens* remedy in any new direction at all. Among the rejected contexts are: violations of federal employees' First Amendment rights by their employers, *Bush v. Lucas,* 462 U.S. 367 (1983); harms suffered incident to military service, *United States v. Stanley,* 483 U.S. 669 (1987); denials of Social Security benefits, *Schweiker,* 487 U.S. at 412; claims against federal agencies, *FDIC v. Meyer,* 510 U.S. 471 (1994); claims against private corporations operating under federal contracts, *Malesko,* 534 U.S. 61 (2001); and claims of retaliation by federal officials against private landowners, *Wilkie,* 551 U.S. at 562.

This case requires us to examine whether allowing this *Bivens* action to proceed would extend *Bivens* to a new "context," and if so, whether such an extension is advisable.

"Context" is not defined in the case law. At a sufficiently high level of generality, any claim can be analogized to some other claim for which a *Bivens* action is afforded, just as at a sufficiently high level of particularity, every case has points of distinction. We construe the word "context" as it is commonly used in law: to reflect a potentially recurring scenario that has similar legal and factual components.

The context of this case is international rendition, specifically, "extraordinary rendition." Extraordinary rendition is treated as a distinct phenomenon in international law. Indeed, law review articles that affirmatively advocate the creation of a remedy in cases like Arar's recognize "extraordinary rendition" as the context. *See, e.g.,* Peter Johnston, Note, *Leaving the Invisible Universe: Why All Victims of*

Extraordinary Rendition Need a Cause of Action Against the United States, 16 J.L. & Pol'y 357, 363 (2007). More particularly, the context of extraordinary rendition in Arar's case is the complicity or cooperation of United States government officials in the delivery of a non-citizen to a foreign country for torture (or with the expectation that torture will take place). This is a "new context": no court has previously afforded a *Bivens* remedy for extraordinary rendition.

Once we have identified the context as "new," we must decide whether to recognize a *Bivens* remedy in that environment of fact and law. The Supreme Court tells us that this is a two-part inquiry. In order to determine whether to recognize a *Bivens* remedy in a new context, we must consider: whether there is an alternative remedial scheme available to the plaintiff; and whether "'special factors counsel[ ] hesitation'" in creating a *Bivens* remedy. *Wilkie,* 551 U.S. at 550 (quoting *Bush,* 462 U.S. at 378).

VIII . . .

. . . [W]e need not decide whether an alternative remedial scheme was available because, "even in the absence of an alternative [remedial scheme], a *Bivens* remedy is a subject of judgment . . . [in which] courts must . . . pay particular heed . . . to any special factors counselling hesitation before authorizing a new kind of federal litigation." *Wilkie,* 551 U.S. at 550. Such special factors are clearly present in the new context of this case, and they sternly counsel hesitation.

IX

When the *Bivens* cause of action was created in 1971, the Supreme Court explained that such a remedy could be afforded because that "case involve[d] no special factors counselling hesitation in the absence of affirmative action by Congress." *Bivens,* 403 U.S. at 396. This prudential limitation was expressly weighed by the Court in *Davis,* 442 U.S. at 245-46, and *Carlson,* 446 U.S. at 18-19, and such hesitation has defeated numerous *Bivens* initiatives, *see, e.g., Stanley,* 483 U.S. at 683-84; [*Chappell v. Wallace,* 462 U.S. 296 (1983)] at 304; *Wilkie,* 551 U.S. at 554-55; [*Dotson v. Griesa,* 398 F.3d 156 (2d Cir. 2005)] at 166-67. Among the "special factors" that have "counsel[ed] hesitation" and thereby foreclosed a *Bivens* remedy are: military concerns, *Stanley,* 483 U.S. at 683-84; *Chappell,* 462 U.S. at 304; separation of powers, *United States v. City of Philadelphia,* 644 F.2d 187, 200 (3d Cir. 1980); the comprehensiveness of available statutory schemes, *Dotson,* 398 F.3d at 166; national security concerns, *Beattie v. Boeing Co.,* 43 F.3d 559, 563 (10th Cir. 1994); and foreign policy considerations, *United States v. Verdugo-Urquidez,* 494 U.S. 259, 274 (1990).

Two principles emerge from this review of case law:

- "Special factors" is an embracing category, not easily defined; but it is limited in terms to factors that provoke "hesitation." While special factors should be substantial enough to justify the absence of a damages remedy for a wrong, no account is taken of countervailing factors that might counsel alacrity or activism, and none has ever been cited by the Supreme Court as a reason for affording a *Bivens* remedy where it would not otherwise exist.
- The only relevant threshold – that a factor "counsels hesitation" – is remarkably low. It is at the opposite end of the continuum from the unflagging duty to exercise jurisdiction. Hesitation is a pause, not a full stop, or an abstention; and to counsel is not to require. "Hesitation" is "counseled" whenever thoughtful discretion would pause even to consider.

With these principles in mind, we adduce, one by one, special factors that bear upon the recognition of a *Bivens* remedy for rendition.

X

Although this action is cast in terms of a claim for money damages against the defendants in their individual capacities, it operates as a constitutional challenge to policies promulgated by the executive. Our federal system of checks and balances provides means to consider allegedly unconstitutional executive policy, but a private action for money damages against individual policymakers is not one of them. A *Bivens* action is sometimes analogized to an action pursuant to 42 U.S.C. §1983, but it does not reach so far as to create the federal counterpart to an action under *Monell v. Department of Social Services,* 436 U.S. 658 (1978). Here, we need not decide categorically whether a *Bivens* action can lie against policymakers because in the context of extraordinary rendition, such an action would have the natural tendency to affect diplomacy, foreign policy, and the security of the nation, and that fact counsels hesitation. Our holding need be no broader.

A. Security and Foreign Policy

The Executive has practiced rendition since at least 1995. *See* Extraordinary Rendition in U.S. Counterterrorism Policy: The Impact on Transatlantic Relations: Joint Hearing Before the Subcomm. on International Organizations, Human Rights, and Oversight and the Subcomm. on Europe of the H. Comm. on Foreign Affairs, 110th Cong. 15 (2007) (statement of Michael F. Scheuer, Former Chief, Bin Laden Unit, CIA). Arar gives "the mid-1990s" as the date for the inception of the policy under which he was sent to Syria for torture. A suit seeking a damages remedy against senior officials who implement such a policy is in critical respects a suit against the government as to which the government has not waived sovereign immunity. Such a suit unavoidably influences government policy, probes government secrets, invades government interests, enmeshes government lawyers, and thereby elicits government funds for settlement. (Canada has already paid Arar $10 million.)

It is a substantial understatement to say that one must hesitate before extending *Bivens* into such a context. A suit seeking a damages remedy against senior officials who implement an extraordinary rendition policy would enmesh the courts ineluctably in an assessment of the validity and rationale of that policy and its implementation in this particular case, matters that directly affect significant diplomatic and national security concerns. It is clear from the face of the complaint that Arar explicitly targets the "policy" of extraordinary rendition; he cites the policy twice in his complaint, and submits documents and media reports concerning the practice. His claim cannot proceed without inquiry into the perceived need for the policy, the threats to which it responds, the substance and sources of the intelligence used to formulate it, and the propriety of adopting specific responses to particular threats in light of apparent geopolitical circumstances and our relations with foreign countries.

The Supreme Court has expressly counseled that matters touching upon foreign policy and national security fall within "an area of

executive action 'in which courts have long been *hesitant* to intrude'"
absent congressional authorization. *Lincoln v. Vigil*, 508 U.S. 182, 192
(1993) (emphasis added) (*quoting Franklin v. Massachusetts*, 505 U.S.
788, 819 (1992) (Stevens, J., concurring in part and concurring in the
judgment)). It "has recognized 'the generally accepted view that foreign
policy was the province and responsibility of the Executive. . . . Thus,
unless Congress specifically has provided otherwise, courts traditionally
have been *reluctant* to intrude upon the authority of the Executive in
military and national security affairs." *Dep't of Navy v. Egan*, 484 U.S.
518, 529-30 (1988) (emphasis added) (*quoting Haig v. Agee*, 453 U.S.
280, 293-94 (1981)). This "hesita[tion]" and "reluctan[ce]" is counseled
by:

- the constitutional separation of powers among the branches of
  government, *see United States v. Curtiss-Wright Exp. Co.*, 299 U.S.
  304, 320-22 (1936) . . .
- the limited institutional competence of the judiciary, *see Boumediene v.
  Bush*, --- U.S. ----, 128 S. Ct. 2229, 2276-77 (2008) ("Unlike the
  President and some designated Members of Congress, neither the
  Members of this Court nor most federal judges begin the day with
  briefings that may describe new and serious threats to our Nation and
  its people. The law must accord the Executive substantial authority to
  apprehend and detain those who pose a real danger to our security."). . . .

B. *Classified Information*

The extraordinary rendition context involves exchanges among the
ministries and agencies of foreign countries on diplomatic, security, and
intelligence issues. The sensitivities of such classified material are "too
obvious to call for enlarged discussion." *Dep't of Navy*, 484 U.S. at 529
(internal quotation marks omitted). Even the probing of these matters
entails the risk that other countries will become less willing to cooperate
with the United States in sharing intelligence resources to counter
terrorism. "At its core," as the panel opinion observed, "this suit arises
from the Executive Branch's alleged determination that (a) Arar was
affiliated with Al Qaeda, and therefore a threat to national security, and
(b) his removal to Syria was appropriate in light of U.S. diplomatic and
national security interests." *Arar*, 532 F.3d at 181. To determine the basis

for Arar's alleged designation as an Al Qaeda member and his subsequent removal to Syria, the district court would have to consider what was done by the national security apparatus of at least three foreign countries, as well as that of the United States. Indeed, the Canadian government-which appears to have provided the intelligence that United States officials were acting upon when they detained Arar-paid Arar compensation for its role in the events surrounding this lawsuit, but has *also* asserted the need for Canada itself to maintain the confidentiality of certain classified materials related to Arar's claims.

C. Open Courts

Allegations of conspiracy among government agencies that must often work in secret inevitably implicate a lot of classified material that cannot be introduced into the public record. Allowing Arar's claims to proceed would very likely mean that some documents or information sought by Arar would be redacted, reviewed *in camera,* and otherwise concealed from the public. Concealment does not bespeak wrongdoing: in such matters, it is just as important to conceal what has *not* been done. Nevertheless, these measures would excite suspicion and speculation as to the true nature and depth of the supposed conspiracy, and as to the scope and depth of judicial oversight. Indeed, after an inquiry at oral argument as to whether classified materials relating to Arar's claims could be made available for review *in camera,* Arar objected to the supplementation of the record with material he could not see. *See* Letter from David Cole, Counsel for Maher Arar (Dec. 23, 2008). After pointing out that such materials are unnecessary to the adjudication of a motion on the pleadings (where the allegations of the complaint must be accepted as true), Arar protested that any materials submitted *ex parte* and *in camera* would not be subject to adversarial testing and that consideration of such documents would be "presumptively unconstitutional" since they would result in a decision "on the basis of secret information available to only one side of the dispute."

The court's reliance on information that cannot be introduced into the public record is likely to be a common feature of any *Bivens* actions arising in the context of alleged extraordinary rendition. This should provoke hesitation, given the strong preference in the Anglo-American legal tradition for open court proceedings, a value incorporated into modern First and Sixth Amendment law. . . .

XI

A government report states that this case involves assurances received from other governments in connection with the determination that Arar's removal to Syria would be consistent with Article 3 of the CAT. Office of Inspector General, Dep't of Homeland Sec., (Unclassified) *The Removal of a Canadian Citizen to Syria* 5, 22, 26-27 (2008). This case is not unique in that respect. Cases in the context of extraordinary rendition are very likely to present serious questions relating to private diplomatic assurances from foreign countries received by federal officials, and this feature of such claims opens the door to graymail.

A. Assurances

The regulations promulgated pursuant to the [Foreign Affairs Reform and Restructuring Act of 1998 ("FARRA"), 8 U.S.C. §1231 note] explicitly authorize the removal of an alien to a foreign country following receipt from that country of sufficiently reliable assurances that the alien will not be tortured. *See* 8 C.F.R. §208.18(c). Should we decide to extend *Bivens* into the extraordinary rendition context, resolution of these actions will require us to determine whether any such assurances were received from the country of rendition and whether the relevant defendants relied upon them in good faith in removing the alien at issue.

Any analysis of these questions would necessarily involve us in an inquiry into the work of foreign governments and several federal agencies, the nature of certain classified information, and the extent of secret diplomatic relationships. An investigation into the existence and content of such assurances would potentially embarrass our government through inadvertent or deliberate disclosure of information harmful to our own and other states. Given the general allocation of authority over foreign relations to the political branches and the decidedly limited experience and knowledge of the federal judiciary regarding such matters, such an investigation would also implicate grave concerns about the separation of powers and our institutional competence. These considerations strongly counsel hesitation in acknowledging a *Bivens* remedy in this context.

B. Graymail

. . . [T]here is further reason to hesitate where, as in this case, the challenged government policies are the subject of classified communications: a possibility that such suits will make the government "vulnerable to 'graymail,' *i.e.,* individual lawsuits brought to induce the [government] to settle a case (or prevent its filing) out of fear that any effort to litigate the action would reveal classified information that may undermine ongoing covert operations," or otherwise compromise foreign policy efforts. *Tenet v. Doe,* 544 U.S. 1, 11 (2005). We cast no aspersions on Arar, or his lawyers; this dynamic inheres in any case where there is a risk that a defendant might "disclose classified information in the course of a trial." *United States v. Pappas,* 94 F.3d 795, 799 (2d Cir. 1996). This is an endemic risk in cases (however few) which involve a claim like Arar's.

The risk of graymail is itself a special factor which counsels hesitation in creating a *Bivens* remedy. There would be hesitation enough in an ordinary graymail case, *i.e.,* where the tactic is employed against the *government,* which can trade settlement cash (or the dismissal of criminal charges) for secrecy. *See Tenet,* 544 U.S. at 11; *Pappas,* 94 F.3d at 799. But the graymail risk in a *Bivens* rendition case is uniquely troublesome. The interest in protecting military, diplomatic, and intelligence secrets is located (as always) in the *government;* yet a *Bivens* claim, by definition, is never pleaded against the government. *See, e.g., Malesko,* 534 U.S. at 70. So in a *Bivens* case, there is a dissociation between the holder of the non-disclosure interest (the government, which cannot be sued directly under *Bivens*) and the person with the incentive to disclose (the defendant, who cannot waive, but will be liable for any damages assessed). In a rendition case, the *Bivens* plaintiff could in effect pressure the individual defendants until the *government* cries uncle. Thus any *Bivens* action involving extraordinary rendition would inevitably suck the government into the case to protect its considerable interests, and – if disclosure is ordered – to appeal, or to suffer the disclosure, or to pay. . . .

In the end, a *Bivens* action based on rendition is – in all but name – a claim against the government. It is not for nothing that Canada (the government, not an individual officer of it) paid Arar $10 million dollars.

XII

In the small number of contexts in which courts have implied a *Bivens* remedy, it has often been easy to identify both the line between constitutional and unconstitutional conduct, and the alternative course which officers should have pursued. The guard who beat a prisoner should not have beaten him; the agent who searched without a warrant should have gotten one; and the immigration officer who subjected an alien to multiple strip searches without cause should have left the alien in his clothes. This distinction may or may not amount to a special factor counseling hesitation in the implication of a *Bivens* remedy. But it is surely remarkable that the context of extraordinary rendition is so different, involving as it does a complex and rapidly changing legal framework beset with critical legal judgments that have not yet been made, as well as policy choices that are by no means easily reached.

Consider: should the officers here have let Arar go on his way and board his flight to Montreal? Canada was evidently unwilling to receive him; it was, after all, Canadian authorities who identified Arar as a terrorist (or did something that led their government to apologize publicly to Arar and pay him $10 million).

Should a person identified as a terrorist by his own country be allowed to board his plane and go on to his destination? Surely, that would raise questions as to what duty is owed to the other passengers and the crew.

Or should a suspected terrorist en route to Canada have been released on the Canadian border – over which he could re-enter the United States virtually at will? Or should he have been sent back whence his plane came, or to some third country? Should those governments be told that Canada thinks he is a terrorist? If so, what country would take him?

Or should the suspected terrorist have been sent to Guantanamo Bay or – if no other country would take him – kept in the United States with the prospect of release into the general population? *See Zadvydas v. Davis*, 533 U.S. 678, 699-700 (2001).

None of this is to say that extraordinary rendition is or should be a favored policy choice. At the same time, the officials required to decide these vexed issues are "subject to the pull of competing obligations." *Lombardi v. Whitman,* 485 F.3d 73, 83 (2d Cir. 2007). Many viable actions they might consider "clash with other equally important governmental responsibilities." *Pena v. DePrisco,* 432 F.3d 98, 114 (2d Cir. 2005) (internal quotation marks omitted). Given the ample reasons for pause already discussed, we need not and do not rely on this consideration in concluding that it is inappropriate to extend *Bivens* to this context. Still, Congress is the appropriate branch of government to decide under what circumstances (if any) these kinds of policy decisions – which are directly related to the security of the population and the foreign affairs of the country – should be subjected to the influence of litigation brought by aliens.

XIII

All of these special factors notwithstanding, we cannot ignore that, as the panel dissent put it, "there is a long history of judicial review of Executive and Legislative decisions related to the conduct of foreign relations and national security." *Arar,* 532 F.3d at 213 (Sack, J., concurring in part and dissenting in part). Where does that leave us? We recognize our limited competence, authority, and jurisdiction to make rules or set parameters to govern the practice called rendition. By the same token, we can easily locate that competence, expertise, and responsibility elsewhere: in Congress. Congress may be content for the Executive Branch to exercise these powers without judicial check. But if Congress wishes to create a remedy for individuals like Arar, it can enact legislation that includes enumerated eligibility parameters, delineated safe harbors, defined review processes, and specific relief to be afforded. Once Congress has performed this task, *then* the courts in a proper case will be able to review the statute and provide judicial oversight to the "Executive and Legislative decisions [which have been made with regard] to the conduct of foreign relations and national security." *Id.* . . .

SACK, Circuit Judge, joined by Judges CALABRESI, POOLER, and PARKER, concurring in part and dissenting in part. . . . We disagree . . . with the majority's continued insistence that Arar cannot employ a

Bivens remedy to seek compensation for his injuries at the hands of government agents. The majority reaches that conclusion by artificially dividing the complaint into a domestic claim that does not involve torture – viz., "[Arar's] claim regarding detention in the United States," – and a foreign claim that does – viz., "[Arar's] claims for detention and torture in Syria." The majority then dismisses the domestic claim as inadequately pleaded and the foreign claim as one that cannot "be asserted under *Bivens*" in light of the opinion's "dominant holding" that "in the context of involuntary rendition, hesitation is warranted by special factors.". . .

As we will explain, . . . the complaint's allegations cannot properly be divided into claims for mistreatment in the United States and "claims for detention and torture in Syria." Arar's complaint of mistreatment sweeps more broadly than that, encompassing a chain of events that began with his interception and detention at New York's John F. Kennedy Airport ("JFK") and continued with his being sent abroad in shackles by government agents with the knowledge that he would likely be tortured as a result. Viewed in this light, we conclude that Arar's allegations do not present a "new context" for a *Bivens* action.

And even were it a new context, we disagree with what appears to be the *en banc* majority's test for whether a new *Bivens* action should be made available: the existence *vel non* of "special factors counselling hesitation." First, we think heeding "special factors" relating to secrecy and security is a form of double counting inasmuch as those interests are fully protected by the state-secrets privilege. Second, in our view the applicable test is not whether "special factors" exist, but whether after "paying particular heed to" them, a *Bivens* remedy should be recognized with respect to at least some allegations in the complaint. Applying that test, we think a *Bivens* remedy is available. . . .

Our overriding concern, however, is with the majority's apparent determination to go to whatever length necessary to reach what it calls its "dominant holding": that a *Bivens* remedy is unavailable. Such a holding is unnecessary inasmuch as the government assures us that this case could likely be resolved quickly and expeditiously in the district court by application of the state-secrets privilege. . . .

II. The Dismissal of the Fourth Claim for Relief . . .

A. *Specification of Defendants' Acts and Conspiracy Allegations* . . .

Arar should not have been required to "name those defendants [who] were personally involved in the alleged unconstitutional treatment." *Arar,* 414 F. Supp. 2d at 287. In actions pursuant to 42 U.S.C. §1983, which are "analog [s]" of the less-common *Bivens* action, *Ashcroft v. Iqbal,*--- U.S. ----, ----, 129 S. Ct. 1937, 1948 (2009) (citation omitted), we allow plaintiffs to "maintain[ ] supervisory personnel as defendants . . . until [they have] been afforded an opportunity through at least brief discovery to identify the subordinate officials who have personal liability." *Davis v. Kelly,* 160 F.3d 917, 921 (2d Cir. 1998) (citing Second Circuit authority).

> Similarly, courts have rejected the dismissal of suits against unnamed defendants described by roles . . . until the plaintiff has had some opportunity for discovery to learn the identities of responsible officials. Once the supervisory officer has inquired within the institution and identified the actual decision-makers of the challenged action, those officials may then submit affidavits based on their personal knowledge of the circumstances.

Id. (citations omitted). . . .

To be sure, the Supreme Court has recently set a strict pleading standard for supervisory liability claims under Bivens against a former Attorney General of the United States and the Director of the FBI." *See Iqbal, supra.* We do not think, however, that the Court has thereby permitted governmental actors who are unnamed in a complaint automatically to escape personal civil rights liability. A plaintiff must, after all, have some way to identify a defendant who anonymously violates his civil rights. We doubt that *Iqbal* requires a plaintiff to obtain his abusers' business cards in order to state a civil rights claim. Put conversely, we do not think that *Iqbal* implies that federal government miscreants may avoid *Bivens* liability altogether through the simple expedient of wearing hoods while inflicting injury. Some manner of proceeding must be made available for the reasons we recognized in *Davis.*

Whether or not there is a mechanism available to identify the "Doe" defendants, moreover, Arar's complaint *does* sufficiently name some individual defendants who personally took part in the alleged violation of his civil rights. The role of defendant J. Scott Blackman, formerly Director of the Regional Office of INS, for example, is, as reflected in the district court's explication of the facts, *see Arar,* 414 F. Supp. 2d at 252-54, set forth in reasonable detail in the complaint. So are at least some of the acts of the defendant Edward J. McElroy, District Director of the INS. . . .

C. Sufficient Pleading under Iqbal

More generally, we think the district court's extended recitation of the allegations in the complaint makes clear that the facts of Arar's mistreatment while within the United States – including the alleged denial of his access to courts and counsel and his alleged mistreatment while in federal detention in the United States – were pleaded meticulously and in copious detail. The assertion of relevant places, times, and events – and names when known – is lengthy and specific. Even measured in light of Supreme Court case law post-dating the district court's dismissal of the fourth claim, which instituted a more stringent standard of review for pleadings, the complaint here passes muster. It does not "offer[ ] 'labels and conclusions' or 'a formulaic recitation of the elements of a cause of action.'" *Iqbal,* 129 S. Ct. at 1949 (quoting *Bell Atl. Corp. v. Twombly,* 550 U.S. 544, 555 (2007)). Nor does it "tender[ ] 'naked assertion[s]' devoid of 'further factual enhancement.'" *Id.* (quoting *Twombly,* 550 U.S. at 557). Its allegations of a constitutional violation are "'plausible on [their] face.'" *Id.* (quoting *Twombly,* 550 U.S. at 555). And, as we have explained, Arar has pled "factual content that allows the court to draw the reasonable inference that the defendant[s][are] liable for the misconduct alleged." *Id.* (quoting *Twombly,* 550 U.S. at 556). We would therefore vacate the district court's dismissal of the Fourth Claim for Relief.

III. The Majority's Interpretation of the Second and Third Claims for Relief . . .

Although Arar pled in his Fourth Claim for Relief what he denominated as a separate "Claim" on the subject of "Domestic

Detention," including allegations about unconstitutional conditions of confinement and denial of access to courts and counsel, the complaint as a whole makes broader allegations of mistreatment while within the borders of the United States. . . .

It may not have been best for Arar to file a complaint that structures his claims for relief so as to charge knowing or reckless subjection to torture, coercive interrogation, and arbitrary detention in Syria (the second and third claims) separately from charges of cruel and inhuman conditions of confinement and "interfere[nce] with access to lawyers and the courts" while in the United States (the fourth claim). But such division of theories is of no legal consequence. "'Factual allegations alone are what matter [ ].'" *Northrop*, 134 F.3d at 46 (quoting *Albert*, 851 F.2d at 571 n.3). The assessment of Arar's complaint must, then, take into account the entire arc of factual allegations that it contains – his interception and arrest; his interrogation, principally by FBI agents, about his putative ties to terrorists; his detention and mistreatment at JFK in Queens and the MDC in Brooklyn; the deliberate misleading of both his lawyer and the Canadian Consulate; and his transport to Washington, D.C. and forced transfer to Syrian authorities for further detention and questioning under torture. Such attention to the complaint's factual allegations, rather than its legal theories, makes perfectly clear that the remaining claims upon which Arar seeks relief are not limited to his "detention or torture in Syria," but include allegations of violations of his due process rights in the United States. The scope of those claims is relevant in analyzing whether a *Bivens* remedy is available.

IV. The "Context" in Which a *Bivens* Remedy Is Sought

The majority's artificial interpretation of the complaint permits it to characterize the "context" of Arar's *Bivens* action as entirely one of "international rendition, specifically, 'extraordinary rendition.'" This permits the majority to focus on the part of the complaint that presents a "new context" for *Bivens* purposes. But when the complaint is considered in light of all of Arar's allegations, his due process claim for relief from his apprehension, detention, interrogation, and denial of access to counsel and courts in the United States, as well as his expulsion to Syria for further interrogation likely under torture, is not at all "new.". . .

C. The New Context Test . . .

If the alleged facts of Arar's complaint were limited to his claim of "extraordinary rendition" to, and torture in, Syria – that is, limited to his allegations that he was transported by the United States government to Syria via Jordan pursuant to a conspiracy or other arrangement among the countries or their agents and mistreated in Syria as a result – as the majority would have it, then we might well agree that we are dealing with a "new context." But. . . the complaint is not so limited. Incarceration in the United States without cause, mistreatment while so incarcerated, denial of access to counsel and the courts while so incarcerated, and the facilitation of torture by others, considered as possible violations of a plaintiff's procedural and substantive due process rights, are hardly novel claims, nor do they present us with a "new context" in any legally significant sense.

We have recognized implied *Bivens* rights of action pursuant to the Due Process Clause, so Arar's claims for relief are not new actions under *Bivens* in that sense. . . . In *Iqbal*, for example, we considered a *Bivens* action brought on, *inter alia,* a Fifth Amendment substantive due process theory. The plaintiff alleged physical mistreatment and humiliation, as a Muslim prisoner, by federal prison officials, while he was detained at the MDC. After concluding, on interlocutory appeal, that the defendants were not entitled to qualified immunity, we returned the matter to the district court for further proceedings. We did not so much as hint either that a *Bivens* remedy was unavailable or that its availability would constitute an unwarranted extension of the *Bivens* doctrine. *Iqbal,* 490 F.3d at 177-78. . . .

Indeed, even the most "international" of Arar's domestic allegations – that the defendants, acting within the United States, sent Arar to Syria with the intent that he be tortured – present no new context for *Bivens* purposes. Principles of substantive due process apply to a narrow band of extreme misbehavior by government agents acting under color of law: mistreatment that is "so egregious, so outrageous, that it may fairly be said to shock the contemporary conscience." *Lombardi v. Whitman,* 485 F.3d 73, 79 (2d Cir.2007) (internal quotation marks omitted). Sending Arar from the United States with the intent or understanding that he will be tortured in Syria easily exceeds the level of outrageousness needed to make out a substantive due process claim. . . .

To be sure, Arar alleges not that the defendants themselves tortured him; he says that they "outsourced" it. But we do not think that the question whether the defendants violated Arar's substantive due process rights turns on whom they selected to do the torturing, or that such "outsourcing" somehow changes the essential character of the acts within the United States to which Arar seeks to hold the defendants accountable. . . .

V. Devising a New *Bivens* Damages Action . . .

B. The Special Factors Identified by the Majority . . .

. . . After *Iqbal,* it would be difficult to argue that Arar's complaint can survive as against defendants who are alleged to have been supervisors with, at most, "knowledge" of Arar's mistreatment. *See Iqbal,* 129 S. Ct. at 1949; *see also id.* at 1955 (Souter, J., dissenting). And to the extent that the United States remains a defendant, perhaps it should be dismissed for want of possible liability under *Bivens* too. But that does not dispose of the case against the lower-level defendants, such as Blackman, McElroy, and the Doe defendants, who are alleged to have personally undertaken purposeful unconstitutional actions against Arar.

It also may be that to the extent actions against "policymakers" can be equated with lawsuits against policies, they may not survive *Iqbal* either. But while those championing Arar's case may in fact wish to challenge extraordinary rendition policy writ large, the relief Arar himself seeks is principally compensation for an unconstitutional implementation of that policy. That is what *Bivens* actions are for. . . .

. . . The other "special factors" cited by the majority focus our attention on the ability of the executive to conduct the business of diplomacy and government in secret as necessary and to protect public and private security. It is beyond dispute that the judiciary must protect that concern. *See, e.g., Doe v. CIA,* 576 F.3d 95 (2d Cir. 2009). But inasmuch as there are established procedures for doing just that, we think treating that need as giving rise to "special factors counseling hesitation" is an unfortunate form of double counting. The problem can be, should be, and customarily is, dealt with case by case by employing the established procedures of the state-secrets doctrine, rather than by barring all such plaintiffs at the courtroom door without further inquiry.

C. *Factors Weighing in Favor of a* Bivens *Action*

At least some factors weigh in favor of permitting a *Bivens* action in this case. We assume, as we are required to, that Arar suffered a grievous infringement of his constitutional rights by one or more of the defendants, from his interception and detention while changing planes at an international airport to the time two weeks later when he was sent off in the expectation – perhaps the intent and expectation – that he would be tortured, all in order to obtain information from him. Breach of a constitutional or legal duty would appear to counsel in favor of some sort of opportunity for the victim to obtain a remedy for it. . . .

VI. The State-Secrets Privilege

[The dissenters argue that the state-secrets privilege is well suited to provide for a ruling on the merits of Arar's claims.] . . .

BARRINGTON D. PARKER, Circuit Judge, joined by Judges CALABRESI, POOLER, and SACK, dissenting: . . . My point of departure from the majority is the text of the Convention Against Torture, which provides that "[n]o exceptional circumstances whatsoever, whether a state of war or a threat of war, internal political instability or any other public emergency, may be invoked as a justification of torture." United Nations Convention Against Torture and Other Cruel, Inhuman, or Degrading Treatment or Punishment Art. 2, cl. 2, December 10, 1984, S. Treaty Doc. No. 100-20, 1465 U.N.T.S. 85 ("Convention Against Torture"). Because the majority has neglected this basic commitment and a good deal more, I respectfully dissent.

Maher Arar credibly alleges that United States officials conspired to ship him from American soil, where the Constitution and our laws apply, to Syria, where they do not, so that Syrian agents could torture him at federal officials' direction and behest. He also credibly alleges that, to accomplish this unlawful objective, agents of our government actively obstructed his access to this very Court and the protections established by Congress. *See* 8 U.S.C. §1252(a)(2)(D) (providing for judicial review of constitutional claims or questions of law raised by an order of removal).

While I broadly concur with my colleagues who dissent, I write separately to underscore the miscarriage of justice that leaves Arar without a remedy in our courts. The majority would immunize official misconduct by invoking the separation of powers and the executive's responsibility for foreign affairs and national security. Its approach distorts the system of checks and balances essential to the rule of law, and it trivializes the judiciary's role in these arenas. To my mind, the most depressing aspect of the majority's opinion is its sincerity. . . .

Notably, the majority opinion does not appear to dispute the notion that Arar has stated an injury under the Fifth Amendment of the Constitution. That is heartening, because, by any measure, the notion that federal officials conspired to send a man to Syria to be tortured "shocks the conscience." *Rochin v. California,* 342 U.S. 165, 172 (1952). What is profoundly disturbing, however, is the Court's pronouncement that it can offer Arar no opportunity to prove his case and no possibility of relief. This conclusion is at odds with the Court's responsibility to enforce the Constitution's protections and cannot, in my view, be reconciled with *Bivens.* The majority is at odds, too, with our own State Department, which has repeatedly taken the position before the world community that this exact remedy is available to torture victims like Arar. If the Constitution ever implied a damages remedy, this is such a case – where executive officials allegedly blocked access to the remedies chosen by Congress in order to deliver a man to known torturers.

The Court's hesitation today immunizes official conduct directly at odds with the express will of Congress and the most basic guarantees of liberty contained in the Constitution. By doing so, the majority risks a government that can interpret the law to suits its own ends, without scrutiny. . . .

I . . .

When presented with an appropriate case or controversy, courts are entitled – indeed obliged – to act, even in instances where government officials seek to shield their conduct behind invocations of "national security" and "foreign policy." *See, e.g., Hamdan v. Rumsfeld,* 548 U.S. 557 723 (2006); *Reid v. Covert,* 354 U.S. 1, 23-30 (1957); *Youngstown [Sheet & Tube Co. v. Sawyer,* 343 U.S. 579 (1952)]. *Compare Ex parte Quirin,* 317 U.S. 1, 19 (1942) (observing the "duty which rests on the courts, in time of war as well as in time of peace, to preserve unimpaired the constitutional safeguards of civil liberty"), *with* Maj. Op. at 42 (suggesting that Arar's allegations do not trigger the Court's "unflagging duty to exercise [its] jurisdiction"). This authority derives directly from the Constitution and goes hand in hand with the responsibility of the courts to adjudicate all manner of cases put before them. . . .

II . . .

. . . [C]ontrary to the majority's suggestion, the courts require no invitation from Congress before considering claims that touch upon foreign policy or national security. In fact, the Supreme Court has demonstrated its willingness to enter this arena against the express wishes of Congress. In *Boumediene v. Bush,* --- U.S. ----, 128 S. Ct. 2229 (2008), the Supreme Court rebuffed legislative efforts to strip the courts of jurisdiction over detainees held at Guantanamo Bay. It held that the writ of habeas corpus extended to the naval base, and that neither Congress nor the executive branch could displace the courts without formally suspending the writ. Importantly, it did so despite the fact that this exercise of judicial power plainly affected the executive's detention of hundreds of enemy combatants and a centerpiece of the war on terror. The Court recognized that habeas proceedings "may divert the attention of military personnel from other pressing tasks" but refused to find these concerns "dispositive." *Id.* at 2261. . . .

POOLER, Circuit Judge, joined by Judges CALABRESI, SACK, and PARKER, dissenting. . . .

II. TVPA . . .

. . . In the Section 1983 context, the Supreme Court has held that private individuals may be liable for joint activities with state actors even where those private individuals had no official power under state law. *Dennis v. Sparks,* 449 U.S. 24, 27-28 (1980). In *Sparks,* the private individuals conspired with a state judge to enjoin the plaintiff's mining operation. The Court held:

[T]o act 'under color of' state law for §1983 purposes doesnot require that the defendant be an officer of the State. It is enough that he is a willful participant in joint action with the State or its agents. Private persons, jointly engaged with state officials in the challenged action, are acting 'under color' of law for purposes of §1983 actions.

Id.; see also Khulumani v. Barclay Nat. Bank Ltd., 504 F.3d 254, 315 (2d Cir. 2007) (Korman, J., concurring in part). Arar alleges that U.S. officials, recognizing that Syrian law was more permissive of torture that U.S. law, contacted an agent in Syria to arrange to have Arar tortured under the authority of Syrian law. Specifically, Arar alleges that U.S. officials sent the Syrians a dossier containing questions, identical to those questions he was asked while detained in the U.S., including one about his relationship with a particular individual wanted for terrorism. He also alleges the Syrian officials supplied U.S. officials with information they extracted from him, citing a public statement by a Syrian official. Assuming the truth of these allegations, defendants' wrongdoing was only possible due to the latitude permitted under Syrian law and their joint action with Syrian authorities. The torture may fairly be attributed to Syria. . . .

Under Section 1983, non-state actors who willfully participate in joint action with state officials, acting under state law, themselves act under color of state law. By analogy, under the TVPA, non-Syrian actors who willfully participate in joint action with Syrian officials, acting under Syrian law, themselves act under color of Syrian law. In *Aldana v. Del Monte Fresh Produce,* 416 F.3d 1242, 1249, 1265 (11th Cir. 2005), the Eleventh Circuit sustained a TVPA claim where plaintiffs alleged that a U.S. corporation "hir[ed] and direct[ed] its employees and/or agents," including a Guatemalan mayor, "to torture the Plaintiffs and threaten them with death." 416 F.3d at 1265. The allegation that the corporation participated in joint action with the Guatemalan official was sufficient. I see no principled reason to apply different rules to the TVPA context than the Section 1983 context, to federal agent defendants than corporate defendants, or to actors in the United States than actors on foreign soil. Arar alleges that defendants, acting in concert with Syrian officials, interrogated him through torture under color of Syrian law, which they could not have accomplished under color of U.S. law alone. . . .

CALABRESI, Circuit Judge, joined by Judges POOLER, SACK, and PARKER, dissenting. . . . In its utter subservience to the executive branch, its distortion of *Bivens* doctrine, its unrealistic pleading standards, its misunderstanding of the TVPA and of § 1983, as well as in its persistent choice of broad dicta where narrow analysis would have sufficed, the majority opinion goes seriously astray. It does so, moreover, with the result that a person – whom we must assume (a) was totally innocent and (b) was made to suffer excruciatingly (c) through the misguided deeds of individuals acting under color of federal law – is effectively left without a U.S. remedy. . . .

All this, as the other dissenters have powerfully demonstrated, is surely bad enough. I write to discuss one last failing, an unsoundness that, although it may not be the most significant to Arar himself, is of signal importance to us as federal judges: the majority's unwavering willfulness. It has engaged in what properly can be described as extraordinary judicial activism. It has violated long-standing canons of restraint that properly must guide courts when they face complex and searing questions that involve potentially fundamental constitutional rights. It has reached out to decide an issue that should not have been resolved at this stage of Arar's case. Moreover, in doing this, the court has justified its holding with side comments (as to other fields of law such as torts) that are both sweeping and wrong. That the majority – made up of colleagues I greatly respect – has done all this with the best of intentions, and in the belief that its holding is necessary in a time of crisis, I do not doubt. But this does not alter my conviction that in calmer times, wise people will ask themselves: how could such able and worthy judges have done that? . . .

[NSL p. 826, CTL p. 480. Substitute the following Supreme Court decision for the lower court decisions in *Humanitarian Law Project* and *United States v. Al-Arian*.]

Holder v. Humanitarian Law Project
United States Supreme Court, 2010
___ S. Ct. ___, 2010 WL 2471055

Chief Justice ROBERTS delivered the opinion of the Court. Congress has prohibited the provision of "material support or resources" to certain foreign organizations that engage in terrorist activity. 18 U.S.C. §2339B(a)(1). That prohibition is based on a finding that the specified organizations "are so tainted by their criminal conduct that any contribution to such an organization facilitates that conduct." Antiterrorism and Effective Death Penalty Act of 1996 (AEDPA), §301(a)(7), 110 Stat. 1247, note following 18 U.S.C. §2339B (Findings and Purpose). . . . Plaintiffs claim that . . . applying the material-support law to prevent them from doing so violates the Constitution. In particular, they claim that the statute is too vague, in violation of the Fifth Amendment, and that it infringes their rights to freedom of speech and association, in violation of the First Amendment. We conclude that the material-support statute is constitutional as applied to the particular activities plaintiffs have told us they wish to pursue. We do not, however, address the resolution of more difficult cases that may arise under the statute in the future. . . .

[The plaintiffs are two U.S. citizens, the Humanitarian Law Project (HLP) (a human rights organization with consultative status to the United Nations), Ralph Fertig (the HLP's president), and others who want to provide support to the Kurdistan Workers' Party (PKK) (founded to establish an independent Kurdish state in southeastern Turkey), and the Liberation Tigers of Tamil Eelam (LTTE) (founded to create an independent Tamil state in Sri Lanka). The PKK and LTTE were each designated a foreign terrorist organization by the United States based on evidence that they committed numerous terrorist attacks, some of which harmed U.S. citizens. Plaintiffs claimed, however, that they want to support only the lawful humanitarian and political activities of the PKK and LTTE with monetary contributions, other tangible aid, legal training, and political advocacy.]

II

Given the complicated 12-year history of this litigation, we pause to clarify the questions before us. Plaintiffs challenge §2339B's prohibition on four types of material support – "training," "expert advice or assistance," "service," and "personnel." They raise three constitutional claims. First, plaintiffs claim that §2339B violates the Due Process Clause of the Fifth Amendment because these four statutory terms are impermissibly vague. Second, plaintiffs claim that §2339B violates their freedom of speech under the First Amendment. Third, plaintiffs claim that §2339B violates their First Amendment freedom of association.

Plaintiffs do not challenge the above statutory terms in all their applications. Rather, plaintiffs claim that §2339B is invalid to the extent it prohibits them from engaging in certain specified activities. With respect to the HLP and Judge Fertig, those activities are: (1) "train[ing] members of [the] PKK on how to use humanitarian and international law to peacefully resolve disputes"; (2) "engag[ing] in political advocacy on behalf of Kurds who live in Turkey"; and (3) "teach[ing] PKK members how to petition various representative bodies such as the United Nations for relief." With respect to the other plaintiffs, those activities are: (1) "train[ing] members of [the] LTTE to present claims for tsunami-related aid to mediators and international bodies"; (2) "offer[ing] their legal expertise in negotiating peace agreements between the LTTE and the Sri Lankan government"; and (3) "engag[ing] in political advocacy on behalf of Tamils who live in Sri Lanka." . . .

III

Plaintiffs claim, as a threshold matter, that we should affirm the Court of Appeals without reaching any issues of constitutional law. They contend that we should interpret the material-support statute, when applied to speech, to require proof that a defendant intended to further a foreign terrorist organization's illegal activities. That interpretation, they say, would end the litigation because plaintiffs' proposed activities consist of speech, but plaintiffs do not intend to further unlawful conduct by the PKK or the LTTE.

We reject plaintiffs' interpretation of §2339B because it is inconsistent with the text of the statute. Section 2339B(a)(1) prohibits "knowingly" providing material support. It then specifically describes the type of knowledge that is required: "To violate this paragraph, a person must have knowledge that the organization is a designated terrorist organization . . ., that the organization has engaged or engages in terrorist activity . . ., or that the organization has engaged or engages in terrorism. . . ." *Ibid.* Congress plainly spoke to the necessary mental state for a violation of §2339B, and it chose knowledge about the organization's connection to terrorism, not specific intent to further the organization's terrorist activities.   Plaintiffs' interpretation is also untenable in light of the sections immediately surrounding §2339B, both of which do refer to intent to further terrorist activity. See §2339A(a) (establishing criminal penalties for one who "provides material support or resources . . . knowing or intending that they are to be used in preparation for, or in carrying out, a violation of" statutes prohibiting violent terrorist acts); §2339C(a)(1) (setting criminal penalties for one who "unlawfully and willfully provides or collects funds with the intention that such funds be used, or with the knowledge that such funds are to be used, in full or in part, in order to carry out" other unlawful acts). Congress enacted §2339A in 1994 and §2339C in 2002. See §120005(a), 108 Stat.2022 (§2339A); §202(a), 116 Stat. 724 (§2339C). Yet Congress did not import the intent language of those provisions into §2339B, either when it enacted §2339B in 1996, or when it clarified §2339B's knowledge requirement in 2004.

Finally, plaintiffs give the game away when they argue that a specific intent requirement should apply only when the material-support statute applies to speech. There is no basis whatever in the text of §2339B to read the same provisions in that statute as requiring intent in some circumstances but not others. It is therefore clear that plaintiffs are asking us not to interpret §2339B, but to revise it. "Although this Court will often strain to construe legislation so as to save it against constitutional attack, it must not and will not carry this to the point of perverting the purpose of a statute." *Scales v. United States,* 367 U.S. 203, 211 (1961).

Scales is the case on which plaintiffs most heavily rely, but it is readily distinguishable. That case involved the Smith Act, which prohibited membership in a group advocating the violent overthrow of the government. The Court held that a person could not be convicted under the statute unless he had knowledge of the group's illegal advocacy and a specific intent to bring about violent overthrow. *Id.*, at 220-222, 229. This action is different: Section 2339B does not criminalize mere membership in a designated foreign terrorist organization. It instead prohibits providing "material support" to such a group. Nothing about *Scales* suggests the need for a specific intent requirement in such a case. The Court in *Scales,* moreover, relied on both statutory text and precedent that had interpreted closely related provisions of the Smith Act to require specific intent. Plaintiffs point to nothing similar here.

We cannot avoid the constitutional issues in this litigation through plaintiffs' proposed interpretation of §2339B.

IV

We turn to the question whether the material-support statute, as applied to plaintiffs, is impermissibly vague under the Due Process Clause of the Fifth Amendment. "A conviction fails to comport with due process if the statute under which it is obtained fails to provide a person of ordinary intelligence fair notice of what is prohibited, or is so standardless that it authorizes or encourages seriously discriminatory enforcement." *United States v. Williams,* 553 U.S. 285, 304 (2008). We consider whether a statute is vague as applied to the particular facts at issue, for "[a] plaintiff who engages in some conduct that is clearly proscribed cannot complain of the vagueness of the law as applied to the conduct of others." *Hoffman Estates v. Flipside, Hoffman Estates, Inc.,* 455 U.S. 489, 495 (1982). We have said that when a statute "interferes with the right of free speech or of association, a more stringent vagueness test should apply." *Id.*, at 499. "But 'perfect clarity and precise guidance have never been required even of regulations that restrict expressive activity.'" *Williams, supra,* at 304 (quoting *Ward v. Rock Against Racism,* 491 U.S. 781, 794 (1989)). . . .

. . . [Cases establish the] rule that "[a] plaintiff who engages in some conduct that is clearly proscribed cannot complain of the vagueness of the law as applied to the conduct of others." *Hoffman Estates, supra,* at 495. That rule makes no exception for conduct in the form of speech. Thus, even to the extent a heightened vagueness standard applies, a plaintiff whose speech is clearly proscribed cannot raise a successful vagueness claim under the Due Process Clause of the Fifth Amendment for lack of notice. And he certainly cannot do so based on the speech of others. Such a plaintiff may have a valid overbreadth claim under the First Amendment, but our precedents make clear that a Fifth Amendment vagueness challenge does not turn on whether a law applies to a substantial amount of protected expression. Otherwise the doctrines would be substantially redundant.

Under a proper analysis, plaintiffs' claims of vagueness lack merit. Plaintiffs do not argue that the material-support statute grants too much enforcement discretion to the Government. We therefore address only whether the statute "provide[s] a person of ordinary intelligence fair notice of what is prohibited." *Williams,* 553 U.S., at 304.

As a general matter, the statutory terms at issue here are quite different from the sorts of terms that we have previously declared to be vague. We have in the past "struck down statutes that tied criminal culpability to whether the defendant's conduct was 'annoying' or 'indecent'– wholly subjective judgments without statutory definitions, narrowing context, or settled legal meanings." *Id.,* at 306; see also *Papachristou v. Jacksonville,* 405 U.S. 156, n.1 (1972) (holding vague an ordinance that punished "vagrants," defined to include "rogues and vagabonds," "persons who use juggling," and "common night walkers" (internal quotation marks omitted)). Applying the statutory terms in this action – "training," "expert advice or assistance," "service," and "personnel" – does not require similarly untethered, subjective judgments.

Congress also took care to add narrowing definitions to the material-support statute over time. These definitions increased the clarity of the statute's terms. See §2339A(b)(2) ("'training' means instruction or teaching designed to impart a specific skill, as opposed to general knowledge"); §2339A(b)(3) ("'expert advice or assistance' means advice or assistance derived from scientific, technical or other specialized knowledge"); §2339B(h) (clarifying the scope of "personnel"). And the knowledge requirement of the statute further reduces any potential for vagueness, as we have held with respect to other statutes containing a similar requirement.

Of course, the scope of the material-support statute may not be clear in every application. But the dispositive point here is that the statutory terms are clear in their application to plaintiffs' proposed conduct, which means that plaintiffs' vagueness challenge must fail. Even assuming that a heightened standard applies because the material-support statute potentially implicates speech, the statutory terms are not vague as applied to plaintiffs.

Most of the activities in which plaintiffs seek to engage readily fall within the scope of the terms "training" and "expert advice or assistance." Plaintiffs want to "train members of [the] PKK on how to use humanitarian and international law to peacefully resolve disputes," and "teach PKK members how to petition various representative bodies such as the United Nations for relief." 552 F.3d at 921 n.1. A person of ordinary intelligence would understand that instruction on resolving disputes through international law falls within the statute's definition of "training" because it imparts a "specific skill," not "general knowledge." §2339A(b)(2). Plaintiffs' activities also fall comfortably within the scope of "expert advice or assistance": A reasonable person would recognize that teaching the PKK how to petition for humanitarian relief before the United Nations involves advice derived from, as the statute puts it, "specialized knowledge." §2339A(b)(3). In fact, plaintiffs themselves have repeatedly used the terms "training" and "expert advice" throughout this litigation to describe their own proposed activities, demonstrating that these common terms readily and naturally cover plaintiffs' conduct.

Plaintiffs respond by pointing to hypothetical situations designed to test the limits of "training" and "expert advice or assistance." They argue that the statutory definitions of these terms use words of degree – like "specific," "general," and "specialized" – and that it is difficult to apply those definitions in particular cases. . . .

Whatever force these arguments might have in the abstract, they are beside the point here. Plaintiffs do not propose to teach a course on geography, and cannot seek refuge in imaginary cases that straddle the boundary between "specific skills" and "general knowledge." We emphasized this point in *Scales,* holding that even if there might be theoretical doubts regarding the distinction between "active" and "nominal" membership in an organization – also terms of degree – the defendant's vagueness challenge failed because his "case present[ed] no such problem." 367 U.S. at 223. . . .

Plaintiffs also contend that they want to engage in "political advocacy" on behalf of Kurds living in Turkey and Tamils living in Sri Lanka. They are concerned that such advocacy might be regarded as "material support" in the form of providing "personnel" or "service[s]," and assert that the statute is unconstitutionally vague because they cannot tell.

As for "personnel," Congress enacted a limiting definition in IRTPA that answers plaintiffs' vagueness concerns. Providing material support that constitutes "personnel" is defined as knowingly providing a person "to work under that terrorist organization's direction or control or to organize, manage, supervise, or otherwise direct the operation of that organization." §2339B(h). The statute makes clear that "personnel" does not cover *independent* advocacy: "Individuals who act entirely independently of the foreign terrorist organization to advance its goals or objectives shall not be considered to be working under the foreign terrorist organization's direction and control." *Ibid.*

"[S]ervice" similarly refers to concerted activity, not independent advocacy. See Webster's Third New International Dictionary 2075 (1993) (defining "service" to mean "the performance of work commanded or paid for by another: a servant's duty: attendance on a superior"; or "an act done for the benefit or at the command of another"). Context confirms that ordinary meaning here. The statute prohibits providing a service "*to* a foreign terrorist organization." §2339B(a)(1) (emphasis added). The use of the word "to" indicates a connection between the service and the foreign group. We think a person of ordinary intelligence would understand that independently advocating for a cause is different from providing a service to a group that is advocating for that cause. . . .

V

A

We next consider whether the material-support statute, as applied to plaintiffs, violates the freedom of speech guaranteed by the First Amendment. Both plaintiffs and the Government take extreme positions on this question. Plaintiffs claim that Congress has banned their "pure political speech." It has not. Under the material-support statute, plaintiffs may say anything they wish on any topic. They may speak and write freely about the PKK and LTTE, the governments of Turkey and Sri Lanka, human rights, and international law. They may advocate before the United Nations. As the Government states: "The statute does not prohibit independent advocacy or expression of any kind." Brief for Government 13. Section 2339B also "does not prevent [plaintiffs] from becoming members of the PKK and LTTE or impose any sanction on them for doing so." *Id.,* at 60. Congress has not, therefore, sought to suppress ideas or opinions in the form of "pure political speech." Rather, Congress has prohibited "material support," which most often does not take the form of speech at all. And when it does, the statute is carefully drawn to cover only a narrow category of speech to, under the direction of, or in coordination with foreign groups that the speaker knows to be terrorist organizations.[4] . . .

[But] [t]he Government is wrong that the only thing actually at issue in this litigation is conduct . . . . [Section] 2339B regulates speech on the basis of its content. Plaintiffs want to speak to the PKK and the LTTE, and whether they may do so under §2339B depends on what they say. If plaintiffs' speech to those groups imparts a "specific skill" or communicates advice derived from "specialized knowledge"– for example, training on the use of international law or advice on petitioning the United Nations – then it is barred. On the other hand, plaintiffs' speech is not barred if it imparts only general or unspecialized knowledge. . . .

B

The First Amendment issue before us is more refined than either plaintiffs or the Government would have it. It is not whether the Government may prohibit pure political speech, or may prohibit material support in the form of conduct. It is instead whether the Government

---

4. The dissent also analyzes the statute as if it prohibited "[p]eaceful political advocacy" or "pure speech and association," without more. Section 2339B does not do that, and we do not address the constitutionality of any such prohibitions. The dissent's claim that our decision is inconsistent with this Court's cases analyzing those sorts of restrictions is accordingly unfounded.

may prohibit what plaintiffs want to do – provide material support to the PKK and LTTE in the form of speech.

Everyone agrees that the Government's interest in combating terrorism is an urgent objective of the highest order. Plaintiffs' complaint is that the ban on material support, applied to what they wish to do, is not "necessary to further that interest." The objective of combating terrorism does not justify prohibiting their speech, plaintiffs argue, because their support will advance only the legitimate activities of the designated terrorist organizations, not their terrorism.

Whether foreign terrorist organizations meaningfully segregate support of their legitimate activities from support of terrorism is an empirical question. When it enacted §2339B in 1996, Congress made specific findings regarding the serious threat posed by international terrorism. See AEDPA §§301(a)(1)-(7), 110 Stat. 1247, note following 18 U.S.C. §2339B (Findings and Purpose). One of those findings explicitly rejects plaintiffs' contention that their support would not further the terrorist activities of the PKK and LTTE: "[F]oreign organizations that engage in terrorist activity are so tainted by their criminal conduct that *any contribution to such an organization* facilitates that conduct." §301(a)(7) (emphasis added).

Plaintiffs argue that the reference to "any contribution" in this finding meant only monetary support. There is no reason to read the finding to be so limited, particularly because Congress expressly prohibited so much more than monetary support in §2339B. Congress's use of the term "contribution" is best read to reflect a determination that any form of material support furnished "to" a foreign terrorist organization should be barred, which is precisely what the material-support statute does. Indeed, when Congress enacted §2339B, Congress simultaneously removed an exception that had existed in §2339A(a) (1994 ed.) for the provision of material support in the form of "humanitarian assistance to persons not directly involved in" terrorist activity. AEDPA §323, 110 Stat. 1255. That repeal demonstrates that Congress considered and rejected the view that ostensibly peaceful aid would have no harmful effects.

We are convinced that Congress was justified in rejecting that view. The PKK and the LTTE are deadly groups. "The PKK's insurgency has claimed more than 22,000 lives." Declaration of Kenneth R. McKune, App. 128, ¶5. The LTTE has engaged in extensive suicide bombings and political assassinations, including killings of the Sri Lankan President, Security Minister, and Deputy Defense Minister. *Id.,* at 130-132; Brief for Government 6-7. "On January 31, 1996, the LTTE exploded a truck bomb filled with an estimated 1,000 pounds of explosives at the Central Bank in Colombo, killing 100 people and injuring more than 1,400. This bombing was the most deadly terrorist incident in the world in 1996." McKune Affidavit, App. 131, ¶6.h. It is not difficult to conclude as Congress did that the "tain[t]" of such violent activities is so great that working in coordination with or at the command of the PKK and LTTE serves to legitimize and further their terrorist means. AEDPA §301(a)(7), 110 Stat. 1247.

Material support meant to "promot[e] peaceable, lawful conduct," Brief for Plaintiffs 51, can further terrorism by foreign groups in multiple ways. "Material support" is a valuable resource by definition. Such support frees up other resources within the organization that may be put to violent ends. It also importantly helps lend legitimacy to foreign terrorist groups – legitimacy that makes it easier for those groups to persist, to recruit members, and to raise funds – all of which facilitate more terrorist attacks. "Terrorist organizations do not maintain *organizational* 'firewalls' that would prevent or deter . . . sharing and commingling of support and benefits." McKune Affidavit, App. 135, ¶11. "[I]nvestigators have revealed how terrorist groups systematically conceal their activities behind charitable, social, and political fronts." M. Levitt, Hamas: Politics, Charity, and Terrorism in the Service of Jihad 2-3 (2006). "Indeed, some designated foreign terrorist organizations use social and political components to recruit personnel to carry out terrorist operations, and to provide support to criminal terrorists and their families in aid of such operations." McKune Affidavit, App. 135, ¶11; Levitt, *supra,* at 2 ("Muddying the waters between its political activism, good works, and terrorist attacks, Hamas is able to use its overt political and charitable organizations as a financial and logistical support network for its terrorist operations").

Money is fungible, and "[w]hen foreign terrorist organizations that have a dual structure raise funds, they highlight the civilian and humanitarian ends to which such moneys could be put." McKune Affidavit, App. 134, ¶9. But "there is reason to believe that foreign terrorist organizations do not maintain legitimate *financial* firewalls between those funds raised for civil, nonviolent activities, and those

ultimately used to support violent, terrorist operations." *Id.,* at 135, ¶12.
Thus, "[f]unds raised ostensibly for charitable purposes have in the past
been redirected by some terrorist groups to fund the purchase of arms
and explosives." *Id.,* at 134, ¶10. See also Brief for Anti-Defamation
League as *Amicus Curiae* 19-29 (describing fundraising activities by the
PKK, LTTE, and Hamas); *Regan v. Wald,* 468 U.S. 222, 243 (1984)
(upholding President's decision to impose travel ban to Cuba "to curtail
the flow of hard currency to Cuba – currency that could then be used in
support of Cuban adventurism"). There is evidence that the PKK and the
LTTE, in particular, have not "respected the line between humanitarian
and violent activities." McKune Affidavit, App. 135, ¶13 (discussing
PKK); see *id.,* at 134 (LTTE).

The dissent argues that there is "no natural stopping place" for the
proposition that aiding a foreign terrorist organization's lawful activity
promotes the terrorist organization as a whole. But Congress has settled
on just such a natural stopping place: The statute reaches only material
support coordinated with or under the direction of a designated foreign
terrorist organization. Independent advocacy that might be viewed as
promoting the group's legitimacy is not covered.

Providing foreign terrorist groups with material support in any form
also furthers terrorism by straining the United States' relationships with
its allies and undermining cooperative efforts between nations to prevent
terrorist attacks. We see no reason to question Congress's finding that
"international cooperation is required for an effective response to
terrorism, as demonstrated by the numerous multilateral conventions in
force providing universal prosecutive jurisdiction over persons involved
in a variety of terrorist acts, including hostage taking, murder of an
internationally protected person, and aircraft piracy and sabotage."
AEDPA §301(a)(5), 110 Stat. 1247, note following 18 U.S.C. §2339B
(Findings and Purpose). The material-support statute furthers this
international effort by prohibiting aid for foreign terrorist groups that
harm the United States' partners abroad: "A number of designated
foreign terrorist organizations have attacked moderate governments with
which the United States has vigorously endeavored to maintain close and
friendly relations," and those attacks "threaten [the] social, economic and
political stability" of such governments. McKune Affidavit, App. 137,
¶16. "[O]ther foreign terrorist organizations attack our NATO allies,

thereby implicating important and sensitive multilateral security arrangements." *Ibid.* . . .

C

In analyzing whether it is possible in practice to distinguish material support for a foreign terrorist group's violent activities and its nonviolent activities, we do not rely exclusively on our own inferences drawn from the record evidence. We have before us an affidavit stating the Executive Branch's conclusion on that question. The State Department informs us that "[t]he experience and analysis of the U.S. government agencies charged with combating terrorism strongly suppor[t]" Congress's finding that all contributions to foreign terrorist organizations further their terrorism. McKune Affidavit, App. 133, ¶8. See *Winter v. Natural Resources Defense Council, Inc.,* 129 S. Ct. 365, 376-377 (2008) (looking to similar affidavits to support according weight to national security claims). In the Executive's view: "Given the purposes, organizational structure, and clandestine nature of foreign terrorist organizations, it is highly likely that any material support to these organizations will ultimately inure to the benefit of their criminal, terrorist functions-regardless of whether such support was ostensibly intended to support non-violent, non-terrorist activities." McKune Affidavit, App. 133, ¶8.

That evaluation of the facts by the Executive, like Congress's assessment, is entitled to deference. This litigation implicates sensitive and weighty interests of national security and foreign affairs. The PKK and the LTTE have committed terrorist acts against American citizens abroad, and the material-support statute addresses acute foreign policy concerns involving relationships with our Nation's allies. See *id.,* at 128-133, 137. We have noted that "neither the Members of this Court nor most federal judges begin the day with briefings that may describe new and serious threats to our Nation and its people." *Boumediene v. Bush,* 553 U.S. 723, 797 (2008). It is vital in this context "not to substitute . . . our own evaluation of evidence for a reasonable evaluation by the Legislative Branch." *Rostker v. Goldberg,* 453 U.S. 57, 68 (1981).

Our precedents, old and new, make clear that concerns of national security and foreign relations do not warrant abdication of the judicial role. We do not defer to the Government's reading of the First

Amendment, even when such interests are at stake. We are one with the dissent that the Government's "authority and expertise in these matters do not automatically trump the Court's own obligation to secure the protection that the Constitution grants to individuals." But when it comes to collecting evidence and drawing factual inferences in this area, "the lack of competence on the part of the courts is marked," *Rostker, supra,* at 65, and respect for the Government's conclusions is appropriate.

One reason for that respect is that national security and foreign policy concerns arise in connection with efforts to confront evolving threats in an area where information can be difficult to obtain and the impact of certain conduct difficult to assess. The dissent slights these real constraints in demanding hard proof – with "detail," "specific facts," and "specific evidence"– that plaintiffs' proposed activities will support terrorist attacks. That would be a dangerous requirement. In this context, conclusions must often be based on informed judgment rather than concrete evidence, and that reality affects what we may reasonably insist on from the Government. The material-support statute is, on its face, a preventive measure – it criminalizes not terrorist attacks themselves, but aid that makes the attacks more likely to occur. The Government, when seeking to prevent imminent harms in the context of international affairs and national security, is not required to conclusively link all the pieces in the puzzle before we grant weight to its empirical conclusions. See *Zemel v. Rusk,* 381 U.S., at 17 ("[B]ecause of the changeable and explosive nature of contemporary international relations, . . . Congress . . . must of necessity paint with a brush broader than that it customarily wields in domestic areas"). . . .

We also find it significant that Congress has been conscious of its own responsibility to consider how its actions may implicate constitutional concerns. First, §2339B only applies to designated foreign terrorist organizations. There is, and always has been, a limited number of those organizations designated by the Executive Branch, see, *e.g.,* 74 Fed. Reg. 29742 (2009); 62 Fed. Reg. 52650 (1997), and any groups so designated may seek judicial review of the designation. Second, in response to the lower courts' holdings in this litigation, Congress added clarity to the statute by providing narrowing definitions of the terms "training," "personnel," and "expert advice or assistance," as well as an explanation of the knowledge required to violate §2339B. Third, in effectuating its stated intent not to abridge First Amendment rights, see

§2339B(i), Congress has also displayed a careful balancing of interests in creating limited exceptions to the ban on material support. The definition of material support, for example, excludes medicine and religious materials. See §2339A(b)(1). In this area perhaps more than any other, the Legislature's superior capacity for weighing competing interests means that "we must be particularly careful not to substitute our judgment of what is desirable for that of Congress." *Rostker, supra,* at 68. Finally, and most importantly, Congress has avoided any restriction on independent advocacy, or indeed any activities not directed to, coordinated with, or controlled by foreign terrorist groups.

At bottom, plaintiffs simply disagree with the considered judgment of Congress and the Executive that providing material support to a designated foreign terrorist organization – even seemingly benign support – bolsters the terrorist activities of that organization. That judgment, however, is entitled to significant weight, and we have persuasive evidence before us to sustain it. Given the sensitive interests in national security and foreign affairs at stake, the political branches have adequately substantiated their determination that, to serve the Government's interest in preventing terrorism, it was necessary to prohibit providing material support in the form of training, expert advice, personnel, and services to foreign terrorist groups, even if the supporters meant to promote only the groups' nonviolent ends.

We turn to the particular speech plaintiffs propose to undertake. First, plaintiffs propose to "train members of [the] PKK on how to use humanitarian and international law to peacefully resolve disputes." 552 F.3d at 92 n.1. Congress can, consistent with the First Amendment, prohibit this direct training. It is wholly foreseeable that the PKK could use the "specific skill[s]" that plaintiffs propose to impart, §2339A(b)(2), as part of a broader strategy to promote terrorism. The PKK could, for example, pursue peaceful negotiation as a means of buying time to recover from short-term setbacks, lulling opponents into complacency, and ultimately preparing for renewed attacks. See generally A. Marcus, Blood and Belief: The PKK and the Kurdish Fight for Independence 286-295 (2007) (describing the PKK's suspension of armed struggle and subsequent return to violence). A foreign terrorist organization introduced to the structures of the international legal system might use the information to threaten, manipulate, and disrupt. This possibility is real, not remote.

Second, plaintiffs propose to "teach PKK members how to petition various representative bodies such as the United Nations for relief." 552 F.3d at 921 n.1. The Government acts within First Amendment strictures in banning this proposed speech because it teaches the organization how to acquire "relief," which plaintiffs never define with any specificity, and which could readily include monetary aid. Indeed, earlier in this litigation, plaintiffs sought to teach the LTTE "to present claims for tsunami-related aid to mediators and international bodies," 552 F.3d at 921 n.1, which naturally included monetary relief. Money is fungible, and Congress logically concluded that money a terrorist group such as the PKK obtains using the techniques plaintiffs propose to teach could be redirected to funding the group's violent activities.

Finally, plaintiffs propose to "engage in political advocacy on behalf of Kurds who live in Turkey," and "engage in political advocacy on behalf of Tamils who live in Sri Lanka." 552 F.3d at 921 n.1. As explained above, plaintiffs do not specify their expected level of coordination with the PKK or LTTE or suggest what exactly their "advocacy" would consist of. Plaintiffs' proposals are phrased at such a high level of generality that they cannot prevail in this preenforcement challenge. See *supra,* at ___; [*Washington State Grange v. Washington State Republican Party*, 552 U.S. 442, 454 (2008)]; *Zemel,* 381 U.S., at 20.

In responding to the foregoing, the dissent fails to address the real dangers at stake. It instead considers only the possible benefits of plaintiffs' proposed activities in the abstract. The dissent seems unwilling to entertain the prospect that training and advising a designated foreign terrorist organization on how to take advantage of international entities might benefit that organization in a way that facilitates its terrorist activities. In the dissent's world, such training is all to the good. Congress and the Executive, however, have concluded that we live in a different world: one in which the designated foreign terrorist organizations "are so tainted by their criminal conduct that any contribution to such an organization facilitates that conduct." AEDPA §301(a)(7). One in which, for example, "the United Nations High Commissioner for Refugees was forced to close a Kurdish refugee camp in northern Iraq because the camp had come under the control of the PKK, and the PKK had failed to respect its 'neutral and humanitarian nature.'" McKune Affidavit, App. 135-136, ¶13. Training and advice on how to work with the United Nations could readily have helped the PKK in its efforts to use the United Nations camp as a base for terrorist activities. . . .

All this is not to say that any future applications of the material-support statute to speech or advocacy will survive First Amendment scrutiny. It is also not to say that any other statute relating to speech and terrorism would satisfy the First Amendment. In particular, we in no way suggest that a regulation of independent speech would pass constitutional muster, even if the Government were to show that such speech benefits foreign terrorist organizations. We also do not suggest that Congress could extend the same prohibition on material support at issue here to domestic organizations. We simply hold that, in prohibiting the particular forms of support that plaintiffs seek to provide to foreign terrorist groups, §2339B does not violate the freedom of speech.

VI

Plaintiffs' final claim is that the material-support statute violates their freedom of association under the First Amendment. Plaintiffs argue that the statute criminalizes the mere fact of their associating with the PKK and the LTTE, thereby running afoul of [prior] decisions . . . and cases in which we have overturned sanctions for joining the Communist Party.

The Court of Appeals correctly rejected this claim because the statute does not penalize mere association with a foreign terrorist organization. As the Ninth Circuit put it: "The statute does not prohibit being a member of one of the designated groups or vigorously promoting and supporting the political goals of the group. . . . What [§2339B] prohibits is the act of giving material support. . . ." 205 F.3d at 1133. Plaintiffs want to do the latter. Our decisions scrutinizing penalties on simple association or assembly are therefore inapposite. *See, e.g., Robel, supra,* at 262 ("It is precisely because th[e] statute sweeps indiscriminately across all types of association with Communist-action groups, without regard to the quality and degree of membership, that it runs afoul of the First Amendment"). . . .

* * *

The Preamble to the Constitution proclaims that the people of the United States ordained and established that charter of government in part to "provide for the common defence." As Madison explained, "[s]ecurity against foreign danger is . . . an avowed and essential object of the American Union." The Federalist No. 41, p. 269 (J. Cooke ed. 1961). We hold that, in regulating the particular forms of support that plaintiffs seek to provide to foreign terrorist organizations, Congress has pursued that objective consistent with the limitations of the First and Fifth Amendments.

The judgment of the United States Court of Appeals for the Ninth Circuit is affirmed in part and reversed in part, and the cases are remanded for further proceedings consistent with this opinion.

It is so ordered.

Justice BREYER, with whom Justices GINSBURG and SOTOMAYOR join, dissenting. Like the Court, and substantially for the reasons it gives, I do not think this statute is unconstitutionally vague. But I cannot agree with the Court's conclusion that the Constitution permits the Government to prosecute the plaintiffs criminally for engaging in coordinated teaching and advocacy furthering the designated organizations' lawful political objectives. In my view, the Government has not met its burden of showing that an interpretation of the statute that would prohibit this speech- and association-related activity serves the Government's compelling interest in combating terrorism. And I would interpret the statute as normally placing activity of this kind outside its scope.

I. . . .

"Coordination" with a group that engages in unlawful activity also does not deprive the plaintiffs of the First Amendment's protection under any traditional "categorical" exception to its protection. The plaintiffs do not propose to solicit a crime. They will not engage in fraud or defamation or circulate obscenity. Cf. *United States v. Stevens,* 130 S. Ct. 1577, 1585 (2010) (describing "categories" of unprotected speech). And the First Amendment protects advocacy even of *unlawful* action so long as that advocacy is not "directed to inciting or producing *imminent*

lawless action and . . . *likely to incite or produce* such action."
Brandenburg v. Ohio, 395 U.S. 444, 447 (1969) *(per curiam)* (emphasis
added). Here the plaintiffs seek to advocate peaceful, *lawful* action to
secure *political* ends; and they seek to teach others how to do the same.
No one contends that the plaintiffs' speech to these organizations can be
prohibited as incitement under *Brandenburg.*

Moreover, the Court has previously held that a person who associates
with a group that uses unlawful means to achieve its ends does not
thereby necessarily forfeit the First Amendment's protection for freedom
of association. See *Scales v. United States,* 367 U.S. 203, 229 (1961)
("[Q]uasi-political parties or other groups that may embrace both legal
and illegal aims differ from a technical conspiracy, which is defined by
its criminal purpose"); see also [*NAACP v. Claiborne Hardware Co.,* 458
U.S. 886, 908 (1982)] ("The right to associate does not lose all
constitutional protection merely because some members of the group
may have participated in conduct or advocated doctrine that itself is not
protected"). Rather, the Court has pointed out in respect to associating
with a group advocating overthrow of the Government through force and
violence: "If the persons assembling have committed crimes elsewhere . . .,
they may be prosecuted for their . . . violation of valid laws. But it is a
different matter when the State, instead of prosecuting them for such
offenses, seizes upon mere participation in a peaceable assembly and a
lawful public discussion as the basis for a criminal charge." [*De Jonge v.
Oregon,* 299 U.S. 353, 365 (1937)] (striking down conviction for
attending and assisting at Communist Party meeting because
"[n]otwithstanding [the party's] objectives, the defendant still enjoyed
his personal right of free speech and to take part in peaceable assembly
having a lawful purpose"). . . .

Not even the "serious and deadly problem" of international terrorism
can require *automatic* forfeiture of First Amendment rights. §301(a)(1),
110 Stat. 1247, note following 18 U.S.C. §2339B. Cf. §2339B(i)
(instructing courts not to "constru[e] or appl[y the statute] so as to
abridge the exercise of right guaranteed under the First Amendment").
After all, this Court has recognized that not "'[e]ven the war power . . .
remove[s] constitutional limitations safeguarding essential liberties.'"
United States v. Robel, 389 U.S. 258, 264 (1967) (quoting *Home
Building & Loan Assn. v. Blaisdell,* 290 U.S. 398, 426 (1934)). See also
Abrams v. United States, 250 U.S. 616, 628 (1919) (Holmes, J.,

dissenting) ("[A]s against dangers peculiar to war, as against others, the principle of the right to free speech is always the same"). Thus, there is no general First Amendment exception that applies here. If the statute is constitutional in this context, it would have to come with a strong justification attached. . . .

The Government does identify a compelling countervailing interest, namely, the interest in protecting the security of the United States and its nationals from the threats that foreign terrorist organizations pose by denying those organizations financial and other fungible resources. I do not dispute the importance of this interest. But I do dispute whether the interest can justify the statute's criminal prohibition. To put the matter more specifically, precisely how does application of the statute to the protected activities before us *help achieve* that important security-related end?

The Government makes two efforts to answer this question. *First,* the Government says that the plaintiffs' support for these organizations is "fungible" in the same sense as other forms of banned support. Being fungible, the plaintiffs' support could, for example, free up other resources, which the organization might put to terrorist ends.

The proposition that the two very different kinds of "support" are "fungible," however, is not *obviously* true. There is no *obvious* way in which undertaking advocacy for political change through peaceful means or teaching the PKK and LTTE, say, how to petition the United Nations for political change is fungible with other resources that might be put to more sinister ends in the way that donations of money, food, or computer training are fungible. It is far from obvious that these advocacy activities can themselves be redirected, or will free other resources that can be directed, towards terrorist ends. Thus, we must determine whether the Government has come forward with evidence to support its claim.

The Government has provided us with no empirical information that might convincingly support this claim. . . .

Second, the Government says that the plaintiffs' proposed activities will "bolste[r] a terrorist organization's efficacy and strength in a community" and "undermin[e] this nation's efforts to *delegitimize and weaken* those groups." Government Brief 56 (emphasis added). In the Court's view, too, the Constitution permits application of the statute to activities of the kind at issue in part because those activities could provide a group that engages in terrorism with "legitimacy." The Court suggests that, armed with this greater "legitimacy," these organizations will more readily be able to obtain material support of the kinds Congress plainly intended to ban – money, arms, lodging, and the like. . . .

But this "legitimacy" justification cannot by itself warrant suppression of political speech, advocacy, and association. Speech, association, and related activities on behalf of a group will often, perhaps always, help to legitimate that group. Thus, were the law to accept a "legitimating" effect, in and of itself and without qualification, as providing sufficient grounds for imposing such a ban, the First Amendment battle would be lost in untold instances where it should be won. Once one accepts this argument, there is no natural stopping place. The argument applies as strongly to "independent" as to "coordinated" advocacy. That fact is reflected in part in the Government's claim that the ban here, so supported, prohibits a lawyer hired by a designated group from filing on behalf of that group an *amicus* brief before the United Nations or even before this Court. . . .

Regardless, the "legitimacy" justification itself is inconsistent with critically important First Amendment case law. Consider the cases involving the protection the First Amendment offered those who joined the Communist Party intending only to further its peaceful activities. In those cases, this Court took account of congressional findings that the Communist Party not only advocated theoretically but also sought to put into practice the overthrow of our Government through force and violence. The Court had previously accepted Congress' determinations that the American Communist Party was a "Communist action organization" which (1) acted under the "control, direction, and discipline" of the world Communist movement, a movement that sought to employ "espionage, sabotage, terrorism, and any other means deemed necessary, to establish a Communist totalitarian dictatorship," and (2) "endeavor[ed]" to bring about "the overthrow of existing governments by . . . force if necessary." *Communist Party of United States v. Subversive Activities Control Bd.,* 367 U.S. 1, 5-6 (1961) (internal quotation marks omitted).

Nonetheless, the Court held that the First Amendment protected an American's right to belong to that party – despite whatever "legitimating" effect membership might have had – as long as the person did not share the party's unlawful purposes. . . . The Government's "legitimating" theory would seem to apply to these cases with equal justifying force; and, if recognized, it would have led this Court to conclusions other than those it reached. . . .

II

For the reasons I have set forth, I believe application of the statute as the Government interprets it would gravely and without adequate justification injure interests of the kind the First Amendment protects. Thus, there is "a serious doubt" as to the statute's constitutionality. [*Crowell v. Benson*, 285 U.S. 22, 62 (1932)]. And where that is so, we must "ascertain whether a construction of the statute is fairly possible by which the question may be avoided." *Ibid.*

I believe that a construction that would avoid the constitutional problem is "fairly possible." In particular, I would read the statute as criminalizing First-Amendment-protected pure speech and association only when the defendant knows or intends that those activities will assist the organization's unlawful terrorist actions. Under this reading, the Government would have to show, at a minimum, that such defendants provided support that they knew was significantly likely to help the organization pursue its unlawful terrorist aims.

A person acts with the requisite knowledge if he is aware of (or willfully blinds himself to) a significant likelihood that his or her conduct will materially support the organization's terrorist ends. On the other hand, for the reasons I have set out, knowledge or intent that this assistance (aimed at lawful activities) could or would help further terrorism simply by helping to legitimate the organization is not sufficient.

This reading of the statute protects those who engage in pure speech and association ordinarily protected by the First Amendment. But it does not protect that activity where a defendant purposefully intends it to help terrorism or where a defendant knows (or willfully blinds himself to the fact) that the activity is significantly likely to assist terrorism. Where the activity fits into these categories of purposefully or knowingly supporting terrorist ends, the act of providing material support to a known terrorist organization bears a close enough relation to terrorist acts that, in my view, it likely can be prohibited notwithstanding any First Amendment interest. Cf. *Brandenburg*, 395 U.S. 444. At the same time, this reading does not require the Government to undertake the difficult task of proving which, as between peaceful and nonpeaceful purposes, a defendant specifically preferred; knowledge is enough.

This reading is consistent with the statute's text. The statute prohibits "*knowingly* provid[ing] *material* support or resources to a foreign terrorist organization." §2339B(a)(1) (emphasis added). Normally we read a criminal statute as applying a *mens rea* requirement to all of the subsequently listed elements of the crime. See *Flores-Figueroa v. United States,* 129 S. Ct. 1886, 1891-1892 (2009). So read, the defendant would have to know or intend (1) that he is *providing* support or resources, (2) that he is providing that support *to a foreign terrorist organization,* and (3) that he is providing support that is *material,* meaning (4) that his support bears a significant likelihood of furthering the organization's terrorist ends.

This fourth requirement flows directly from the statute's use of the word "material." That word can mean being of a physical or worldly nature, but it also can mean "being of real importance or great consequence." Webster's Third New International Dictionary 1392 (1961). Here, it must mean the latter, for otherwise the statute, applying only to physical aid, would not apply to speech at all. See also §2339A(b)(1) (defining "'material support or resources'" as "any property, *tangible or intangible* " (emphasis added)). And if the statute applies only to support that would likely be of real importance or great consequence, it must have importance or consequence in respect to the organization's terrorist activities. That is because support that is not significantly likely to help terrorist activities, for purposes of this statute, neither has "importance" nor is of "great consequence." . . .

Thus, textually speaking, a statutory requirement that the defendant *knew* the support was material can be read to require the Government to show that the defendant knew that the consequences of his acts had a significant likelihood of furthering the organization's terrorist, not just its lawful, aims.

I need not decide whether this is the only possible reading of the statute in cases where "material support" takes the form of "currency," "property," "monetary instruments," "financial securities," "financial services," "lodging," "safehouses," "false documentation or identification," "weapons," "lethal substances," or "explosives," and the like. §2339A(b)(1). Those kinds of aid are inherently more likely to help an organization's terrorist activities, either directly or because they are fungible in nature. Thus, to show that an individual has provided support of those kinds will normally prove sufficient for conviction (assuming the statute's other requirements are met). But where support consists of pure speech or association, I would indulge in no such presumption. Rather, the Government would have to prove that the defendant knew he was providing support significantly likely to help the organization pursue its unlawful terrorist aims (or, alternatively, that the defendant intended the support to be so used). . . .

III

Having interpreted the statute to impose the *mens rea* requirement just described, I would remand the cases so that the lower courts could consider more specifically the precise activities in which the plaintiffs still wish to engage and determine whether and to what extent a grant of declaratory and injunctive relief were warranted. . . .

[NSL p. 866, insert after Note 10. CTL p. 540, substitute for *United States v. Abu Marzook* and Notes 1-4.]

United States v. Abu Ali
United States Court of Appeals, Fourth Circuit, 2008
528 F.3d 210

WILKINSON, MOTZ and TRAXLER, Circuit Judges: [Ahmed Omar Abu Ali was born in the United States of Saudi parents. He was sent to Saudi Arabia for college education. While attending school there, he became affiliated with an Al Qaeda cell. In the course of meetings with Al Qaeda operatives in Saudi Arabia, Abu Ali suggested "assassinations or kidnappings of members of the U.S. Senate, the U.S. Army, and the Bush administration, a plan to rescue the prisoners at Guantánamo Bay, and plans to blow up American warplanes on U.S. bases and at U.S. ports, similar to the USS Cole operation." The cell began his training to reenter the United States as a "sleeper," for purposes of conducting later terrorist acts.

However, the Saudi counterterrorist agency Mabahith arrested Abu Ali before his training was completed and interrogated him. It also notified the FBI, which suggested questions for the interrogation. Eventually, the Saudi authorities surrendered Abu Ali to the United States, where he was tried for providing material support to a foreign terrorist organization, among several counts, partly on the basis of statements he made during the Saudi interrogation. When he challenged the admissibility of this evidence on the grounds that he had been tortured, the Saudi authorities made two Mabahith agents available for depositions in Saudi Arabia. Abu Ali's counsel attended the depositions and questioned the witnesses, but Abu Ali was not permitted to attend. At trial, the court also admitted unredacted versions of classified evidence that his defense team had only seen in redacted form before trial. He was convicted, and this appeal followed.] . . .

Unlike some others suspected of terrorist acts and designs upon the United States, Abu Ali was formally charged and tried according to the customary processes of the criminal justice system. Persons of good will may disagree over the precise extent to which the formal criminal justice process must be utilized when those suspected of participation in terrorist cells and networks are involved. There should be no disagreement, however, that the criminal justice system does retain an important place in the ongoing effort to deter and punish terrorist acts without the sacrifice of American constitutional norms and bedrock values. As will be apparent herein, the criminal justice system is not without those attributes of adaptation that will permit it to function in the post-9/11 world. These adaptations, however, need not and must not come at the expense of the requirement that an accused receive a fundamentally fair trial. In this case, we are satisfied that Abu Ali received a fair trial, though not a perfect one, and that the criminal justice system performed those functions which the Constitution envisioned for it. The three of us unanimously express our conviction that this is so in this opinion, which we have jointly authored.

Some differences do exist, however, among the panel members. Judge Wilkinson and Judge Traxler join in the opinion in its entirety. Judge Motz dissents [in parts not here relevant.] . . .

IV.

We next address Abu Ali's claim that the taking of the depositions of the Saudi Mabahith officials in Riyadh violated his Sixth Amendment

Confrontation Clause rights. We hold that the procedures developed by the district court to meet the extraordinary circumstances of this case adequately protected Abu Ali's Sixth Amendment rights. We therefore reject his claim.

A.

We briefly summarize the facts relevant to his Confrontation Clause claim here. On June 8, 2003, the Mabahith arrested Abu Ali on suspicion that he was a member of the al-Faq'asi terrorist cell. Soon after his detention, Abu Ali confessed to his involvement with the cell when confronted with the fact that several other detained cell members had identified him. On July 18, 2003, while still in Saudi custody, Abu Ali wrote a handwritten confession which he was videotaped reading on July 24, 2003. The government offered both Abu Ali's handwritten and videotaped confessions as evidence at trial.

Abu Ali argued that he was tortured by the Mabahith and that his confessions were therefore involuntary. In depositions taken pursuant to Rule 15 of the Federal Rules of Criminal Procedure, Abu Ali's two principal interrogators both denied that they had ever tortured Abu Ali or were aware of any other Saudi government official engaging in such behavior. Transcripts of this testimony were made part of the record in the district court's hearing on Abu Ali's motion to suppress his confession and a videotape of the deposition (as redacted pursuant to the court's order) was played at trial and made part of the trial record.

B.

Abu Ali claims that his Sixth Amendment Confrontation Clause right was violated because he was not physically present when the Rule 15 depositions of the Mabahith officers were taken. Since the government planned to introduce the depositions at trial, Abu Ali claims that he should have been physically present when the Mabahith officers were deposed. This argument is premised on the well-accepted notion that "eye-to-eye" contact between the accused and his accuser is more likely to lead to the truth. See Coy v. Iowa, 487 U.S. 1012 (1988) ("It is always more difficult to tell a lie about a person 'to his face' than 'behind his back.'").

Abu Ali's absence at the Rule 15 deposition was the result of the logistical arrangements the trial court made to deal with the practical difficulties of securing testimony from the Mabahith officers. As Saudi citizens who reside in Saudi Arabia, the Mabahith officers were beyond the subpoena power of the district court. Given this limitation, the United States government officially inquired into whether the Saudi Arabian government would allow the officers to testify at trial in the United States. The Saudi government denied this request, but permitted the officers to sit for depositions in Riyadh. As represented by counsel for the United States, this was a first in Saudi-American relations: the Saudi government had never before allowed such foreign access to a Mabahith officer.

Given the possibility of taking the deposition in Riyadh, the district court found it impractical for Abu Ali to travel to Saudi Arabia for two reasons. First, it would have been difficult for United States Marshals to maintain custody of Abu Ali while in Saudi Arabia. Second, the fact that Abu Ali committed his offenses in Saudi Arabia might subject him to prosecution overseas, complicating – if not precluding – his return to the United States to face trial. In fact, the government represented at oral argument that Abu Ali never asked the district court to allow him to travel to Saudi Arabia for the depositions, and we find no evidence in the record to dispute this claim.

Given these practical difficulties – witnesses who could only testify in Saudi Arabia and a defendant unable to go to Saudi Arabia – the trial court attempted to fashion deposition procedures that would best preserve Abu Ali's Confrontation Clause right. At the court's directive, two defense attorneys, including Abu Ali's lead attorney, attended the depositions in Saudi Arabia, while a third attorney sat with Abu Ali in Virginia. Two attorneys for the government and a translator were also present in the room in Saudi Arabia while the Mabahith officers were being deposed.

A live, two-way video link was used to transmit the proceedings to a courtroom in Alexandria. This permitted Abu Ali and one of his attorneys to see and hear the testimony contemporaneously; it also allowed the Mabahith officers to see and hear Abu Ali as they testified. A court reporter in Alexandria transcribed the testimony in real time, and both the witnesses and Abu Ali were videotaped during the depositions, so that the jury could see their reactions. The trial court presided over the deposition testimony of the Mabahith officials from the courtroom in Alexandria, ruling on objections as they arose. Furthermore, Abu Ali was able to communicate via cell phone with his defense counsel in Saudi Arabia during the frequent breaks in the proceedings. In addition, the court was willing to stop the depositions if Abu Ali's counsel in Saudi Arabia wanted to consult with their client.

Having fashioned these procedures, the district court presided over seven days of deposition testimony from several Saudi Mabahith officers involved in the arrest, detention, and interrogation of Abu Ali. The subject matter of the depositions encompassed all aspects of Abu Ali's experience with the Saudi criminal justice system, including the manner of his arrest, the length of his interrogation, the conditions of his confinement, the Mabahith's methods of questioning, and the circumstances surrounding his confessions.

Of critical importance was the testimony of two Saudi government officials, a Brigadier General and a Captain in the Mabahith, who presided over the interrogation of Abu Ali. These officers stated that Abu Ali was not blindfolded, handcuffed, or shackled in any way during his interrogation, and that he was provided with food, water, and access to a bathroom during breaks in questioning. Both the Brigadier General and the Captain adamantly denied that they directed, participated in, or were aware of any government official using physical force or psychological coercion against Abu Ali.

Abu Ali's counsel actively participated throughout these depositions, objecting frequently during the government's direct examination and cross-examining each of the witnesses at length. In particular, Abu Ali's counsel were able to question the interrogating officers about Abu Ali's claims that he was tortured and beaten; deprived of sleep, food, and water; and denied use of a bathroom and mattress.

C.

The Confrontation Clause of the Sixth Amendment provides that "[i]n all criminal prosecutions, the accused shall enjoy the right . . . to be confronted with the witnesses against him." U.S. Const. amend. VI. This clause traditionally affords "the defendant a face-to-face meeting with witnesses appearing before the trier of fact." *Coy,* 487 U.S. at 1016.

However, the right of the defendant to physically confront the witnesses against him is not absolute.

In *Maryland v. Craig*, 497 U.S. 836 (1990), the Supreme Court held that a district court may constitutionally admit testimony taken in the physical absence of the defendant so long as two conditions are met. *Id.* at 850. First, the denial of "face-to-face confrontation" must be "necessary to further an important public policy." *Id.* Second, the district court must ensure that protections are put in place so that "the reliability of the testimony is otherwise assured." *Id.* We find that both of *Craig*'s conditions are satisfied in this case.

First, the Supreme Court has long acknowledged that "no governmental interest is more compelling than the security of the Nation." *Haig v. Agee,* 453 U.S. 280, 307 (1981). . . . This case – in which the defendant is charged with crimes targeting American civilians and the President of the United States – plainly implicates this vital interest. This is not to suggest that a generalized interest in law enforcement is sufficient to satisfy the first prong of *Craig*. *Craig* plainly requires a public interest more substantial than convicting someone of a criminal offense. The prosecution of those bent on inflicting mass civilian casualties or assassinating high public officials is, however, just the kind of important public interest contemplated by the *Craig* decision.

Insistence on face-to-face confrontation may in some circumstances limit the ability of the United States to further its fundamental interest in preventing terrorist attacks. It is unquestionable that the struggle against terrorism is one of global dimension and that the United States depends upon its allies for logistical support and intelligence in this endeavor. This cooperation can result in foreign officials possessing information vital to prosecutions occurring in American courts. If the government is flatly prohibited from deposing foreign officials anywhere but in the United States, this would jeopardize the government's ability to prosecute terrorists using the domestic criminal justice system.

Thus, the district court reasonably determined that it was necessary in this case for the Mabahith officers to testify without the defendant physically present. Given the Saudi government's insistence that the Mabahith officers could only testify in Saudi Arabia and given that the defendant, for reasons of security or personal volition, could not travel overseas, requiring face-to-face confrontation here would have precluded the government from relying on the Saudi officers' important testimony. This would, to put it mildly, have greatly hindered efforts to prosecute the defendant, because the circumstances surrounding the confession bore crucially on any jury assessment of its voluntariness. The Sixth Amendment is not so inflexible as to require this outcome. *See Mattox v. United States*, 156 U.S. 237, 243 (1895) (noting that "[t]he law in its wisdom declares that the rights of the public shall not be wholly sacrificed in order that an incidental benefit may be preserved to the accused").

The second prong of the *Craig* test requires a district court to make certain that, absent face-to-face confrontation, "the reliability of the testimony is otherwise assured." *Craig*, 497 U.S. at 850. In *Craig*, the Court provided a blueprint on how to satisfy this requirement when it noted that "the presence of [the] other elements of confrontation – oath, cross-examination, and observation of the witness'[s] demeanor – adequately ensures that the testimony is both reliable and subject to rigorous adversarial testing in a manner functionally equivalent to that accorded live, in-person testimony." *Id.* at 851.

These "other elements" are present here. First, the Saudi witnesses testified under oath. While the oath used in this case, at the suggestion of defense counsel, was apparently an oath used in the Saudi criminal justice system, we cannot conclude, without more, that such an oath failed to serve its intended purpose of encouraging truth through solemnity. The oath used here was similar in most respects to the oath used in American judicial proceedings, and the appellant raised no objection to the oath in his briefs. Second, as discussed earlier, defense counsel was able to cross-examine the Mabahith witnesses extensively. Finally, the defendant, judge, and jury were all able to observe the demeanor of the witnesses. Both the defendant and the judge were able to view the witnesses as they testified via two-way video link, and the jury watched a videotape of the deposition at trial. This videotape presented side-by-side footage of the Mabahith officers testifying and the defendant's simultaneous reactions to the testimony.

In fact, the procedures used in this case were in some ways more protective of the defendant's interests than those used in *Craig*. While the Court in *Craig* approved the use of one-way video testimony, *see Craig*, 497 U.S. at 860, the depositions in this case were taken via a two-way video link. This two-way link meant that the witnesses were able to view the defendant as they testified, a protection not present in *Craig*.

. . . There is simply no evidence in the record that would lead this court to conclude that the defendant did not have a constitutionally sufficient chance to cross-examine the Mabahith witnesses. . . .

We thus find there to be no violation of the Confrontation Clause under *Craig*. The district court properly found that logistical and international necessities required the Mabahith officials to testify without the defendant present in order to further the government's undoubted national security interests. Furthermore, the procedures designed by the district court to replicate the "rigorous adversarial testing" present in a face-to-face confrontation plainly meet the reliability prong of *Craig*. . . .

VI.

Abu Ali also challenges the district court's handling of certain classified information under the provisions of the Classified Information Procedures Act ("CIPA"), 18 U.S.C. App. 3, §§1-16 (West 2000 & Supp. 2007).[13] Abu Ali's primary contention is that the district court violated his Sixth Amendment Confrontation Clause rights by admitting as evidence unredacted versions of two classified documents that Abu Ali had only been permitted to view in a redacted form, and by refusing to allow Abu Ali and his lead trial counsel to attend and participate in the hearings conducted under CIPA to discuss the classified evidence. . . .

A.

The Sixth Amendment guarantees that "[i]n all criminal prose-cutions, the accused shall enjoy . . . the right to be confronted with the witnesses against him." U.S. Const. amend. VI. Its "main and essential purpose . . . is to secure for the opponent the opportunity of cross-examination." *Delaware v. Van Arsdall,* 475 U.S. 673, 678 (1986). However, the right "means more than being allowed to confront the witness physically." *Id.* "[T]he principal evil at which the Confrontation Clause was directed was the civil-law mode of criminal procedure, and

---

13. These issues were separately raised via classified briefs and argued in closed proceedings before this panel.

350 National Security Law/Counterterrorism Law

particularly its use of *ex parte* examinations as evidence against the accused." *Crawford v. Washington,* 541 U.S. 36, 54 (2004). Thus, while this is not the ordinary case, we think the criminal defendant's right to confront witnesses necessarily encompasses his right to also see any documentary evidence that such witnesses offer at trial as evidence to support a conviction. *Cf. Abourezk v. Reagan,* 785 F.2d 1043, 1060 (D.C. Cir. 1986) ("It is a hallmark of our adversary system that we safeguard party access to evidence tendered in support of a requested court judgment. The openness of judicial proceedings serves to preserve both the appearance and the reality of fairness in the adjudications of United States courts. It is therefore the firmly held main rule that a court may not dispose of the merits of a case on the basis of *ex parte, in camera* submissions.").

A defendant's right to see the evidence that is tendered against him *during* trial, however, does not necessarily equate to a right to have classified information disclosed to him *prior* to trial. Evidentiary privileges may serve as valid bases to block the disclosure of certain types of evidence, and the validity of such privileges may be tested by in camera and ex parte proceedings before the court "for the limited purpose of determining whether the asserted privilege is genuinely applicable." *Id.* As a general rule, "[i]f the court finds that the claimed privilege does not apply, then the other side must be given access to the information." *Id.* If the court finds that the privilege does apply, then it may preclude access to the information. But neither scenario results in the conviction of a defendant "based upon evidence he was never permitted to see and to rebut." *Id.*

In the area of national security and the government's privilege to protect classified information from public disclosure, we look to CIPA for appropriate procedures. . . .

C.

With these principles in mind, we turn first to Abu Ali's Confrontation Clause challenge to the government's introduction at trial of two unredacted, classified documents that memorialized communications between Sultan Jubran [an Al Qaeda operative] and Abu Ali in the days following the May 2003 safe house raids conducted by the Saudi officials in Medina, as well as to his exclusion from the CIPA proceedings in which these communications were discussed.

1. . . .

[Only one of Abu Ali's lawyers obtained a security clearance. The government disclosed to the security-cleared lawyer unredacted copies of evidence it intended to declassify and introduce at trial, but explained that it would take some precautions to prevent public disclosure of the unredacted documents. It also afforded Abu Ali's non-cleared lawyers only redacted versions of the same documents.]

. . . The first declassified document was dated May 27, 2003, and read as follows:

> Peace, How are you and how is your family? I hope they are good. I heard the news about the children's sickness. I wish them a speedy recovery, God willing. Anyway, please keep in touch. Greetings to the group, Hani.

The government intended to demonstrate that "Hani" was a known alias of Abu Ali and that "news about the children's sickness" was a coded reference to the raids conducted by the Mabahith and the arrest of the Medina cell members. The second declassified document was dated June 6, 2003, and read as follows:

> To my brother, Peace to you with God's mercy and blessings. Thank God, I am fine. I was saved from the accident by a great miracle. I ask God that I would be thankful to Him. I have no idea about the others. However, according to what one doctor mentioned, 'Adil was not with them, thank God. The important thing is to get yourself ready for the medical checkup because you may have an appointment soon. Therefore, you must keep yourself ready by refraining from eating high fat meals and otherwise.

With regard to this communication, the government intended to demonstrate that the term "accident" was also a coded reference to the safe house raids. According to the government's theory, Sultan Jubran was advising Abu Ali that he did not know which cell members had escaped and which were captured, but that he and al-Faq'asi (a/k/a "Adil"), had escaped, and warning that Abu Ali might also be at risk.

A comparison of the classified and unclassified documents reveals that the declassified versions provided the dates, the opening salutations, the entire substance of the communications, and the closings, and had only been lightly redacted to omit certain identifying and forensic information.

On October 19, 2005, the government filed an in camera, ex parte motion pursuant to §4 of CIPA, seeking a protective order prohibiting testimony and lines of questioning that would lead to the disclosure of the classified information during the trial. *See* 18 U.S.C. App. 3 §4. The government advised that the classified portions of the communications could not be provided to Abu Ali and his uncleared counsel because they contained highly sensitive information which, if confirmed in a public setting, would divulge information detrimental to national security interests. The district court granted the government's motion by in camera, ex parte, sealed order. However, the district court ruled that the United States could use the "silent witness rule" to disclose the classified information to the jury at trial.[18] . . .

3.

Having carefully considered the circumstances and evidence below, we conclude that the district court's determination that the redacted classified information need not be disclosed to the defendant, his uncleared counsel, and the public was not an abuse of discretion. Nor do we think that the district court's exclusion of Abu Ali and his uncleared

---

18. The "silent witness" rule was described in *United States v. Zettl*, 835 F.2d 1059, 1063 (4th Cir. 1987), as follows.

[T]he witness would not disclose the information from the classified document in open court. Instead, the witness would have a copy of the classified document before him. The court, counsel and the jury would also have copies of the classified document. The witness would refer to specific places in the document in response to questioning. The jury would then refer to the particular part of the document as the witness answered. By this method, the classified information would not be made public at trial but the defense would be able to present that classified information to the jury.

Id.

counsel from the CIPA proceedings ran afoul of the Confrontation Clause. The district court's admission of the classified versions of the documents as evidence for consideration by the jury without disclosing the same versions to Abu Ali, however, was clearly contrary to the rights guaranteed to Abu Ali by the Confrontation Clause.

We begin with the district court's exclusion of Abu Ali and his uncleared counsel from the CIPA proceedings. The district court was presented with a §4 motion by the government to protect the classified information and a §5 motion, made at a later date, by Abu Ali that he be allowed to disclose that information. Initially, the district court found the redacted, unclassified version of the communications to be adequate to meet the defendant's need for information. CIPA expressly provides for such redactions of classified information from documents sought or required to be produced to the defendant, and the determination may be based upon an ex parte showing that the disclosure would jeopardize national security interests. The district court appropriately balanced the interests and made a reasonable determination that disclosure of the redacted information was not necessary to a fair trial.

There was likewise no abuse of discretion in the district court's decision to preclude Abu Ali's uncleared counsel from cross-examining the government's witnesses about the redacted information, which would have effectively disclosed the classified information that the court had already ruled need not be disclosed. A defendant and his counsel, if lacking in the requisite security clearance, must be excluded from hearings that determine what classified information is material and whether substitutions crafted by the government suffice to provide the defendant adequate means of presenting a defense and obtaining a fair trial. Thus, the mere exclusion of Abu Ali and his uncleared counsel from the CIPA hearings did not run afoul of CIPA or Abu Ali's Confrontation Clause rights.

We also conclude that the district court struck an appropriate balance between the government's national security interests and the defendant's right to explore the manner in which the communications were obtained and handled. Abu Ali and his uncleared counsel were provided with the substance of the communications, the dates, and the parties involved, and CIPA-cleared defense counsel was provided with the classified versions and afforded unfettered opportunity to cross-examine the government's witnesses concerning these matters. At the conclusion of the examinations, defense counsel pointed to no specific problem with the issues explored. The district court also expressly considered Abu Ali's rights under the Confrontation Clause and determined that public examination of these witnesses was not necessary to prevent infringement of them. Having fully considered the record and the classified information ourselves, we agree. Uncleared defense counsel were not entitled to disclose the classified information via their questioning of the witnesses about their roles in extracting, sharing, transferring, and handling the communications, and Abu Ali, who was ably represented by counsel at the hearing on this issue, was not deprived of his right to confrontation or to a fair trial merely because he and his uncleared counsel were not also allowed to attend.

The error in the case, which appears to have originated in the October 2005 CIPA proceeding, was that CIPA was taken one step too far. The district court did not abuse its discretion in protecting the classified information from disclosure to Abu Ali and his uncleared counsel, in approving a suitable substitute, or in determining that Abu Ali would receive a fair trial in the absence of such disclosure. But, for reasons that remain somewhat unclear to us, the district court granted the government's request that the complete, unredacted classified document could be presented to the jury via the "silent witness" procedure. The end result, therefore, was that the jury was privy to the information that was withheld from Abu Ali.

As noted above, CIPA contemplates and authorizes district courts to prevent the disclosure of classified information, as was done in this case, so long as it does not deprive the defendant of a fair trial. CIPA also authorizes restrictions upon the questioning of the witnesses to ensure that classified information remains classified. Indeed, even the "silent witness" procedure contemplates situations in which the jury is provided classified information that is withheld from the public, but not from the defendant. In addition, CIPA provides district courts wide discretion to evaluate and approve suitable substitutions to be presented to the jury. CIPA does not, however, authorize courts to provide classified documents to the jury when only such substitutions are provided to the defendant. Nor could it. There is a stark difference between ex parte submissions from prosecutors which protect the disclosure of irrelevant, nonexculpatory, or privileged information, and situations in which the government seeks to use *ex parte* information in court as evidence to obtain a conviction. And, the notion that such "safeguards against wide-ranging discovery . . . would be sufficient to justify a conviction on secret evidence is patently absurd." *Id.*; *see also United States v. Innamorati,* 996 F.2d 456, 488 (1st Cir. 1993) (finding no error in prosecutor's ex parte submission of information for consideration as to whether it must be disclosed to the defendant, but noting that "there [was] no question . . . of convictions based upon secret evidence furnished to the factfinder but withheld from the defendants").

The same can be said for the evidence here. If classified information is to be relied upon as evidence of guilt, the district court may consider steps to protect some or all of the information from unnecessary public disclosure in the interest of national security and in accordance with CIPA, which specifically contemplates such methods as redactions and substitutions so long as these alternatives do not deprive the defendant of a fair trial. However, the government must at a minimum provide the same version of the evidence to the defendant that is submitted to the jury. We do not balance a criminal defendant's right to see the evidence which will be used to convict him against the government's interest in protecting that evidence from public disclosure. If the government does not want the defendant to be privy to information that is classified, it may either declassify the document, seek approval of an effective substitute, or forego its use altogether. What the government cannot do is hide the evidence from the defendant, but give it to the jury. Such plainly violates the Confrontation Clause.

D.

Having determined that submission of the classified documents to the jury ran afoul of Abu Ali's Confrontation Clause rights, we turn now to consider whether that error was harmless. We conclude that it was. . . .

VIII. . . .

For the foregoing reasons, the judgment is affirmed in part, reversed in part, and remanded for further proceedings consistent with this decision.

Affirmed in Part, Reversed in Part, and Remanded.

[Dissenting opinion of DIANA GRIBBON MOTZ, Circuit Judge, omitted.]

[NSL p. 866, CTL p. 540. Insert after *United States v. Abu Ali*.]

United States v. Rosen

United States District Court, Eastern District of Virginia, 2007

487 F. Supp. 2d 703

ELLIS, District Judge. This Espionage Act (18 U.S.C. §793) prosecution involves a substantial amount of classified information the government contends is information relating to the national defense ("NDI")[19] and for this reason the government seeks to avoid public disclosure of this material in the course of the trial. To this end, the government, by motion pursuant to §6 of the Classified Information Procedures Act ("CIPA"),[20] has proposed utilizing a procedure at trial whereby substantial quantities of classified information would be disclosed to the Court, the jury, and counsel, but withheld from the public. This novel proposal, if allowed, would effectively close a substantial portion of the trial. Accordingly, defendants challenge this proposed procedure on the grounds that it is neither authorized by CIPA nor constitutionally permissible.

I.

Both defendants are charged with conspiracy to communicate NDI to persons not authorized to receive it, in violation of 18 U.S.C. §793(g), (e). Rosen is additionally charged with aiding and abetting alleged co-conspirator Lawrence Franklin's unauthorized communication of NDI to persons not authorized to receive it, in violation of 18 U.S.C. §§793(d) and 2. The superceding indictment generally alleges that over a course of several years, defendants cultivated various sources of information within the United States government, obtained NDI from those sources, and then disseminated that NDI to others not authorized to receive it, including co-workers, journalists, and foreign government officials. For

---

19. It is important to recognize that NDI and classified material may not be coextensive sets. . . . While classified status may be probative of information's NDI status, it is not conclusive.

20. 18 U.S.C. App. 3.

a more complete recitation of the facts alleged in the superceding indictment, as well as a more precise delineation of the government's burden of proof, see *United States v. Rosen*, 445 F. Supp. 2d. 602 (E.D. Va. 2006) [*infra* p. 436] . . . .

III.

[After defendants proposed to offer classified information in their defense at trial and objected to the government's proposed substitutions pursuant to CIPA], "[t]he government . . . proposed a procedure for handling this material at trial and it is this proposal that is at issue here. The government's proposal is novel; no published opinion has been found or cited in which the precise procedure proposed here was judicially approved or used. Simply put, the government proposes that while the jury, the Court, and counsel will, for the most part, have access to the unredacted classified material, the public will not. Instead, the public, in the course of the trial, will see and hear only the substitutions that have passed through the CIPA §6(c) process. In other words, and putting to one side the not insubstantial practical problems inherent in conducting a trial pursuant to the government's proposed procedure, its use would surely exclude the public from substantial and critical parts of the trial. This result is evident from a more detailed description of the proposed procedure.

The government's proposal is, in effect, a variant and a substantial expansion of the so-called "silent witness rule," a rule that has been used and judicially approved in certain, but not all circumstances. . . . As noted, the effect of using the procedure in this case would be the exclusion of the public from substantial portions of the trial.

The proposed procedure would work as follows: for each classified document discussed at trial, the Court, the witness, counsel, and the jurors would have the unredacted classified document in front of them, either in paper form or via computer screens viewable only by those persons. The public, however, would see only a redacted version. When counsel or a witness wishes to direct the jury to a classified portion of the document, counsel and the witness would refer to the page, paragraph and line numbers, with the Court, opposing counsel, and the jury following along, but members of the public could not follow along because they would be unaware of the specific information referenced by counsel or the witness. And, the witness answering the questions about the document would not be permitted to refer to specific language or information in the document, except by use of certain codes. For example, to rebut the government's contention that certain material is NDI, defendants will likely wish to call witnesses to compare various public source documents with the alleged NDI. To do so effectively may well require the witness to refer to specific language or contents of both the public source document and the alleged NDI. Anticipating this, the government proposes that the witness would not speak the names of certain specific countries, foreign persons, etc., but would instead use a code (e.g., "Country A," "Report X," "Foreign Person Y," "Foreign Person Z," etc.) provided also to counsel, the Court, and the jury. Moreover, this code would change with respect to different alleged overt acts, presumably to prevent the public from inferring the meaning of the generic designations or otherwise breaking the code. For example, if a witness discussing a particular alleged disclosure is instructed to refer to Monaco as Country A, a different witness (or even the same witness) discussing another alleged disclosure might use Country B or C to refer to Monaco.

Likewise, when recordings discussing classified information are played, the government proposes that the Court, counsel, witness, and jury listen on special headphones to the entire recording. The public, however, would not hear the full recording; instead, the recorded conversations would be played aloud in the courtroom, but where classified information is discussed in the recording, the public version would revert to static. Also, the public would receive only a redacted transcript of the conversations.

In sum, the novel and distinctive feature of the government's proposed procedure is that the public is walled off from seeing and hearing everything the jury, the Court, the attorneys and the witnesses see and hear. What the public does not see or hear is the heart of the case, namely the classified material the government claims is the NDI that the defendants allegedly received and distributed without authorization. A further, related novel and distinctive feature of the government's proposal relates to the jury. Although jurors will see and hear classified material, they, of course, will not have received security clearances for this purpose. Nor has this ever been otherwise in cases involving classified material, for a variety of reasons including the substantial time and effort typically required for such clearances to be completed and the substantial question whether it is constitutionally permissible to exclude jurors because they could not pass a security clearance investigation. The government's remedy for this anomaly is simply to have the jurors instructed that they cannot disclose to anyone the classified material they will see and hear during the trial.

With this description in mind, the analysis now proceeds to address the following questions:

(i) Whether the government's proposed procedure is explicitly or implicitly authorized by CIPA.

(ii) Whether the government's proposed procedure violates the right to a public trial, guaranteed to defendants by the Sixth Amendment and to the public by the First Amendment.

IV.

A.

The government urges that the use of the silent witness rule, codes, and redacted recordings are "substitutions" authorized by CIPA. Defendants disagree, noting the government's proposed procedure is nowhere authorized by CIPA, either explicitly or implicitly. Defendants are correct, a conclusion that follows from CIPA's plain language, but also from the fact that the government's proposed procedure simply cannot fit within CIPA's confines even assuming the statute's plain language would not otherwise preclude it.

Analysis of this statutory argument properly focuses on CIPA §6(c) and §8(b) . . . . As noted, CIPA §6(c) allows the government to move that in lieu of disclosing classified information at trial, a "substitution" be used, which could take the form of a summary of the information or a presumably sanitized statement of facts the classified statement would tend to prove. Importantly, no substitutions can be used unless there is a judicial finding that the substitution provides defendants with "substantially the same ability to make his defense as would disclosure of the specific classified information." Consistent with this, CIPA §8(b) also permits introduction and use at trial of redacted versions of classified materials unless "the whole ought in fairness to be considered."

Significantly, neither §6(c) nor §8(b) explicitly authorize[s] or state[s] that "substitutions" may be made available to the public and the jury on different terms. CIPA is at best silent on this issue. Yet, this silence should not be construed as implicitly authorizing the government's proposal. To the contrary, it seems clear that CIPA envisions that "substitutions," if not unfair to defendants, will be used at a public trial in identical form for both the jury and the public. While it is true, as reflected in CIPA's legislative history, that "Congress expected trial judges to fashion creative solutions in the interests of justice for classified information problems,"[9] there is no evidence that Congress expected this creativity to extend to adopting procedures that effectively close the trial to the public. Indeed, given the strong presumption in the law that trials will be open and that evidence will be fully aired in public, CIPA's silence about whether "substitutions" and "excisions" can be made available to the public and jury on different terms should be interpreted as a prohibition on doing so. Closing a trial, even partially, is a highly unusual result disfavored by the law. A statute, even one regulating the use of classified information, should not be construed as authorizing a trial closure based on Congress' mere silence or use of ambiguous language. Rather, because a trial closure implicates important constitutional rights, CIPA should not be read to authorize closure absent a clear and explicit statement by Congress in the statutory language.

In short, CIPA only authorizes the use of substitutions to avoid disclosure of classified information *to the public and the jury,* provided defendant's right to present a defense is not impaired; this authority is not the authority to close a trial to the public.

B.

Even assuming, *arguendo,* that the CIPA provision allowing "substitutions" might be stretched to encompass the government's proposed procedure, there is no doubt that the procedure would not pass muster under CIPA's fairness requirements. Where, as here, a central

---

9. United States v. North, 713 F. Supp. 1452 (D.D.C. 1989) (citing H. Rep. No. 96-1436, 1980 U.S.C.C.A.N. 4294).

issue in the case is whether the government's alleged NDI is indeed genuinely NDI, and the proposed procedure would amount to a wholesale use of the silent witness rule to cover all of the alleged NDI, it cannot be said that the procedure affords defendants "substantially the same ability to make [their] defense as would disclosure of the specific classified information." CIPA §6(c). A few examples vividly illustrate this point.

As noted, the government in this case has the burden of proving beyond a reasonable doubt that the alleged NDI is indeed NDI. To this end, the government will likely invite witnesses to compare the substance of certain of defendants' emails, telephone conversations, or faxes with certain alleged NDI to show that defendants had obtained NDI and were disseminating it without authorization. Defendants, of course, may wish to show, and indeed to emphasize, the dissimilarities between the alleged NDI and the information they obtained. Plainly, they would be significantly hobbled in doing so by use of the government's proposed procedure, inasmuch as the specific information could not be used in open court. The silent comparison of paragraphs or sentences, even where supplemented by codes, would effectively preclude defense counsel from driving home important points to the jury.

Similarly, it is apparent that defendants intend at trial to rebut the government's claim that certain material is NDI by having witnesses compare the alleged NDI to contemporaneous public domain material. Once again, the proposed procedure would unfairly impact defendants' ability to establish this defense. In this context, the silent witness rule, applied across the board as the government proposes here, essentially robs defendants of the chance to make vivid and drive home to the jury their view that the alleged NDI is no such thing, as essentially similar material was abundant in the public domain. Importantly in this respect, it is hard to see how defendants could effectively show, via the silent witness rule, that the details of differences between public source material and the alleged NDI are neither minor nor trivial. . . .

. . . In short, the use of codes would render virtually impossible an effective line of cross-examination vital to the defense. . . .

Yet another fatal defect in the fairness of the proposed procedure is apparent from the way in which it would hamper defendants should they choose to testify. Clearly, the proposed procedure would unfairly hinder defendants in their effort to explain why they believed any information they sought to obtain, the information they received, and the information they disclosed to others was not NDI. In this regard, defendants must be able to explain precisely what they knew and when, and from whom or what they learned it, and why they did not believe the material was NDI they were not authorized to have, or otherwise lacked the requisite *mens rea.* Yet, the proposed procedure would unfairly hinder defendants from doing so. For example, statements like "I heard from Foreign Person C the fact about Country X, reflected at Exhibit A page 3 paragraph 4 line 2 – well, except for the last clause – and so when I asked Franklin for confirmation of that fact, I thought I was asking for a matter of public record," may provide some exculpatory description of defendants' state of mind, assuming the jury could decode the statement quickly enough to follow the questioning. Yet, it would be difficult, if not impossible, for defendants to explain fully why they believed the information they sought or had was in the public domain without revealing details about the information, the identity and reliability of Person C, etc. Because the proposed procedure shackles defendants in this way, it cannot pass muster under CIPA.

Finally, it must be noted that the government's proposed frequently-changing system of coded references not only invites juror confusion, but virtually guarantees it. Given the sheer number of substitutions and the proliferation of coded phrases, varying from witness to witness and overt act to overt act, the likelihood of juror confusion would be a sufficient ground, by itself, for rejecting the wholesale proposed substitutions under CIPA §6(c). . . .

V.

Defendants' challenge to the government's proposed procedure rests on constitutional as well as statutory grounds. Specifically, defendants argue that even if CIPA's language can be stretched to cover the government's proposed procedure, that procedure nonetheless fails as a violation of defendants' Sixth Amendment right to a public trial and the public's First Amendment right to a trial open to public scrutiny. Thus, even if the procedure passed muster under CIPA, constitutional analysis is nonetheless required. This follows, defendants argue, because the proposed procedure effectively excludes the public from essential portions of the trial.[20]

Nor is there any doubt that the portions of the trial that would be closed to the public are critical portions of the trial. It is clear that the government's proposal precludes the public from hearing and evaluating the evidence on a crucial and contested element of the case, namely, whether the information at issue is NDI and whether defendants knew it to be such. Moreover, the quality and quantity of material the government proposes to exclude from public view is significant. Testimony about the putative NDI at issue in seven of the alleged nine disclosures would be partially closed to the public, as would the recordings and documents corresponding to this NDI. Notably, the government's proposed procedure would treat even certain related public domain documents, including news reports, as if they were classified documents. In short, in the circumstances of this case, the government's proposal is clearly equivalent to sealing essential aspects of the trial.

The analysis of defendants' constitutional argument properly begins with the recognition that defendants and the public have a fundamental right to a trial open to the public. The right to a public trial contributes to just adjudication, stimulates public confidence in the judicial system, and ensures that the public is fairly apprised of the proceedings in cases of public concern. A public trial contributes to just adjudication in several ways: (i) requiring witness[es]' testimony to be public deters perjury; (ii) requiring a judge's rulings to be made in public deters partiality and bias; and (iii) requiring prosecutors to present their charges and evidence publicly deters prosecutorial vindictiveness and abuse of power. In these ways, the presence of the public encourages accurate factfinding and wise use of judicial and prosecutorial discretion, thereby contributing to

---

20. It is noteworthy in this respect that the government sensibly appears to have abandoned its original position that the proposed use of the silent witness rule, coded testimony, and redacted recordings does not close the trial because the public would be present in the courtroom. This argument, if credited, leads to the absurd result that a trial unintelligible to the public is still "open" to the public simply because the public is physically present to see and hear what they cannot understand. The public's physical presence, by itself, does not guarantee that a trial is public; it is also necessary that the trial be reasonably comprehensible to the physically present public.

public confidence that justice has prevailed at trial. In short, justice must not only be done, it must be seen to be done.

Given the important interests at stake, it is now well-settled that defendants in criminal cases and the public both have a right to a trial open to public scrutiny. *See Press-Enterprise Co. v. Superior Court of California*, 464 U.S. 501, 510 (1984) (public's First Amendment right); *Waller v. Georgia*, 467 U.S. 39, 44-45 (1984) (defendant's Sixth Amendment right). It is also well-settled that the standard governing whether the public trial right has been infringed is the same whether the right is asserted by the press under the First Amendment or by a defendant under the Sixth Amendment. *Waller*, 467 U.S. at 46-47. Under this constitutional standard, a trial is presumptively open, and may be closed only if certain criteria are met. These criteria are set forth in *Press-Enterprise* and its progeny, as follows:

> (1) an "overriding interest" must exist to close the trial,
>
> (2) the closure is no broader than necessary to protect that interest,
>
> (3) the court considers reasonable alternatives to closure, and
>
> (4) the court makes specific findings on the record concerning the existence of the overriding interest, the breadth of the closure, and the unavailability of alternatives to facilitate appellate review.

Press-Enterprise, 464 U.S. at 510. As the proponent of closing the proceedings, the government bears a "weighty" burden to establish that closure is permissible. *Press-Enterprise*, 464 U.S. at 509-10. Decisions to close trials must be made on a case by case basis, with attention to the facts and circumstances of each case; statutes *per se* requiring closure in certain circumstances are impermissible. *Globe Newspaper Co. v. Superior Court*, 457 U.S. 596, 611 n.27 (1982). Finally, before trials may be closed, the public must be given notice and an opportunity to be heard. *In re Knight Publishing Co.*, 743 F.2d 231, 234-35 (4th Cir. 1984). An erroneous denial of a public trial is a structural error not amenable to harmless error analysis. *Bell*, 236 F.3d at 165 (citing cases).

Each of the four *Press-Enterprise* elements is separately considered.

1. Overriding Interest

The government claims that its interest in protecting classified information is a compelling and overriding one, and has cited numerous cases in support of this claim. While it is true, as an abstract proposition, that the government's interest in protecting classified information can be a qualifying compelling and overriding interest, it is also true that the government must make a specific showing of harm to national security in specific cases to carry its burden in this regard. The government's *ipse dixit* that information is damaging to national security is not sufficient to close the courtroom doors nor to obtain the functional equivalent, namely trial by code. *Press-Enterprise* and *In re Washington Post* require more; they require a judicial inquiry into the legitimacy of the asserted national security interest, and specific findings, sealed if necessary, about the harm to national security that would ensue if the request to close the trial is not granted. *See Press-Enterprise*, 464 U.S. at 510; *In re Washington Post*, 807 F.2d 383, 391-92 (4th Cir. 1986) (rejecting the government's argument that courts should defer to Executive Branch assertions that trial closures are necessary for national security reasons, and stating that a proceeding cannot be closed merely because the case implicated CIPA at an earlier stage). Moreover, the government's *ipse dixit* is insufficient whether it appears by way of classified status, or the bald assertion of counsel that information is damaging to national security. Thus, granting that national security concerns can justify appropriately tailored trial closures, the government nonetheless bears the burden of demonstrating, as a factual matter, that harm to national security would result from failing to close the trial.

Here, the government has not met its burden; instead, it has done no more than to invoke "national security" broadly and in a conclusory fashion, as to all the classified information in the case. Of course, classification decisions are for the Executive Branch, and the information's classified status must inform an assessment of the government's asserted interests under *Press-Enterprise*. But ultimately, trial judges must make their own judgment about whether the government's asserted interest in partially closing the trial is compelling or overriding. As noted, a generalized assertion of "national security interests," whether by virtue of the information's classified status or upon representation of counsel, is not alone sufficient to overcome the presumption in favor of open trials. Here, the government has not proffered any evidence about danger to national security from airing the evidence publicly, let alone an item-by-item description of the harm to national security that will result from disclosure at trial of each specific piece of information as to which closure is sought, as required by *Press-Enterprise.*

Moreover, quite aside from the government's failure to provide any evidence of harm to national security from an open trial, the government's assertion of an overriding interest justifying a trial closure is undermined by the substance of the proposed procedure, to wit, that the jury and uncleared witnesses will be permitted to receive unredacted classified information. Given that the government appears willing to trust its confidential information to jurors, alternates, and uncleared witnesses, including (potentially) defendants, it is difficult to credit fully the government's claim that the classified information at issue is deserving of rigorous protection.

The government urges that this proposed disclosure to the jury does not reflect any inconsistency on its part, because the jurors could be instructed never to disclose the classified information they received at trial. Yet such an instruction appears patently unfair here, because it would suggest to the jury that the information at issue is NDI. Nor is this a minor consideration given that the status of the information as NDI is a central issue in the case, and indeed an element of the charged crime as to which the government bears the burden of proof beyond a reasonable doubt. An instruction that the jurors must treat the information they receive as a closely-held government secret is not easily reconciled with the instruction that the jury is the sole judge of the facts of the case and that it alone determines whether the information at issue is NDI, *i.e.,* whether it is closely held and potentially damaging to national security if revealed. While the two instructions are not flatly contradictory, they would be beyond the capacity of most jurors to reconcile . . . .

In short, the government's asserted overriding interest is not treated as such by the government itself, given that the putative NDI will be disclosed to uncleared jurors and witnesses. And while the government's cited cases support the notion that national security interests *can be* sufficiently compelling to justify a partial closure of the trial, they also require that the government satisfy *Press-Enterprise* by adequately supporting its motion with a description of the specific harm to national security that would ensue from disclosure. The government has not done so here. Accordingly, its motion fails under the first prong of *Press-Enterprise.*

2. Narrowly Tailored

For the same reasons, there is no basis to conclude that the government's proposal is narrowly tailored to protect any national security interests. Since the government has not identified with specificity which of the classified information to be kept from public view would harm national security if disclosed to the broader public, or how the national security would be affected, it is impossible to evaluate whether the proposed closure is as narrowly tailored as possible to protect that asserted interest.

3. Alternatives

Likewise, assuming that an overriding interest exists here because disclosure of some or all of the classified information at issue would damage national security, it is evident that reasonable alternatives to closure exist here. To wit, the government could propose conventional CIPA §6(c) substitutions that would be given to the jury and the public in the same form. Whether these substitutions would pass CIPA §6(c) fairness standards is another question not here presented.

4. Findings

Although the conclusions concerning the other *Press-Enterprise* factors obviate the need for factual findings, the absence of any affidavit describing the ensuing harms to national security should the trial not be closed is noteworthy. A highly detailed explanation of the ensuing harms to national security is especially necessary to make the thorough factual findings required for a closure when, as here, much of the classified information at issue is not self-evidently damaging to national security. . . .

VI.

To summarize, the wholesale use of the silent witness rule, coded testimony, and redacted recordings effectively closes the trial. This procedure is not a "substitution" authorized by CIPA, and even if it were, it would not afford defendants substantially the same opportunity to present their defense as the specific classified information. Moreover, even if the procedure passed muster under CIPA, it nonetheless would have to satisfy the *Press-Enterprise* test because it effectively closes portions of the trial. The proposed procedure does not; the government's showing of an overriding interest in protecting sensitive national security information has been insufficient to this point, and the government's claim that the information at issue is damaging to the national security if publicly disclosed is belied by its own proposal to release the information to uncleared persons. This opinion does not foreclose the government from proposing specific §6(c) substitutions that pass CIPA muster. Nor does this opinion foreclose consideration of or narrowly limited use of the silent witness rule where the government provides a specific factual basis for a claim that public disclosure would damage the national security.

For these reasons, defendants' motion to strike must be granted, and the government's motion to close the trial, styled a CIPA §6(c) motion, must be denied. At the government's request and with no objection from defendants, entry of an appropriate Order will be delayed to afford the government time to consider how to proceed with respect to the CIPA process.

[NSL p. 875, CTL p. 555. Insert at end of chapter.]

Letter from Attorney General Eric Holder to Senator Mitch McConnell Regarding Umar Farouk Abdulmutallab
Feb. 3, 2010
http://www.justice.gov/cjs/docs/ag-letter-2-3-10.pdf

[This letter may be found *supra* p. 276.]

[NSL p. 906, insert at the end of Note 8. CTL p. 587, substitute for Military Commissions Act of 2006.]

Military Commissions Act of 2009

Pub. L. No. 111-84, tit. XVIII, 123 Stat. 2190, 2574-2614

SEC. 1801. SHORT TITLE.

This title may be cited as the "Military Commissions Act of 2009."

SEC. 1802. MILITARY COMMISSIONS.

Chapter 47A of title 10, United States Code, is amended to read as follows:

SUBCHAPTER I – GENERAL PROVISIONS

§948a. Definitions

In this chapter:

(1) ALIEN. – The term "alien" means an individual who is not a citizen of the United States.

(2) CLASSIFIED INFORMATION. – The term "classified information" means the following:

(A) Any information or material that has been determined by the United States Government pursuant to statute, Executive order, or regulation to require protection against unauthorized disclosure for reasons of national security.

(B) Any restricted data, as that term is defined in section 11y. of the Atomic Energy Act of 1954 (42 U.S.C. 2014(y)).

(3) COALITION PARTNER. – The term "coalition partner," with respect to hostilities engaged in by the United States, means any State or armed force directly engaged along with the United States in such hostilities or providing direct operational support to the United States in connection with such hostilities.

(4) GENEVA CONVENTION RELATIVE TO THE TREATMENT OF PRISONERS OF WAR. – The term "Geneva Convention Relative to

the Treatment of Prisoners of War" means the Convention Relative to the Treatment of Prisoners of War, done at Geneva August 12, 1949 (6 UST 3316).

(5) GENEVA CONVENTIONS. – The term "Geneva Conventions" means the international conventions signed at Geneva on August 12, 1949.

(6) PRIVILEGED BELLIGERENT. – The term "privileged belligerent" means an individual belonging to one of the eight categories enumerated in Article 4 of the Geneva Convention Relative to the Treatment of Prisoners of War.

(7) UNPRIVILEGED ENEMY BELLIGERENT. – The term "unprivileged enemy belligerent" means an individual (other than a privileged belligerent) who –

    (A) has engaged in hostilities against the United States or its coalition partners;

    (B) has purposefully and materially supported hostilities against the United States or its coalition partners; or

    (C) was a part of al Qaeda at the time of the alleged offense under this chapter.

(8) NATIONAL SECURITY. – The term "national security" means the national defense and foreign relations of the United States.

(9) HOSTILITIES. – The term "hostilities" means any conflict subject to the laws of war.

§948b. Military commissions generally

(a) PURPOSE. – This chapter establishes procedures governing the use of military commissions to try alien unprivileged enemy belligerents for violations of the law of war and other offenses triable by military commission.

(b) AUTHORITY FOR MILITARY COMMISSIONS UNDER THIS CHAPTER. – The President is authorized to establish military commissions under this chapter for offenses triable by military commission as provided in this chapter.

(c) CONSTRUCTION OF PROVISIONS. – The procedures for military commissions set forth in this chapter are based upon the procedures for trial by general courts-martial under chapter 47 of this title (the Uniform Code of Military Justice). Chapter 47 of this title does not, by its terms, apply to trial by military commission except as specifically provided therein or in this chapter, and many of the provisions of chapter 47 of this title are by their terms inapplicable to military commissions. The judicial construction and application of chapter 47 of this title, while instructive, is therefore not of its own force binding on military commissions established under this chapter.

(d) INAPPLICABILITY OF CERTAIN PROVISIONS. –

(1) The following provisions of this title shall not apply to trial by military commission under this chapter:

(A) Section 810 (article 10 of the Uniform Code of Military Justice), relating to speedy trial, including any rule of courts-martial relating to speedy trial.

(B) Sections 831(a), (b), and (d) (articles 31(a), (b), and (d) of the Uniform Code of Military Justice), relating to compulsory self-incrimination.

(C) Section 832 (article 32 of the Uniform Code of Military Justice), relating to pretrial investigation.

(2) Other provisions of chapter 47 of this title shall apply to trial by military commission under this chapter only to the extent provided by the terms of such provisions or by this chapter.

(e) GENEVA CONVENTIONS NOT ESTABLISHING PRIVATE RIGHT OF ACTION. – No alien unprivileged enemy belligerent subject to trial by military commission under this chapter may invoke the Geneva Conventions as a basis for a private right of action.

§948c. Persons subject to military commissions

Any alien unprivileged enemy belligerent is subject to trial by military commission as set forth in this chapter.

§948d. Jurisdiction of military commissions

A military commission under this chapter shall have jurisdiction to try persons subject to this chapter for any offense made punishable by this chapter, sections 904 and 906 of this title (articles 104 and 106 of the Uniform Code of Military Justice), or the law of war, whether such offense was committed before, on, or after September 11, 2001, and may, under such limitations as the President may prescribe, adjudge any punishment not forbidden by this chapter, including the penalty of death when specifically authorized under this chapter. A military commission is a competent tribunal to make a finding sufficient for jurisdiction.

SUBCHAPTER II – COMPOSITION OF MILITARY COMMISSIONS . . .

§948h. Who may convene military commissions

Military commissions under this chapter may be convened by the Secretary of Defense or by any officer or official of the United States designated by the Secretary for that purpose.

§948i. Who may serve on military commissions

(a) IN GENERAL. – Any commissioned officer of the armed forces on active duty is eligible to serve on a military commission under this chapter, including commissioned officers of the reserve components of the armed forces on active duty, commissioned officers of the National Guard on active duty in Federal service, or retired commissioned officers recalled to active duty. . . .

§948j. Military judge of a military commission

(a) DETAIL OF MILITARY JUDGE. – A military judge shall be detailed to each military commission under this chapter. The Secretary of Defense shall prescribe regulations providing for the manner in which military judges are so detailed to military commissions. The military judge shall preside over each military commission to which such military judge has been detailed. . . .

§948k. Detail of trial counsel and defense counsel

(a) DETAIL OF COUNSEL GENERALLY. – (1) Trial counsel and military defense counsel shall be detailed for each military commission under this chapter. . . .

§948m. Number of members; excuse of members; absent and additional members

(a) NUMBER OF MEMBERS. – (1) Except as provided in paragraph (2), a military commission under this chapter shall have at least five members. . . .

SUBCHAPTER III – PRE-TRIAL PROCEDURE . . .

§948q. Charges and specifications

(a) CHARGES AND SPECIFICATIONS. – Charges and specifications against an accused in a military commission under this chapter shall be signed by a person subject to chapter 47 of this title under oath before a commissioned officer of the armed forces authorized to administer oaths and shall state –

(1) that the signer has personal knowledge of, or reason to believe, the matters set forth therein; and

(2) that such matters are true in fact to the best of the signer's knowledge and belief.

(b) NOTICE TO ACCUSED. – Upon the swearing of the charges and specifications in accordance with subsection (a), the accused shall be informed of the charges and specifications against the accused as soon as practicable.

§948r. Exclusion of statements obtained by torture or cruel, inhuman, or degrading treatment; prohibition of self-incrimination; admission of other statements of the accused

(a) EXCLUSION OF STATEMENTS OBTAIN BY TORTURE OR CRUEL, INHUMAN, OR DEGRADING TREATMENT. – No statement obtained by the use of torture or by cruel, inhuman, or degrading treatment (as defined by section 1003 of the Detainee Treatment Act of 2005 (42 U.S.C. 2000dd)), whether or not under color of law, shall be admissible in a military commission under this chapter, except against a person accused of torture or such treatment as evidence that the statement was made.

(b) SELF-INCRIMINATION PROHIBITED. – No person shall be required to testify against himself or herself at a proceeding of a military commission under this chapter.

(c) OTHER STATEMENTS OF THE ACCUSED. – A statement of the accused may be admitted in evidence in a military commission under this chapter only if the military judge finds –

(1) that the totality of the circumstances renders the statement reliable and possessing sufficient probative value; and

(2) that –

(A) the statement was made incident to lawful conduct during military operations at the point of capture or during closely related active combat engagement, and the interests of justice would best be served by admission of the statement into evidence; or

(B) the statement was voluntarily given.

(d) DETERMINATION OF VOLUNTARINESS. – In determining for purposes of subsection (c)(2)(B) whether a statement was voluntarily given, the military judge shall consider the totality of the circumstances, including, as appropriate, the following:

(1) The details of the taking of the statement, accounting for the circumstances of the conduct of military and intelligence operations during hostilities.

(2) The characteristics of the accused, such as military training, age, and education level.

(3) The lapse of time, change of place, or change in identity of the questioners between the statement sought to be admitted and any prior questioning of the accused. . . .

SUBCHAPTER IV – TRIAL PROCEDURE . . .

§949a. Rules

(a) PROCEDURES AND RULES OF EVIDENCE. – Pretrial, trial, and post-trial procedures, including elements and modes of proof, for cases triable by military commission under this chapter may be prescribed by the Secretary of Defense. Such procedures may not be contrary to or inconsistent with this chapter. Except as otherwise provided in this chapter or chapter 47 of this title, the procedures and rules of evidence applicable in trials by general courts-martial of the United States shall apply in trials by military commission under this chapter.

(b) EXCEPTIONS. –

(1) In trials by military commission under this chapter, the Secretary of Defense, in consultation with the Attorney General, may make such exceptions in the applicability of the procedures and rules of evidence otherwise applicable in general courts-martial as may be required by the unique circumstances of the conduct of military and intelligence operations during hostilities or by other practical need consistent with this chapter.

(2) Notwithstanding any exceptions authorized by paragraph (1), the procedures and rules of evidence in trials by military commission under this chapter shall include, at a minimum, the following rights of the accused:

(A) To present evidence in the accused's defense, to cross-examine the witnesses who testify against the accused, and to examine and respond to all evidence admitted against the accused on the issue of guilt or innocence and for sentencing, as provided for by this chapter.

(B) To be present at all sessions of the military commission (other than those for deliberations or voting), except when excluded under section 949d of this title.

(C) (i) When none of the charges preferred against the accused are capital, to be represented before a military commission by civilian counsel if provided at no expense to the Government, and by either the defense counsel detailed or the military counsel of the accused's own selection, if reasonably available.

(ii) When any of the charges preferred against the accused are capital, to be represented before a military commission in accordance with clause (i) and, to the greatest extent practicable, by at least one additional counsel who is learned in applicable law relating to capital cases and who, if necessary, may be a civilian and compensated in accordance with regulations prescribed by the Secretary of Defense.

(D) To self-representation, if the accused knowingly and competently waives the assistance of counsel, subject to the provisions of paragraph (4).

(E) To the suppression of evidence that is not reliable or probative.

(F) To the suppression of evidence the probative value of which is substantially outweighed by –

(i) the danger of unfair prejudice, confusion of the issues, or misleading the members; or

(ii) considerations of undue delay, waste of time, or needless presentation of cumulative evidence.

(3) In making exceptions in the applicability in trials by military commission under this chapter from the procedures and rules otherwise applicable in general courts-martial, the Secretary of Defense may provide the following:

(A) Evidence seized outside the United States shall not be excluded from trial by military commission on the grounds that the evidence was not seized pursuant to a search warrant or authorization.

(B) A statement of the accused that is otherwise admissible shall not be excluded from trial by military commission on grounds of alleged coercion or compulsory self-incrimination so long as the evidence complies with the provisions of section 948r of this title.

(C) Evidence shall be admitted as authentic so long as –

(i) the military judge of the military commission determines that there is sufficient evidence that the evidence is what it is claimed to be; and

(ii) the military judge instructs the members that they may consider any issue as to authentication or identification of evidence in determining the weight, if any, to be given to the evidence.

(D) Hearsay evidence not otherwise admissible under the rules of evidence applicable in trial by general courts-martial may be admitted in a trial by military commission only if –

(i) the proponent of the evidence makes known to the adverse party, sufficiently in advance to provide the adverse party with a fair opportunity to meet the evidence, the proponent's intention to offer the evidence, and the particulars of the evidence (including information on the circumstances under which the evidence was obtained); and

(ii) the military judge, after taking into account all of the circumstances surrounding the taking of the statement, including the degree to which the statement is corroborated, the indicia of reliability within the statement itself, and whether the will of the declarant was overborne, determines that –

(I) the statement is offered as evidence of a material fact;

(II) the statement is probative on the point for which it is offered;

(III) direct testimony from the witness is not available as a practical matter, taking into consideration the physical location of the witness, the unique circumstances of military and intelligence operations during hostilities, and the adverse impacts on military or intelligence operations that would likely result from the production of the witness; and

(IV) the general purposes of the rules of evidence and the interests of justice will best be served by admission of the statement into evidence. . . .

§949b. Unlawfully influencing action of military commission and United States Court of Military Commission Review

(a) MILITARY COMMISSIONS. –

(1) No authority convening a military commission under this chapter may censure, reprimand, or admonish the military commission, or any member, military judge, or counsel thereof, with respect to the findings or sentence adjudged by the military commission, or with respect to any other exercises of its or their functions in the conduct of the proceedings. . . .

§949c. Duties of trial counsel and defense counsel . . .

(b) DEFENSE COUNSEL. – . . .

(2) The accused may be represented by military counsel detailed under section 948k of this title or by military counsel of the

accused's own selection, if reasonably available.

(3) The accused may be represented by civilian counsel if retained by the accused, provided that such civilian counsel –

(A) is a United States citizen;

(B) is admitted to the practice of law in a State, district, or possession of the United States, or before a Federal court;

(C) has not been the subject of any sanction of disciplinary action by any court, bar, or other competent governmental authority for relevant misconduct;

(D) has been determined to be eligible for access to information classified at the level Secret or higher; and

(E) has signed a written agreement to comply with all applicable regulations or instructions for counsel, including any rules of court for conduct during the proceedings.

(4) If the accused is represented by civilian counsel, military counsel shall act as associate counsel. . . .

(6) Defense counsel may cross-examine each witness for the prosecution who testifies before a military commission under this chapter.

(7) Civilian defense counsel shall protect any classified information received during the course of representation of the accused in accordance with all applicable law governing the protection of classified information, and may not divulge such information to any person not authorized to receive it.

§949d. Sessions . . .

(c) CLOSURE OF PROCEEDINGS. –

(1) The military judge may close to the public all or part of the proceedings of a military commission under this chapter.

(2) The military judge may close to the public all or a portion of the proceedings under paragraph (1) only upon making a specific finding that such closure is necessary to –

(A) protect information the disclosure of which could reasonably be expected to cause damage to the national security, including intelligence or law enforcement sources, methods, or activities; or

(B) ensure the physical safety of individuals.

(3) A finding under paragraph (2) may be based upon a presentation, including a presentation ex parte or in camera, by either trial counsel or defense counsel.

(d) EXCLUSION OF ACCUSED FROM CERTAIN PROCEEDINGS. – The military judge may exclude the accused from any portion of a proceeding upon a determination that, after being warned by the military judge, the accused persists in conduct that justifies exclusion from the courtroom –

(1) to ensure the physical safety of individuals; or

(2) to prevent disruption of the proceedings by the accused. . . .

§949j. Opportunity to obtain witnesses and other evidence

(a) IN GENERAL. –

(1) Defense counsel in a military commission under this chapter shall have a reasonable opportunity to obtain witnesses and other evidence as provided in regulations prescribed by the Secretary of Defense. The opportunity to obtain witnesses and evidence shall be comparable to the opportunity available to a criminal defendant in a court of the United States under article III of the Constitution.

(2) Process issued in military commissions under this chapter to compel witnesses to appear and testify and to compel the production of other evidence –

(A) shall be similar to that which courts of the United States having criminal jurisdiction may lawfully issue; and

(B) shall run to any place where the United States shall have jurisdiction thereof.

(b) DISCLOSURE OF EXCULPATORY EVIDENCE. –

(1) As soon as practicable, trial counsel in a military commission under this chapter shall disclose to the defense the existence of any evidence that reasonably tends to –

(A) negate the guilt of the accused of an offense charged; or

(B) reduce the degree of guilt of the accused with respect to an offense charged.

(2) The trial counsel shall, as soon as practicable, disclose to the defense the existence of evidence that reasonably tends to impeach the credibility of a witness whom the government intends to call at trial.

(3) The trial counsel shall, as soon as practicable upon a finding of guilt, disclose to the defense the existence of evidence that is not subject to paragraph (1) or paragraph (2) but that reasonably may be viewed as mitigation evidence at sentencing.

(4) The disclosure obligations under this subsection encompass evidence that is known or reasonably should be known to any government officials who participated in the investigation and prosecution of the case against the defendant. . . .

§949m. Number of votes required

(a) CONVICTION. – No person may be convicted by a military commission under this chapter of any offense, except as provided in section 949i(b) of this title [relating to a finding of guilt after a guilty plea] or by concurrence of two-thirds of the members present at the time the vote is taken.

(b) SENTENCES. –

(1) Except as provided in paragraphs (2) and (3), sentences shall be determined by a military commission by the concurrence of two-thirds of the members present at the time the vote is taken.

(2) No person may be sentenced to death by a military commission, except insofar as –

(A) the penalty of death has been expressly authorized under this chapter, chapter 47 of this title, or the law of war for an offense of which the accused has been found guilty;

(B) trial counsel expressly sought the penalty of death by filing an appropriate notice in advance of trial;

(C) the accused was convicted of the offense by the concurrence of all the members present at the time the vote is taken; and

(D) all members present at the time the vote was taken concurred in the sentence of death.

(3) No person may be sentenced to life imprisonment, or to confinement for more than 10 years, by a military commission under this chapter except by the concurrence of three-fourths of the members present at the time the vote is taken.

(c) NUMBER OF MEMBERS REQUIRED FOR PENALTY OF DEATH. –

(1) Except as provided in paragraph (2), in a case in which the penalty of death is sought, the number of members of the military commission under this chapter shall be not less than 12 members. . . .

SUBCHAPTER V – CLASSIFIED INFORMATION PROCEDURES . . .

§949p-1. Protection of classified information: applicability of subchapter

(a) PROTECTION OF CLASSIFIED INFORMATION. – Classified information shall be protected and is privileged from disclosure if disclosure would be detrimental to the national security. Under no circumstances may a military judge order the release of classified information to any person not authorized to receive such information.

(b) ACCESS TO EVIDENCE. – Any information admitted into evidence pursuant to any rule, procedure, or order by the military judge shall be provided to the accused.

(c) DECLASSIFICATION. – Trial counsel shall work with the original classification authorities for evidence that may be used at trial to ensure that such evidence is declassified to the maximum extent possible, consistent with the requirements of national security. . . .

[The rules set out in the balance of this subchapter for discovery, admission, and protection of classified information during a military commission are substantially similar to those in the Classified Information Procedures Act, 18 U.S.C. app., which is described in NSL pp. 857-866 and CTL pp. 530-539, and in this *Supplement* at pp. 344-370. An important exception is that classified information may be admitted into evidence in a military commission proceeding, subject to sealing and protective orders against disclosure. See §949p-7.]

SUBCHAPTER VI – SENTENCES . . .

§949u. Execution of confinement

(a) IN GENERAL. – Under such regulations as the Secretary of Defense may prescribe, a sentence of confinement adjudged by a military commission under this chapter may be carried into execution by confinement –

(1) in any place of confinement under the control of any of the armed forces; or

(2) in any penal or correctional institution under the control of the United States or its allies, or which the United States may be allowed to use.

(b) TREATMENT DURING CONFINEMENT BY OTHER THAN THE ARMED FORCES. – Persons confined under subsection (a)(2) in a penal or correctional institution not under the control of an armed force are subject to the same discipline and treatment as persons confined or committed by the courts of the United States or of the State, District of Columbia, or place in which the institution is situated.

SUBCHAPTER VII – POST-TRIAL PROCEDURE AND REVIEW OF MILITARY COMMISSIONS . . .

§950b. Review by the convening authority

(a) NOTICE TO CONVENING AUTHORITY OF FINDINGS AND SENTENCE. – The findings and sentence of a military commission under this chapter shall be reported in writing promptly to the convening authority after the announcement of the sentence. . . .

(c) ACTION BY CONVENING AUTHORITY. – . . .

(2) The convening authority is not required to take action on the findings of a military commission under this chapter. If the convening authority takes action on the findings, the convening authority may, in the sole discretion of the convening authority, only –

(A) dismiss any charge or specification by setting aside a finding of guilty thereto; or

(B) change a finding of guilty to a charge to a finding of guilty to an offense that is a lesser included offense of the offense stated in the charge.

(3) (A) The convening authority shall take action on the sentence of a military commission under this chapter.

(B) Subject to regulations prescribed by the Secretary of Defense, action under this paragraph may be taken only after consideration of any matters submitted by the accused . . . .

(C) In taking action under this paragraph, the convening authority may, in the sole discretion of the convening authority, approve, disapprove, commute, or suspend the sentence in whole or in part. The convening authority may not increase a sentence beyond that which is found by the military commission. . . .

(d) ORDER OF REVISION OR REHEARING. –

(1) Subject to paragraphs (2) and (3), the convening authority of a military commission under this chapter may, in the sole discretion of the convening authority, order a proceeding in revision or a rehearing.

(2) (A) Except as provided in subparagraph (B), a proceeding in revision may be ordered by the convening authority if –

(i) there is an apparent error or omission in the record; or

(ii) the record shows improper or inconsistent action by the military commission with respect to the findings or sentence that can be rectified without material prejudice to the substantial rights of the accused.

(B) In no case may a proceeding in revision –

(i) reconsider a finding of not guilty of a specification or a ruling which amounts to a finding of not guilty;

(ii) reconsider a finding of not guilty of any charge, unless there has been a finding of guilty under a specification laid under that charge, which sufficiently alleges a violation; or

(iii) increase the severity of the sentence unless the sentence prescribed for the offense is mandatory.

(3) A rehearing may be ordered by the convening authority if the convening authority disapproves the findings and sentence and states the reasons for disapproval of the findings. If the convening authority disapproves the finding and sentence and does not order a rehearing, the convening authority shall dismiss the charges. . . .

§950c. Appellate referral; waiver or withdrawal of appeal

(a) AUTOMATIC REFERRAL FOR APPELLATE REVIEW. – [Unless the right of review is waived by the accused], in each case in which the final decision of a military commission under this chapter (as approved by the convening authority) includes a finding of guilty, the

convening authority shall refer the case to the United States Court of
Military Commission Review. Any such referral shall be made in
accordance with procedures prescribed under regulations of the
Secretary. . . .

§950d. Interlocutory appeals by the United States

(a) INTERLOCUTORY APPEAL. – Except as provided in
subsection (b), in a trial by military commission under this chapter, the
United States may take an interlocutory appeal to the United States Court
of Military Commission Review of any order or ruling of the military
judge –
    (1) that terminates proceedings of the military commission with
respect to a charge or specification;
    (2) that excludes evidence that is substantial proof of a fact
material in the proceeding;
    (3) that relates to a matter under subsection (c) or (d) of section
949d of this title; or
    (4) that, with respect to classified information –
        (A) authorizes the disclosure of such information;
        (B) imposes sanctions for nondisclosure of such information; or
        (C) refuses a protective order sought by the United States to
prevent the disclosure of such information.
    (b) LIMITATION. – The United States may not appeal under
subsection (a) an order or ruling that is, or amounts to, a finding of not
guilty by the military commission with respect to a charge or
specification. . . .
    (g) APPEALS COURT TO ACT ONLY WITH RESPECT TO
MATTER OF LAW. – In ruling on an appeal under paragraph (1), (2), or
(3) of subsection (a), the appeals court may act only with respect to
matters of law. . . .

§950f. Review by United States Court of Military Commission Review

(a) ESTABLISHMENT. – There is a court of record to be known as
the "United States Court of Military Commission Review" (in this
section referred to as the "Court"). The Court shall consist of one or

more panels, each composed of not less than three appellate military judges. For the purpose of reviewing decisions of military commissions under this chapter, the Court may sit in panels or as a whole, in accordance with rules prescribed by the Secretary of Defense. . . .

(d) STANDARD AND SCOPE OF REVIEW. – In a case reviewed by the Court under this section, the Court may act only with respect to the findings and sentence as approved by the convening authority. The Court may affirm only such findings of guilty, and the sentence or such part or amount of the sentence, as the Court finds correct in law and fact and determines, on the basis of the entire record, should be approved. In considering the record, the Court may weigh the evidence, judge the credibility of witnesses, and determine controverted questions of fact, recognizing that the military commission saw and heard the witnesses. . . .

§950g. Review by United States Court of Appeals for the District of Columbia Circuit; writ of certiorari to Supreme Court

(a) EXCLUSIVE APPELLATE JURISDICTION. – Except as provided in subsection (b), the United States Court of Appeals for the District of Columbia Circuit shall have exclusive jurisdiction to determine the validity of a final judgment rendered by a military commission (as approved by the convening authority and, where applicable, the United States Court of Military Commission Review) under this chapter.

(b) EXHAUSTION OF OTHER APPEALS. – The United States Court of Appeals for the District of Columbia Circuit may not review a final judgment described in subsection (a) until all other appeals under this chapter have been waived or exhausted. . . .

(e) REVIEW BY SUPREME COURT. – The Supreme Court may review by writ of certiorari pursuant to section 1254 of title 28 the final judgment of the United States Court of Appeals for the District of Columbia Circuit under this section. . . .

SUBCHAPTER VIII – PUNITIVE MATTERS . . .

§950p. Definitions; construction of certain offenses; common circumstances

(a) DEFINITIONS. – In this subchapter:

(1) The term "military objective" means combatants and those objects during hostilities which, by their nature, location, purpose, or use, effectively contribute to the war-fighting or war-sustaining capability of an opposing force and whose total or partial destruction, capture, or neutralization would constitute a definite military advantage to the attacker under the circumstances at the time of an attack.

(2) The term "protected person" means any person entitled to protection under one or more of the Geneva Conventions, including civilians not taking an active part in hostilities, military personnel placed out of combat by sickness, wounds, or detention, and military medical or religious personnel.

(3) The term "protected property" means any property specifically protected by the law of war, including buildings dedicated to religion, education, art, science, or charitable purposes, historic monuments, hospitals, and places where the sick and wounded are collected, but only if and to the extent such property is not being used for military purposes or is not otherwise a military objective. The term includes objects properly identified by one of the distinctive emblems of the Geneva Conventions, but does not include civilian property that is a military objective.

(b) CONSTRUCTION OF CERTAIN OFFENSES. – The intent required for offenses under paragraphs (1), (2), (3), (4), and (12) of section 950t of this title precludes the applicability of such offenses with regard to collateral damage or to death, damage, or injury incident to a lawful attack.

(c) COMMON CIRCUMSTANCES. – An offense specified in this subchapter is triable by military commission under this chapter only if the offense is committed in the context of and associated with hostilities.

(d) EFFECT. – The provisions of this subchapter codify offenses that have traditionally been triable by military commission. This chapter does not establish new crimes that did not exist before the date of the enactment of this subchapter, as amended [on October 28, 2009], but rather codifies those crimes for trial by military commission. Because the provisions of this subchapter codify offenses that have traditionally been triable under the law of war or otherwise triable by military commission, this subchapter does not preclude trial for offenses that occurred before the date of the enactment of this subchapter, as so amended. . . .

§950t. Crimes triable by military commission

The following offenses shall be triable by military commission under this chapter at any time without limitation:

(1) MURDER OF PROTECTED PERSONS. – Any person subject to this chapter who intentionally kills one or more protected persons shall be punished by death or such other punishment as a military commission under this chapter may direct.

(2) ATTACKING CIVILIANS. – Any person subject to this chapter who intentionally engages in an attack upon a civilian population as such, or individual civilians not taking active part in hostilities, shall be punished, if death results to one or more of the victims, by death or such other punishment as a military commission under this chapter may direct, and, if death does not result to any of the victims, by such punishment, other than death, as a military commission under this chapter may direct.

(3) ATTACKING CIVILIAN OBJECTS. – Any person subject to this chapter who intentionally engages in an attack upon a civilian object that is not a military objective shall be punished as a military commission under this chapter may direct.

(4) ATTACKING PROTECTED PROPERTY. – Any person subject to this chapter who intentionally engages in an attack upon protected property shall be punished as a military commission under this chapter may direct.

(5) PILLAGING. – Any person subject to this chapter who intentionally and in the absence of military necessity appropriates or seizes property for private or personal use, without the consent of a person with authority to permit such appropriation or seizure, shall be punished as a military commission under this chapter may direct.

(6) DENYING QUARTER. – Any person subject to this chapter who, with effective command or control over subordinate groups, declares, orders, or otherwise indicates to those groups that there shall be

no survivors or surrender accepted, with the intent to threaten an adversary or to conduct hostilities such that there would be no survivors or surrender accepted, shall be punished as a military commission under this chapter may direct.

(7) TAKING HOSTAGES. – Any person subject to this chapter who, having knowingly seized or detained one or more persons, threatens to kill, injure, or continue to detain such person or persons with the intent of compelling any nation, person other than the hostage, or group of persons to act or refrain from acting as an explicit or implicit condition for the safety or release of such person or persons, shall be punished, if death results to one or more of the victims, by death or such other punishment as a military commission under this chapter may direct, and, if death does not result to any of the victims, by such punishment, other than death, as a military commission under this chapter may direct.

(8) EMPLOYING POISON OR SIMILAR WEAPONS. – Any person subject to this chapter who intentionally, as a method of warfare, employs a substance or weapon that releases a substance that causes death or serious and lasting damage to health in the ordinary course of events, through its asphyxiating, bacteriological, or toxic properties, shall be punished, if death results to one or more of the victims, by death or such other punishment as a military commission under this chapter may direct, and, if death does not result to any of the victims, by such punishment, other than death, as a military commission under this chapter may direct.

(9) USING PROTECTED PERSONS AS A SHIELD. – Any person subject to this chapter who positions, or otherwise takes advantage of, a protected person with the intent to shield a military objective from attack or to shield, favor, or impede military operations, shall be punished, if death results to one or more of the victims, by death or such other punishment as a military commission under this chapter may direct, and, if death does not result to any of the victims, by such punishment, other than death, as a military commission under this chapter may direct.

(10) USING PROTECTED PROPERTY AS A SHIELD. – Any person subject to this chapter who positions, or otherwise takes advantage of the location of, protected property with the intent to shield a military objective from attack, or to shield, favor, or impede military operations, shall be punished as a military commission under this chapter may direct.

(11) TORTURE. –

(A) OFFENSE. – Any person subject to this chapter who commits an act specifically intended to inflict severe physical or mental pain or suffering (other than pain or suffering incidental to lawful sanctions) upon another person within his custody or physical control for the purpose of obtaining information or a confession, punishment, intimidation, coercion, or any reason based on discrimination of any kind, shall be punished, if death results to one or more of the victims, by death or such other punishment as a military commission under this chapter may direct, and, if death does not result to any of the victims, by such punishment, other than death, as a military commission under this chapter may direct.

(B) SEVERE MENTAL PAIN OR SUFFERING DEFINED. – In this paragraph, the term "severe mental pain or suffering" has the meaning given that term in section 2340(2) of title 18.

(12) CRUEL OR INHUMAN TREATMENT. – Any person subject to this chapter who subjects another person in their custody or under their physical control, regardless of nationality or physical location, to cruel or inhuman treatment that constitutes a grave breach of common Article 3 of the Geneva Conventions shall be punished, if death results to the victim, by death or such other punishment as a military commission under this chapter may direct, and, if death does not result to the victim, by such punishment, other than death, as a military commission under this chapter may direct.

(13) INTENTIONALLY CAUSING SERIOUS BODILY INJURY. –

(A) OFFENSE. – Any person subject to this chapter who intentionally causes serious bodily injury to one or more persons, including privileged belligerents, in violation of the law of war shall be punished, if death results to one or more of the victims, by death or such other punishment as a military commission under this chapter may direct, and, if death does not result to any of the victims, by such punishment, other than death, as a military commission under this chapter may direct.

(B) SERIOUS BODILY INJURY DEFINED. – In this para-graph, the term "serious bodily injury" means bodily injury which involves –

(i) a substantial risk of death;

(ii) extreme physical pain;

(iii) protracted and obvious disfigurement; or

(iv) protracted loss or impairment of the function of a bodily member, organ, or mental faculty.

(14) MUTILATING OR MAIMING. – Any person subject to this chapter who intentionally injures one or more protected persons by disfiguring the person or persons by any mutilation of the person or persons, or by permanently disabling any member, limb, or organ of the body of the person or persons, without any legitimate medical or dental purpose, shall be punished, if death results to one or more of the victims, by death or such other punishment as a military commission under this chapter may direct, and, if death does not result to any of the victims, by such punishment, other than death, as a military commission under this chapter may direct.

(15) MURDER IN VIOLATION OF THE LAW OF WAR. – Any person subject to this chapter who intentionally kills one or more persons, including privileged belligerents, in violation of the law of war shall be punished by death or such other punishment as a military commission under this chapter may direct. . . .

(23) HIJACKING OR HAZARDING A VESSEL OR AIRCRAFT. – Any person subject to this chapter who intentionally seizes, exercises unauthorized control over, or endangers the safe navigation of a vessel or aircraft that is not a legitimate military objective shall be punished, if death results to one or more of the victims, by death or such other punishment as a military commission under this chapter may direct, and, if death does not result to any of the victims, by such punishment, other than death, as a military commission under this chapter may direct.

(24) TERRORISM. – Any person subject to this chapter who intentionally kills or inflicts great bodily harm on one or more protected persons, or intentionally engages in an act that evinces a wanton disregard for human life, in a manner calculated to influence or affect the conduct of government or civilian population by intimidation or coercion, or to retaliate against government conduct, shall be punished, if death results to one or more of the victims, by death or such other punishment as a military commission under this chapter may direct, and, if death does not result to any of the victims, by such punishment, other than death, as a military commission under this chapter may direct.

(25) PROVIDING MATERIAL SUPPORT FOR TERRORISM. –

(A) OFFENSE. – Any person subject to this chapter who

provides material support or resources, knowing or intending that they are to be used in preparation for, or in carrying out, an act of terrorism (as set forth in paragraph (24) of this section), or who intentionally provides material support or resources to an international terrorist organization engaged in hostilities against the United States, knowing that such organization has engaged or engages in terrorism (as so set forth), shall be punished as a military commission under this chapter may direct.

(B) MATERIAL SUPPORT OR RESOURCES DEFINED. – In this paragraph, the term "material support or resources" has the meaning given that term in section 2339A(b) of title 18.

(26) WRONGFULLY AIDING THE ENEMY. – Any person subject to this chapter who, in breach of an allegiance or duty to the United States, knowingly and intentionally aids an enemy of the United States, or one of the co-belligerents of the enemy, shall be punished as a military commission under this chapter may direct.

(27) SPYING. – Any person subject to this chapter who, in violation of the law of war and with intent or reason to believe that it is to be used to the injury of the United States or to the advantage of a foreign power, collects or attempts to collect information by clandestine means or while acting under false pretenses, for the purpose of conveying such information to an enemy of the United States, or one of the co-belligerents of the enemy, shall be punished by death or such other punishment as a military commission under this chapter may direct.

(28) ATTEMPTS. –

(A) IN GENERAL. – Any person subject to this chapter who attempts to commit any offense punishable by this chapter shall be punished as a military commission under this chapter may direct.

(B) SCOPE OF OFFENSE. – An act, done with specific intent to commit an offense under this chapter, amounting to more than mere preparation and tending, even though failing, to effect its commission, is an attempt to commit that offense.

(C) EFFECT OF CONSUMMATION. – Any person subject to this chapter may be convicted of an attempt to commit an offense although it appears on the trial that the offense was consummated.

(29) CONSPIRACY. – Any person subject to this chapter who conspires to commit one or more substantive offenses triable by military commission under this subchapter, and who knowingly does any overt

act to effect the object of the conspiracy, shall be punished, if death results to one or more of the victims, by death or such other punishment as a military commission under this chapter may direct, and, if death does not result to any of the victims, by such punishment, other than death, as a military commission under this chapter may direct.

(30) SOLICITATION. – Any person subject to this chapter who solicits or advises another or others to commit one or more substantive offenses triable by military commission under this chapter shall, if the offense solicited or advised is attempted or committed, be punished with the punishment provided for the commission of the offense, but, if the offense solicited or advised is not committed or attempted, shall be punished as a military commission under this chapter may direct.

(31) CONTEMPT. – A military commission under this chapter may punish for contempt any person who uses any menacing word, sign, or gesture in its presence, or who disturbs its proceedings by any riot or disorder.

(32) PERJURY AND OBSTRUCTION OF JUSTICE. – A military commission under this chapter may try offenses and impose such punishment as the military commission may direct for perjury, false testimony, or obstruction of justice related to the military commission. . . .

SEC. 1807. SENSE OF CONGRESS ON MILITARY COMMISSION SYSTEM.

It is the sense of Congress that –

(1) the fairness and effectiveness of the military commissions system under chapter 47A of title 10, United States Code (as amended by section 1802), will depend to a significant degree on the adequacy of defense counsel and associated resources for individuals accused, particularly in the case of capital cases, under such chapter 47A; and

(2) defense counsel in military commission cases, particularly in capital cases, under such chapter 47A of title 10, United States Code (as so amended), should be fully resourced as provided in such chapter 47A.

[NSL p. 906, CTL p. 587. Insert after Military Commissions Act of 2009.]

Remarks by President Barack Obama, Protecting Our Security and Our Values

National Archives, Washington, D.C.

May 21, 2009

[These remarks are set forth *supra* p. 256.]

[NSL p. 954, insert at the end of the Insurrection Act excerpt. CTL p. 679, add at the end of Note 1.]

Section 333 of the Insurrection Act was amended again in 2008 to restore its original language. National Defense Authorization Act for Fiscal Year 2008, Pub. L. 110-181, §1068(a)(1), 122 Stat. 3, 325 (2008). It now reads:

10 U.S.C. §333. Interference with State and Federal law

The President, by using the militia or the armed forces, or both, or by any other means, shall take such measures as he considers necessary to suppress, in a State, any insurrection, domestic violence, unlawful combination, or conspiracy, if it –

(1) so hinders the execution of the laws of that State, and of the United States within the State, that any part or class of its people is deprived of a right, privilege, immunity, or protection named in the Constitution and secured by law, and the constituted authorities of that State are unable, fail, or refuse to protect that right, privilege, or immunity, or to give that protection; or

(2) opposes or obstructs the execution of the laws of the United States or impedes the course of justice under those laws.

In any situation covered by clause (1), the State shall be considered to have denied the equal protection of the laws secured by the Constitution.

[NSL p. 969, CTL p. 697. Insert following Note 4.]

Six weeks after the terrorist attacks of 9/11, John C. Yoo and Robert J. Delahunty wrote a memorandum for the Justice Department's Office of Legal Counsel concerning the Defense Department's authority for the domestic use of military force to combat terrorist activities. The 37-page memorandum may be viewed at http://www.usdoj.gov/opa/documents/memomilitaryforcecombatus10232001.pdf. It described the President's powers very expansively, concluding that

> the President has ample constitutional and statutory authority to deploy the military against international or foreign terrorists operating within the United States. We further believe that the use of such military force generally is consistent with constitutional standards, and that it need not follow the exact procedures that govern law enforcement operations.

The memorandum was not released to the public when it was written, and its influence on military planning and policy is unknown. On October 6, 2008, the Yoo/Delahunty memorandum was repudiated in substantial part by another OLC memorandum authored by Steven G. Bradbury, set forth below. Both memoranda were made public on March 2, 2009, after the Obama administration took office.

October 23, 2001 OLC Opinion Addressing the Domestic Use of Military Force to Combat Terrorist Activities

U.S. Department of Justice, Office of Legal Counsel

October 6, 2008

available at http://www.fas.org/irp/agency/doj/olc/caution.pdf

Memorandum for: The Files

From: Steven G. Bradbury, Principal Deputy Assistant Attorney
      General

The purpose of this memorandum is to advise that caution should be exercised before relying in any respect on the Memorandum for Alberto

R. Gonzales, Counsel to the President, and William J. Haynes II, General Counsel, Department of Defense, from John C. Yoo, Deputy Assistant Attorney General, and Robert J. Delahunty, Special Counsel, Office of Legal Counsel, *Re: Authority for Use of Military Force to Combat Terrorist Activities Within the United States* (Oct. 23, 2001) ("10/23/01 Memorandum") as precedent of the Office of Legal Counsel, and that certain propositions stated in the 10/23/01 Memorandum, as described below, should not be treated as authoritative for any purpose.

It is important to understand the context of the 10/23/01 Memorandum. It was the product of an extraordinary – indeed, we hope, a unique – period in the history of the Nation: the immediate aftermath of the attacks of 9/11. Perhaps reflective of this context the 10/23/01 Memorandum did not address specific and concrete policy proposals, rather it addressed in general terms the broad contours of hypothetical scenarios involving possible domestic military contingencies that senior policy-makers feared might become a reality in the uncertain wake of the catastrophic terrorist attacks of 9/11. Thus, the 10/23/01 Memorandum represents a departure, although perhaps for understandable reasons, from the preferred practice of OLC to render formal opinions only with respect to specific and concrete policy proposals and not to undertake a general survey of a broad area of the law or to address general or amorphous hypothetical scenarios that implicate difficult questions of law.

We also judge it necessary to point out that the 10/23/01 Memorandum states several specific propositions that are either incorrect or highly questionable. The memorandum's treatment of the following propositions is not satisfactory and should not be treated as authoritative for any purpose:

- The memorandum concludes in part V, pages 25-34, that the Fourth Amendment would not apply to domestic military operations, designed to deter and prevent further terrorist attacks. This conclusion does not reflect the current views of this Office. The Fourth Amendment is fully applicable to domestic military operations, though the application of the Fourth Amendment's essential "reasonableness" requirement to particular circumstances will be sensitive to the exigencies of military actions. The 10/23/01 Memorandum itself concludes in part VI, pages 34-37, that domestic military operations necessary to prevent or address further catastrophic terrorist attacks within the United States likely would satisfy the Fourth Amendment's reasonableness requirement, if the Fourth Amendment were held to apply; thus, the erroneous conclusion in part V was not necessary to the opinion.

- Part V of the memorandum also contains certain broad statements on page 24 suggesting that First Amendment speech and press rights and other guarantees of individual liberty under the Constitution would potentially be subordinated to overriding military necessities. These statements, too, were unnecessary to the opinion, are overbroad and general, and are not sufficiently grounded in the particular circumstances of a concrete scenario, and therefore cannot be viewed as authoritative.

- The memorandum concludes in part IV(A), pages 16-20, that the domestic deployment of the Armed Forces by the President to prevent and deter terrorism would fundamentally serve a military purpose rather than a law enforcement purpose, and therefore the Posse Comitatus Act, 18 U.S.C. §1385 (2000), would not apply to such operations. Although the "military purpose" doctrine is a well-established limitation on the applicability of the Posse Comitatus Act, the broad conclusion reached in part IV(A) of the 10/23/01 Memorandum is far too general and divorced from specific facts and circumstances to be useful as an authoritative precedent of OLC.

- The memorandum, on pages 20-31, treats the Authorization for Use of Military Force ("AUMF"), enacted by Congress in the immediate wake of 9/11, Pub. L. No. 107-40, 115 Stat. 224 (Sept. 18, 2001), as a statutory exception to the Posse Comitatus Act's restriction on the use of the military for domestic law enforcement. The better view, however, is that a reasonable and necessary use of military force taken under the authority of the AUMF would be a military action, potentially subject to the established "military purpose" doctrine, rather than a law enforcement action.

- The memorandum reasons, on pages 21-22, that in the aftermath of the 9/11 attacks, the Insurrection Act, 10 U.S.C. §333 (2000), would provide general authority for the President to deploy the military domestically to prevent and deter future terrorist attacks; whereas, consistent with the longstanding interpretation of the Executive Branch, any particular application of the Insurrection Act to authorize the use of the military for law enforcement purposes would require the presence of an actual obstruction of the execution of federal law or a breakdown in the ability of state authorities to protect federal rights.

For all of the foregoing reasons, we have concluded that appropriate caution should be exercised before relying in any respect on the 10/23/01 Memorandum as a precedent of OLC, and that particular propositions identified above should not be treated as authoritative. We have advised the Counsel to the President, the Acting General Counsel of the Department of Defense, and appropriate offices within the Department of Justice of these conclusions.

[NSL p. 979. Substitute for Exec. Order No. 13,292.]

Executive Order No. 13,526, Classified National Security Information
75 Fed. Reg. 707 (Dec. 29, 2009)

This order prescribes a uniform system for classifying, safeguarding, and declassifying national security information, including information relating to defense against transnational terrorism. Our democratic principles require that the American people be informed of the activities of their Government. Also, our Nation's progress depends on the free flow of information both within the Government and to the American people. Nevertheless, throughout our history, the national defense has required that certain information be maintained in confidence in order to protect our citizens, our democratic institutions, our homeland security, and our interactions with foreign nations. Protecting information critical to our Nation's security and demonstrating our commitment to open Government through accurate and accountable application of classification standards and routine, secure, and effective declassification are equally important priorities.

NOW, THEREFORE, I, Barack Obama, by the authority vested in me as President by the Constitution and the laws of the United States of America, [hereby order] as follows:

PART 1 – ORIGINAL CLASSIFICATION

Section 1.1. Classification Standards.

(a) Information may be originally classified under the terms of this order only if all of the following conditions are met:

(1) an original classification authority is classifying the information;

(2) the information is owned by, produced by or for, or is under the control of the United States Government;

(3) the information falls within one or more of the categories of information listed in section 1.4 of this order; and

(4) the original classification authority determines that the unauthorized disclosure of the information reasonably could be expected to result in damage to the national security, which includes defense against transnational terrorism, and the original classification authority is able to identify or describe the damage.

(b) If there is significant doubt about the need to classify information, it shall not be classified. This provision does not:

(1) amplify or modify the substantive criteria or procedures for classification; or

(2) create any substantive or procedural rights subject to judicial review.

(c) Classified information shall not be declassified automatically as a result of any unauthorized disclosure of identical or similar information.

(d) The unauthorized disclosure of foreign government information is presumed to cause damage to the national security.

Sec. 1.2. Classification Levels.

(a) Information may be classified at one of the following three levels:

(1) "Top Secret" shall be applied to information, the unauthorized disclosure of which reasonably could be expected to cause exceptionally grave damage to the national security that the original classification authority is able to identify or describe.

(2) "Secret" shall be applied to information, the unauthorized disclosure of which reasonably could be expected to cause serious damage to the national security that the original classification authority is able to identify or describe.

(3) "Confidential" shall be applied to information, the unauthorized disclosure of which reasonably could be expected to cause damage to the national security that the original classification authority is able to identify or describe.

(b) Except as otherwise provided by statute, no other terms shall be used to identify United States classified information.

(c) If there is significant doubt about the appropriate level of classification, it shall be classified at the lower level.

Sec. 1.3. Classification Authority.

(a) The authority to classify information originally may be exercised only by:

(1) the President and the Vice President;

(2) agency heads and officials designated by the President; and

(3) United States Government officials delegated this authority . . . .

Sec. 1.4. Classification Categories.

Information shall not be considered for classification unless its unauthorized disclosure could reasonably be expected to cause identifiable or describable damage to the national security in accordance with section 1.2 of this order, and it pertains to one or more of the following:

(a) military plans, weapons systems, or operations;

(b) foreign government information;

(c) intelligence activities (including covert action), intelligence sources or methods, or cryptology;

(d) foreign relations or foreign activities of the United States, including confidential sources;

(e) scientific, technological, or economic matters relating to the national security;

(f) United States Government programs for safeguarding nuclear materials or facilities;

(g) vulnerabilities or capabilities of systems, installations, infrastructures, projects, plans, or protection services relating to the national security; or

(h) the development, production, or use of weapons of mass destruction.

Sec. 1.5. Duration of Classification.

(a) At the time of original classification, the original classification authority shall establish a specific date or event for declassification based on the duration of the national security sensitivity of the information. Upon reaching the date or event, the information shall be automatically declassified. Except for information that should clearly and demonstrably be expected to reveal the identity of a confidential human source or a human intelligence source or key design concepts of weapons of mass destruction, the date or event shall not exceed the time frame established in paragraph (b) of this section.

(b) If the original classification authority cannot determine an earlier specific date or event for declassification, information shall be marked for declassification 10 years from the date of the original decision, unless the original classification authority otherwise determines that the sensitivity of the information requires that it be marked for declassification for up to 25 years from the date of the original decision. . . .

(d) No information may remain classified indefinitely. Information marked for an indefinite duration of classification under predecessor orders, for example, marked as "Originating Agency's Determination Required," or classified information that contains incomplete declassification instructions or lacks declassification instructions shall be declassified in accordance with part 3 of this order.

Sec. 1.6. Identification and Markings.

(a) At the time of original classification, the following shall be indicated in a manner that is immediately apparent:

(1) one of the three classification levels defined in section 1.2 of this order;

(2) the identity, by name and position, or by personal identifier, of the original classification authority;

(3) the agency and office of origin, if not otherwise evident;

(4) declassification instructions . . . ; and

(5) a concise reason for classification that, at a minimum, cites the applicable classification categories in section 1.4 of this order. . . .

(c) With respect to each classified document, the agency originating the document shall, by marking or other means, indicate which portions are classified, with the applicable classification level, and which portions are unclassified. . . .

Sec. 1.7. Classification Prohibitions and Limitations.

(a) In no case shall information be classified, continue to be maintained as classified, or fail to be declassified in order to:

(1) conceal violations of law, inefficiency, or administrative error;

(2) prevent embarrassment to a person, organization, or agency; . . . .

(b) Basic scientific research information not clearly related to the national security shall not be classified.

(c) Information may not be reclassified after declassification and release to the public under proper authority unless:

(1) the reclassification is personally approved in writing by the agency head based on a document-by-document determination by the agency that reclassification is required to prevent significant and demonstrable damage to the national security;

(2) the information may be reasonably recovered without bringing undue attention to the information; . . . .

(d) Information that has not previously been disclosed to the public under proper authority may be classified or reclassified after an agency has received a request for it under the Freedom of Information Act (5 U.S.C. 552), the Presidential Records Act, 44 U.S.C. 2204(c)(1), the Privacy Act of 1974 (5 U.S.C. 552a), or the mandatory review provisions of section 3.5 of this order . . . .

Sec. 1.8. Classification Challenges. . . .

(b) . . . [A]n agency head or senior agency official shall establish procedures under which authorized holders of information, including authorized holders outside the classifying agency, are encouraged and expected to challenge the classification of information that they believe is improperly classified or unclassified. These procedures shall ensure that:

(1) individuals are not subject to retribution for bringing such actions;

(2) an opportunity is provided for review by an impartial official or panel; and

(3) individuals are advised of their right to appeal agency decisions to the Interagency Security Classification Appeals Panel (Panel) established by section 5.3 of this order. . . .

Sec. 1.9. Fundamental Classification Guidance Review.

(a) Agency heads shall complete on a periodic basis a comprehensive review of the agency's classification guidance, particularly classification guides, to ensure the guidance reflects current circumstances and to identify classified information that no longer requires protection and can be declassified. . . .

PART 3 – DECLASSIFICATION AND DOWNGRADING

Sec. 3.1. Authority for Declassification.

(a) Information shall be declassified as soon as it no longer meets the standards for classification under this order. . . .

(d) It is presumed that information that continues to meet the classification requirements under this order requires continued protection. In some exceptional cases, however, the need to protect such information may be outweighed by the public interest in disclosure of the information, and in these cases the information should be declassified. . . .

(g) No information may be excluded from declassification under section 3.3 of this order based solely on the type of document or record in which it is found. Rather, the classified information must be considered on the basis of its content. . . .

Sec. 3.3. Automatic Declassification.

(a) Subject to paragraphs (b)-(d) and (g)-(j) of this section, all classified records that (1) are more than 25 years old and (2) have been determined to have permanent historical value under title 44, United States Code, shall be automatically declassified whether or not the records have been reviewed. . . .

(b) An agency head may exempt from automatic declassification under paragraph (a) of this section specific information, the release of which should clearly and demonstrably be expected to:

(1) reveal the identity of a confidential human source, a human intelligence source, a relationship with an intelligence or security service of a foreign government or international organization, or a nonhuman intelligence source; or impair the effectiveness of an intelligence method currently in use, available for use, or under development;

(2) reveal information that would assist in the development, production, or use of weapons of mass destruction;

(3) reveal information that would impair U.S. cryptologic systems or activities;

(4) reveal information that would impair the application of state-of-the-art technology within a U.S. weapon system;

(5) reveal formally named or numbered U.S. military war plans that remain in effect, or reveal operational or tactical elements of prior plans that are contained in such active plans;

(6) reveal information, including foreign government information, that would cause serious harm to relations between the United States and a foreign government, or to ongoing diplomatic activities of the United States;

(7) reveal information that would impair the current ability of United States Government officials to protect the President, Vice President, and other protectees for whom protection services, in the interest of the national security, are authorized;

(8) reveal information that would seriously impair current national security emergency preparedness plans or reveal current

vulnerabilities of systems, installations, or infrastructures relating to the national security; or

(9) violate a statute, treaty, or international agreement that does not permit the automatic or unilateral declassification of information at 25 years. . . .

(e) Information exempted from automatic declassification under this section shall remain subject to the mandatory and systematic declassification review provisions of this order.

(j) At least 1 year before information is subject to automatic declassification under this section, an agency head or senior agency official shall notify the Director of the Information Security Oversight Office, serving as Executive Secretary of the Panel, of any specific information that the agency proposes to exempt from automatic declassification under paragraphs (b) and (h) of this section. . . .

(2) The Panel may direct the agency not to exempt the information or to declassify it at an earlier date than recommended. An agency head may appeal such a decision to the President through the National Security Advisor. The information will remain classified while such an appeal is pending. . . .

Sec. 3.5. Mandatory Declassification Review.

(a) Except as provided in paragraph (b) of this section, all information classified under this order or predecessor orders shall be subject to a review for declassification by the originating agency if:

(1) the request for a review describes the document or material containing the information with sufficient specificity to enable the agency to locate it with a reasonable amount of effort;

(2) the document or material containing the information responsive to the request is not contained within an operational file exempted from search and review, publication, and disclosure under 5 U.S.C. 552 in accordance with law; and

(3) the information is not the subject of pending litigation.

(b) Information originated by the incumbent President or the incumbent Vice President; the incumbent President's White House Staff or the incumbent Vice President's Staff; committees, commissions, or boards appointed by the incumbent President; or other entities within the Executive Office of the President that solely advise and assist the incumbent President is exempted from the provisions of paragraph (a) of this section. . . .

(c) Agencies conducting a mandatory review for declassification shall declassify information that no longer meets the standards for classification under this order. They shall release this information unless withholding is otherwise authorized and warranted under applicable law. . . .

(e) . . . [A]gency heads shall . . . provide a means for administratively appealing a denial of a mandatory review request, and for notifying the requester of the right to appeal a final agency decision to the Panel. . . .

Sec. 3.6. Processing Requests and Reviews.

. . . [I]n response to a request for information under the Freedom of Information Act, the Presidential Records Act, the Privacy Act of 1974, or the mandatory review provisions of this order:

(a) An agency may refuse to confirm or deny the existence or nonexistence of requested records whenever the fact of their existence or nonexistence is itself classified under this order or its predecessors. . . .

Sec. 3.7. National Declassification Center

(a) There is established within the National Archives a National Declassification Center to streamline declassification processes, facilitate quality-assurance measures, and implement standardized training regarding the declassification of records determined to have permanent historical value. . .

PART 4 – SAFEGUARDING

Sec. 4.1. General Restrictions on Access.

(a) A person may have access to classified information provided that:

(1) a favorable determination of eligibility for access has been made by an agency head or the agency head's designee;

(2) the person has signed an approved nondisclosure agreement; and

(3) the person has a need-to-know the information. . . .

(g) Consistent with law, executive orders, directives, and regulations, each agency head or senior agency official, or with respect to the Intelligence Community, the Director of National Intelligence, shall establish controls to ensure that classified information is used, processed, stored, reproduced, transmitted, and destroyed under conditions that provide adequate protection and prevent access by unauthorized persons. . . .

[NSL p. 993. Add following Note 1.]

The Freedom of Information Act (FOIA)
Office of the Attorney General
March 19, 2009
available at http://www.fas.org/sgp/foia/ag031909.pdf

Memorandum for: Heads of Executive Departments and Agencies

From: The Attorney General

The Freedom of Information Act (FOIA), 5 U.S.C. §552, reflects our nation's fundamental commitment to open government. This memorandum is meant to underscore that commitment and to ensure that it is realized in practice.

A Presumption of Openness

As President Obama instructed in his January 21 FOIA Memorandum, "The Freedom of Information Act should be administered with a clear presumption: In the face of doubt, openness prevails." This presumption has two important implications.

First, an agency should not withhold information simply because it may do so legally. I strongly encourage agencies to make discretionary disclosures of information. An agency should not withhold records merely because it can demonstrate, as a technical matter, that the records fall within the scope of a FOIA exemption.

Second, whenever an agency determines that it cannot make full disclosure of a requested record, it must consider whether it can make partial disclosure. Agencies should always be mindful that the FOIA requires them to take reasonable steps to segregate and release non-exempt information. Even if some parts of a record must be withheld, other parts either may not be covered by a statutory exemption, or may be covered only in a technical sense unrelated to the actual impact of disclosure.

At the same time, the disclosure obligation under the FOIA is not absolute. The Act provides exemptions to protect, for example, national security, personal privacy, privileged records, and law enforcement interests. But as the President stated in his memorandum, "The Government should not keep information confidential merely because public officials might be embarrassed by disclosure, because errors and failures might be revealed, or because of speculative or abstract fears."

Pursuant to the President's directive that I issue new FOIA guidelines, I hereby rescind the Attorney General's FOIA Memorandum of October 12, 2001, which stated that the Department of Justice would defend decisions to withhold records "unless they lack a sound legal basis or present an unwarranted risk of adverse impact on the ability of other agencies to protect other important records."

Instead, the Department of Justice will defend a denial of a FOIA request only if (1) the agency reasonably foresees that disclosure would harm an interest protected by one of the statutory exemptions, or (2) disclosure is prohibited by law. . . .

FOIA Is Everyone's Responsibility

Application of the proper disclosure standard is only one part of ensuring transparency. Open government requires not just a presumption of disclosure but also an effective system for responding to FOIA requests. . . .

I would like to emphasize that responsibility for effective FOIA administration belongs to all of us – it is not merely a task assigned to an agency's FOIA staff. We all must do our part to ensure open government. . . .

. . . FOIA professionals should be mindful of their obligation to work "in a spirit of cooperation" with FOIA requesters, as President Obama has directed. Unnecessary, bureaucratic hurdles have no place in the "new era of open Government" that the President has proclaimed.

Working Proactively and Promptly

Open government requires agencies to work proactively and respond to requests promptly. The President's memorandum instructs agencies to "use modern technology to inform citizens what is known and done by their Government." Accordingly, agencies should readily and systematically post information online in advance of any public request. Providing more information online reduces the need for individualized requests and may help reduce existing backlogs. When information not previously disclosed is requested, agencies should make it a priority to respond in a timely manner. Timely disclosure of information is an essential component of transparency. Long delays should not be viewed as an inevitable and insurmountable consequence of high demand. . . .

[NSL p. 997. Add the following new Note after Note 10.]

11. *Amendments to FOIA.* On December 31, 2007, Congress amended FOIA by enacting the Open Government Act of 2007, Pub. L. No. 110-175, 121 Stat. 2524. Highlights are described in a Senate Judiciary Committee Report, S. Rep. No. 110-59 (2007):

III. SECTION-BY-SECTION SUMMARY OF THE BILL . . .

Sec. 3. Protection of fee status for news media

This section amends 5 U.S.C. 552(a)(4)(A)(ii) to make clear that independent journalists are not barred from obtaining fee waivers solely because they lack an institutional affiliation with a recognized news media entity. In determining whether to grant a fee waiver, an agency shall consider the prior publication history of the requestor. If the requestor has no prior publication history and no current affiliation with a news organization, the agency shall review the requestor's plans for disseminating the requested material and whether those plans include distributing the material to a reasonably broad audience.

Sec. 4. Recovery of attorney fees and litigation costs

This section, the so-called *Buckhannon* fix, amends 5 U.S.C. 552(a)(4)(E) to clarify that a complainant has substantially prevailed in a FOIA lawsuit, and is eligible to recover attorney fees, if the complainant has obtained relief through a judicial or administrative order or if the pursuit of a claim was the catalyst for the voluntary or unilateral change in position by the opposing party. The section responds to the Supreme Court's ruling in *Buckhannon Board and Care Home, Inc. v. West Virginia Dep't of Health and Human Resources*, 532 U.S. 598 (2001), which eliminated the "catalyst theory" of attorney fee recovery under certain Federal civil rights laws. Requestors have raised concerns that the holding in *Buckhannon* could be extended to FOIA cases. This section clarifies that *Buckhannon*'s holding does not and should not apply to FOIA litigation. . . .

Sec. 6. Time limits for agencies to act on requests

The section clarifies that the 20-day time limit on responding to a FOIA request commences on the date on which the request is first received by the agency. Further, the section states that if the agency fails to respond within the 20-day limit, the agency may not then [assess search fees, except under "unusual or exceptional" circumstances].

Sec. 7. Individualized tracking numbers for requests and status information

Requires agencies to establish tracking systems by assigning a tracking number to each FOIA request; notifying a requestor of the tracking number within ten days of receiving a request; and establishing a telephone or Internet tracking system to allow requesters to easily obtain information on the status of their individual requests, including an estimated date on which the agency will complete action on the request. . . .

Sec. [9.] Openness of agency records maintained by a private entity

This section clarifies that agency records kept by private contractors licensed by the government to undertake record keeping functions remain subject to FOIA just as if those records were maintained by the relevant government agency. . . .

[NSL p. 1011. Insert at the end of Note 8.]

American Civil Liberties Union v. Dep't of Defense, 543 F.3d 59 (2d Cir. 2008), concerned a FOIA request for as many as 2,000 photographs depicting prisoner abuse by U.S. forces at detention facilities in Iraq and Afghanistan, including Abu Ghraib Prison. On September 22, 2008, the Court of Appeals ruled that the photographs could not be withheld under Exemption 7(F), as records compiled for law enforcement purposes whose release "could reasonably be expected to endanger the life or physical safety of any individual." Neither, said the court, could release of the photographs, as redacted, reasonably be expected to constitute an "unwarranted invasion of personal privacy" that would justify withholding under Exemptions 6 or 7(C).

The Bush administration immediately challenged the decision, and on March 11, 2009, the Court of Appeals denied a rehearing en banc. The Obama administration first decided not to petition the Supreme Court for a writ of certiorari, then on August 7, 2009, it reversed course and filed such a petition.

Meanwhile, a rider to the FY 2010 Homeland Security Appropriations Act, supported by the Obama administration, was aimed squarely at the pending litigation.

Department of Homeland Security Appropriations Act, 2010
Pub. L. No. 111-83, §§564-565,
123 Stat. 2142, 2184-2185 (Oct. 28, 2009)

Sec. 564.

(a) SHORT TITLE. – This section may be cited as the "OPEN FOIA Act of 2009."

(b) SPECIFIC CITATIONS IN STATUTORY EXEMPTIONS. – Section 552(b) of title 5, United States Code, is amended by striking paragraph (3) and inserting the following:

(3) specifically exempted from disclosure by statute (other than section 552b of this title), if that statute –

(A) (i) requires that the matters be withheld from the public in such a manner as to leave no discretion on the issue; or

(ii) establishes particular criteria for withholding or refers to particular types of matters to be withheld; and

(B) if enacted after the date of enactment of the OPEN FOIA Act of 2009, specifically cites to this paragraph.

Sec. 565.

(a) SHORT TITLE. – This section may be cited as the "Protected National Security Documents Act of 2009."

(b) Notwithstanding any other provision of the law to the contrary, no protected document, as defined in subsection (c), shall be subject to disclosure under section 552 of title 5, United States Code or any proceeding under that section.

(c) DEFINITIONS. – In this section:

(1) PROTECTED DOCUMENT. – The term "protected document" means any record –

(A) for which the Secretary of Defense has issued a certification, as described in subsection (d), stating that disclosure of that record would endanger citizens of the United States, members of the United States Armed Forces, or employees of the United States Government deployed outside the United States; and

(B) that is a photograph that –

(i) was taken during the period beginning on September 11, 2001, through January 22, 2009; and

(ii) relates to the treatment of individuals engaged, captured, or detained after September 11, 2001, by the Armed Forces of the United States in operations outside of the United States.

(2) PHOTOGRAPH. – The term "photograph" encompasses all photographic images, whether originals or copies, including still photographs, negatives, digital images, films, video tapes, and motion pictures.

(d) CERTIFICATION. –

(1) IN GENERAL. – For any photograph described under subsection (c)(1), the Secretary of Defense shall issue a certification

if the Secretary of Defense determines that disclosure of that
photograph would endanger citizens of the United States, members
of the United States Armed Forces, or employees of the United
States Government deployed outside the United States. . . .

Secretary of Defense Robert Gates exercised the certification
authority granted in this legislation on November 13 to withhold the
photographs sought by the ACLU. Two weeks later the petition for
certiorari was granted, and the Second Circuit judgment was vacated and
remanded for further consideration in light of the new FOIA amendment.
Dep't of Defense v. ACLU, 130 S. Ct.777 (2009).

[NSL p. 1016. Add at the end of the page.]

Executive Order No. 13,489
Presidential Records
74 Fed. Reg. 4669 (Jan. 21, 2009)

By the authority vested in me as President by the Constitution and
the laws of the United States of America, and in order to establish
policies and procedures governing the assertion of executive privilege by
incumbent and former Presidents in connection with the release of
Presidential records by the National Archives and Records Administration (NARA) pursuant to the Presidential Records Act of 1978, it is
hereby ordered as follows:

Section 1. Definitions.

For purposes of this order:
(a) "Archivist" refers to the Archivist of the United States or his
designee. . . .
(e) "Presidential records" refers to those documentary materials
maintained by NARA pursuant to the Presidential Records Act, including
Vice Presidential records. . . .
(g) A "substantial question of executive privilege" exists if NARA's
disclosure of Presidential records might impair national security

(including the conduct of foreign relations), law enforcement, or the deliberative processes of the executive branch. . . .

Sec. 2. Notice of Intent to Disclose Presidential Records.

(a) When the Archivist provides notice to the incumbent and former Presidents of his intent to disclose Presidential records pursuant to section 1270.46 of the NARA regulations, the Archivist, using any guidelines provided by the incumbent and former Presidents, shall identify any specific materials, the disclosure of which he believes may raise a substantial question of executive privilege. However, nothing in this order is intended to affect the right of the incumbent or former Presidents to invoke executive privilege with respect to materials not identified by the Archivist. . . .

(b) Upon the passage of 30 days after receipt by the incumbent and former Presidents of a notice of intent to disclose Presidential records, the Archivist may disclose the records covered by the notice, unless during that time period the Archivist has received a claim of executive privilege by the incumbent or former President or the Archivist has been instructed by the incumbent President or his designee to extend the time period for a time certain and with reason for the extension of time provided in the notice. . . .

Sec. 3. Claim of Executive Privilege by Incumbent President.

(a) Upon receipt of a notice of intent to disclose Presidential records, the Attorney General . . . and the Counsel to the President shall review as they deem appropriate the records covered by the notice and consult with each other, the Archivist, and such other executive agencies as they deem appropriate concerning whether invocation of executive privilege is justified.

(b) The Attorney General and the Counsel to the President, in the exercise of their discretion and after appropriate review and consultation under subsection (a) of this section, may jointly determine that invocation of executive privilege is not justified. The Archivist shall be notified promptly of any such determination.

(c) If either the Attorney General or the Counsel to the President believes that the circumstances justify invocation of executive privilege, the issue shall be presented to the President by the Counsel to the President and the Attorney General.

(d) If the President decides to invoke executive privilege, the Counsel to the President shall notify the former President, the Archivist, and the Attorney General in writing of the claim of privilege and the specific Presidential records to which it relates. After receiving such notice, the Archivist shall not disclose the privileged records unless directed to do so by an incumbent President or by a final court order.

Sec. 4. Claim of Executive Privilege by Former President.

(a) Upon receipt of a claim of executive privilege by a living former President, the Archivist shall consult with the Attorney General . . . , the Counsel to the President, and such other executive agencies as the Archivist deems appropriate concerning the Archivist's determination as to whether to honor the former President's claim of privilege or instead to disclose the Presidential records notwithstanding the claim of privilege. Any determination under section 3 of this order that executive privilege shall not be invoked by the incumbent President shall not prejudice the Archivist's determination with respect to the former President's claim of privilege.

(b) In making the determination referred to in subsection (a) of this section, the Archivist shall abide by any instructions given him by the incumbent President or his designee unless otherwise directed by a final court order. The Archivist shall notify the incumbent and former Presidents of his determination at least 30 days prior to disclosure of the Presidential records, unless a shorter time period is required in the circumstances set forth in section 1270.44 of the NARA regulations. . . .

Sec. 6.

Revocation. Executive Order 13233 of November 1, 2001, is revoked.

[NSL p. 1050. Add this case after Note 5.]

El-Masri v. United States

United States Court of Appeals, Fourth Circuit, 2007

479 F.3d 296, *cert. denied*, 128 S. Ct. 373 (2007)

KING, Circuit Judge. Khaled El-Masri appeals from the dismissal of his civil action against former Director of Central Intelligence George Tenet, three corporate defendants, ten unnamed employees of the Central Intelligence Agency (the "CIA"), and ten unnamed employees of the defendant corporations. In his Complaint in the Eastern District of Virginia, El-Masri alleged that the defendants were involved in a CIA operation in which he was detained and interrogated in violation of his rights under the Constitution and international law. The United States intervened as a defendant in the district court, asserting that El-Masri's civil action could not proceed because it posed an unreasonable risk that privileged state secrets would be disclosed. By its Order of May 12, 2006, the district court agreed with the position of the United States and dismissed El-Masri's Complaint. *See El-Masri v. Tenet*, 437 F. Supp. 2d 530, 541 (E.D. Va. 2006) (the "Order"). On appeal, El-Masri contends that the district court misapplied the state secrets doctrine and erred in dismissing his Complaint. As explained below, we affirm.

I.

A.

On December 6, 2005, El-Masri, a German citizen of Lebanese descent, filed his Complaint in this case, alleging, in substance, as follows: on December 31, 2003, while travelling in Macedonia, he was detained by Macedonian law enforcement officials; after twenty-three days in Macedonian custody, he was handed over to CIA operatives, who flew him to a CIA-operated detention facility near Kabul, Afghanistan; he was held in this CIA facility until May 28, 2004, when he was transported to Albania and released in a remote area; and Albanian officials then picked him up and took him to an airport in Tirana, Albania, from which he travelled to his home in Germany. The

Complaint asserted that El-Masri had not only been held against his will, but had also been mistreated in a number of other ways during his detention, including being beaten, drugged, bound, and blindfolded during transport; confined in a small, unsanitary cell; interrogated several times; and consistently prevented from communicating with anyone outside the detention facility, including his family or the German government. El-Masri alleged that his detention and interrogation were

> carried out pursuant to an unlawful policy and practice devised and implemented by defendant Tenet known as "extraordinary rendition": the clandestine abduction and detention outside the United States of persons suspected of involvement in terrorist activities, and their subsequent interrogation using methods impermissible under U.S. and international laws.

Complaint ¶3.

According to the Complaint, the corporate defendants provided the CIA with an aircraft and crew to transport El-Masri to Afghanistan, pursuant to an agreement with Director Tenet, and they either knew or reasonably should have known that "Mr. El-Masri would be subjected to prolonged arbitrary detention, torture and cruel, inhuman, or degrading treatment in violation of federal and international laws during his transport to Afghanistan and while he was detained and interrogated there." Complaint ¶61. El-Masri also alleges that CIA officials "believed early on that they had the wrong person," and that Director Tenet was notified in April 2004 that "the CIA had detained the wrong person" in El-Masri. *Id.* ¶43.

The Complaint alleged three separate causes of action. The first claim was against Director Tenet and the unknown CIA employees, pursuant to *Bivens v. Six Unknown Named Agents of Federal Bureau of Narcotics*, 403 U.S. 388 (1971), for violations of El-Masri's Fifth Amendment right to due process. Specifically, El-Masri contends that Tenet and the defendant CIA employees contravened the Due Process Clause's prohibition against subjecting anyone held in United States custody to treatment that shocks the conscience or depriving a person of liberty in the absence of legal process. El-Masri's second cause of action was initiated pursuant to the Alien Tort Statute (the "ATS"), and alleged that each of the defendants had contravened the international legal norm against prolonged arbitrary detention. The third cause of action was also asserted under the ATS, and maintained that each defendant had violated international legal norms prohibiting cruel, inhuman, or degrading treatment.

On March 8, 2006, the United States filed a Statement of Interest in the underlying proceedings, pursuant to 28 U.S.C. §517, and interposed a claim of the state secrets privilege. The then Director of the CIA, Porter Goss, submitted two sworn declarations to the district court in support of the state secrets privilege claim. The first declaration was unclassified, and explained in general terms the reasons for the United States' assertion of privilege. The other declaration was classified; it detailed the information that the United States sought to protect, explained why further court proceedings would unreasonably risk that information's disclosure, and spelled out why such disclosure would be detrimental to the national security (the "Classified Declaration"). . . . On March 13, 2006, the United States formally moved to intervene as a defendant in the district court proceedings. Contemporaneous with seeking to intervene as a defendant, the United States moved to dismiss the Complaint, contending that its interposition of the state secrets privilege precluded the litigation of El-Masri's causes of action.

El-Masri responded that the state secrets doctrine did not necessitate dismissal of his Complaint, primarily because CIA rendition operations, including El-Masri's alleged rendition, had been widely discussed in public forums. In support of this contention, Steven Macpherson Watt, a human rights adviser to the American Civil Liberties Union, filed a sworn declaration in the district court, dated April 7, 2006, in which he asserted that United States officials – including Secretary of State Condoleezza Rice, White House Press Secretary Scott McClellan, and Directors Tenet and Goss – had publicly acknowledged that the United States had conducted renditions. Watt also observed that international human rights organizations had issued statements on various United States rendition operations, including El-Masri's alleged rendition, and that at least one such release had described the use of privately owned aircraft in the renditions of El-Masri and others. Additionally, according to Watt, the European Parliament and the Council of Europe had commenced investigations into possible European cooperation in United States renditions, and similar inquiries were pending in eighteen European countries.

Watt further asserted that "[m]edia reports on the rendition program generally, and Mr. El-Masri's rendition specifically, are too numerous to assemble." Watt Declaration ¶26. According to Watt, these media reports revealed the existence of secret CIA detention facilities where some rendition subjects were held, as well as the United States' "modus operandi" for conducting renditions: "masked men in an unmarked jet seize their target, cut off his clothes, put him in a blindfold and jumpsuit, tranquilize him and fly him away." *Id.* ¶26(vi). And, Watt represented, the news media had documented some of the details of El-Masri's alleged rendition, including the underlying "decision-making process" and the roles of the German and Macedonian governments. *Id.* ¶26(viii).

On May 12, 2006, . . . the district court concluded that the claim of the state secrets privilege was valid, and that, "given the application of the privilege to this case, the United States' motion to dismiss must be . . . granted." *See* Order, 437 F. Supp. 2d at 541. El-Masri has appealed from the Order and corresponding judgment of dismissal . . . .

II.

El-Masri maintains on appeal that the district court misapplied the state secrets doctrine in dismissing his Complaint without requiring any responsive pleadings from the defendants or permitting any discovery to be conducted. Importantly, El-Masri does not contend that the state secrets privilege has no role in these proceedings. To the contrary, he acknowledges that at least some information important to his claims is likely to be privileged, and thus beyond his reach. But he challenges the court's determination that state secrets are so central to this matter that any attempt at further litigation would threaten their disclosure. As explained below, we conclude that the district court correctly assessed the centrality of state secrets in this dispute. We therefore affirm its Order and the dismissal of El-Masri's Complaint.

A.

1. . . .

[Here the court reviews the holdings of the Supreme Court in *United States v. Reynolds*, 345 U.S. 1, 10 (1953), and *Totten v. United States*, 92

U.S. 105 (1875), and related matters.]

2.

A court faced with a state secrets privilege question is obliged to resolve the matter by use of a three-part analysis. At the outset, the court must ascertain that the procedural requirements for invoking the state secrets privilege have been satisfied. Second, the court must decide whether the information sought to be protected qualifies as privileged under the state secrets doctrine. Finally, if the subject information is determined to be privileged, the ultimate question to be resolved is how the matter should proceed in light of the successful privilege claim.

a.

The procedural requirements for invoking the state secrets privilege are set forth in *Reynolds* . . . .

b.

After a court has confirmed that the *Reynolds* procedural prerequisites are satisfied, it must determine whether the information that the United States seeks to shield is a state secret, and thus privileged from disclosure. This inquiry is a difficult one, for it pits the judiciary's search for truth against the Executive's duty to maintain the nation's security. The *Reynolds* Court recognized this tension, observing that "[j]udicial control over the evidence in a case cannot be abdicated to the caprice of executive officers" – no matter how great the interest in national security – but that the President's ability to preserve state secrets likewise cannot be placed entirely at the mercy of the courts. 345 U.S. at 9-10. Moreover, a court evaluating a claim of privilege must "do so without forcing a disclosure of the very thing the privilege is designed to protect."

The *Reynolds* Court balanced those concerns by leaving the judiciary firmly in control of deciding whether an executive assertion of the state secrets privilege is valid, but subject to a standard mandating restraint in the exercise of its authority. A court is obliged to honor the Executive's assertion of the privilege if it is satisfied, "from all the circumstances of the case, that there is a reasonable danger that compulsion of the evidence will expose military matters which, in the interest of national security, should not be divulged." *Reynolds,* 345 U.S. at 10. In assessing the risk that such a disclosure might pose to national security, a court is obliged to accord the "utmost deference" to the responsibilities of the executive branch. [*United States v. Nixon*, 418 U.S. 683 (1974)], at 710. Such deference is appropriate not only for constitutional reasons, but also practical ones: the Executive and the intelligence agencies under his control occupy a position superior to that of the courts in evaluating the consequences of a release of sensitive information. In the related context of confidentiality classification decisions, we have observed that "[t]he courts, of course, are ill-equipped to become sufficiently steeped in foreign intelligence matters to serve effectively in the review of secrecy classifications in that area." *United States v. Marchetti*, 466 F.2d 1309, 1318 (4th Cir. 1972). The executive branch's expertise in predicting the potential consequences of intelligence disclosures is particularly important given the sophisticated nature of modern intelligence analysis, in which "[t]he significance of one item of information may frequently depend upon knowledge of many other items of information," and "[w]hat may seem trivial to the uninformed, may appear of great moment to one who has a broad view of the scene and may put the questioned item of information in its proper context." *Id.* In the same vein, in those situations where the state secrets privilege has been invoked because disclosure risks impairing our foreign relations, the President's assessment of the diplomatic situation is entitled to great weight.

The Executive bears the burden of satisfying a reviewing court that the *Reynolds* reasonable-danger standard is met. A court considering the Executive's assertion of the state secrets privilege, however, must take care not to "forc[e] a disclosure of the very thing the privilege is designed to protect" by demanding more information than is necessary. *Reynolds,* 345 U.S. at 8. Frequently, the explanation of the department head who has lodged the formal privilege claim, provided in an affidavit or personal declaration, is sufficient to carry the Executive's burden. *See, e.g., Sterling v. Tenet*, 416 F.3d 338, 345 (4th Cir. 2005) (relying on declarations of CIA Director); *Reynolds,* 345 U.S. at 5 (relying on Claim of Privilege by Secretary of Air Force and affidavit of Air Force Judge Advocate General). In some situations, a court may conduct an in camera examination of the actual information sought to be protected, in order to ascertain that the criteria set forth in *Reynolds* are fulfilled. *See Sterling,* 416 F.3d at 345. The degree to which such a reviewing court should probe depends in part on the importance of the assertedly privileged information to the position of the party seeking it. *See Reynolds,* 345 U.S. at 11. "Where there is a strong showing of necessity, the claim of privilege should not be lightly accepted. . . ." *Id.* On the other hand, "even the most compelling necessity cannot overcome the claim of privilege if the court is ultimately satisfied that military secrets are at stake." *Id.* Indeed, in certain circumstances a court may conclude that an explanation by the Executive of why a question cannot be answered would itself create an unacceptable danger of injurious disclosure. *See id.* at 9. In such a situation, a court is obliged to accept the executive branch's claim of privilege without further demand. *See id.*

After information has been determined to be privileged under the state secrets doctrine, it is absolutely protected from disclosure – even for the purpose of in camera examination by the court. On this point, *Reynolds* could not be more specific: "When . . . the occasion for the privilege is appropriate, . . . the court should not jeopardize the security which the privilege is meant to protect by insisting upon an examination of the evidence, even by the judge alone, in chambers." 345 U.S. at 10. Moreover, no attempt is made to balance the need for secrecy of the privileged information against a party's need for the information's disclosure; a court's determination that a piece of evidence is a privileged state secret removes it from the proceedings entirely. *See id.* at 11.

c.

The effect of a successful interposition of the state secrets privilege by the United States will vary from case to case. If a proceeding involving state secrets can be fairly litigated without resort to the privileged information, it may continue. But if "'the circumstances make clear that sensitive military secrets will be so central to the subject matter of the litigation that any attempt to proceed will threaten disclosure of the privileged matters,' dismissal is the proper remedy." *Sterling,* 416 F.3d at 348 (quoting *DTM Research, LLC v. AT & T Corp.,* 245 F.3d 327, 334 (4th Cir. 2001)). The Supreme Court has recognized that some matters are so pervaded by state secrets as to be incapable of judicial resolution once the privilege has been invoked. *See Totten,* 92 U.S. at 107; *Reynolds,* 345 U.S. at 11 n.26. Although *Totten* has come to primarily represent a somewhat narrower principle – a categorical bar on actions to enforce secret contracts for espionage – it rested, as we have already observed, on the proposition that a cause cannot be maintained if its trial would inevitably lead to the disclosure of privileged information. *See* 92 U.S. at 107. And in *Reynolds,* while concluding that dismissal was unnecessary because the privileged information was peripheral to the plaintiffs' action, the Court made clear that where state secrets form the very subject matter of a court proceeding, as in *Totten,* dismissal at the pleading stage – "without ever reaching the question of evidence" – is appropriate. *See* 345 U.S. at 11 n.26. In a recent decision unanimously reaffirming *Totten*'s validity, the Supreme Court approvingly quoted *Reynolds*'s discussion of *Totten* as a matter in which dismissal on the pleadings was appropriate because the very subject matter of the action was a state secret. *See Tenet v. Doe,* 544 U.S. 1, 9 (2005).

Our own decisions applying the state secrets privilege have also recognized that, in certain proceedings, the unavailability of privileged state secrets as evidence will necessarily lead to dismissal. In *Farnsworth Cannon, Inc. v. Grimes,* an action alleging tortious interference with a classified contract to perform services for the Navy, our en banc Court affirmed the district court's dismissal on state secrets grounds. *See* 635 F.2d 268 (4th Cir. 1980). We reasoned that privileged secrets were so central to the dispute that "[i]n an attempt to make out a prima facie case during an actual trial, the plaintiff and its lawyers would have every incentive to probe as close to the core secrets as the trial judge would permit." *Id.* at 281. "Such probing in open court," we concluded, "would inevitably be revealing," and dismissal was therefore warranted. *Id.*

In *Fitzgerald v. Penthouse International, Ltd.,* in 1985, we affirmed the district court's dismissal, under the state secrets doctrine, of an action alleging that a magazine article on the Navy's classified marine mammal program had libelously accused the plaintiff of espionage. *See* 776 F.2d 1236, 1237-38 (4th Cir. 1985). There, the Secretary of the Navy had filed a public declaration asserting that the plaintiff's plan to call witnesses with knowledge of the Navy's classified program risked the disclosure of military secrets, since those witnesses could be questioned about the secret information to which they were privy. *See id.* at 1242. In addition, the Secretary filed a separate, classified declaration that elaborated on his reasons for asserting the state secrets privilege in the case. *See id.* at 1243 n.9. From all the circumstances, we concluded that "there was simply no way this particular case could be tried without compromising sensitive military secrets," and ruled that the district court had not erred in dismissing it. *Id.* at 1243.

More recently, in our 2005 *Sterling* decision, we affirmed the dismissal of a Title VII action initiated by an African-American CIA officer alleging unlawful discriminatory practices by CIA management. *See* 416 F.3d at 341. We concluded that state secrets were so central to that proceeding that it could not be litigated given the Executive's invocation of the privilege. *Id.* at 346-48. The evidence in the dispute would have consisted primarily of documents and testimony regarding the assignments and performance evaluations of CIA operatives, and many of the necessary witnesses were individuals whose very identities were state secrets. *Id.* at 347-48. Indeed, as Judge Wilkinson explained, "the whole object of the suit and of the discovery [was] to establish a fact that is a state secret – namely, the methods and operations of the Central Intelligence Agency." *Id.* at 348 (internal quotation marks and citation omitted). In those circumstances, dismissal was deemed appropriate.

Our sister circuits have likewise recognized that the unavailability of privileged information may, in some instances, necessarily lead to dismissal. *See Kasza v. Browner*, 133 F.3d 1159, 1170 (9th Cir. 1998) (affirming dismissal, on state secrets grounds, of action alleging that Air Force had unlawfully handled hazardous waste in classified operating area); *Black v. United States*, 62 F.3d 1115, 1118-19 (8th Cir. 1995) (affirming dismissal, on state secrets grounds, of action alleging that executive branch officials had engaged in "campaign of harassment and psychological attacks" against plaintiff); *Bareford v. Gen. Dynamics Corp.*, 973 F.2d 1138, 1140 (5th Cir. 1992) (affirming dismissal, on state secrets grounds, of action alleging manufacturing and design defects in military weapons system); *Halkin v. Helms*, 690 F.2d 977, 981 (D.C. Cir. 1982) (affirming dismissal, on state secrets grounds, of action alleging unlawful CIA surveillance); *cf. Tenenbaum v. Simonini*, 372 F.3d 776, 777-78 (6th Cir. 2004) (affirming summary judgment because no defense was available without resort to privileged state secrets).

3.

To summarize, our analysis of the Executive's interposition of the state secrets privilege is governed primarily by two standards. First, evidence is privileged pursuant to the state secrets doctrine if, under all the circumstances of the case, there is a reasonable danger that its disclosure will expose military (or diplomatic or intelligence) matters which, in the interest of national security, should not be divulged. *See Reynolds,* 345 U.S. at 10. Second, a proceeding in which the state secrets privilege is successfully interposed must be dismissed if the circumstances make clear that privileged information will be so central to the litigation that any attempt to proceed will threaten that information's disclosure. *See Sterling,* 416 F.3d at 348; *see also Reynolds,* 345 U.S. at 11 n.26; *Totten,* 92 U.S. at 107. With these controlling principles in mind, and being cognizant of the delicate balance to be struck in applying the state secrets doctrine, we proceed to our analysis of El-Masri's contentions.

B.

1. . . .

a.

The heart of El-Masri's appeal is his assertion that the facts essential to his Complaint have largely been made public, either in statements by United States officials or in reports by media outlets and foreign governmental entities. He maintains that the subject of this action is simply "a rendition and its consequences," and that its critical facts – the CIA's operation of a rendition program targeted at terrorism suspects, plus the tactics employed therein – have been so widely discussed that litigation concerning them could do no harm to national security. As a result, El-Masri contends that the district court should have allowed his case to move forward with discovery, perhaps with special procedures imposed to protect sensitive information.

El-Masri's contention in that regard, however, misapprehends the nature of our assessment of a dismissal on state secrets grounds. The controlling inquiry is not whether the general subject matter of an action can be described without resort to state secrets. Rather, we must ascertain whether an action can be *litigated* without threatening the disclosure of such state secrets. Thus, for purposes of the state secrets analysis, the "central facts" and "very subject matter" of an action are those facts that are essential to prosecuting the action or defending against it.

El-Masri is therefore incorrect in contending that the central facts of this proceeding are his allegations that he was detained and interrogated under abusive conditions, or that the CIA conducted the rendition program that has been acknowledged by United States officials. Facts such as those furnish the general terms in which El-Masri has related his story to the press, but advancing a case in the court of public opinion, against the United States at large, is an undertaking quite different from prevailing against specific defendants in a court of law. If El-Masri's civil action were to proceed, the facts central to its resolution would be the roles, if any, that the defendants played in the events he alleges. To establish a prima facie case, he would be obliged to produce admissible evidence not only that he was detained and interrogated, but that the defendants were involved in his detention and interrogation in a manner that renders them personally liable to him. Such a showing could be made only with evidence that exposes how the CIA organizes, staffs, and supervises its most sensitive intelligence operations. With regard to Director Tenet, for example, El-Masri would be obliged to show in detail how the head of the CIA participates in such operations, and how information concerning their progress is relayed to him. With respect to the defendant corporations and their unnamed employees, El-Masri would have to demonstrate the existence and details of CIA espionage contracts, an endeavor practically indistinguishable from that categorically barred by *Totten* and *Tenet v. Doe*. See *Totten v. United States*, 92 U.S. 105, 107 (1875) (establishing absolute bar to enforcement of confidential agreements to conduct espionage, on ground that "public policy forbids the maintenance of any suit in a court of justice, the trial of which would inevitably lead to the disclosure of matters which the law itself regards as confidential"); *Tenet v. Doe*, 544 U.S. 1, 10-11 (2005) (reaffirming *Totten* in unanimous decision). Even marshalling the evidence necessary to make the requisite showings would implicate privileged state secrets, because El-Masri would need to rely on witnesses whose identities, and evidence the very existence of which, must remain confidential in the interest of national security. *See Sterling,* 416 F.3d at 347 ("[T]he very methods by which evidence would be gathered in this case are themselves problematic.").

b.

Furthermore, if El-Masri were somehow able to make out a prima facie case despite the unavailability of state secrets, the defendants could not properly defend themselves without using privileged evidence. The main avenues of defense available in this matter are to show that El-Masri was not subject to the treatment that he alleges; that, if he was subject to such treatment, the defendants were not involved in it; or that, if they were involved, the nature of their involvement does not give rise to liability. Any of those three showings would require disclosure of information regarding the means and methods by which the CIA gathers intelligence. If, for example, the truth is that El-Masri was detained by the CIA but his description of his treatment is inaccurate, that fact could be established only by disclosure of the actual circumstances of his detention, and its proof would require testimony by the personnel involved. Or, if El-Masri was in fact detained as he describes, but the operation was conducted by some governmental entity other than the CIA, or another government entirely, that information would be privileged. Alternatively, if the CIA detained El-Masri, but did so without Director Tenet's active involvement, effective proof thereof would require a detailed explanation of how CIA operations are supervised. Similarly, although an individual CIA officer might demonstrate his lack of involvement in a given operation by disclosing that he was actually performing some other function at the time in question, establishing his alibi would likely require him to reveal privileged information.

Moreover, proof of the involvement – or lack thereof – of particular CIA officers in a given operation would provide significant information on how the CIA makes its personnel assignments. Similar concerns would attach to evidence produced in defense of the corporate defendants and their unnamed employees. And, like El-Masri's prima facie case, any of the possible defenses suggested above would require the production of witnesses whose identities are confidential and evidence the very existence of which is a state secret. We do not, of course, mean to suggest that any of these hypothetical defenses represents the true state of affairs in this matter, but they illustrate that virtually any conceivable response to El-Masri's allegations would disclose privileged information.

c.

It is clear from precedent that the "central facts" or "very subject matter" of a civil proceeding, for purposes of our dismissal analysis, are those facts necessary to litigate it – not merely to discuss it in general terms. In *Bareford v. General Dynamics Corp.*, several plaintiffs who had been injured or whose decedents had died in the 1987 missile attack on the U.S.S. Stark in the Persian Gulf initiated an action against the manufacturers of the vessel's weapons system, alleging that the system had been defectively manufactured and designed. *See* 973 F.2d 1138, 1140 (5th Cir. 1992). Those allegations, like El-Masri's, could be set forth without revealing state secrets; the plaintiffs' assertion that a Navy weapons system was defective was not, in itself, detrimental to national security. The facts central to the resolution of the proceeding, however, were whether the weapons system was intended to destroy the missile that struck the Stark and, if so, why it failed. Those critical factual questions could not be answered, the Fifth Circuit concluded, without threatening disclosure of privileged state secrets, and thus dismissal was appropriate. *See id.* at 1143-44. . . .

[Here the court reviews other similar Court of Appeals decisions.]

In light of these decisions, we must reject El-Masri's view that the existence of public reports concerning his alleged rendition (and the CIA's rendition program in general) should have saved his Complaint from dismissal. Even if we assume, arguendo, that the state secrets privilege does not apply to the information that media outlets have published concerning those topics, dismissal of his Complaint would nonetheless be proper because the public information does not include the facts that are central to litigating his action. Rather, those central facts – the CIA means and methods that form the subject matter of El-Masri's claim – remain state secrets. Consequently, pursuant to the standards that El-Masri has acknowledged as controlling, the district court did not err in dismissing his Complaint at the pleading stage.

2.

El-Masri also contends that, instead of dismissing his Complaint, the district court should have employed some procedure under which state secrets would have been revealed to him, his counsel, and the court, but withheld from the public. Specifically, he suggests that the court ought to have received all the state secrets evidence in camera and under seal, provided his counsel access to it pursuant to a nondisclosure agreement (after arranging for necessary security clearances), and then conducted an in camera trial. We need not dwell long on El-Masri's proposal in this regard, for it is expressly foreclosed by *Reynolds,* the Supreme Court decision that controls this entire field of inquiry. *Reynolds* plainly held that when "the occasion for the privilege is appropriate, . . . the court should not jeopardize the security which the privilege is meant to protect by insisting upon an examination of the evidence, even by the judge alone, in chambers." 345 U.S. at 10. El-Masri's assertion that the district court erred in not compelling the disclosure of state secrets to him and his lawyers is thus without merit.

C.

In addition to his analysis under the controlling legal principles, El-Masri presents a sharp attack on what he views as the dire constitutional and policy consequences of dismissing his Complaint. He maintains that the district court's ruling, if affirmed, would enable the Executive to unilaterally avoid judicial scrutiny merely by asserting that state secrets are at stake in a given matter. More broadly, he questions the very application of the state secrets doctrine in matters where "egregious executive misconduct" is alleged, contending that, in such circumstances, the courts' "constitutional duty to review executive action" should trump the procedural protections traditionally accorded state secrets.

Contrary to El-Masri's assertion, the state secrets doctrine does not represent a surrender of judicial control over access to the courts. As we have explained, it is the court, not the Executive, that determines whether the state secrets privilege has been properly invoked. In order to successfully claim the state secrets privilege, the Executive must satisfy the court that disclosure of the information sought to be protected would expose matters that, in the interest of national security, ought to remain secret. Similarly, in order to win dismissal of an action on state secrets grounds, the Executive must persuade the court that state secrets are so central to the action that it cannot be fairly litigated without threatening their disclosure. The state secrets privilege cannot be successfully interposed, nor can it lead to dismissal of an action, based merely on the Executive's assertion that the pertinent standard has been met.

In this matter, the reasons for the United States' claim of the state secrets privilege and its motion to dismiss were explained largely in the Classified Declaration, which sets forth in detail the nature of the information that the Executive seeks to protect and explains why its disclosure would be detrimental to national security. We have reviewed the Classified Declaration, as did the district court, and the extensive information it contains is crucial to our decision in this matter. El-Masri's contention that his Complaint was dismissed based on the Executive's "unilateral assert[ion] of a need for secrecy" is entirely unfounded. It is no doubt frustrating to El-Masri that many of the specific reasons for the dismissal of his Complaint are classified. An inherent feature of the state secrets privilege, however, is that the party against whom it is asserted will often not be privy to the information that the Executive seeks to protect. That El-Masri is unfamiliar with the Classified Declaration's explanation for the privilege claim does not imply, as he would have it, that no such explanation was required, or that the district court's ruling was simply an unthinking ratification of a conclusory demand by the executive branch.

We also reject El-Masri's view that we are obliged to jettison procedural restrictions – including the law of privilege – that might impede our ability to act as a check on the Executive. Indeed, El-Masri's position in that regard fundamentally misunderstands the nature of our relationship to the executive branch. El-Masri envisions a judiciary that possesses a roving writ to ferret out and strike down executive excess. Article III, however, assigns the courts a more modest role: we simply decide cases and controversies. Thus, when an executive officer's liability for official action can be established in a properly conducted judicial proceeding, we will not hesitate to enter judgment accordingly. But we would be guilty of excess in our own right if we were to disregard settled legal principles in order to reach the merits of an executive action that would not otherwise be before us – especially when the challenged action pertains to military or foreign policy. We decline to follow such a course, and thus reject El-Masri's invitation to rule that the state secrets doctrine can be brushed aside on the ground that the President's foreign policy has gotten out of line.

D.

As we have observed in the past, the successful interposition of the state secrets privilege imposes a heavy burden on the party against whom the privilege is asserted. *See Sterling,* 416 F.3d at 348 ("We recognize that our decision places, on behalf of the entire country, a burden on Sterling that he alone must bear."). That party loses access to evidence that he needs to prosecute his action and, if privileged state secrets are sufficiently central to the matter, may lose his cause of action altogether. Moreover, a plaintiff suffers this reversal not through any fault of his own, but because his personal interest in pursuing his civil claim is subordinated to the collective interest in national security. *See id.* ("[T]here can be no doubt that, in limited circumstances like these, the fundamental principle of access to court must bow to the fact that a nation without sound intelligence is a nation at risk."); *Fitzgerald,* 776 F.2d at 1238 n.3 ("When the state secrets privilege is validly asserted, the result is unfairness to individual litigants – through the loss of important evidence or dismissal of a case – in order to protect a greater public value"). In view of these considerations, we recognize the gravity of our conclusion that El-Masri must be denied a judicial forum for his Complaint, and reiterate our past observations that dismissal on state secrets grounds is appropriate only in a narrow category of disputes. *See Sterling,* 416 F.3d at 348; *Fitzgerald,* 776 F.2d at 1241-42. Nonetheless, we think it plain that the matter before us falls squarely within that narrow class, and we are unable to find merit in El-Masri's assertion to the contrary. . . .

Affirmed.

NOTE

On August 13, 2007, the American Bar Association adopted a resolution declaring:

That the American Bar Association supports procedures and standards designed to ensure that whenever possible, federal civil cases are not dismissed based solely on the state secrets privilege; and

. . . That, in furtherance of this objective the American Bar Association urges Congress to enact legislation governing federal civil cases implicating the state secrets privilege . . . .

[NSL p. 1050. Insert the following proposed legislation after *El-Masri v. United States.*]

State Secrets Protection Act
S. 417, 111th Cong. (2009)

A BILL

To enact a safe, fair, and responsible state secrets privilege Act.

Be it enacted by the Senate and House of Representatives of the United States of America in Congress assembled,

SECTION 1. SHORT TITLE.

This Act may be cited as the State Secrets Protection Act.

SEC. 2. STATE SECRETS PROTECTION.

(a) In General – Title 28 of the United States Code is amended by adding after chapter 180, the following:

CHAPTER 181 – STATE SECRETS PROTECTION

Sec. 4051. Definitions

In this chapter –
(1) the term "evidence" means any document, witness testimony, discovery response, affidavit, object, or other material that could be

admissible in court under the Federal Rules of Evidence or discoverable under the Federal Rules of Civil Procedure; and

(2) the term "state secret" refers to any information that, if disclosed publicly, would be reasonably likely to cause significant harm to the national defense or foreign relations of the United States.

Sec. 4052. Rules governing procedures related to this chapter

(a) Documents – A Federal court –

(1) shall determine which filings, motions, and affidavits, or portions thereof, submitted under this chapter shall be submitted ex parte;

(2) may order a party to provide a redacted, unclassified, or summary substitute of a filing, motion, or affidavit to other parties; and

(3) shall make decisions under this subsection taking into consideration the interests of justice and national security.

(b) Hearings –

(1) In Camera Hearings –

(A) In General – Except as provided in subparagraph (B), all hearings under this chapter shall be conducted in camera.

(B) Exception – A court may not conduct a hearing under this chapter in camera based on the assertion of the state secrets privilege if the court determines that the hearing relates only to a question of law and does not present a risk of revealing state secrets.

(2) Ex Parte Hearings – A Federal court may conduct hearings or portions thereof ex parte if the court determines, following in camera review of the evidence, that the interests of justice and national security cannot adequately be protected through the measures described in subsections (c) and (d).

(3) Record of Hearings – . . . The court shall seal all records to the extent necessary to protect national security.

(c) Attorney Security Clearances –

(1) In General – A Federal court shall, at the request of the United States, limit participation in hearings conducted under this chapter, or access to motions or affidavits submitted under this chapter, to attorneys with appropriate security clearances, if the court

determines that limiting participation in that manner would serve the interests of national security. The court may also appoint a guardian ad litem with the necessary security clearances to represent any party for the purposes of any hearing conducted under this chapter. . . .

(3) Court Oversight – If the United States fails to provide a security clearance necessary to conduct a hearing under this chapter in a reasonable period of time, the court may review in camera and ex parte the reasons of the United States for denying or delaying the clearance to ensure that the United States is not withholding a security clearance from a particular attorney or class of attorneys for any reason other than protection of national security.

(d) Protective Orders – A Federal court may issue a protective order governing any information or evidence disclosed or discussed at any hearing conducted under this chapter if the court determines that issuing such an order is necessary to protect national security.

(e) Opinions and Orders – Any opinions or orders issued under this chapter may be issued under seal or in redacted versions if, and to the extent that, the court determines that such measure is necessary to protect national security.

(f) Special Masters – A Federal court may appoint a special master or other independent advisor who holds the necessary security clearances to assist the court in handling a matter subject to this chapter.

Sec. 4053. Procedures for answering a complaint

(a) Intervention – The United States may intervene in any civil action in order to protect information the Government determines may be subject to the state secrets privilege.

(b) Impermissible as Grounds for Dismissal Prior to Hearings – Except as provided in section 4055, the state secrets privilege shall not constitute grounds for dismissal of a case or claim. . . .

Sec. 4054. Procedures for determining whether evidence is protected from disclosure by the state secrets privilege

(a) Asserting the State Secrets Privilege – The United States may, in any civil action to which the United States is a party or in any other civil action before a Federal or State court, assert the state secrets privilege as a ground for withholding information or evidence in discovery or for preventing the disclosure of information through court filings or through the introduction of evidence.

(b) Supporting Affidavit – In each instance in which the United States asserts the state secrets privilege with respect to an item of information or evidence, the United States shall provide the court with an affidavit signed by the head of the executive branch agency with responsibility for, and control over, the state secrets involved explaining the factual basis for the claim of privilege. The United States shall make public an unclassified version of the affidavit.

(c) Hearing – A Federal court shall conduct a hearing, consistent with the requirements of section 4052, to examine the items of evidence that the United States asserts are subject to the state secrets privilege, as well as any affidavit submitted by the United States in support of any assertion of the state secrets privilege, and to determine the validity of any assertion of the state secrets privilege made by the United States.

(d) Review of Evidence –

(1) Submission of Evidence – In addition to the affidavit provided under subsection (b), and except as provided in paragraph (2) of this subsection, the United States shall make all evidence the United States claims is subject to the state secrets privilege available for the court to review, consistent with the requirements of section 4052, before any hearing conducted under this section.

(2) Sampling in Certain Cases – If the volume of evidence the United States asserts is protected by the state secrets privilege precludes a timely review of each item of evidence, or the court otherwise determines that a review of all of that evidence is not feasible, the court may substitute a sufficient sampling of the evidence . . . .

(3) Index of Materials – The United States shall provide the court with a manageable index of evidence it contends is subject to the state secrets privilege by formulating a system of itemizing and indexing that would correlate statements made in the affidavit provided under subsection (b) with portions of the evidence the United States asserts is subject to the state secrets privilege. The index shall be specific enough to afford the court an adequate foundation to review the basis of the invocation of the privilege by the United States.

(e) Determinations as to Applicability of State Secrets Privilege –

(1) In General – . . . An item of evidence is subject to the state secrets privilege if it contains a state secret, or there is no possible means of effectively segregating it from other evidence that contains a state secret.

(2) Admissibility and Disclosure –

(A) Privileged Evidence – If the court agrees that an item of evidence is subject to the state secrets privilege, that item shall not be disclosed or admissible as evidence.

(B) Non-privileged Evidence – If the court determines that an item of evidence is not subject to the state secrets privilege, the state secrets privilege does not prohibit the disclosure of that item to the opposing party or the admission of that item at trial, subject to the Federal Rules of Civil Procedure and the Federal Rules of Evidence.

(3) Standard of Review – The court shall give substantial weight to an assertion by the United States relating to why public disclosure of an item of evidence would be reasonably likely to cause significant harm to the national defense or foreign relations of the United States. The court shall weigh the testimony of a Government expert in the same manner as the court weighs, and along with, any other expert testimony in the applicable case.

(f) Non-Privileged Substitute – If the court finds that material evidence is subject to the state secrets privilege and it is possible to craft a non-privileged substitute for that privileged material evidence that provides a substantially equivalent opportunity to litigate the claim or defense as would that privileged material evidence, the court shall order the United States to provide such a substitute, which may consist of –

(1) a summary of such privileged information;

(2) a version of the evidence with privileged information redacted;

(3) a statement admitting relevant facts that the privileged information would tend to prove; or

(4) any other alternative as directed by the court in the interests of justice and protecting national security.

(g) Refusal To Provide Non-Privileged Substitute – In a suit against the United States or an officer or agent of the Unites States acting in the official capacity of that officer or agent, if the court orders the United

States to provide a non-privileged substitute for evidence in accordance with this section, and the United States fails to comply, the court shall resolve the disputed issue of fact or law to which the evidence pertains in the non-government party's favor.

Sec. 4055. Procedures when evidence protected by the state secrets privilege is necessary for adjudication of a claim or counterclaim

After reviewing all pertinent evidence, privileged and non-privileged, a Federal court may dismiss a claim or counterclaim on the basis of the state secrets privilege only if the court determines that –

(1) it is impossible to create for privileged material evidence a non-privileged substitute under section 4054(f) that provides a substantially equivalent opportunity to litigate the claim or counterclaim as would that privileged material evidence;

(2) dismissal of the claim or counterclaim would not harm national security; and

(3) continuing with litigation of the claim or counterclaim in the absence of the privileged material evidence would substantially impair the ability of a party to pursue a valid defense to the claim or counterclaim.

Sec. 4057. Security procedures

(a) In General – The security procedures established under the Classified Information Procedures Act (18 U.S.C. App.) by the Chief Justice of the United States for the protection of classified information shall be used to protect against unauthorized disclosure of evidence protected by the state secrets privilege.

(b) Rules – The Chief Justice of the United States, in consultation with the Attorney General, the Director of National Intelligence, and the Secretary of Defense, may create additional rules or amend the rules to implement this chapter . . . .

Sec. 4058. Reporting

(a) Assertion of State Secrets Privilege –

(1) In General – The Attorney General shall submit to the

Permanent Select Committee on Intelligence and the Committee on the Judiciary of the House of Representatives and the Select Committee on Intelligence and the Committee on the Judiciary of the Senate a report on any case in which the United States asserts the state secrets privilege, not later than 30 calendar days after the date of such assertion. . . .

[NSL p. 1050. Add this memorandum after the proposed State Secrets Protection Act.]

Memorandum from the Attorney General Regarding Policies and Procedures Governing Invocation of the State Secrets Privilege

Sept. 23, 2009

http://www.justice.gov/opa/documents/state-secret-privileges.pdf

I am issuing today new Department of Justice policies and administrative procedures that will provide greater accountability and reliability in the invocation of the state secrets privilege in litigation. The Department is adopting these policies and procedures to strengthen public confidence that the U.S. Government will invoke the privilege in court only when genuine and significant harm to national defense or foreign relations is at stake and only to the extent necessary to safeguard those interests. The policies and procedures set forth in this Memorandum are effective as of October 1. 2009. and the Department shall apply them in all cases in which a government department or agency thereafter seeks to invoke the state secrets privilege in litigation.

1. Standards for Determination

A. Legal Standard. The Department will defend an assertion of the stale secrets privilege ("privilege") in litigation when a government department or agency seeking to assert the privilege makes a sufficient showing that assertion of the privilege is necessary to protect information the unauthorized disclosure of which reasonably could be expected to cause significant harm to the national defense or foreign relations ("national security'") of the United States. With respect to classified information, the Department will defend invocation of the privilege to protect information properly classified pursuant to Executive Order 12958, as amended, or any successor order, at any level of classification, so long as the unauthorized disclosure of such information reasonably could be expected to cause significant harm to the national security of the United States. With respect to information that is nonpublic but not classified, the Department will also defend invocation of the privilege so long as the disclosure of such information reasonably could be expected to cause significant harm to the national security of the United States.

B. Narrow Tailoring. The Department's policy is that the privilege should be invoked only to the extent necessary to protect against the risk of significant harm to national security. The Department will seek to dismiss a litigant's claim or case on the basis of the state secrets privilege only when doing so is necessary to protect against the risk of significant harm to national security.

C. Limitations. The Department will not defend an invocation of the privilege in order **to:** (i) conceal violations of the law, inefficiency, or administrative error; (ii) prevent embarrassment to a person, organization, or agency of the United States government; (iii) restrain competition; or (iv) prevent or delay the release of information the release of which would not reasonably be expected to cause significant harm to national security.

2. Initial Procedures for Invocation of the Privilege

A. Evidentiary Support. A government department or agency seeking invocation of the privilege in litigation must submit to the Division in the Department with responsibility for the litigation in question[1] a detailed declaration based on personal knowledge that

---

1. The question whether to invoke the privilege typically arises in civil litigation. Requests for invocation of the privilege in those cases shall be addressed to the Civil Division. The question whether to invoke the privilege also may arise in cases handled by the Environment and Natural Resources Division (ENRD), and requests for invocation of the privilege shall be addressed to ENRD in those instances. It is also possible that a court may require the Government to satisfy the standards for invoking the privilege in criminal proceedings. *See United States v. Araf,* 533 F.3d 72, 78-80 (2d Cir. 2008); *but*

specifies in detail: (i) the nature of the information that must be protected from unauthorized disclosure; (ii) the significant harm to national security that disclosure can reasonably be expected to cause; (iii) the reason why unauthorized disclosure is reasonably likely to cause such harm; and (iv) any other information relevant to the decision whether the privilege should be invoked in litigation.

B. Recommendation from the Assistant Attorney General. The Assistant Attorney General for the Division responsible for the matter shall formally recommend in writing whether or not the Department should defend the assertion of the privilege in litigation. In order to make a formal recommendation to defend the assertion of the privilege, the Assistant Attorney General must conclude, based on a personal evaluation of the evidence submitted by the department or agency seeking invocation of the privilege, that the standards set forth in Section 1(a) of this Memorandum are satisfied. The recommendation of the Assistant Attorney General shall be made in a timely manner to ensure that the State Secrets Review Committee has adequate time to give meaningful consideration to the recommendation.

3. State Secrets Review Committee

A. Review Committee. A State Secrets Review Committee consisting of senior Department of Justice officials designated by the Attorney General will evaluate the Assistant Attorney General's recommendation to determine whether invocation of the privilege in litigation is warranted.

B. Consultation. The Review Committee will consult as necessary and appropriate with the department or agency seeking invocation of the privilege in litigation and with the Office of the Director of National Intelligence. The Review Committee must engage in such consultation prior to making any recommendation against defending the invocation of the privilege in litigation.

---

see *United States* v. *Rosen,* 557 F.3d 192, 198 (4th Cir. 2009). In such instances, requests to submit filings to satisfy that standard shall be directed to the National Security Division.

C. Recommendation by the Review Committee. The Review Committee shall make a recommendation to the Deputy Attorney General, who shall in turn make a recommendation to the Attorney General.[2] The recommendations shall be made in a timely manner to ensure that the Attorney General has adequate time to give meaningful consideration to such recommendations.

4. Attorney General Approval

A. Attorney General Approval. The Department will not defend an assertion of the privilege in litigation without the personal approval of the Attorney General (or, in the absence or recusal of the Attorney General, the Deputy Attorney General or the Acting Attorney General).

B. Notification to Agency or Department Head. In the event that the Attorney General does not approve invocation of the privilege in litigation with respect to some or all of the information a requesting department or agency seeks to protect, the Department will provide prompt notice to the head of the requesting department or agency.

C. Referral to Agency or Department Inspector General. If the Attorney General concludes that it would be proper to defend invocation of the privilege in a case, and that invocation of the privilege would preclude adjudication of particular claims, but that the case raises credible allegations of government wrongdoing, the Department will refer those allegations to the Inspector General of the appropriate department or agency for further investigation, and will provide prompt notice of the referral to the head of the appropriate department or agency.

5. Reporting to Congress

The Department will provide periodic reports to appropriate oversight committees of Congress with respect to all cases in which the Department invokes the privilege on behalf of departments or agencies in litigation, explaining the basis for invoking the privilege.

6. Classification Authority

The department or agency with classification authority over information

---

2. In civil cases, the review committee's recommendation should be made through the Associate Attorney General to the Deputy Attorney General, who shall in turn make a recommendation to the Attorney General.

potentially subject to an invocation of the privilege at all times retains its classification authority under Executive Order 12958, as amended, or any successor order.

7. No Substantive or Procedural Rights Created

This policy statement is not intended to, and does not, create any right or benefit, substantive or procedural, enforceable at law or in equity, by any party against the United States, its departments, agencies, or entities, its officers, employees, or agents, or any other person.

[NSL p. 1077. Add the following case after Note 7.]

United States v. Rosen
United States District Court, Eastern District of Virginia, 2006
445 F. Supp. 2d 602, *as amended*, 2006 WL 5049154

ELLIS, District Judge. In this Espionage Act prosecution, defendants Steven Rosen and Keith Weissman have been charged in Count I of a superseding indictment with conspiring to transmit information relating to the national defense[1] to those not entitled to receive it, in violation of 18 U.S.C. §793(g) [providing criminal liability for co-conspirators]. Defendants, by pretrial motion, attack the constitutionality of §793 in three ways. First, they argue that the statute, as applied to them, is unconstitutionally vague in violation of the Due Process Clause of the Fifth Amendment. Second, they argue that the statute, as applied to them, abridges their First Amendment right to free speech and their First Amendment right to petition the government. Third, defendants assert the First Amendment rights of others by attacking the statute as facially overbroad. In the alternative, defendants urge the Court to avoid these constitutional issues by interpreting the statute as applying only to the transmission of tangible items, *i.e.*, documents, tapes, discs, maps and the like.

In addition, defendant Rosen has been charged in Count III of the superseding indictment with aiding and abetting the transmission of information relating to the national defense to one not entitled to receive

---

1. The phrase "information relating to the national defense" will sometimes be referred to herein as NDI.

it, in violation of 18 U.S.C. §793(d) and 2. He seeks dismissal of this count on the ground that the facts alleged in the superseding indictment in support of this count are legally insufficient.

I.

During the period of the conspiracy alleged in Count I, defendants Rosen and Weissman were employed by the American Israel Public Affairs Committee (AIPAC) in Washington, D.C. AIPAC is a pro-Israel organization that lobbies the United States executive and legislative branches on issues of interest to Israel, especially U.S. foreign policy with respect to the Middle East. Rosen was AIPAC's Director of Foreign Policy Issues . . . . Rosen did not have a security clearance during the period of the alleged conspiracy . . . . Defendant Weissman was AIPAC's Senior Middle East Analyst . . . . Alleged co-conspirator Lawrence Franklin worked on the Iran desk in the Office of the Secretary of the Department of Defense (DOD) and held a top secret security clearance during the alleged conspiracy.[3]

In general, the superseding indictment alleges that in furtherance of their lobbying activities, defendants (i) cultivated relationships with government officials with access to sensitive U.S. government information, including NDI, (ii) obtained the information from these officials, and (iii) transmitted the information to persons not otherwise entitled to receive it, including members of the media, foreign policy analysts, and officials of a foreign government.

The government's recitation of the acts constituting the conspiracy begins on April 13, 1999, when Rosen told an unnamed foreign official (FO-1) that he had "picked up an extremely sensitive piece of intelligence" which he described as "codeword protected intelligence." Rosen proceeded to relate this piece of intelligence, which concerned terrorist activities in Central Asia, to the foreign official. . . . The superseding indictment alleges further that Weissman's role in the conspiracy became

---

3. On October 5, 2005, Franklin pled guilty to one count of conspiracy to communicate national defense information to one not entitled to receive it, in violation of 18 U.S.C. §§793(d) and (g), and to one count of conspiracy to communicate classified information to an agent of a foreign government in violation of 50 U.S.C. §783 and 18 U.S.C. §371.

apparent on June 11, 1999, when Weissman told the same foreign official that he had learned of a "secret FBI, classified FBI report" relating to
the Khobar Towers bombing from three different sources, including an
official of the United States government. Later that day, Weissman told
FO-1 that he had interested a member of the media in the report.

According to the superseding indictment, roughly eighteen months
later, on December 12, 2000, Rosen and Weissman met with a United
States government official (USGO-1) who had access to classified
information relating to U.S. strategy pertaining to a certain Middle East
country. Following this meeting, Rosen allegedly had a conversation
with a member of the media in which he communicated classified
information relating to the U.S. government's deliberations on its
strategy towards that particular Middle Eastern country. . . .

In August 2002, Rosen was introduced to Franklin through a contact
at the DOD. Rosen, Weissman, Franklin and another DOD employee
finally met nearly six months later, on February 12, 2003. At this
meeting, Franklin disclosed to Rosen and Weissman information relating
to a classified draft internal United States government policy document
concerning a certain Middle Eastern country. . . . Rosen met with FO-2
and discussed the same draft internal policy document that Franklin had
discussed with Rosen and Weissman. . . .

[The court goes on to describe in some detail a number of other
instances in which Rosen and Weissman allegedly knowingly received
classified information and passed it on to other AIPAC employees,
foreign officials, and journalists.]

The superseding indictment also charges Rosen with aiding and
abetting Franklin in the latter's violation of 18 U.S.C. §793(d). Specifically, Rosen is alleged to have aided and abetted Franklin's March 17,
2003 transmission by fax of the document he had created from the
classified draft internal policy document related to a certain Middle
Eastern country.

Rosen and Weissman have challenged the constitutionality of Count
I of the superseding indictment on three separate but related grounds.
First, the defendants argue that the government's application of 18
U.S.C. §793(e) in this prosecution violates the Fifth Amendment's Due
Process Clause under the vagueness doctrine because the statute's
indeterminate language failed to provide these defendants with adequate
warning that their conduct was proscribed. In addition to this as-applied

vagueness claim, defendants make two arguments based on the guarantees of the First Amendment. First, they argue that their conduct, as alleged in the superseding indictment, may not be proscribed without transgressing the First Amendment's guarantees of free speech and the right to petition the government. Second, even assuming the statute's constitutional application here, they raise a facial challenge to the statute pursuant to the First Amendment's well-recognized overbreadth doctrine. Finally, in a separate motion to dismiss, Rosen challenges the sufficiency of the allegation that he aided and abetted Franklin's violation of §793(d). Each of these contentions is separately addressed.

II.

The operative statute at issue in defendant's constitutional challenge is codified at 18 U.S.C. §793 and provides, in pertinent part, as follows:

[Subsections (d) and (e) are set forth at casebook p. 1067.]

(g) If two or more persons conspire to violate any of the foregoing provisions of this section, and one or more of such persons do any act to effect the object of the conspiracy, each of the parties to such conspiracy shall be subject to the punishment provided for the offense which is the object of the conspiracy.

18 U.S.C. §793. A brief history of this statute provides necessary context and helps illuminate the analysis of the questions presented. . . .

[After a lengthy discussion, the court ruled that §793 applies to information transmitted in oral, as well as tangible, form.]

Defendants' first constitutional challenge to the statute is based on the principle that the Due Process clause of the Fifth Amendment prohibits punishment pursuant to a statute so vague that "men of common intelligence must necessarily guess at its meaning and differ as to its application." *United States v. Lanier*, 520 U.S. 259, 266 (1997) (quoting *Connally v. General Constr. Co.*, 269 U.S. 385, 391 (1926)). . . .

IV. . . .

C.

. . . [A]ny inherent vagueness in the terms "relating to the national defense" or "entitled to receive" as used in §§793(d) and (e) is cured through the judicial glosses that have been added to these phrases. To the extent that oral transmission of information relating to the national defense makes it more difficult for defendants to know whether they are violating the statute, the statute is not thereby rendered unconstitutionally vague because the statute permits conviction only of those who "willfully" commit the prohibited acts and do so with bad faith. So construed, both phrases pass Fifth Amendment muster; they are not unconstitutionally vague as applied to these defendants.

D.

Seeking to avoid this conclusion, defendants argue that notwithstanding the clarity of the statute's language, the application of the statute to these defendants is so novel and unprecedented that it violates the fair warning prong of the vagueness doctrine. As explained *supra*, the constitutionally required clarity of a statute may be provided through the gloss of judicial interpretation, and it is precisely the judicial glosses on §793 that save the statute from defendants' vagueness challenge. The corollary of this principle is that "due process bars courts from applying a novel construction of a criminal statute to conduct that neither the statute nor any prior judicial decision has fairly disclosed to be within its scope." *Lanier*, 520 U.S. at 266. . . . [T]he test . . . is whether the language and application of the statute has provided defendants adequate warning that their conduct was proscribed. Section 793, as applied here, meets this test; its language and history provided adequate warning to these defendants that the statute proscribed the alleged conduct.

Defendants argue that the present prosecution represents a novel construction of the statute which they could not have anticipated because "leaks" of classified information by non-governmental persons have never been prosecuted under this statute. The statute's plain language rebuts this argument.[38] It is clear from this plain language that defendants' conduct, as alleged in the superseding indictment is within the sweep of the statute. . . . [T]he defendants here cannot argue persuasively that the result reached here amounts to an unforeseeable judicial enlargement of §793.

And, it is useful in this regard to address defendants' frequent use of the term "leak" in advancing their argument that there was not constitutionally adequate notice that the statute reached the alleged conduct. The term "leak," at bottom, connotes in this context, an unpermitted or unauthorized transmission or transfer of information, which of course, is an act plainly within §793, assuming all the other requirements are met. So, labeling an event a "leak" does not remove the event from the statute's scope. At best, the term "leak" is a euphemism used to imply or suggest to a careless reader that the transmission of the information was somehow authorized. Whether the "leaks" or transmissions of information in this case were authorized is likely to be a sharply controverted issue in this case and if the government does not carry its burden of showing that the transfers of information were unauthorized, the prosecution fails. But the analysis here proceeds, as it must, on the superseding indictment's allegations, including the allegation that all transmissions of NDI were unauthorized. At this point, therefore, defendants frequent use of "leak" as a characterization of what occurred is unavailing.

Also unsuccessful is defendants' claim that past applications of the statute fail to provide fair warning that the statute could be applied to the facts alleged in the superseding indictment. [*United States v. Morison*, 844 F.2d 1057 (4th Cir. 1988)] itself rebuts this claim. Notably, in *Morison* the Fourth Circuit considered the very similar argument that the statute was intended to apply only to classic espionage cases and therefore did not apply to Morison's "leak" to a news publication. In rejecting this argument, the Fourth Circuit noted the rarity of prosecutions under §793(e), but stated

---

38. In amending the statute in 1950, Congress made it quite clear that the statute was intended to apply to the transmission of national defense information by non-government employees by adding subsection (e). . . .

that the rarity of prosecution under the statutes does not indicate that the statutes were not to be enforced as written. We think in any event, the rarity of use of the statute as a basis for prosecution is at best a questionable basis for nullifying the clear language of the statute, and we think the revision of 1950 and its reenactment of section 793(d) demonstrate that Congress did not consider such statute meaningless or intend that the statute and its prohibitions were to be abandoned.

Morison, 844 F.2d at 1067. The Fourth Circuit's reasoning in rejecting Morison's challenge is equally applicable to the defendants here, and therefore, for the same reasons, defendants' vagueness challenge based on the novelty of this prosecution fails as well.

V.

The defendants' next constitutional challenge rests on the First Amendment's guarantees of free speech and the right to petition the government for grievances. . . . Defendants' First Amendment challenge exposes the inherent tension between the government transparency so essential to a democratic society and the government's equally compelling need to protect from disclosure information that could be used by those who wish this nation harm. In addressing this tension, it is important to bear in mind that the question to be resolved here is not whether §793 is the optimal resolution of this tension, but whether Congress, in passing this statute, has struck a balance between these competing interests that falls within the range of constitutionally permissible outcomes.

As an initial matter, it is necessary to confront the government's proposed categorical rule that espionage statutes cannot implicate the First Amendment. This contention overreaches. In the broadest terms, the conduct at issue – collecting information about United States' foreign policy and discussing that information with government officials (both United States and foreign), journalists, and other participants in the foreign policy establishment – is at the core of the First Amendment's guarantees. *See Mills v. Alabama,* 384 U.S. 214, 218 (1966) ("[T]here is practically universal agreement that a major purpose of [the First] Amendment was to protect the free discussion of governmental affairs."). And, even under a more precise description of the conduct – the passing of government secrets relating to the national defense to those not entitled to receive them in an attempt to influence United States foreign policy – the application of §793 to the defendants is unquestionably still deserving of First Amendment scrutiny. . . .

Given that the application of the statute to these defendants warrants First Amendment scrutiny, the question then becomes whether Congress may nonetheless penalize the conduct alleged in the superseding indictment, for while the invocation of "national security" does not free Congress from the restraints of the First Amendment, it is equally well established that the invocation of the First Amendment does not "provide immunity for every possible use of language," *Frohwerk v. U.S.*, 249 U.S. 204, 206 (1919), and that "the societal value of speech must, on occasion, be subordinated to other values and considerations." *Dennis v. United States*, 341 U.S. 494, 503 (1951). As Justice Frankfurter aptly put it in *Dennis:*

> The demands of free speech in a democratic society as well as the interest in national security are better served by a candid and informed weighing of the competing interests, within the confines of the judicial process, than by announcing dogmas too inflexible for the non-Euclidian problems to be solved.

Dennis, 341 U.S. at 524-25 (Frankfurter, J., concurring). Thus, to determine, on any given occasion, whether the government's interest prevails over the First Amendment, courts must begin with "an assessment of the competing societal interests" at stake, *Morison,* 844 F.2d at 1082, and proceed to the "delicate and difficult task" of weighing those interests "to determine whether the resulting restriction on freedom can be tolerated." *United States v. Robel*, 389 U.S. 258, 264 (1967).

As already noted, the defendants' First Amendment interests at stake in this prosecution, and those of the third parties raised by defendants, are significant and implicate the core values the First Amendment was designed to protect. The collection and discussion of information about the conduct of government by defendants and others in the body politic is indispensable to the healthy functioning of a representative government, for "[a]s James Madison put it in 1822: 'A popular Government, without popular information, or a means of acquiring it, is but a Prologue to a Farce or a Tragedy; or, perhaps both.'" *Morison,* 844 F.2d at 1081

(Wilkinson, J., concurring) (quoting 9 Writings of James Madison 103
(G. Hunt ed., 1910)). This is especially so in the context of foreign
policy because, as Justice Stewart observed in the Pentagon Papers case:

> In the absence of the government checks and balances present in other areas
> of our national life, the only effective restraint upon executive policy and
> power in the areas of national defense and international affairs may lie in an
> enlightened citizenry-in an informed and critical public opinion which alone
> can here protect the values of democratic government.

New York Times v. United States, 403 U.S. 713, 728 (1971) (Stewart J.,
concurring). . . .

But importantly, the defendants here are not accused merely of
disclosing government secrets, they are accused of disclosing NDI, *i.e.*,
government secrets the disclosure of which could threaten the security of
the nation. And, however vital an informed public may be, it is well
established that disclosure of certain information may be restricted in
service of the nation's security, for "[i]t is 'obvious and unarguable' that
no governmental interest is more compelling than the security of the
Nation." *Haig v. Agee*, 453 U.S. 280, 307 (1981). And, as the Supreme
Court has repeatedly noted, one aspect of the government's paramount
interest in protecting the nation's security is the government's "compelling interest in protecting both the secrecy of information important to
our national security and the appearance of confidentiality so essential to
the effective operation of our foreign intelligence service." [*Snepp v.
United States*, 444 U.S. 507 (1980),] at 509 n.3. Thus, the right to free
speech and the value of an informed citizenry is not absolute and must
yield to the government's legitimate efforts to ensure "the environment
of physical security which a functioning democracy requires." *Morison,*
844 F.2d at 1082. This point is best expressed in the Supreme Court's
pithy phrase that "while the Constitution protects against the invasion of
individual rights, it is not a suicide pact." [*Aptheker v. Sec'y of State*,
378 U.S. 500 (1964),] at 509.

Of course, the abstract proposition that the rights protected by the
First Amendment must at times yield to the need for national security
does not address the concrete issue of whether the §793, as applied here,
violates the First Amendment. This determination depends on whether
§793 is narrowly drawn to apply only to those instances in which the

government's need for secrecy is legitimate, or whether it is too
indiscriminate in its sweep, seeking in effect, to excise the cancer of
espionage with a chainsaw instead of a scalpel. In this respect, the first
clause of §793(e) implicates only the defendants' right to disclose,
willfully, information the government has sought to keep confidential
due to the potential harm its disclosure poses to the national security in
situations in which the defendants have reason to believe that such
disclosure could be used to injure the United States or aid a foreign
government. Likewise, §793(d), which defendants are charged with
conspiring to violate, implicates the same interests, but is limited to those
people – generally government employees or contractors – with authorized possession of the information. Thus, it seems fair to say that §793,
taken together with its judicial glosses, is more the result of a legislative
scalpel and not a chainsaw. This, however, does not end the analysis.

As defendants correctly argue, the analysis of the First Amendment
interests implicated by §§793(d) and (e) depends on the relationship to
the government of the person whose First Amendment rights are
implicated. In this respect, there are two classes of people roughly
correlating to those subject to prosecution under §793(d) and those
subject to prosecution under §793(e). The first class consists of persons
who have access to the information by virtue of their official position.
These people are most often government employees or military
personnel with access to classified information, or defense contractors
with access to classified information, and are often bound by contractual
agreements whereby they agree not to disclose classified information.
As such, they are in a position of trust with the government. The second
class of persons are those who have no employment or contractual
relationship with the government, and therefore have not exploited a
relationship of trust to obtain the national defense information they are
charged with disclosing, but instead generally obtained the information
from one who has violated such a trust.

There can be little doubt, as defendants readily concede, that the
Constitution permits the government to prosecute the first class of
persons for the disclosure of information relating to the national defense
when that person knew that the information is the type which could be
used to threaten the nation's security, and that person acted in bad faith,
i.e., with reason to believe the disclosure could harm the United States or
aid a foreign government. Indeed, the relevant precedent teaches that the

Constitution permits even more drastic restraints on the free speech rights of this class of persons. . . .

. . . For this reason, the government may constitutionally punish government employees like Franklin for the willful disclosure of national defense information, and if the government proves the defendants conspired with Franklin in his commission of that offense, they may be subject to prosecution, as well. 18 U.S.C. §793(g).

But the analysis must go beyond this because the defendants are also charged with conspiring to violate §793(e) for their own disclosures of NDI to those not entitled to receive it. In this regard, they belong in the second class of those subject to prosecution under §793 – namely, those who have not violated a position of trust with the government to obtain and disclose information, but have obtained the information from one who has. The defendants argue that unlike Morison, Marchetti or Snepp, they did not agree to restrain their speech as part of their employment, and accordingly their First Amendment interests are more robust. . . .

One possible implication . . . is that a special relationship with the government is necessary before the government may constitutionally punish the disclosure of information relating to the national defense. Seizing upon this possible implication, defendants here contend that the First Amendment bars Congress from punishing those persons, like defendants, without a special relationship to the government for the disclosure of NDI. In essence, their position is that once a government secret has been leaked to the general public and the first line of defense thereby breached, the government has no recourse but to sit back and watch as the threat to the national security caused by the first disclosure multiplies with every subsequent disclosure. This position cannot be sustained. Although the question whether the government's interest in preserving its national defense secrets is sufficient to trump the First Amendment rights of those not in a position of trust with the government is a more difficult question, and although the authority addressing this issue is sparse, both common sense and the relevant precedent point persuasively to the conclusion that the government can punish those outside of the government for the unauthorized receipt and deliberate retransmission of information relating to the national defense.

Of course, in some instances the government's interest is so compelling, and the defendant's purpose so patently unrelated to the values of the First Amendment, that a constitutional challenge is easily dismissed. The obvious example is the unauthorized disclosure of troop movements or military technology to hostile foreign powers by non-governmental persons, conduct typically prosecuted under §794. But this is not such a case; the government has not charged the defendants under §794(a), and therefore the most relevant precedent, although it dealt with the freedom of press, is the Supreme Court's decision in *New York Times Co. v. United States*, 403 U.S. 713 (1971) (per curiam). . . . [A] close reading of [the concurring] opinions indicates that the result may have been different had the government sought to prosecute the newspapers under §793(e) subsequent to the publication of the Pentagon Papers. [Here the court analyzed these opinions. *See also* casebook pp. 1090-1093.] While the Supreme Court's discussion of the application of §793(e) to the newspapers is clearly *dicta,* lower courts "are bound by the Supreme Court's considered *dicta* almost as firmly as by the Court's outright holdings, particularly when, as here, a *dictum* is of recent vintage and not enfeebled by any subsequent statement." *McCoy v. Massachusetts Institute of Technology*, 950 F.2d 13, 19 (1st Cir. 1991). In sum, Congress's attempt to provide for the nation's security by extending punishment for the disclosure of national security secrets beyond the first category of persons within its trust to the general populace is a reasonable, and therefore constitutional[,] exercise of its power. . . .

. . . [E]ven when a person is charged with the transmission of intangible "information" the person had "reason to believe could be used to the injury of the United States," the application of the statute without the requirement that disclosure of the information be potentially harmful to the United States would subject non-governmental employees to prosecution for the innocent, albeit negligent, disclosure of information relating to the national defense. Punishing defendants engaged in public debate for unwittingly harming a legitimate government interest is inconsistent with the Supreme Court's First Amendment jurisprudence. Limiting the set of information relating to the national defense to that information which the defendant *knows,* if disclosed, is potentially harmful to the United States, by virtue of the statute's willfulness requirement, avoids this problem. Thus, for these reasons, information relating to the national defense, whether tangible or intangible, must necessarily be information which if disclosed, is potentially harmful to the United States, and the defendant must know that disclosure of the information is potentially harmful to the United States. The alternative construction simply is not sustainable. So limited, the statute does not violate the defendants' First Amendment guarantee of free speech.

For essentially the same reasons, §793, as applied to these defendants, does not violate the defendants' First Amendment right to petition the government for grievances. The Supreme Court has stated that "[t]he right to petition is cut from the same cloth as the other guarantees of [the First] Amendment, and is an assurance of a particular expression of freedom." *McDonald v. Smith*, 472 U.S. 479, 482 (1985). Indeed, "this right is implicit in 'the very idea of government, republican in form.'" *Id.* . . . For this reason, defendants contend that §793 cannot constitutionally be applied to their alleged conduct.

This argument suffers the same fatal flaws as defendants' argument under the First Amendment's free speech guarantee. Like the First Amendment's guarantee of free speech, the right to petition the government for grievances is not absolute, and may be validly regulated. *See California Motor Transport v. Trucking Unlimited*, 404 U.S. 508, 514-15 (1972) ("First Amendment rights may not be used as the means or pretext for achieving 'substantive evils'") (citing *NAACP v. Button*, 371 U.S. 415, 444 (1963)). . . . [T]he right to petition the government is validly restrained if the government does so for a legitimate purpose. And because the government's vital and legitimate national security interest is validly served through these statutes, the defendants' right to petition the government, like their right to free speech, must yield. . . .

[The court then rejected the defendants' challenge based on the overbreadth doctrine.]

VII.

In the end, it must be said that this is a hard case, and not solely because the parties' positions and arguments are both substantial and complex. It is also a hard case because it requires an evaluation of whether Congress has violated our Constitution's most sacred values, enshrined in the First and the Fifth Amendment, when it passed legislation in furtherance of our nation's security. The conclusion here is that the balance struck by §793 between these competing interests is constitutionally permissible because (1) it limits the breadth of the term "related to the national defense" to matters closely held by the government for the legitimate reason that their disclosure could threaten our collective security; and (2) it imposes rigorous scienter requirements as a condition for finding criminal liability.

The conclusion that the statute is constitutionally permissible does not reflect a judgment about whether Congress could strike a more appropriate balance between these competing interests, or whether a more carefully drawn statute could better serve both the national security and the value of public debate. Indeed, the basic terms and structure of this statute have remained largely unchanged since the administration of William Howard Taft. The intervening years have witnessed dramatic changes in the position of the United States in world affairs and the nature of threats to our national security. The increasing importance of the United States in world affairs has caused a significant increase in the size and complexity of the United States' military and foreign policy establishments, and in the importance of our nation's foreign policy decision making. Finally, in the nearly one hundred years since the passage of the Defense Secrets Act mankind has made great technological advances affecting not only the nature and potential devastation of modern warfare, but also the very nature of information and communication. These changes should suggest to even the most casual observer that the time is ripe for Congress to engage in a thorough review and revision of these provisions to ensure that they reflect both these changes, and contemporary views about the appropriate balance between our nation's security and our citizens' ability to engage in public debate about the United States' conduct in the society of nations.

An appropriate Order will issue.

[NSL p. 1091. Add the following case after Note 7.]

United States v. Rosen

United States District Court, Eastern District of Virginia, 2006
445 F. Supp. 2d 602

[The opinion is set forth *supra* p. 441.]

[CTL p. 733. Replace all of Chapter 23 – Suing Terrorists and Their Supporters with material found on the "Professor Materials" section of the casebook's website.]